A HISTORY OF SOUTHEAST ASIA

A HISTORY OF SOUTHEAST ASIA

ARTHUR COTTERELL

 **Marshall Cavendish**
Editions

Reprinted 2015, 2017

Project editor: Lee Mei Lin
Design by Lynn Chin Nyuk Ling

Published by Marshall Cavendish Editions
An imprint of Marshall Cavendish International

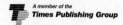

A member of the
Times Publishing Group

Other Marshall Cavendish Offices
Marshall Cavendish Corporation. 99 White Plains Road, Tarrytown NY 10591-9001, USA • Marshall Cavendish International (Thailand) Co Ltd. 253 Asoke, 12th Flr, Sukhumvit 21 Road, Klongtoey Nua, Wattana, Bangkok 10110, Thailand • Marshall Cavendish (Malaysia) Sdn Bhd, Times Subang, Lot 46, Subang Hi-Tech Industrial Park, Batu Tiga, 40000 Shah Alam, Selangor Darul Ehsan, Malaysia

Marshall Cavendish is a registered trademark of Times Publishing Limited

National Library Board Singapore Cataloguing in Publication Data

Cotterell, Arthur.
A history of Southeast Asia / Arthur Cotterell. – Singapore : Marshall Cavendish Editions, 2014.
pages cm
ISBN : 978-981-4361-02-6 (paperback)
Southeast Asia--Civilization. 2. Southeast Asia--Antiquities. 3. Southeast Asia--History.
I. Title.
DS525
959 -- dc23   OCN864455899

Printed in Singapore by Fabulous Printers Pte Ltd

On the cover: a seventeenth-century Dutch map by William Janzsoon Blaeu.

For
Yong Yap

CONTENTS

PART THREE: MODERN SOUTHEAST ASIA

PREFACE

"You lost, sir," a Land Dyak student informed me one Monday morning at the Anglican school where I taught in Kuching, capital of newly independent Sarawak and one of the states in the Federation of Malaysia. The previous Saturday in mid-1967 I had travelled to his longhouse at Giam, some 30 kilometres into the jungle. The local art club had arranged for its members to sketch there, and so we were expected.

Unexpected though was our reception because, across the rapids which gave the longhouse its name, and beneath a large Union Jack, stood the headman wearing a smart blue suit. Once ferried safely across to the opposite bank, the headman expressed his joy at our arrival, for the good reason that assistance was urgently required with a debate taking place that evening. He told me his suit was a present from a departing district officer, while the flag dated from 1946, the year in which the last white rajah ceded Sarawak to Britain. Both were obviously intended to make my wife and I feel welcome, over and above the generous hospitality shown to longhouse visitors.

After checking that we had no objection to ceremonies involving the ritual slaughter of several chickens, the consumption of their blood and an elaborate sword display, we settled down to a meal of rice and arak, an extremely strong rice wine. At a distance from this traditional reception of guests, I noticed a group of young men clustered around one who was playing a guitar. When I asked about their absence from the meal, the headman told me that it formed the subject of the debate. The young men had said that such traditional customs were out of date and the longhouse should convert to Christianity, and this was the issue to be settled by a vote of all the inhabitants after our departure.

But the headman was uneasy. He feared the debate would be too one-sided, since not enough reasons could be found to oppose the adoption

A "spirit" carving. For Dyaks birds are messengers

of Christianity. He wondered if I might help with suggestions as to why conversion should be rejected. In this Lord Jim situation, I racked my brains for Dyak examples of wise inaction. Pointing out how indigenous plants grew better than imported varieties, the story of Foolish Alois came to mind. This comical character is renowned for always making the wrong decisions. Offered a half share in a banana plant, he chose to cut off the leaves at the top, entirely ignoring the main stem and the roots. How could anyone be certain then that the Christian faith was not unlike Foolish Alois' leaves? If it failed to transplant successfully and withered as they had done, the longhouse would have given up its traditional beliefs for nothing.

On the way back to Kuching, I reflected on the impact that evangelical preachers were having on isolated longhouses. The Sarawak government had sanctioned missionary activity provided it was accompanied by social benefits—an American hospital had opened close by. But what struck me most about the visit to Giam was the thoroughly democratic nature of the longhouse. Its spokesman, the besuited headman, possessed no hereditary privilege; his chief concern was to ensure fair and open discussion. The Land Dyaks living in the longhouse would decide its future, once everyone who wished to express an opinion had done so. They did and Foolish Alois was consigned to history.

Conversion hardly changed, however, the longhouse's relationship with the spirit world. Even though Christianity provided an additional defence against the malignant spirits lurking in the jungle, it still left plenty of scope for the unseen powers that haunt Southeast Asia. Whether they are called nats in Myanmar, nak ta in Cambodia, ba in Vietnam, tujul in Java or hantu in Borneo, belief in their influence on human affairs is unshakeable. That they existed in Kuching was

A Balinese lady offers flowers at a garden shrine

confirmed when a Sea Dyak clergyman informed me how he was often molested by ghosts in the school's grounds. During the Second World War its buildings were used as an interrogation centre by the Japanese military police, the dreaded Kempeitai. The neighbouring girls' school housed an army brothel, its "comfort women" forcibly recruited from Korea and Taiwan.

Bomo, the Malay word for "black magic", exactly sums up the outlook of Austronesian speakers, who dispersed around 3000 BC from the Yangzi delta. Besides the Malayan peninsula, southern Thailand and central Vietnam, they occupied the whole of maritime Southeast Asia so that belief about communication with spirits through trances, sometimes by means of transvestite specialists as in Sulawesi, is common throughout the islands. Indian ideas have been influential, as indeed have been the teachings of Islam, but bomo remains central to Southeast Asia's eclectic heritage. Watching women collecting in a plastic bag their snipped locks from the floor of a hairdressing salon reveals how magical manipulation is still feared today. Not dissimilar anxieties can be observed among mainland Southeast Asians, even in ultra-modern Singapore.

Hardly surprising then in 1991 was the television announcement by Myanmar's military strongman General Saw Maung that he did not use black magic; nor was there any reaction a few years earlier in Cambodia when a suspicious magistrate obliged a witness to swear the truth of his testimony by a nak ta, whose dwelling place was a tree next to the courthouse. The witness changed his story once an oath invoked the wrath of an indigenous spirit rather than the one he had already sworn on the Buddhist scriptures. By far the most dramatic instance of bomo was the spell placed in 2009 on Susilo Bambang Yudhoyono, Indonesia's first directly elected president. He said the "revolving clouds" sent against him by an ill-disposed sorcerer proved to be a greater challenge than the Acehnese tsunami.

This survey of Southeast Asian history, from early times until the present, attempts to place key events in a cultural context. Without an appreciation of how Chinese, Indian, Moslem and European ideas have interacted with traditional beliefs, there is little chance of understanding modern Southeast Asian polities and peoples. Open though the region has always been to the outside world, located as it is at the junction of several ocean routes, Southeast Asia's unique character essentially stems from an adaptation to landscape, water and climate. Active volcanoes and high mountains, great rivers and turbulent seas, dense jungle and teeming wildlife, monsoon rain and seasonal drought—these are the factors that have shaped one of the most distinctive and fascinating parts of the globe. They never act as a mere backdrop to events, but form the dynamic which determines available choices for action.

A recent example of how flooding thwarted the territorial ambitions of the Republic of Indonesia occurred in 1962–63, at the start of President Sukarno's confrontation with Malaysia. Banking on a sympathetic reception from the peoples of Sarawak, Indonesian infiltrators were largely shunned because Commonwealth forces had already earned their undying affection. Along the strategically important Limbang river, which reaches the South China Sea near Brunei, the volume of flood water was such that its tributaries ran uphill. A 10-metre rise in the river level was quite beyond the protection afforded by the stilts on which longhouses and villages were built. So helicopters rescued frightened and drenched people from the roofs of their homes and the tops of trees, while assault craft distributed food and medical supplies. Although in counter-insurgency terms this operation would be described as "winning hearts and minds", for Sarawakians it was simply the response expected from friends in an environment subject to extreme emergencies.

In publishing this book I must acknowledge the invaluable contributions made by several people. First of all my wife Yong Yap, through the translation of documents from Asian languages; second, Graham Guest, an old friend whose amazingly extensive archive of pre-1900 illustrations, Imperial Images, furnished material in the early chapters; third, Ray Dunning the creator of the maps and illustrations spread throughout the text; and last but not least, my former publisher Chris Newson, who recognized the need for an illustrated survey of Southeast Asian history.

INTRODUCTION

Even though the pattern of migration is by no means clear in prehistoric times, the original homeland of most Southeast Asian peoples was southern China, and especially the Yangzi river delta. When these ancient population movements began, not later than 3000 BC, this area was not of course Chinese. The cradle of China's civilization was situated much farther north, on the flood plain of the Yellow river.

The shift southwards of China's centre of gravity only began with the unification of the north under Qin Shi Huangdi, the first emperor. Although this determined ruler primarily built the Great Wall to protect his subjects from nomad raids, he also wished to halt any drift of farmers to the north, where they might abandon agriculture and take up stock rearing, thus strengthening the nomad economy. To encourage a southward population movement instead, imperial armies had, by 210 BC, extended Qin Shi Huangdi's authority as far south to present-day Hong Kong. While the southern peoples were by no means assimilated or firmly controlled, they were irrevocably tied to the Chinese empire. The same fate almost befell the Vietnamese, once the Han dynasty that followed the Qin house added northern Vietnam to the imperial defences. Not for a millennium would the Vietnamese finally assert their independence.

This event is surprising because by then nomad pressure had already pushed the Chinese capital southwards. After 1127 it was located in Hangzhou, over 500 kilometres to the south of the Yellow river. Song emperors could never reconcile themselves to Hangzhou being a permanent capital, but residence in this long-established trading centre altered their attitude toward commerce. Because the profits from maritime trade with Southeast Asian countries were so enormous, Emperor Gao Zong asked his ministers in 1145 whether it was better to derive the bulk of the empire's revenue from a levy on merchant enterprise rather than taxing the people.

Yet tributary relations with China had been a regular feature of Southeast Asian diplomacy from early times. Although maritime exchange appears to have been initially stimulated by Arab traders who brought frankincense to Sumatran ports, exchanging this perfume for other goods, the onward China trade came to dominate the Southeast Asian market. The Sumatran state of Srivijaya grew rich on the strength of its special relationship with China, with King Jayanasa sending an embassy there in 695.

China also maintained close relations with mainland Southeast Asian states, so that our knowledge of the earliest ones owes much to the reports of Chinese envoys. In the 240s these visitors were amazed at the wealth of Funan, a state located on the Mekong river, quite close to modern Phnom Penh. Equally revealing is their account of Sriksetra's defences, a Pyu settlement that flourished in the Irrawaddy river valley during the same period. The Sanskrit name "Sriksetra", meaning "hallowed field", indicates the influence of India. Yet there was a profound difference between the Southeast Asian perceptions of the Indians and the Chinese. Whereas India was looked upon as the source of religious ideas, China was always expected to play a political role. With the exception of northern Vietnam, the Indian view of divine kingship initially held sway in all Southeast Asian polities.

In chapter 1, the Indian impact on early Burma is obvious in the development of Pagan as a great Buddhist centre of learning, which began with the conversion of King Anawrahta by a monk who hailed from the Mon city of Thaton. But this monarch remained realistic about the likely response of his subjects to the new religion, and he incorporated worship of nats, the indigenous spirits of Burma, in Buddhism to make it more accessible. His son Kyanzittha, who came to the throne in 1084, even claimed in a previous life to have worshipped the Buddha in the company of Thagyamin, king of the nats. Throughout Southeast Asia the spirit world has always been part of everyday life, as indeed it still is today, even in Chinese-influenced northern Vietnam. There Daoism, China's own spiritual alternative to the this-worldly tenor of Confucius' teachings, chimed with indigenous Vietnamese ideas to the extent that they survived in association with Buddhism.

Anawrahta's patronage of the Buddhist faith assisted its spread in mainland Southeast Asia. Following the Mongol destruction of Pagan in 1287, Burma was still regarded as staunchly Buddhist. The hundreds of brick-built stupas and temples standing at Pagan today bear witness to this early enthusiasm for Indian religious ideas, just as the impressive ruins of Angkor show a parallel Khmer commitment.

Chapter 2 describes the rise of the earliest Cambodian kings and their eventual choice of Angkor as a capital, situated on the shore of the great inland lake, the Tonle Sap. Despite the Khmers embracing both Hinduism and Buddhism, the caste system did not transfer from India, unlike Indonesia where its social distinctions are currently followed by the Balinese. Helped though Khmer rulers were by brahmins in becoming devarajas, "god kings", these Indian priests never succeeded in monopolizing early Cambodian belief. The democratic outlook of the Buddha, who rejected the whole system of hereditary classes, prevented the brahmins from achieving any social superiority. A person's position, the Buddha maintained, was determined not by birth but worth, by conduct and by character, rather than descent.

Chapter 3 begins with China's tremendous impact on Vietnam. Like Korea on the edge of northern China, however, Vietnam received Chinese civilization without losing its identity. Its Southeast Asian language —a part of the Austroasiatic group of tongues which also includes Khmer and Mon—provided a sure defence against total assimilation, once it was customary for educated Vietnamese to learn to speak and write Chinese alongside their native speech. The Chams, who blocked the southern expansion of Vietnam until 1471, spoke an Austronesian language similar to the languages of maritime Southeast Asia. These seafarers had migrated from the Yangzi delta, populating islands as far west as Madagascar and as far east as Hawaii. The vast majority of Austronesian speakers, however, settled in the Indonesian archipelago where there are now 300 distinct peoples who communicate in 250 separate languages.

That was the reason why Sukarno, Indonesia's first president, insisted that teachers in primary schools used Bahasa Indonesia, the national language. Based on the Malay spoken in central Sumatra, it contained additional elements from other tongues, above all Javanese. From his earliest years, Sukarno had been aware of language differences because his Javanese father was a teacher in the employ of the Dutch, who married a local girl when he was working in Bali.

Vietnam's long involvement with China left such an indelible mark that France called its colonial empire of Vietnam, Laos and Cambodia by the name of Indochina. It signals the meeting point of two diametrically opposed cultures: religion-oriented India and secular China. Not that the Chinese were without any beliefs of their own; rather the Confucian emphasis on family morality tended to minimize concern about the afterlife. "I stand in awe of the spirits," Confucius remarked, "but keep them at a distance."

The growth of states in maritime Southeast Asia is the subject of chapter 4. There strategically located Srivijaya took advantage of international trade passing through the Straits of Malacca, besides acting as a stopover for Buddhist monks travelling between China and India. Arriving in 671, the Chinese monk Yijing was astonished by the generous support given to Buddhist monasteries by Srivijayan kings. A legacy of this early prosperity was the survival of Malay as the language of learning, after the decline of Palembang as a trading port. Emperor Gao Zong's encouragement of seaborne trade opened up commercial opportunities in China for the rest of the Indonesian archipelago, which Javanese rulers were quick to exploit. Yet Srivijaya was also knocked off course as a trading empire by the Cholas, a south Indian dynasty which attacked Malaya and Sumatra in the eleventh century. The ultimate beneficiary of this intervention was Majapahit, a powerful state in eastern Java. Its rise to prominence occurred after the Mongols sent in 1292 an expeditionary force to punish King Kertanagara of Singhasari, who had refused to send hostages to Beijing and tattooed the faces of Kubilai Khan's ambassadors.

Because Kertanagara's own son-in-law, Raden Vijaya, so willingly acknowledged Mongol hegemony, the new capital that he founded at Majapahit was free to develop a trading network greater than Srivijaya had ever achieved. It stretched as far east as New Guinea and as far north as the Philippines. Its most famous king was Hayam Wuruk, who ruled until 1389 with the guidance of his chief minister Gajah Mada.

Chapter 5 reviews the changed situation in Burma after the abandonment of Pagan. The late Burmese revival was centred upon Toungoo, a city in the remote Sittang river valley. From there Toungoo kings reunited the country, destroyed the rival Thai kingdom of Ayudhya in 1767, and fended off the Portuguese as well as the French. Already weapons of European manufacture were changing the nature of warfare in Burma as stone and brick replaced wood for the construction of fortifications. Despite British efforts to establish an agreed frontier between India and Burma, the newly founded Konbaung dynasty let negotiations drift and its commanders invade areas under Calcutta's protection. The result was the First Anglo-Burmese War which ended in 1826 with the British acquisition of Manipur, Assam, Arakan and Tennasserim.

Turmoil also affected late Cambodia. Unlike Pagan, however, the Mongols were not directly responsible for Angkor's fall, but their conquest of Nanzhou had an indirect impact on the Khmer empire, because the disappearance of this belligerent power accelerated the southern migration of the Thai from their homeland in Yunnan. Soon there was a patchwork of Thai principalities stretching continuously from the Vietnamese border across the Mekong and Chaophraya rivers to the Gulf of Martaban. None of these jostling kingdoms attained sufficient power to dominate its neighbours, and it was not until the foundation of Ayudhya in 1351 that the Thai became a really significant force in mainland Southeast Asia.

The rise and fall of Ayudhya is described in chapter 6, along with the end of Khmer power. The Thai made Angkor so unsafe that, after a siege in 1431, the Cambodian capital shifted downriver to Lovek and then Phnom Penh, where one Khmer king considered Christian baptism as a means of securing military aid from Spain. Despite the antagonism between the Thai and the Cambodians, the former were deeply impressed by the splendour of Angkor and borrowed its culture wholesale. Particularly attractive was the last great Khmer king, Jayavarman VII, who died in 1218. More than any other ruler, Jayavarman tried to integrate Buddhist concepts with Hindu ideas of kingship. As a consequence, he was looked upon as a living Buddha, whose compassion for his people explained the reason for his occupation of the throne. It was a view of monarchy that the Thai found most congenial.

In chapter 7 we note the severe travails of late Vietnam. Notwithstanding the immense contribution to Vietnamese civilization made by Emperor Le Thanh Tong, his quarrelsome children undermined the country's unity and, from 1672 until 1806, Vietnam was divided into two separate states. The Nguyen dynasty ruled the south from Hue, while the Trinh family controlled the north through a series of puppet Le emperors. The reunion of Vietnam under the Nguyen emperors seemed to usher in a new golden age at the start of the nineteenth century, but its Chinese-style administration proved no match for the French, who occupied Saigon in 1859. As did Qing China during the Second Opium War, Vietnam had little chance of resisting territorial demands when backed with modern weaponry, and by 1874 there were French concessions as far north as the city of Hanoi and the port of Haiphong.

Similar military pressure had turned the Indonesian archipelago into a Dutch preserve. Chapter 8 is devoted to the late island powers of Malacca, Aceh, Mataram, Brunei and the Philippines. It also offers an account of Portuguese, Spanish, Dutch and British intervention. Once Ming China had withdrawn its navy from the "Southern Oceans" in the mid-fifteenth century, these European powers gained the false impression that they were the earliest navigators of Asian waters. Had Vasco da Gama rounded the Cape of Good Hope seventy years before his first voyage to India in 1498, the Portuguese admiral would have found his own vessels of 300 tonnes sailing alongside a Chinese fleet with ships of 1,500 tonnes.

By the time the Portuguese captured Malacca in 1511, China had ceased to bother with the sea, possibly for the reason that the removal of the capital northwards to Beijing had focused attention on the Great Wall as the empire's critical line of defence. So in maritime Southeast Asia the local states were left to resist European colonialism on their own. Sultan Agung of Mataram twice invested Batavia, the headquarters of the Dutch East India Company on the site of present-day Jakarta, but without a navy he could not prevent its resupply from the sea. After the failure of a second siege in 1629, Sultan Agung recognized that the Dutch were not going to be easily expelled, as did other Javanese rulers.

The Dutch gradually pushed the Portuguese out of Southeast Asia with the exception of the Lesser Sunda islands and Timor. They ignored the Spaniards in the Philippines and maintained an uneasy relationship with the British in the Straits of Malacca. Although Spain's alliance with France in the Seven Years War brought an English East India Company expedition to Manila in 1762, the Spanish colonial authorities were allowed to resume control when peace was agreed. A victim of the peace agreement was Diego Silang, a nationalist who briefly tried to free the Philippines from Spain. He was assassinated at the instance of the local Catholic clergy.

In chapter 9 modern times begin with the colonial era, which reached its climax in the Greater East Asia Co-Prosperity Sphere, Japan's abortive attempt to carve out an empire of its own. A surprising development was the American colony of the Philippines, which was not simply an unforeseen consequence of the Spanish-American War of 1898. President William McKinley had already decided to advance the position of the United States in the Pacific by means of the annexation of key islands. Aware of the threat posed to stability by a modernized and aggressive Japan, McKinley thought he had discovered a solution to American weakness in Asia with the acquisition of the Philippines as well as Guam. The US navy was pleased to add the excellent anchorage at Luzon's Subic Bay to the facilities then being built at Pearl Harbor, in newly annexed Hawaii.

The 1941 Japanese assault on Pearl Harbor resulted as much from Japanese frustration at American double-standards as wartime strategy. Tokyo could never understand how the first people to escape from the clutches of European colonialism could presume to restrain Japan's own imperial ambitions, while becoming in Southeast Asia colonialists themselves. Chapter 10 follows the rise and fall of the Greater East Asia Co-Prosperity Sphere, a euphemism for ruthless Japanese exploitation of Southeast Asian peoples, and looks at the beginning of decolonization following the defeat of Japan. This process of European withdrawal was greatly facilitated by the sweeping 1945 election victory of the Labour Party in Britain. Because the Labour Party was committed to the replacement of the British empire with a Commonwealth of free nations, Britain avoided colonial wars that so troubled the French and the Dutch.

Chapters 11 and 12, the final chapters, bring this history of Southeast Asia to a close. While the British conducted an orderly withdrawal from empire, after the historic decision to grant India and Burma early independence, the Dutch and the French tried to retain their colonies in a totally changed world. For the Vietnamese, who led resistance to France in mainland Southeast Asia, the anti-colonial struggle proved devastating once the United States became involved. The Second Vietnam War is a salutary lesson of how misconceived were so many actions during the Cold War. Washington simply failed to grasp Ho Chi Minh's essential aim: the reunification of the Vietnamese homeland.

For Filipinos, the Pacific dimension of the Second World War made no difference to the agreed date of their independence, 4 July 1946. But the wanton destruction of Manila cast a shadow over this event, since the city suffered as much damage as Warsaw and Budapest during their liberation. As did Thailand and Myanmar, the new name for Burma, the Philippines learned that democracy provided no ready solution to popular unrest, although so far it has managed to avoid a military coup. The Republic of Indonesia's chequered history since gaining independence from Holland in 1949 was largely the result of military interference with its government. The dramatic fall of President Suharto in 1998 seemed to promise a return to democratic standards, but not until 2004 did Indonesia's first directly elected president take office.

Although corruption has blighted politics in Malaysia as well as Indonesia, the Federation has managed the post-colonial period rather well, even though it needed Commonwealth help to deter President Sukarno's territorial ambitions during the 1960s. Yet Malaysia shares a cavalier attitude to the environment with Indonesia, its rainforests currently disappearing at truly alarming rate. Besides the impact of climate change, the replacement of forest by oil palm estates might prove to be a key factor in maritime Southeast Asia's future decline. Outstandingly different, and much more successful, is Singapore's emergence as a modern city-state. As Lee Kuan Yew commented in 2013, its survival depends upon remaining "a very open economy". Yet he added: "If there is turbulence in Southeast Asia, we will take a hit." All that Singapore can do, "is to take the world as it is; it is too small to change it. But we can try to maximize the space we have among the big 'trees' in the region." More worrying than external challenges, however, are the internal ones, and especially that posed by the attitude of young Singaporeans. According to a ninety-year-old Lee Kuan Yew, the younger generation simply "takes for granted Singapore's affluence."

LIST OF MAPS

All maps drawn by Ray Dunning.

PHOTO CREDITS

Preface

Pg xiii   A Balinese lady offers flowers at a garden shrine.
           Source: Arthur Cotterell

Chapter 1

Pg 13   The Shwezigon stupa at Pagan. *Source: Ray Dunning*

Pg 14   Nats, the indigenous spirits of Burma. *Source: Ray Dunning*

Pg 18   The appearance of Kyanzittha's famous Ananda temple has
           changed little since its completion in 1105.
           Source: Ray Dunning

Pg 24   Two views of a reclining Buddha at Pagan. Theravada
           Buddhism always favoured large statues.
           Source: Ray Dunning

Pg 27   The brooding presence of the Dhammayan temple.
           Source: Ray Dunning

Pg 30   A remorseful Narapatisithu started building the
           Gadawpalin temple, but it was completed by his successor
           in the 1210s. *Source: Ray Dunning*

Pg 31   The Htilominlo temple. *Source: Ray Dunning*

Pg 33   Some of the surviving temples at Pagan today.
           Source: Ray Dunning

EARLY
SOUTHEAST ASIA

1

EARLY BURMA

In the City of Righteousness the encircling walls are morality,
the moat is conscience, the ramparts over the city-gates are
understanding, the watch-towers are energy, the pillars are
faith, the gate-keeper is concentration, and the palace is
wisdom.

The Milindapanha

"Shall we go back to Pagan?" King Narathihapate asked his chief queen
in 1287. "We cannot", she pointed out because "there are with us but
few courtiers". Then she added, it was the harshness of his rule that had
alienated so many of his subjects—nobles, monks and soldiers alike.
"If you enter Pagan alone, you are bound to suffer at the hands of your
enemy." That these belonged to the Mongols was also his fault; against
the advice of his ministers, Narathihapate had executed Kubilai Khan's
envoys. "It is nobler to take poison now," the queen said, "than have your
blood gush out from the thrust of a sword." That the fatal dose had been
prepared by a rebellious son named Thihathu, whose men captured the
royal barge at the city of Prome, caused the king to wish in future lives
that he would have only daughters. Then Narathihapate ate the poisoned
food and died.

This account of the end of Pagan's last ruler comes from *The Glass
Palace Chronicle (Hmannan Yazawin)*, compiled by royal command in
1829. Interest then in Burma's first great kingdom is hardly surprising.
British India was already threatening Burmese independence, which
would be extinguished fifty-six years later by the deposition of King

Thibaw at Mandalay. What the Konbaung dynasty was trying to do in 1829 was extol the memory of Pagan, one of the foremost states of early Southeast Asia. Its founders were the ancestors of the modern Burmans who arrived in the north of the country during the ninth century. Their Sino-Tibetan language is quite different from Mon, the tongue belonging to the ancient inhabitants of the lowlands and a close relation of Khmer, the speech of the Cambodians. Nor does Burmese have any connection with the languages spoken by the Shan and the Karens, hill-dwellers along the country's eastern border.

Even though the history of Burma until modern times often comprised a struggle between the kingdoms of the interior and the kingdoms of the Irrawaddy delta, there were cleavages within both Upper and Lower Burma that contributed to the rise and fall of dynasties too. That such a pattern, involving the not infrequent restoration of government after a period of decline, was accepted as normal by Burmese peoples had much to do with Theravada Buddhism. Yet these dramatic changes in the effectiveness of royal authority were a political phenomenon common to all the countries of Southeast Asia. Just as the Javanese distinguished between two eras of time, a golden age of royal prestige and prosperity as opposed to a mad age of anarchy and natural disasters, so in Burma periods of joy alternating with those of misery were viewed as the inevitable condition of humanity.

The ten royal laws—generosity, morality, self-sacrifice, integrity, kindness, austerity, calmness, non-violence, patience and harmony—that were believed to guarantee the stability of a kingdom derived ultimately from the Buddha, whose teachings in India had been taken up with enthusiasm by the Mauryan emperor Asoka. During the 260s BC he had endeavoured to expand his empire through righteousness rather than warfare. In the process Asoka turned Buddhism into a pan-Asian faith, two and a half centuries after the Buddha's death. One of the Mauryan ruler's sons was even despatched as a missionary to Sri Lanka, whence Burma eventually received the Theravada version of the religion.

In the centuries after the passing of Mauryan power, Buddhism in India split into many schools, the two most famous of which are Mahayana, "the great ferry boat" and Hinayana, "the small ferry boat". A possible cause of this event may have been the large number of brahmins

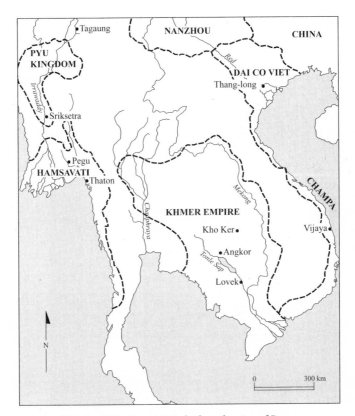

Mainland Southeast Asia before the rise of Pagan

entering the Buddhist order of monks, because brahminical delight in the elaboration of doctrine took the Mahayana version of the faith away from the directness of the Buddha's original message and allowed the development of a pantheon of buddhas and bodhisattvas. The bodhisattva indeed came to be regarded as the supreme example of compassion in that he or she was prepared to postpone buddhahood in order to lead others to enlightenment, so much so that Mahayana apologists were pleased to distinguish between a bodhisattva's unselfishness and the selfishness of a Hinayana monk, who sought personal salvation in the seclusion of a cloister.

This argument in part accounts for the name Hinayana, which can also be translated as the "inferior way", a Mahayana term of abuse that has been unwittingly adopted by some Western commentators on Buddhism.

This Mon bronze reveals much earlier worship
of the Buddha than Burman enthusiasm at Pagan

There were in fact several major schools of Buddhist thought besides Mahayana, including the Theravada one that evolved in Sri Lanka. But Theravada's closeness to the Buddha's final instruction to his disciples—reliance on monastic discipline to ensure the safe transmission of his message from generation to generation—should not tempt us to think that its canon preserves the original words of the Buddha. Theravada Buddhism relies extensively on commentaries such as the *Milindapanha*, the "Questions of King Milinda", and the *Visuddhimagga*, "Path of Purity", written by the Sri Lankan monk Buddhaghosa. This renowned scholar, whose name means "the voice of the Buddha", received a joyous welcome when around 400 he made his way to Thaton, then an important Mon city in Lower Burma. He may well have brought with him one of the Buddha's teeth but what he certainly left behind on his return home were the standard texts of Theravada Buddhism.

Unlike the array of punishments meted out by the denizens of hell between incarnations according to Mahayana doctrine, Theravada denied that there was any intermediate stage between death and rebirth. All that mattered was the karmic effect of previous lives in determining the nature of the next existence. This more straightforward approach goes a long way in explaining the practice among Theravada men of becoming monks, at least for a short time during their lives. In Burma it would give a genuinely popular foundation to the imported religion, while acting as a reminder of the dedication of monks who pursue enlightenment through humility, chastity and austerity.

The Earliest States

According to *The Glass Palace Chronicle*, the earliest kingdom in Burma was founded by an Indian prince, Abhiraja. Called Tagaung or "drum ferry", it was the northernmost of the early walled cities in Upper Burma. Excavations have uncovered curved city defences, a shrine belonging to a tutelary guardian, burial urns, bronze bells, iron furnaces and terracotta roof tiles. After King Abhiraja's death, his two sons quarrelled over the succession to the throne, and as a result the people split into two antagonistic groups. Civil war would have ensued, *The Glass Palace*

A Mon "chedi" or stupa

Chronicle tells us, had not the princes been prepared to submit to a contest of strength without recourse to arms. It was agreed that the prince whose followers completed building an almshouse during the night would become the next king. Whereas the followers of the elder prince used brick and wood so that their almshouse was still unfinished at sunrise, those who followed the younger prince used bamboo and thatch and were able to finish construction on time. Thus it was that the younger prince ascended the throne and the elder prince along with his followers left Tagaung and settled in Arakan.

Later Tagaung was sacked by raiders from the north but the city recovered under Dhajaraja, another Indian prince. The new ruler claimed to be related to the Buddha, whose own social position was most probably magnified in Buddhist texts to that of a prince. More likely the son of a prominent citizen of Kapilavastu, a city in a republic situated near the foothills of the Himalayas, the Buddha was given an exalted status so that he might have had a realistic choice between a career as a great king or a great sage. A prophecy had said he would only choose the latter if he were made aware of suffering in the world: this happened when he encountered a tottering old man, bent double over his walking stick, an incurable invalid and, last but not least, a corpse being carried to the cremation ground. The serene calm of a hermit suggested a course of action and, abandoning throne and family, he wandered off as an ascetic, determined to discover the true nature of things.

The stark choice between ruling as a universal monarch, or living as a sage on the brink of buddhahood, always fascinated Burmese kings. For the rulers of Pagan it was an article of faith, with King Kyanzittha boldly proclaiming that he was actually both. In unstable Burma, the dual role chimed with Theravada Buddhism's notion of a cycle of swings between morality and immorality, between periods of wealth and poverty. While a universal monarch might restore order, his subjects still required spiritual guidance to fulfil their destinies.

Bhinnakaraja, the last king of Tagaung, was forced to move southwards down the Sittaung valley to a new capital close to present-day Beinnaka. *The Glass Palace Chronicle* records how "the kingdom of Tagaung perished... and its people were divided into three groups". The first group travelled east, the second west, and the third settled in the south

A bas-relief of the Buddha at Sriksetra, dating from the fifth century

at Beinnaka "with Bhinnakaraja and his chief queen Nagahsein". The cause of this dispersal was in all probability the Pyus, the vanguard of the Burman tribes who pushed their way down the Irrawaddy to the site of their famous foundation of Sriksetra, near modern Prome. Tagaung must have been a stopping place, one of the small kingdoms they overran on the drive southwards, because a large number of Pyu burial urns have been unearthed there.

Sriksetra, "hallowed field" or "auspicious land", receives scant notice in *The Glass Palace Chronicle*, but Chinese sources reveal that it was once a city of considerable size. Aerial photographs indicate circular defences nearly 15 kilometres in length; along the southern perimeter there are two or three walls placed close together. A Chinese envoy sent to Sriksetra saw these fortifications. "They take one day's march to go completely round," he noted with amazement. "There was a deep moat and walls of glazed brick pierced by a dozen gates fitted with carved and gilded wooden doors." The city walls enclosed an area of nearly 30 square kilometres, making Sriksetra the largest known Pyu settlement. According to local traditions, the city was actually built by the Hindu gods with Indra at their head. Sriksetra was supposed to be a replica of Sudarsana, Indra's own

A Mon or Pyu guardian spirit, embossed on a silver plaque

residence on Mount Meru, the cosmic mountain. The city's remains show a decided attempt at a circular layout even though complete regularity has not been achieved. Its thirty-two gates are said to represent either the number of vassal chiefdoms that acknowledged Sriksetra's power or the thirty-two gods who helped Indra with the construction work. In later capitals a square form was substituted for the circular, but a definite cosmological dimension remained: near the centre of Mandalay, the throne belonging to the last kings of Burma stood beneath a seven-tiered tower that was identified with Mount Meru. Built as a model capital in 1857, Mandalay's layout was conceived in the likeness of the heavenly constellations revolving around the cosmic mountain. Thus the audience chamber in the palace could be said to be situated at the very centre of the universe.

Beyond the double and triple walls running along the southern edge of Sriksetra, a couple of massive stupas are still standing, thanks to later repairs undertaken by Pagan kings. But it is unlikely that they added the stone slabs carved with images of the Buddha, since these steles imitate Indian styles dating from before the rise of Pagan. In spite of local legend regarding the Buddha's prediction about the future glory of Sriksetra, we know that Hindu deities received worship in the city. On a visit to Burma, the Buddha is supposed to have said that Sriksetra would become a great city. When a mole presented him with dirt from his burrow, the Buddha predicted that for this act of kindness, the tiny creature in a future incarnation would become Sriksetra's first king and be named Duttabaung.

Under the Gupta dynasty, which ruled northern India from the fourth century to roughly 550, there was a resurgence of Hinduism along with the system of hereditary classes. In rejecting such social divisions, the Buddha had always maintained that a person's position is determined not by birth but worth, by conduct and by character, rather than descent. This democratic idea was not to be lost in Southeast Asia because Buddhism was India's most enduring export there. How far the Indian caste system transferred is still a matter of debate, except in staunchly Hindu Bali. And of course the prophet Muhammad's insistence on spiritual equality was to sweep away lingering social distinctions in the rest of the Indonesian archipelago, once Islam spread widely during the fifteenth century. It would appear in Burma that Hindu deities were always accommodated within the framework of Buddhist belief, in a similar way to the nats, the indigenous spirits associated with trees, rocks, fields and waterfalls. At Pagan we know that the court worshipped snakes, a survival from pre-Buddhist times despite the use of the Indian term nagas.

In the second century the Pyus had contact with Indian culture, directly via eastern India and Sri Lanka and indirectly perhaps via Lower Burma. As a consequence, their religious outlook combined Buddhism, Hinduism and animism with the tradition of urn burial. In the royal burials at Sriksetra, the respect accorded to these different beliefs can be observed in the inscriptions on individual stone urns. Indian-derived names and dates identify the ashes of the deceased who were laid to rest in traditional fashion. So we read:

On the 9th day of the 7th month of the year 41 King Sri Vikrama died. He was 57 years, two months and 24 days old.

On the 20th day of the 9th month in the year 44 King Singha Vikrama died. He was 80 years old.

The dates refer to the Saka era that in India had replaced the Buddhist one under the Guptas. Translating them gives 160 for the death of Sri Vikrama and 163 for Singha Vikrama. The relationship between the two kings is uncertain, except that the older man may have been a stop-gap choice after the former's sudden death.

The economy of Sriksetra depended entirely upon irrigation. Rainfall was adequate for growing rice but through water-management along secondary streams, yields were greatly increased. The other Burman tribes who followed the Pyus and stayed in Upper Burma were obliged by the drier climate to intensify irrigation-based cultivation. The strength of their great city of Pagan, with its numerous Buddhist monasteries, lay in a location that was destined to become one of Burma's key irrigated areas. In the eleventh century the scale of the agricultural surplus was sufficient for Pagan to control Lower Burma, a conquest that would facilitate a growing cultural exchange with India and with the Theravada stronghold of Sri Lanka.

The end of Sriksetra remains a mystery. A possibility is a raid in 832 from Nanzhou, a belligerent state in the present-day Chinese province of Yunnan. But 656 has been advanced as an earlier end-date: an inscription at Pagan suggests that Sriksetra ceased being the Pyu capital then. The abandonment of a capital was not an unusual event in Southeast Asia, as Angkor Wat notably demonstrates. It seems that in fact Sriksetra was destroyed during the reign of King Anawrahta, who did much to extend Pagan's authority into Lower Burma. Before his death in 1077, when he was gored by a wild buffalo, Anawrahta is said to have razed the city to the ground lest Sriksetra became a stronghold for rebels. Another casualty of Anawrahta's southern campaigns was the Mon city of Thaton, situated near the Three Pagodas Pass to central Thailand. The city was stormed in 1056 as a result of its ruler's refusal to hand over Buddhist scriptures, including those brought from Sri Lanka by Buddhaghosa. And an inscription at Pagan confirms that King Manuha of Thaton was kept as a captive until his death and that his descendants stayed on there.

The Mon kingdom of Hamsavati, of which Thaton may well have been a vassal state, was left intact because later on Prince Kyanzittha was sent by Anawrahta to assist in the defence of its capital Pegu, then threatened by a Shan attack. Apparently Kyanzittha's archers achieved

The Shwezigon stupa at Pagan

Nats, the indigenous spirits of Burma

amazingly accurate shots during a practice session among the city's cucumber beds, before they so intimidated the Shan raiders that these hillmen flung away their weapons and fled, leaving their chieftains to be taken prisoner.

The Rise of Pagan

At first the kingdom of Pagan seems to have been but one among several competing city-states in Upper Burma. A gradual accretion of power, however, was by no means secure before the reign of Anawrahta, who was crowned in 1044. Straddling the Irrawaddy river, the kingdom that he inherited was still tiny, measuring around 250 kilometres from north to south and 100 kilometres from east to west. Anawrahta's initial act was to offer the throne to his father, but the old man preferred to spend his final years in a monastery. This gesture may have been intended to placate public opinion, because Anawrahta had slain his foster-brother in the struggle for power. The murder troubled his own sleep for months until Thagyamin, the king of the nats, appeared in a dream with this advice:

> O King, if you wish to atone for your evil deed and your brother's death, then build many pagodas, cave retreats, monasteries and alms houses, and share the merit with him. Also dig wells, ponds, canals and ditches, and share the merit with him.

Here the advice given by the chief indigenous spirit neatly accounts for Pagan's two outstanding features: extensive irrigation schemes and endless religious building. In and around the city, Burman enthusiasm for the Buddhist faith raised a forest of brick-built stupas, temples and monasteries; today more than 3,000 still bear witness to Pagan's fame as an early centre for Theravada learning.

Anawrahta's own conversion to Theravada Buddhism was due to a Mon monk from Thaton, who had travelled northwards to evangelize the people of Upper Burma. The monk dwelt in a secluded hermitage some distance from Pagan, until one day a forester, wondering what this man wearing a yellow robe was doing there, took him to King Anawrahta. As soon as he saw the monk, the king recognized the goodness of the mendicant and gave him alms. At court, where the monk was invited to reside, the teaching of the Buddha had such an immense impact that Anawrahta decided to champion this version of the Hinayana faith in Southeast Asia. Yet to establish it firmly within his own kingdom, he urgently needed a set of the scriptures because the monk had brought no books with him. Hence his decision to seek immediate assistance from Thaton, by force if necessary.

At the time, the invasion of Sri Lanka by the Hindu Chola dynasty from southern India cut off Burma from this scriptural source of supply, although some maintain that Anawrahta received Theravadan scriptures from a grateful Sri Lankan king for the military assistance he provided against the Cholas. That Anawrahta was successful in his religious mission can be seen from the fact that in 1073, King Vijayabahu of Sri Lanka, desiring to rehabilitate the Buddhist community on the island after more than seventy years of Chola rule, requested that Pagan send a group of Burman and Mon monks to conduct ordination there. The great Buddhaghosa would have been delighted at this turn of events, because it more than justified the time he had spent in Thaton.

In following Thagyamin's advice for the improvement of Pagan's agricultural base, Anawrahta was able to draw upon the irrigation skills of the Thai-speaking Shan hillmen, from whom he received tribute. Mon rice-growers in Lower Burma did not depend on irrigation, but on the management of runoff and waterway floods. In Upper Burma, where rainfall was adversely affected by the Arakan mountains, such an approach to agriculture was out of the question. Even more so was it inappropriate to the hillsides cultivated by the Shan tribes, whose livelihood relied on mastery of land unsuited to growing wet rice. The Shan farmers had to evolve a sophisticated method of water control along with a type of rice that could flourish on dry land or land with limited flooding. Their early-ripening variety of rice would transform Burmese agriculture as it later did farming in large parts of Thailand. Yet Anawrahta found the establishment of an irrigation system far from easy. One of his queens, the sister of a Shan chieftain, finally offered herself as a sacrificial victim to the waters and, after her ritual execution, she was regarded as the guardian spirit of weirs. Access to the agricultural expertise and the military manpower of the Shan gave Pagan distinct political advantages, but these highlanders were a double-edged sword.

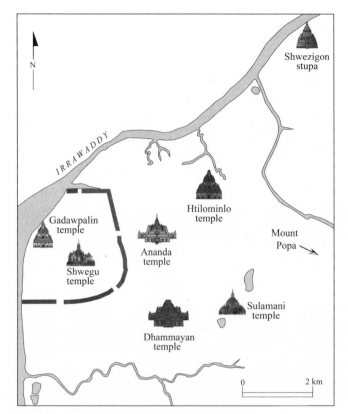

Pagan and its chief monuments

Without Anawrahta's timely marriages to the daughters of leading Shan chieftains, a general coalition would have formed against Pagan.

As soon as he ascended the throne, Anawrahta had given careful thought to his queens. A princess was needed and he accepted Panchakalyani, the only daughter of the king of Vesali in Bengal, as his chief queen; quite possibly because she was reputed to have been miraculously born of a certain fruit. On the long journey across Arakan, the Burman envoy in charge of the bridal party fell in love with her, and with an eye to hiding his improper behaviour from Anawrahta, he sent back at every stage, one of the princess's attendants with the result that when she arrived at the gates of Pagan, only a few attendants were left. Anawrahta received her with honour and installed Panchakalyani in the palace, until a courtier intimated that since her escort was so small, she

The appearance of Kyanzittha's famous Ananda temple
has changed little since its completion in 1105

could not be a true princess. Exiled to the remote village on the Chindwin river, she gave birth to the future king Kyanzittha.

Whether or not Kyanzittha was the envoy's son, he lived like a prince but with a much lower status than that accorded to the heir apparent, Anawrahta's son Sawlu, whose mother may well have been Shan. Kyanzittha always declared that his own mother was "born of bael-fruit stock". Some scepticism has been directed at the story of Kyanzittha's own affair with the Pegu princess Hkin U, because it seems no more than a repeat of the envoy's dalliance—like father, like son. Yet *The Glass Palace Chronicle* tells us that during Anawrahta's reign, the city of Pegu was attacked by a Shan army, and Anawrahta sent Kyanzittha to drive off the attackers. The inhabitants of Pegu comprised a mixture of Mons and Indians, whose king had accepted the suzerainty of Pagan. After he had relieved the city, its king asked Kyanzittha to escort one of his daughters to Anawrahta as an expression of his gratitude. On arrival at Pagan, Hkin U was duly made a queen, but once the liaison with Kyanzittha was discovered, the prince had to flee for his life. Not until after Anawrahta's death would he be recalled by King Sawlu, although his stay was short-lived because Kyanzittha took up again with Hkin U. When he became king himself, Kanzittha raised the Pegu princess to be one of his queens.

After the conquest of Thaton, Anawrahta turned his attention to northern Arakan, where the local ruler quickly acknowledged Pagan's authority. The relationship was hardly onerous because Anawrahta was content to leave an hereditary monarchy in place, and not appoint governors of his own. Pagan never exercised direct authority over the peoples living in the hills and mountains of Upper Burma, nor did it seek to uproot loyal dynasties situated elsewhere. Unquestioned obedience was only forthcoming in the immediate area around the capital, a stronghold from which Burman expeditions could be sent wherever a political crisis arose, such as the Shan assault on Pegu.

A fundamental weakness at Pagan, however, was the fact that economic progress centred on the endowment of Buddhist temples. Eager to acquire religious merit that would benefit them and their families in both this and future lives, aristocrats and members of the royal family handed over to Buddhist monks enormous estates along with their peasant farmers. No doubt this increased agricultural output through

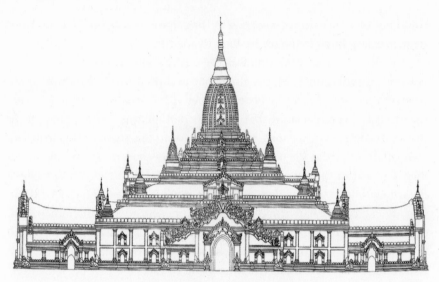

The Ananda temple's elevation

the reclamation of marginal land and increased craft production through a concentration of manpower, but the new prosperity did not directly benefit the royal exchequer because it was tax-exempt.

Of the 10,000 brick structures that once surrounded Pagan, the foundations associated with Anawrahta are few. He is supposed to have started in 1059 the Shwezigon, one of the earliest and largest buildings: its three square terraces are believed to be his work, although Kyanzittha certainly added the drum. *The Glass Palace Chronicle* relates how for the Shwezigon stupa, Anawrahta had tried to get from Sri Lanka a tooth belonging to the Buddha. His ambassadors failed to obtain the relic but were given instead a miraculous duplicate that possessed the faculty to reproduce itself on the voyage back to Burma. When the ship came up the Irrawaddy to Pagan, the king waded into the river up to his neck and bore the casket, containing the duplicate tooth, on his head all the way back to the Shwezigon. By then, there were in fact four teeth.

Mon captions incised on panels depicting the previous lives of the Buddha, and inserted into the walls of the terraces, suggest that the Shwezigon can be attributed to both Anawrahta and Kyanzittha. Mon influence was at its height in Pagan during the residence of King Manuha's family. More than any other building the Shwezigon was the inspiration for later rulers, putting Kyanzittha's own Ananda temple quite in the shade. Named after the Buddha's cousin and favourite disciple Ananda, the golden tower of this magnificent temple rises above brilliant white walls decorated with a series of reliefs celebrating the ministry of the Buddha, while at its centre there are four statues of him in gilded wood. Yet Anawrahta himself remained realistic about his espousal of Theravada Buddhism. He allowed representations of nat spirits to be placed around the Shwezigon because he said: "People will not come for the sake of the new faith. Let them come for their old deities and gradually they will be converted."

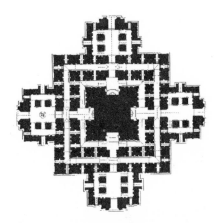

The plan of the Ananda temple

Anawrahta's son Sawlu took a similar view and restored a nat shrine south of Pagan, when he prepared to intercept a rebel Mon army marching up from Pegu. In this hour of peril for the kingdom, Sawlu recalled exiled Kyanzittha and together they faced the rebels, but a crushing defeat resulted in the Pagan king's capture. Kyanzittha risked his life to save him, but was unsuccessful, and the rebel leader Yamankan put Sawlu to death. What annoyed Kyanzittha most about the whole business was how unnecessary the reverse was, because the king had refused to heed his warning about the danger involved in a night attack. The Burman army had stumbled into marshes long before it reached the rebel host.

City of Virtue and Merit

Having refused an offer of the throne because Sawlu was still alive, Kyanzittha went in disguise to the rebel camp and was carrying the king to safety on his shoulders, when Sawlu had second thoughts about his rescuer's motives and wondered if he was being abducted for a foul purpose. After all, both he and his father had treated Kyanzittha badly. So Sawlu cried out that he was being stolen away. In disgust Kyanzittha threw his ungrateful burden aside and plunged into the Irrawaddy to make good his own escape. "Then die, you fool," Kyanzittha shouted, "at the hands of the Mon." Because the rebels were moving northwards to invest Pagan, Kyanzittha was obliged to seek refuge in the Chindwin valley. But Yamankan lacked sufficient strength to take Pagan by storm, and its refusal to surrender meant that he had to get ready for Kyanzittha's counter-attack. Moving further upstream to the locality where Ava was later built, the rebels constructed a fortified encampment and awaited the next move of the Burmans. It was not long coming. Kyanzittha rallied large numbers to his standard and, after conducting rituals pleasing to the nats, he marched against Yamankan, whom he overcame through a tough fight.

Invested in 1084 as the new king of Pagan, Kyanzittha showed at once the restraint that caused him to be recognized as a ruler worthy of this city of religious merit. He announced that the throne should eventually return to Anawrahta's line. So, in due course, he gave his only daughter to Sawlu's son, and when she gave birth to a boy named Alaungsithu, Kyanzittha anointed him king, saying: "My lord, my grandson, this is your throne and I am your servant—a mere caretaker." Kyanzittha told his courtiers how this public act of piety resulted from the timely protection afforded him by an enormous naga when he was a fugitive. That he believed the snake was none other than the saviour god Vishnu should come as no surprise: Theravadan Buddhism was now established strongly enough at Pagan for Hindu and Mahayana ideas to be tolerated without fear of theological complications. In a previous life, Kyanzittha even claimed to have worshipped the Buddha in the company of Thagyamin, king of the nats. One Hindu temple remains standing within the old city walls of Pagan. It may have been a royal place of worship, possibly where Kyanzittha gave thanks to Vishnu, who is depicted lying asleep on the cosmic serpent Ananta. The temple would of course have served Indian merchants living in the capital as well.

Temples at Pagan were designed for worshippers to enter a sanctum that contained one or more statues of the Buddha. Burman architects worked with only two basic ground plans but they achieved an amazing variety of forms. One is based on a solid brick core encircled by a vaulted corridor, while the other has a vaulted inner sanctum, often surrounded by a covered corridor. Kyanzittha's famous foundation, the Ananda

The "Rosetta Stone" of Burma, showing inscriptions
in Pyu on the left and Burmese on the right

temple, possesses a solid core with two encircling corridors, which are
entered from four spacious porches. Half-barrel arches, an innovation
at Pagan, transfer the thrust of the main superstructure across the two
corridors to the earth. For its decoration, especially for the bas-reliefs,
Kyanzittha looked to Mon traditions. It needs to be recalled that at this
time the Mon language was spoken in Pagan.

The exterior symmetry of the Ananda temple remains its distinctive
feature. Each side of the building is perfectly balanced by pediments
that rise to the base of the central tower, a slender golden pagoda. The
principal entrance was probably on the west, as the narrative sculpture
begins on that side. To appreciate the extent of the narrative it is necessary
to walk round the outside of the temple and then along its inner corridors.
Sculptures, bas-reliefs and murals once presented pilgrims with a detailed

Two views of a reclining Buddha at Pagan.
Theravada Buddhism always favoured large statues

account of the Buddha's mission. Though much smaller in scale, the
Ananda temple recalls most closely the purpose behind the construction
of Borobudur, the great stupa erected by the Sailendra dynasty in central
Java. We are fortunate that in 1885 the lower basement of Borobudur was
uncovered: inscribed there was guidance for the sculptors who worked on
its granite blocks from 778 until 824. They were instructed to carve scenes
that touched upon karma, the cause and effect of reincarnation. What the

Sailendra kings wished to show their subjects at Borobudur was the true path each individual must tread to reach buddhahood.

Stupas, such as Anawrahta's Shwezigon, are usually bell-shaped. From the very beginning of the Buddhist faith, they were reserved for relics of the Buddha. Stupas ultimately descend from the memorial tombs of Magadha, as the Ganges valley was called in ancient times. But they were regarded as the very symbol of Buddhism, once this religion spread across Southeast Asia. Because many temples in Burma have been capped with stupa-like superstructures, or at least rounded towers, there tends to be a degree of confusion over stupas and pagodas. And the practice of burying relics inside the fabric of large brick-built temples, either behind or beneath sanctums, only serves to blur any meaningful distinction between their roles.

Besides arranging for the repair of neglected Buddhist monuments in northern India, Kyanzittha was also on good terms with the Chola rulers in the south of the subcontinent. An inscription at Pagan goes so far as to claim that Kyanzittha converted a Chola prince to the teachings of the Buddha by a personal letter written on gold leaves. The Tamil Cholas had emerged as a dominant Indian power during the same period of Pagan's rise to supremacy in Burma. They invaded Sri Lanka, sacked a number

A procession depicted at Pagan

of neighbouring kingdoms, and launched seaborne raids as far away as the Indonesian archipelago. The first confrontation between the Cholas and the Srivijayans, whose Sumatra-based trading empire controlled the Straits of Malacca, may have taken place in 1017, to be followed by a bigger attack on Srivijayan ports in 1025. A third Chola offensive occurred in the 1070s. These expeditions are testimony of a formidable navy that turned the Bay of Bengal into a Chola lake, until overstretch allowed their enemies in India to eclipse the Cholas in the twelfth century.

By Kyanzittha's death in 1112, Pagan was unchallenged and subject rulers accepted both its political and religious authority. On his deathbed Kyanzittha was moved by the pious attitude of his son Yazakumar, who at the king's request had already agreed to relinquish the throne. Not only did he graciously accept the elevation of his cousin, the young Alaungsithu in his stead, but even more he dedicated his own estates to assist with Kyanzittha's accumulation of merit. An inscription in four languages—Mon, Pyu, Burmese and Pali, the language of Theravada Buddhism—explains how Yazakumar honoured Kyanzittha one year after his father passed away. Often called the "Rosetta Stone of Burma", their parallel rendering of the dedication has proved invaluable for the decipherment of Pyu. That this proto-Burman language was employed at all, affirms the continued existence of the Pyus in the kingdom of Pagan. Even though Sriksetra may have been reduced to a ruin, Pyu cultural influence was far from extinguished.

The merit gained by temple building, either through commissions from the king or members of the royal family, was always considered to be in the national interest; because royal merit could be shared by all. Yazakumar is quite explicit about this intention at the close of his inscription: it records his desire for "the attainment of divine wisdom". He even threatens his descendants with ignorance, if they neglect the maintenance of his inscription. "Let none of them ever see the Buddha."

In the same manner Alaungsithu, the grandson of Anawrahta and Kyanzittha's successor, raised works of merit wherever he went. *The Glass Palace Chronicle* relates how sailing from Bassein, he visited the Malayan peninsula, Arakan and Bengal. Possibly his long periods of absence from Pagan engendered a bitter rivalry between his sons, left kicking their heels in the empty palace. As Alaungsithu grew old and travelled less frequently, he could not but notice the unpleasantness at court and settled on Narathu as his successor. It proved to be an unwise choice. From his earliest years the tutor-monk Panthagu had been fearful of this prince's destiny. Everything he taught him, Narathu already seemed to know: a ready understanding that made it impossible for Panthagu to tell what the young prince really thought about anything.

When the eighty-one-year-old Alaungsithu fell gravely ill in 1167, Narathu believed his moment had come. Quickly he removed his unconscious father to the Shwegu temple, Alaungsithu's favourite place of worship. Narathu must have believed that the king would soon die there, but in the quiet stillness of the temple he regained his strength and demanded to know why he was not in the palace. Hearing of this unexpected improvement, Narathu hastened to his father and secretly smothered him with a blanket. During Alaungsithu's funeral, however, there was a definite sign that mischief had been done: light broke out of the earth where the king's body was being cremated. Now certain about what had happened, Narathu's oldest brother arrived in Pagan but, before he could expose the patricidal prince, he succumbed to poison himself. Enthroned, Narathu discovered that he was unloved by his subjects, while

The brooding presence of the Dhammayan temple

Burmese court ladies

to his face Panthagu said: "No greater baseness and shame has ever been joined in a single human being than you. All your deeds are accursed!" Taken aback though he was by this denunciation, the new king did not dare to harm the venerable monk, who quit the kingdom for Sri Lanka.

Desperate to end his unpopularity and deal with his own guilt, Narathu heeded the advice of the nat Mahagiri, whose shrine he had visited on Mount Popa. The nat informed Narathu that this was the second occasion on which he had been born a king and committed an evil deed. The only way to improve his karma, and avoid yet another repetition of such a fate, was to "build a great temple in honour of the Enlightened One and ignite the Light of Holy Truth". So it was that Narathu raised the Dhammayan, the largest of all Pagan's temples. Yet he found no peace of mind during its building and his courtiers believed the king to be possessed by a demon nat. Everyone lived in fear of his mood swings, often accentuated by bouts of heavy drinking.

It was therefore a relief when, in 1170, Narathu fell victim to assassins sent by the king of Pateikkaya, whose daughter had been executed for showing Narathu insufficient respect as one of his queens. Having generously provided for the families of eight of his palace guards, the Pateikkaya ruler dispatched these men to Pagan in order to avenge his daughter's killing. Disguised as brahmins, the assassins gained access to the throne room. They approached Narathu with their hands outstretched in benediction, until they were close enough to draw the daggers concealed under their robes and slay the king. Once the mission was accomplished, they killed each other where they stood.

The pyramidal Dhammayan temple remains enigmatic, a brooding presence that cannot be ignored today in Pagan. For as Panthagu predicted, "the people will shun the temple and creep past it fearfully, remembering the builder's evil deeds". Some Burmans maintain that, in the 1760s, the inner corridor was filled with rubble at the instigation of a hermit monk in order to trap the evil spirit that had possessed Narathu. Two other suggestions concerning this unprecedented action are both unsatisfactory. The first would explain the desecration as the consequence of a Sri Lankan raid in 1165, arising from a Burman prohibition on the export of elephants. Sri Lankan naval forces sailing all the way up the Irrawaddy seems hardly more plausible than the second idea that it was the Mongols who picked out the Dhammayan temple for special treatment. The legendary tamer of the resident demon therefore seems the best candidate, especially if the monk persuaded apprehensive villagers to assist him by carrying great quantities of rocks and stones to the temple.

Pagan's Fall

The Sinhalese version of the raid actually plays down its impact on Pagan. Of a fleet that set sail only six ships reached Burma, as the rest were driven off course by winds and landed on other shores. The warships that reached Lower Burma inflicted damage mostly around Bassein, where soldiers were killed, villages burned, and captives enslaved. "Trees were smashed," a chronicle relates, "like the rampage of drunken elephants." A telling comment in the light of the reason for the conflict, the refusal of Pagan to export these creatures any longer. What King Parakrambahu of Sri Lanka

A remorseful Narapatisithu started building the Gadawpalin temple,
but it was completed by his successor in the 1210s

intended by the seaborne attack was a warning that the cordial relations
between the community of monks in his own kingdom and its counterpart
in Burma could not be taken as a guarantee of international accord.

Although a Mongol invasion usually is said to have been responsible
for Pagan's downfall, the kingdom was in decline throughout the
thirteenth century. The unimpeded growth of monastic property, already
in excess of 60 per cent of the cultivated land in Upper Burma, had the
effect of reducing tax revenue as well as the pool of manpower available
to Pagan kings. So short of soldiers was Narathu that he had to press
monks into armed levies, regardless of their vow to spill no blood. In the
name of Buddhist purification, the throne did from time to time remove
unsuitable monks and recover control over their land, but these purges

failed to restore royal finances, so that kings progressively lost the ability to reward courtiers and commanders, upon whose loyalty they ultimately depended.

In 1170 Narathu's son Naratheinkha briefly became king. His reign was as short as that of his father's because, like Narathu, he could not control his passions. *The Glass Palace Chronicle* relates how on seeing the beautiful wife of his brother, Naratheinkha "trembled so much that he was unable to stand upright". Sending his brother Narapatisithu away on a false errand, the king seized his sister-in-law and raised her as his queen. Once Narapatisithu learned of this, assassins rode to Pagan to slay his wayward brother. Yet a short temper was equally characteristic of Narapatisithu, who ordered the execution of Anantathuriya, Naratheinkha's tutor. In one of the most celebrated poems in Burmese literature, the condemned man accepted death without rancour, and declared how the new king

The Htilominlo temple

was blameless, since his present fate was nothing more than the effect of karma, the sum total of Anantathuriya's own past actions. "Danger and death are constant foes and in this world must ever be so." Though in no hurry to pass to another existence, Anantathuriya acknowledged that he could not progress beyond his current condition without undergoing a rebirth. "Mortals last not and fall away. It is the law," he wrote, because all were subject to the endless round of reincarnation.

When the poem was read aloud in court, and Narapatisithu grasped the profound wisdom it expressed, he commanded, "Set him free." But the executioners told the king that the deed was already done. Blaming them for not showing him the poem first, he condemned the executioners to death as well. Then the king told his courtiers that in future no man should be slain, no matter how angry he might appear, until one month had lapsed. "Let him die," Narapatisithu said, "only when he ought to die. If he ought to live, release him at that time."

Afterwards, a remorseful Narapatisithu embarked on an unprecedented programme of religious construction. At Pagan he built the Gadawpalin and Sulamani temples, while another eleven are credited to him elsewhere in Upper Burma. Described as the most refined of Pagan's temples, the Gadawpalin temple is situated close to the Irrawaddy, within the old city walls; its slender pagoda recalls a rocket about to lift off from its launch pad. Begun by Narapatisithu but finally completed by his successor Nantaungmya in the 1210s, the Gadawpalin contains four monumental images of the Buddha and possesses miniature stupas on its terraces. Although an earthquake in 1975 unfortunately damaged the stucco, some of the original wall paintings are still intact.

On his deathbed a seventy-four-year-old Narapatisithu had enjoined his sons to rule with mercy and justice, living peacefully together after he passed away. His wish was answered to the extent that they accepted the youngest son Nantaungmya as the king without protest. It helped that Nantaungmya preferred to pray at a pagoda than rule the realm, thereby delegating all decisions to his older brothers. He was also called Htilominlo, "he whom the umbrella chose as king", because a white umbrella had confirmed his elevation by miraculously inclining towards him. While his brothers happily directed the council of ministers on his behalf, Nantaungmya continued the temple-building programme started

Some of the surviving temples at Pagan today

by his father. Nantaungmya's even more pious son took even less interest in government, but a shortage of funds meant that he had to be content with memorising the scriptures rather than building more temples.

Pagan's penultimate king was Uzana, who unashamedly enjoyed the pleasures of life, and was content to marry country girls. One of his favourite queens was a peasant woman whom he encountered in 1250 when ascending Mount Popa to hold the annual Mahagiri festival. Worship here may well go back to Tagaung times because legend associates sculptures on its summit with one of its kings. Because this ruler is supposed to have feared the strength belonging to Nga Tin De, the son of a local blacksmith, he persuaded his queen to invite this man to Tagaung. Trusting in the judgement of the queen, who happened to be his sister, Nga Tin De fell into the king's trap and was burned alive. So upset by the treachery was the queen that she stepped into the same fire, made intensely hot with great bellows. The incinerated brother and sister then combined as the nat Mahagiri, an appropriate reincarnation because Mount Popa is in fact the core of an extinct volcano. Respect for this spiritual occupant of Mount Popa is by no means over today. When in 1955 there was seepage from a newly constructed dam in the vicinity, the Burmese government offered prayers to Mahagiri until the problem disappeared, even after heavy rain.

Uzana's delight in hunting sealed his fate in 1254, when a wild elephant trampled him to death. Whether a similar pleasure in drinking contributed to the fatal accident we do not know, but somehow the king slipped to the ground. *The Glass Palace Chronicle* simply states that the cornered elephant ripped through the girth ropes securing the royal saddle.

Pagan's last ruler Narathihapate, the son of Uzana by a concubine, was placed on the throne by ministers unwilling to countenance the elevation of the heir apparent. The lack of respect shown by this prince to these high officials persuaded them that he would be unbearable as a king. That such an action could happen at all is an indication of the weakened authority of the royal house. So insecure did Narathihapate feel that he seriously considered stopping the construction of a temple because a rumour circulated to the effect that its completion would coincide with the kingdom's collapse. On the day of its dedication "a covered way was built from the palace to the pagoda. Beneath it bamboo mats covered in cloth were laid as a pathway fitting for the royal family and the nobility". Although little enthusiasm greeted the event, the degree of indifference never approached the scale of that shown at the Dhammayan temple's dedication, Narathu's infamous construction. But it was not temple building that would bring trouble to Pagan, for the king's execution of ambassadors sent by Kubilai Khan provoked the Mongols to invade Burma. Narathihapate had ordered their deaths because these men refused to take off their shoes sufficiently often. In vain did his ministers recommend that, instead of turning the Mongols into an unnecessary enemy, the king should protest to Kubilai Khan about the patent lack of ceremony.

The Mongol attack has been colourfully described by Marco Polo, who provides a detailed, though perhaps not entirely accurate, account of the battle of Ngasaunggyan. The Venetian traveller would have heard about it during his time as an official in Kubilai Khan's court. To block the Mongol advance, Narathihapate assembled his forces at a strategic point on the route that the invaders would have to take to reach Pagan. Marco Polo writes that their numbers were enormous because the king was determined that "the Great Khan should never feel inclined to send another army to Burma". Notable were "two thousand large elephants, on each of which was set a wooden castle of great strength, carrying from twelve to sixteen soldiers".

Elephants were important on the battlefield because of their psychological effect, especially when directed against opponents unfamiliar with Southeast Asian warfare. At Ngasaunggyan, the horses of the Mongols took such fright at the sight of the elephants that they simply would not face the Pagan forces. Besides the sheer bulk of the elephant, it could be made to trumpet, unleashing a furious and frightening noise.

To deal with the elephant corps, which formed the vanguard of an army of some 40,000 men, the Mongol general swiftly adopted new tactics. His own numbers amounted to no more than 12,000 horsemen. Having tethered their unsettled horses in a nearly forest, the Mongols advanced across open ground on foot and showered the elephants with arrows. "Within a short space of time the advancing elephants were all badly wounded." Marco Polo continues:

> When the elephants felt the smart of the arrows that pelted them like heavy rain, they turned in flight towards the king's men in such a turmoil that it seemed as if all the world were tumbling to bits. They did not stop till they reached the trees and then plunged in and smashed their castles and wrecked and ruined everything... When the Mongols saw this, they did not lose a moment, but sprang to horse and charged down upon the king's army. They began their attack with arrows, and a deadly onslaught it was, for the king and his men put up a stubborn resistance. When their arrows were used up, they set hands to swords and clubs and laid about them lustily, dealing mighty blows... So loud was the tumult and uproar that the thunder of heaven would have gone unheard.

Firearms would later reduce the effectiveness of elephants, because of the terror caused by the sounds and flashes of guns. Artillery most disturbed these great creatures: no amount of training could overcome their fright. It is clear, however, that the discomfiture of the Burman army at Ngasaunggyan was not decisive, because in the following year Kubilai Khan ordered a second campaign. Narathihapate is said in *The Glass Palace Chronicle* to have pulled down hundreds of pagodas to improve the defences of Pagan but when, in 1287, the Mongols eventually arrived in strength, the king fled the city. Having lost whatever prestige he had left, one of Narathihapate's sons exploited the popular sense of outrage to poison the fugitive king. Marco Polo claims that the Mongols did not loot or burn Pagan on the express orders of Kubilai Khan, who is supposed to have spared its religious buildings because he appreciated how previous kings had built them for the welfare of their souls. "And this is not surprising," he adds, "for the good reason that the Mongols never touch the property of the dead."

Marco Polo is quite mistaken about Mongol attitudes. Genghis Khan was careful not to antagonize other people's deities, but the looting of tombs gave him no concern at all. The secret location of his own grave indicates how he expected no privileged treatment himself after death. His grandson Kubilai Khan had few scruples either: he allowed the pillage of Chinese imperial tombs to make up the shortfall in government revenue caused by his expensive foreign wars. In spite of claims that it ended amid blood and flame, the brief Mongol occupation of Pagan was not heavy-handed for contemporary paintings of Mongol horsemen by local artists reflect curiosity rather than shock. They were simply the new overlords. That a diminished state survived at Pagan into the fourteenth century is apparent from new monastic donations. Yet it was the Mongols who paved the way for Pagan's fall, because their conquest of nearby Nanzhou freed Thai chieftains from any restraint, with the result that the Shan overran Upper Burma and the Thai pressed Angkor hard. Most destructive of all were the Shan invasions from 1359 until 1368. The extensive damage to stupas and pagodas evident at present-day Pagan was either the work of Shan tribesmen then, or marauding soldiers during the unsettled years of the seventeenth and eighteenth centuries.

2

EARLY CAMBODIA

Rice can be harvested three or four times a year, the reason being that all four seasons are like our fifth and sixth months, with days that know no frost.

Zhou Daguan's Record of Zhenla

At the start of 2003, Thailand's embassy was ransacked and set ablaze by Cambodian protestors angered at a Thai television star's assertion that the Angkor temples rightfully belonged to Thailand. Southeast Asian newspapers carried photographs of a portrait of Thailand's King Rama IX being trampled underfoot and the burning of the Thai flag. The authorities did not bother to step in when the violence spread to Thai-owned businesses in Phnom Penh. Anger had been simmering for days in the Cambodian capital over the Angkor claim and it boiled over with a rumour of attacks on Cambodian residents in Bangkok.

Thailand issued an ultimatum: either the Cambodian government protect Thai nationals or a commando unit would be sent to restore order in Phnom Penh. Although this threatened action became unnecessary once the police regained control of the capital's streets, the Cambodian premier made no apology but said of the offending starlet that "her life is not worth a patch of grass around Angkor Wat". Relations between Thailand and Cambodia only improved with payment for the damaged property, which Thai businessmen were advised by their own government not to exaggerate in compensation claims. Settlement still cost Cambodia, nonetheless, 8 per cent of its foreign currency reserves.

For Cambodians the very idea that Angkor does not form part of their heritage is unthinkable. Today Cambodia is a small country, covering a mere 180,000 square kilometres, but at the height of Angkor's power it embraced not only the lower Mekong valley which has been absorbed into Vietnam, but also large parts of present-day Thailand as well as southern Laos. Yet the furore in 2003 arose from more recent events than any denial of early greatness. Cambodians had not forgotten it was Thai pressure in 1431 which caused the capital to shift from Angkor to Lovek and, later, Phnom Penh; nor that it was Thai cooperation with the Japanese in the run up to the Second World War that caused the temporary loss of their western provinces, including the site of Angkor. Not until 1947 were they returned to Cambodia.

Pre-Angkor history remains far from clear. The earliest documented states in Southeast Asia arose in the lower reaches of the Mekong river and along the southern coasts of Cambodia and Vietnam, where they profited from maritime trade between India and China. Prior to the development of different sailing routes touching upon Indonesian ports, they were the most prosperous polities. Their subsequent decline may have given the Khmers, as the early Cambodians are known, an opportunity to expand towards the coast and take them over. The Khmers were essentially an agricultural people with little interest in the sea or international commerce, although their economy benefited from regular injections of war booty. Above all, their wealth derived from the abundant rice crops that the rich alluvial soils and plentiful waters of the Mekong so readily sustained. Such is the volume of water flowing down this river during the monsoon that it raises by many metres the level of the Tonle Sap, the inland lake adjacent to Angkor. After the rainy season is over, the Tonle Sap resumes its former condition leaving large areas of fertile soil around its shores awaiting the planting of rice.

Funan

The most important maritime state occupied by the Khmers was Funan, whose Southeast Asian name is unknown. Because no inscription gives any clue as to what it was called, the Chinese designation for this kingdom is used. Located on the Mekong quite close to modern Phnom Penh, its capital in Sanskrit was named Vyadhapura, "the city of hunters". It was linked by a canal some 90 kilometres in length to a port at Oc Eo, which

A rather stiff representation of Vishnu from Funan

acted as an emporium and was defended by palisaded ramparts and a moat sporting crocodiles.

Funan's active involvement with international commerce was fully appreciated in China, which sent during the 240s ambassadors who noted the wealth of the kingdom. "Many of their cups and plates are silver," we are informed, "while taxes are paid in gold, silver, pearls and perfumes." Already Indian influence was apparent in the script which resembled "the characters used by Central Asians". Later Chinese envoys were more explicit about the Indian connection, reporting "numerous brahmins who have come in search of riches... and Buddhist monasteries with both monks and nuns". The favour enjoyed by brahmins at the Funan court resulted from the wholesale import of religious and political ideas from the subcontinent. As in the Indonesian archipelago, where rulers were to espouse Buddhism as well as Hinduism, monks and priests became advisers on court ritual, besides acting as astrologers and scribes. All this activity must have shaped Funan's foundation myth of a brahmin's

In spite of a preference for Vishnu in Funan, this linga celebrates Brahma, Shiva and Vishnu

election as the first king. It tells how a certain Kaundinya led the resistance on an Indian merchant ship to an attack by a female pirate chief, whom the Chinese called Liu Ye, "Willow Leaf". Afterwards, Liu Ye married the brave brahmin, but only after he had drunk the local waters. The couple then established a kingdom based on Indian lines.

The Khmers inherited this myth but with slight modifications. They came to believe that a local dragon-princess had paddled out to greet the brahmin, who fired from a magic bow an arrow into her boat so that she agreed to marry him. Before the wedding ceremony, Kaundinya gave the dragon-princess clothes to wear and in exchange her father, a mighty dragon-lord, enlarged her dowry by drinking up the water that covered the land. He also built them a fine capital and changed the name of the country to Kambuja. It is tempting to see in the story of a blessing from an existing overlord the origin of the water-control schemes that were needed to sustain cultivation at Angkor, in the drier interior. The dragon-lord's lowering of the flood waters patently recalls the annual rise and fall of the Tonle Sap, an agricultural lifeline that was supplemented by the digging of massive reservoirs around the Khmer capital.

The early supremacy of Funan in international trade also depended on its agricultural resources. Prior to ships passing through the Straits of Malacca, cargoes were transported overland across the narrow Isthmus of Kra in southern Thailand. Merchants then boarded other vessels, sailing along the coastline of the Gulf of Thailand until they reached Funan. Whereas the land at Kra was heavily forested and its soils unsuited to intensive cultivation, Funan's alluvial soil could grow rice without irrigation. Regular surpluses were thus able to feed large numbers of merchants and seamen in Funan, while they waited for a change in the monsoon pattern of winds. Though they might have had to stay a couple of months, the system of winds provided a swift and reliable means of sailing to China from July onwards.

Yet this geographical advantage was not destined to last. Chinese envoys at Funan learned of ports on the great island of Sumatra, where a rival network for the India-China trade was already in existence. By the seventh century the inevitable had happened—the decline of Funan's prosperity led to its conquest by the Khmer kingdom of Zhenla. A Chinese source recounts how "Zhenla was formally a vassal of Funan, but Zhenla overran and subdued it".

That Funan embraced more than Hinduism is evident in this sculpture of Avalokitesvara, the Buddhist epitome of mercy and compassion

The take-over of Funan should perhaps not be regarded as an outright attack. Rather it may have represented no more than a change of dynasty, because Funan contained Mon-Khmer speakers in addition to seafarers from the Indonesian archipelago. Since they spoke Khmer or related languages, a new Khmer king would have meant very little to the majority of its inhabitants. Quite likely the Funan population felt attracted to the emerging Khmer civilization and opted to join it.

For the other residents of Funan the situation was not so simple as that facing the Mon and the Khmer. But their gradual departure from Oc Eo was not the result of politics but a marked absence of trading vessels. These Austronesian speakers had begun to disperse from the Yangzi delta around 3000 BC, settling in all the Southeast Asian islands as well as Taiwan. A substantial number of them founded the kingdom of Champa in what is now central Vietnam. Its Indianized kings claimed descent from a more illustrious figure than the brahmin Kaundinya: their forbear was none other than Bhrigu. In the *Mahabharata*, India's longest epic poem, Bhrigu officiated at his fellow seer Daksha's sacrifice to Vishnu. An uninvited Shiva tore into the worshippers with a violence that left gods and goddesses injured. Bhrigu himself was lucky just to lose his beard. The catastrophic event ensured that Cham kings were always careful to include Shiva in all their sacrifices. Given that the Chams spoke an Austronesian language, they could communicate more easily with traders sailing from Sumatra and Java, a circumstance that may well have contributed to Funan's final withdrawal from seaborne commerce.

Zhenla

The name Zhenla, used by the Chinese to describe Cambodia, remains unexplained. No Sanskrit or Khmer word sounds remotely like it. Another reason for uncertainty is that initially the Chinese distinguished between two Zhenlas, one located in the Mekong delta and the other upriver, perhaps near present-day Wat Phu in southern Laos. According to a Chinese record, the capital of inland Zhenla was near "a mountain, on the summit of which a temple stood, always guarded by a thousand soldiers". Here each year "the king himself came to conduct a human sacrifice during the night". The indigenous spirit to whom the bloody offering was made eventually became identified with Shiva, whose early popularity can be traced to an association with earthly and ancestral deities, the nak ta. This was strengthened during the Angkor period by the identification of Shiva with the monarch. As late as 1877, human sacrifices to Shiva's consort, the goddess Uma, still took place in Cambodia at the start of the agricultural cycle.

Ancestral spirits of place, the nak ta are a survival of pre-Indian beliefs. Their propitiation has always been the province of specialist mediums, as elsewhere in Southeast Asia, although spirits dwelling close to villages and towns do communicate directly with the ordinary people. They are believed to inhabit trees, mounds and stones. Most feared are the nak ta found in deserted places or dense forests, where they suffered violent deaths. Though spirit shrines are sited throughout Cambodia, and often possess sculptures of a particular nak ta, the level of cultic attention does not compare to that paid in Burma to the nats. There is no equivalent of Thagyamin, the supreme Burmese spirit.

The gods of Zhenla were then a mix of Indian deities and indigenous spirits. From the start of inscriptions in the seventh century, Sanskrit was employed for religious purposes: it spoke to the heavenly gods in verse.

Mainland Southeast Asia around 1220

Khmer, on the other hand, remained the language of the people and used prose to announce royal decisions, keep track of temple administration, and stipulate the duties of peasants and slaves.

Buddhism did not come to dominate the religious outlook of Cambodia until after the abandonment of Angkor, where the greatest temples are Hindu. Some are Buddhist, but not of the Theravada school, which only reached Angkor in the period of its decline. The most famous Buddhist monument is the Bayon, built by King Jayavarman VII in the 1190s, after his defeat of the Chams. As yet, there is no firm agreement as to the Buddhist doctrines that inspired its construction. The central image is a portrait of the monarch as the Buddha, sheltered beneath the umbrella-like hood of Muchalinda. This gigantic serpent had facilitated the attainment of enlightenment by preventing the Buddha from being disturbed during a frightful storm. Yet we cannot assume that the Bayon's message is the triumph of Buddhism over the Hindu pantheon because its decoration comprises bas-reliefs depicting historical events rather than the usual subjects of Indian mythology. All that can be deduced is an interest in everyday scenes akin to those carved at Borobudur in central Java. For the Bayon, however, we lack the key available for the great Javanese stupa, whose sculptors were instructed to illustrate karma, the trigger for the endless round of rebirth.

The political make-up of Zhenla was in fact more complicated than the Chinese realized. Instead of two main states, there were several principalities gathered in a loose alliance under the most powerful ruler, whose kingdom was probably located near the Tonle Sap. After this king's death, yet another powerful leader named Isanavarman established a kingdom that stretched across the Mekong and reached the coast, absorbing lands once belonging to Funan. His was the first Khmer embassy to be sent to China in 616.

This ascetic's head recalls the "divine yogi" Shiva, the Hindu deity with whom Khmer kings associated themselves

The final seventh-century king of note was Jayavarman I, whose mother was related to Isanavarman's family. He tightened control over vassal princes, supervised religious foundations, strengthened the legal code, and appointed to important posts men from outside the royal family. An administration had emerged that required the direction of a determined ruler, a trait that the king possessed in abundance according to inscriptions describing him as "the living incarnation of victory, the scourge of his enemies, lord of the lands he inherited from his ancestors, and conqueror of yet more lands". A further inscription describes how Jayavarman I's court included brahmins. One of their sons was awarded the governorship of an outlying part of the kingdom, whose dense forests were the refuge of savage rebels. Through his restoration of peace there, the brahmin's son opened the way for the appointment of his family to high office. A younger brother was successively commander of the royal guard, custodian of the royal regalia, chief of the rowers and, last but not least, a provincial governor supported by a force of a thousand soldiers.

From the time of Jayavarman I onwards the ruler claimed authority over all Khmer speakers as well as other peoples like the Mon who were resident within his kingdom. It was a claim publicly demonstrated at the close of the eighth century by Jayavarman II, when he moved his court to Angkor.

The Founding of Angkor

Because Jayavarman II and his son, Javarman III, left no inscriptions of their own, a degree of scepticism has arisen about the roles they played in founding Angkor. Information gleaned from later accounts of their activities reveal how they shifted the kingdom's centre of gravity to the northern shore of the Tonle Sap, not far from the site of that monumental city. What cannot be in doubt, however, is the connection between the choice of location for their capital and the devaraja rite.

This solemn acknowledgement of a devaraja (often translated as "god king" but probably not meaning that the king was seen as a god) began in 802 with Jayavarman II on Mount Mahendra, present-day Phnom Kulen to the northwest of Angkor. Not until the 980s would Yasovarman I be acknowledged as such on a hill at Angkor itself, then laid out within a three-kilometre square. One text relates the details of the ceremony.

> A brahmin full of zeal, employing his knowledge and experience in divine matters, brings together the essence of the scriptures, and then, for the well-being of the world, he performs the success-ensuring ritual of the devaraja.

Justification for this ceremony derives from the political ideas of Manu, a Hindu lawgiver who lived in the third century. Then Manu not only confirmed the caste system as the ideal method of social organization but, even more, he explained the divine nature of kingship. "Because a king is formed of particles from the great gods," he wrote, "he surpasses all created beings and, like the sun, he scorches eyes and hearts, so that none may look upon him."

The consecration on Mount Mahendra was critical for Jayavarman II. Henceforth he was regarded as a favourite of Shiva, and sharing to some extent in his power. Such a great king would ensure that "the Khmers are no longer dependent on Java". This unexpected reference to the Indonesian island has been explained by a period of residence at the Sailendra court. Conflict over the succession may have prompted the future king to spend a couple of years abroad. He is recorded as returning from Java in 800. Should Jayavarman II have gone into temporary exile, a central Javanese kingdom does not seem a plausible place to stay. Given that the Srivijayans controlled the coastlines of Sumatra, western Java, eastern Borneo and the Malayan peninsula, he could have more easily gone to one of Srivijaya's satellites, before firmly establishing himself on the Khmer throne.

Dynastic succession was never straightforward among the Khmers. The crown did not necessarily pass from father to son, for the good reason that an entitlement to rule could also be claimed through the female line. Indravarman I, who ruled from 877 until 889, did not have any relationship with Jayavarman III or his predecessor Jayavarman II. With flexible rules governing succession, it is hardly surprising that Indravarman I's elevation to the throne was fiercely contested. Chaotic though these arrangements may seem to us now, intense competition among Khmer princes helped to produce a high level of competence in those who managed to become kings. "Invincible" is how Indravarman I described himself: mercy was reserved only for "his enemies who turned their backs in surrender, or who placed themselves under his protection".

Violent struggles between contending members of the royal family caused no dismay to the Khmers, who regarded conflict as a normal part of life. Rulers were expected to compete for hegemony, slaying their opponents without a second thought. Royal swords were always "red with the blood". And with no permanent standing forces, the experience of war was something that every able-bodied man knew at first hand. In an emergency, the great men of the provinces were responsible for supplying troops for royal service. The palace guard formed the core of a Khmer army, but hastily raised and poorly-equipped peasants filled its ranks. This was what Zhou Daguan noticed as a member of a Mongol embassy sent to Angkor in 1296 by Kubilai Khan's successor, Timur. "The soldiers go naked and barefoot. In their right hand they carry a spear, and in the left hand a shield. They have nothing that could be called bows and arrows, body armour, helmets, or the like." Ordinary people were ordered out to do battle, Zhou Daguan adds, "often with no good strategy or training".

Indravarman I had announced his elevation to the throne by the digging of a huge reservoir, 3.8 kilometres long and 800 metres wide, immediately after the coronation. Nothing like this had ever been seen before. His second innovative project was the construction of two temple complexes. The first is known today as Preah Ko, "sacred bull", named after a sculpture of Nandi, Shiva's mount, found within its precinct. The milk-white bull is conspicuous outside the entrances to the god's temples. Preah Ko comprises a group of tower shrines dedicated to

As Zhou Daguan observed in 1296, the equipment of the Khmer soldier was rudimentary

Indravarman's parents, his maternal grandparents, and to the dynasty's founder Jayavarman II and his wife, signalling the special favour bestowed on Khmer monarchs by Shiva. The second temple was the Bakong, the first of the royal shrines set on pyramids that became the hallmark of the Angkor kingdom. This temple was a replica of the world mountain of Hindu mythology, Mount Meru. The axis of the universe and the abode of the gods, Mount Meru's symbolic presence was meant to underline Indravarman I's intimacy with the supernatural realm. As he put it in 881, "the king, like a god, dispenser of riches, has erected a linga named Indresvara, here". Indresvara actually combines the name of the king with a title belonging to Shiva, meaning "lord of all".

It was Indravarman's son, Yasovarman I, who decided to focus Khmer society upon Angkor, known until the fourteenth century as Yasodhapura, "glory-bearing city". Having survived a bitter struggle for the throne, King Yasovarman endowed temples, surrounded Angkor with earthen ramparts, and imported the devaraja ritual from his father's capital. At the latter he honoured his parents by raising a temple, now called Lolei, on an island in the middle of his father's great reservoir, and opened a new road from there to Angkor. East of Phnom Bakheng, Yasovarman I dug an even bigger reservoir measuring 6.5 kilometres long and 3 kilometres wide. Along its southern shore he supported temples dedicated to Shiva and Vishnu, as well as the Buddha.

The reservoirs built by father and son were obviously intended to supplement the annual flooding of the Tonle Sap, which covered an enormous area during the monsoon. According to Zhou Daguan,

> for six months the country has rain, for six months no rain at all. From the fourth to the ninth month it rains every day, with the rain falling in the afternoon. The high water mark of the Great Lake can reach nearly thirty metres, completely submerging even very tall trees except for the tips. Families living by the shore all move to higher ground. But from the tenth to the third month there is not a drop of rain. Only small boats can cross the Great Lake, whose waters are no more than a metre or so deep. Then the families move back down to the shore again.

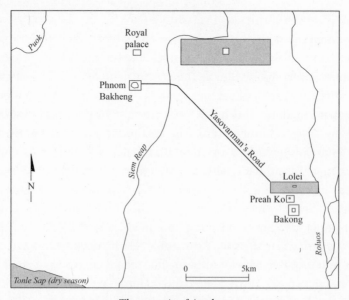

The genesis of Angkor

Once the Tonle Sap resumed its normal level, there was scope for transplanting rice on the recently flooded land, but during the dry season water from artificial lakes and ponds was needed for the paddies. We appreciate now how sophisticated the irrigation system was at Angkor, where run-off water from Tonle Sap's tributaries—the Puok, the Siem Reap, and the Roluos rivers—was retained in swampy areas and then distributed across fields through a network of ditches.

It seems more than likely that effective rice cultivation allowed the Khmer heartland to sustain over one million inhabitants during the reign of Suryavarman II, the builder of Angkor Wat. This early twelfth-century population figure is about half the number of Burmans then living around Pagan in Upper Burma.

The reasons for Yasovarman's relocation of the capital are not explained in any inscription, although the prime motive seems to have been the Phnom Bakheng, a striking but not overwhelming hill standing at the centre of a monumental city. That its name means "Mount Mighty Ancestor" tells us how he envisaged the temple-mountain on its summit to be a constant reminder of his glorious reign, once his remains had been interred within its structure. Thirteen other Khmer rulers copied his example with the result that Angkor was gradually transformed into a city of the semi-divine dead, a baffling practice for Zhou Daguan, who could not discover if "the kings buried in towers... were corpses or just their bones".

China neither designed a capital around the sanctity of a ruler nor gave precedence in its layout to mausoleums. Except for the ancestral temple, the realms of the sacred and the secular were at all times kept firmly apart. While some Chinese emperors were drawn more than others to the spirit world, the this-worldly tenor of Confucian philosophy set the prevailing tone for dealings with the supernatural. As Confucius remarked, "I stand in awe of the spirits but keep them at a distance." While the Khmers incarnated Indian deities in their living kings, the Chinese populated the spiritual realm with bureaucrats. This level-headed approach, which the Vietnamese adopted from China, accounts for their profound disdain for both Cham and Cambodian traditions.

In spite of a bitterly disputed accession, Yasovarman I established the Khmer kingdom as a major power, capable of warding off Cham

A battle scene carved on the outer wall of the Bayon

and Indonesian raids. One inscription mentions a naval victory "over thousands of warships with white sails". We know very little about his two sons who succeeded him, but by 921 a brother of one of the late king's wives had set up a rival city at Koh Ker, some 85 kilometres distant from Angkor. There the usurper raised monuments of enormous dimensions, his own temple-mountain reaching a height of 18 metres, the tallest temple erected in Cambodia with the sole exception of Angkor Wat. The death of Yasovarman I's second son in 928 finally allowed the upstart uncle to be accepted as the legitimate sovereign: he took the title of Jayavarman IV. The colossal self-esteem of this ruler, whose inscriptions assert that Shiva dwelt within him, "the god who is the king", explains the temporary abandonment of Angkor. Not until the 940s would the city become the capital again. One of his nephews, Rajendravarman II, "restored the holy city, long deserted, and embellished its houses with gold, and its palaces with precious stones, like the dwellings of the gods". Following the example of Yasovarman I, the new king built in the middle of the reservoir that this ruler had dug to the east of Phnom Bakheng, a complex of towers dedicated to the memory of his parents. As was usual practice for Khmer royalty, they were represented by statues of Shiva and the goddess Uma.

With the deaths of Rajendravarman II in 968 and his son Jayavarman V in 1001, the first era of Angkor's kingship ends. The strength of Hindu influence can be judged from the social prestige enjoyed by brahmins, one of whom married Jayavarman V's sister. We are aware of the presence of brahmins, possibly of Indian descent, from the inscriptions they left in temples. Yet, as far as we can tell, the Indian caste system was never introduced, possibly because high Khmer officials were also attracted to the more democratic teachings of the Buddha.

The Great Kings

The society that Khmer kings ruled was fundamentally agricultural. And they controlled their farming subjects through two administrative networks: one religious, the other secular. In the case of temple lands, which were not automatically tax exempt like Pagan, appointed officials had to satisfy the throne about the proper use of resources, human and animal. Powerful families endowed local temples, often dedicated to the ancestral spirits, whose priests maintained contact with the large temples in Angkor. Through these central religious institutions a proportion of the wealth generated in the provinces was funnelled to the royal exchequer. The king sanctioned each family's control over local temples and, if dissatisfied with their running, he could revoke that authority.

The second network focused on non-temple farming communities which were liable for taxes in kind—labour work and military service. Their lives were also dominated by the great provincial families, but they were at the beck and call of the monarchy, whose demands for manpower could be heavy when temples, reservoirs and embankments were under construction. "Like a father cherished by his children," claimed Jayavarman V, "he dried the tears of his afflicted subjects." That this ruler actually admitted the harsh lot of the peasantry should not be overlooked; well might farmers acknowledge how prosperity was guaranteed by their semi-divine kings, but they also knew the extent of their own efforts in bringing it to fruition.

Khmer rulers were more careful in their handling of the aristocracy. They had to keep the great landowners on their side by the bestowal of honours and the revenues from newly acquired territory. It is more than likely that almost constant warfare was driven by the need for kings to buy loyalty afresh in every generation. High rank would mean nothing without the means of conspicuous display. Expensive parasols with fringes falling almost to the ground distinguished nobles from the rest of the population. At festivals celebrated nearly every month in Angkor, the cost of lavish entertainment fell upon their purses. According to Zhou Daguan, the New Year was welcomed with incredible extravagance:

> A large stage is set up in front of the royal palace. There is room for over a thousand people. Everywhere there are lanterns and flowers. Facing the stage, on a bank more than a hundred metres away, are tall wooden structures, like the scaffolding used to make a pagoda. They must be over seventy metres high. Every night they put up three or four of these, or five or six of them, and set out fireworks and firecrackers on their tops. The various provincial officials and the great houses cover all the costs.

> When night comes the king is invited to watch, and he lights the fireworks, which can be seen many kilometres away. The firecrackers shake the ground. All the officials and members of the royal family give their share of huge candles and betel nuts, and spend a very great deal. The king also invites foreign envoys as spectators. Things go on in this way for fifteen days before coming to an end.

Lesser events doubtless took place in the provinces, where the peasantry enjoyed a respite from back-breaking work in the fields. Below these free farmers were the enslaved.

Slavery remains a thorny problem because slaves in the Khmer kingdom had many levels of social status, different origins, and a variety of duties. "All family slaves," Zhou Daguan reports, "are savages purchased to work as servants. Most families have a hundred or more; a few have ten or twenty; only the poorest have none at all. These savages are people from the mountains." It was not until a French protectorate was imposed on Cambodia in 1863 that slave raids ceased.

Domestic slaves formed the lowest rank in Khmer society, whether they worked indoors as servants or as labourers in the fields. Above them

An Angkor Wat depiction of Suryavarman II
giving orders to his ministers

was a whole series of gradations that culminated in "temple slaves", who may have enjoyed priestly status. The enslaved at temples could have duties ranging from manual labour to ritually important tasks such as the preparation of food for the gods. There are records of "temple slaves" buying land and even owning their own slaves. Because it was regarded as an honour to enter temple service, well-born women were known to have voluntarily given up their freedom to work in the largest temples. Other Khmers became slaves through poverty: either sold as children by impoverished families or enslaved as debtors when adults.

To what extent was Angkor founded on slavery? No precise answer can be given. In every Southeast Asian country there were slaves, although in Upper Burma their numbers always tended to be small. In Angkor, the free and the enslaved lived together. Yet Zhou Daguan points out how a respectful distance was carefully preserved between Khmer masters and their slaves, who on entering a house "must kneel, join hands in greeting, and bow down to the floor before they can venture forward".

And these servants were "never allowed to sit or sleep indoors". Rulers of course made extensive use of slaves taken in raids as well as prisoners of war: they worked on projects beyond the strength of the Khmers, and especially for Jayavarman VII's reconstruction of Angkor after the water-borne Cham attack of 1177. This king's bloody revenge against Champa and his building programme appears to have imposed a crushing burden on his subjects, already under pressure from the migrating Thai.

Angkor Thom is the present-day name given to the moats and enclosures that Jayavarman VII built to redefine the capital. Despite subscribing to the Buddhist faith himself, the king had to assert in a physical form his entitlement to reign as a divine favourite. Faces of Jayavarman VII as a bodhisattva might decorate the 23-metre-high entrance gateways, and his temple tomb refer to the Buddha rather than Shiva or Vishnu, but the approach to Angkor Thom speaks of Hinduism with gods, nagas and demons carved on balustrades alongside the four main roads. From these traditional representations alone the city derived its cosmic significance. Without this public reference to Hinduism, and by implication to the devaraja ceremony, Jayavarman VII's own ritual circumambulation of the new capital would not have been accepted as that of a king taking rightful possession of both the new city and the old kingdom. The carved balustrades allowed him to integrate Buddhist concepts with Khmer ideas of kingship: a future Buddha's compassion for his subjects explained his occupation of the throne. It was a view of monarchy that the Thai would find most attractive.

Jayavarman VII was the last of the great Khmer warrior-kings. His most illustrious predecessors, Suryavarman I and Suryavarman II, ruled from 1006 to 1049 and from 1113 to 1150 respectively. The first Suryavarman—the royal title means "favoured by the sun god"—was a usurper. He dated his accession to the year 1002, when in fact two rivals also claimed the throne. Inscriptions tell of a civil war in which sacred buildings were damaged before Suryavarman I "seized the kingdom in the midst of a host of other kings". This happened no later than his installation at Angkor in 1009. One new element in his rise to supreme power was patronage of Buddhism, which has led to a belief that some of the temple destruction then arose from religious conviction. Given the inclusive Khmer approach to imported Indian beliefs, it seems incredible that

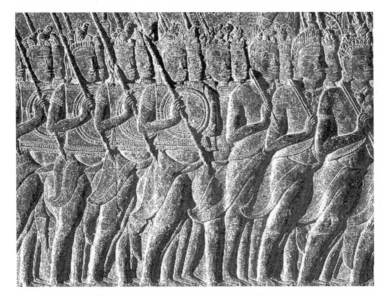

An army of Khmer soldiers and their Thai allies on the march

iconoclasm was ever perpetrated in Suryavarman I's name. The new king had, for a start, powerful allies among the priestly families that dominated Angkor, then a partly depopulated capital. Any disdain that he may have shown towards certain religious establishments was probably the result of political and economic factors: he deliberately punished aristocrats who were slow to side with him by confiscating much of their wealth and curtailing their support of religious foundations.

Suryavarman I's sponsorship of Buddhism in no way interrupted the Hindu-based reverence for kingship. "During his reign," an inscription tells us, "members of the priestly families officiated for the devaraja as before." The king even persuaded a brahmin to give up his priestly duties and marry one of his sisters-in-law. The favoured courtier "restored the temples that had suffered damage when the king led forth his army". Yet the newly installed ruler was so keen on the issue of loyalty that he obliged 4000 officials to publicly swear a solemn blood oath. Its text was inscribed on the walls of a new palace, a key part of which was as follows:

> We officials of the first, second, third and fourth division, cut our hands at
> the moment of swearing in the presence of the sacred fire, the sacred jewel,

the brahmins and the Buddhist monks, offering our lives and our devotion totally to His Majesty Sri Suryavarmandeva, the legitimate king...

If we continue to live in the service of the king, we will die in our devotion to him when the time comes. If a problem arises for His Majesty the King that involves our travelling afar, we will investigate it according to our oath. If there should be one among us who does not keep faith with this oath, let royal punishment chastise him severely. If there are among us any traitors who do not keep faith with this oath, may they be reborn in the thirty-two places of hell forever. If we faithfully keep this oath, may our Sovereign Lord who enjoys absolute legitimate authority, give orders for the upkeep of worthy foundations in our villages and for the support of our families. May we obtain in this world and in the future the just recompense of those who are devoted to their master.

The comprehensive nature of this oath was necessary for Suryavarman I, whose tenuous claim depended on his maternal forbears. What he endeavoured to achieve through it was the prevention of any other prince making a claim to the throne.

Angkor Wat, Suryavarman II's great contribution to the Khmer capital

In the provinces Suryavarman I underlined his authority by erecting linga shrines, situated at the four cardinal points to signal his dominion over the four quarters of the Khmer world. His realm was evidently as extensive as that of his predecessors, since his writ extended to Lopburi in the lower Chaophraya valley. The city appears to have been a provincial centre of administration. Before his accession and after his death, Lopburi asserted its own independence from Angkor, sending diplomatic missions to China requesting recognition as a separate Southeast Asian state. But it was restored to the Khmer kingdom in the 1130s by Suryavarman II. As far as the Khmers were concerned, Lopburi comprised a vassal kingdom of Mon and Thai peoples. Bas-reliefs

A striking portrait of the monkey god Hanuman at Angkor Wat

at Angkor depict the levies that its kings were compelled to send as a reinforcement of the Khmer army. With the waning of Angkor's power, Lopburi once again enjoyed a certain eminence until it was taken over in the fourteenth century by the Thai state of Ayudhya.

Under Suryavarman I Angkor expanded from its heartland in the Mekong valley and round the Tonle Sap to incorporate the Mun valley, north of the Dangrek mountain range. Inscriptions discovered near Ban Khamoy refer to the donation of rice, cloth, slaves, buffaloes and cattle to a Buddhist temple set up by the king. Remains of several reservoirs show that it must have once been a substantial foundation. A further Buddhist complex at Phimai, also now in Thailand, mentions Suryavarman I making an offering of rice for its support. Like the land around the Tonle Sap, farmers growing rice in the area drained by the Mun river relied on seasonal flooding as well as water from artificial lakes and ponds. At Angkor itself, Suryavarman I dug the largest reservoir of all, which still holds a considerable body of water today. Measuring 8 by 2 kilometres, its capacity of 70 million cubic metres was urgently required to sustain a resurgent population. It seems that during his reign there was a marked increase in the numbers living in the kingdom as a whole, so that possibly the Khmer were more numerous than their slaves.

On the death of Suryavarman I in 1049, he received the posthumous title of Nirvanapada, "the king who has gone to nirvana". He was believed to have achieved the goal of all Buddhists; namely, escape from the sufferings involved in the endless round of rebirth. Few of his successors exercised much authority beyond the city of Angkor until, in 1113, Suryavarman II came to the throne by force of arms. Even though he was related to a sister of two previous kings, he had no hesitation in slaying his great-uncle, the aged Dharanindravarman I. Another unifying monarch, Suryavarman II was a young man when crowned. According to one of his inscriptions, he won a crucial engagement against a rival prince by an act of bravery, when "leaving the body of his army on the battlefield... he rushed towards the elephant of his enemy, killing him as a garuda on the slope of a mountain might kill a deadly serpent".

The reference to "the golden sun bird Garuda", the vehicle of the saviour god Vishnu, is telling for Suryavarman II built Angkor Wat, the most spectacular of all Khmer monuments, as a thanks offering to this deity. Angkor Wat's spacious galleries exhibit the chief mythical exploits of Vishnu in a series of bas-reliefs, side by side with representations of the court and the army. Because Suryavarman II envisaged himself as a partial incarnation of Vishnu, rather than Shiva, he arranged for Angkor Wat to be an earthly replica of Vishnu's celestial home, Vaikuntha. A Hindu temple has always been a copy, on a reduced scale, of the heavenly paradise of the god being worshipped.

Because no inscription mentions Angkor Wat, we are ignorant of its original name. Angkor Wat, to present-day Cambodians, means a city turned into a Buddhist monastery. This Vishnu temple remains the most famous of all Angkor's monuments, its outer enclosure measuring 815 by 1,000 metres with a moat 200 metres wide. The main entrance is on the western side, a direction associated with the Hindu god. Apart from the bas-reliefs that refer to Suryavarman II's own reign, the rest are reminders of Vishnu's all-pervading presence: the root of his name, vish, means "to

One of the eighty-eight Hindu gods involved in "churning the ocean"

pervade". Just how potent his powers of preservation and restoration were believed to have been in Angkor is evident in the avatars, or "descents", celebrated by Suryavarman II. "When order, justice, or mortals are endangered," Vishnu remarked, "I come down to Earth." Though devotees of Shiva propose no less than twenty-eight incarnations for their own deity, the avatars of Vishnu hold centre stage in Hindu mythology.

At Angkor Wat, Vishnu appears among other incarnations, as the tortoise Kurma, the boar Varaha, as well as the heroes Rama and Krishna. That on his death in 1150 Suryavarman II received the posthumous title of Paramvishnuloka, "he who has joined the realm of the great Vishnu", can leave us in no doubt as to the function of Angkor Wat. It was a public statement of the king's own divinity and of his close kinship with the gods. After he passed away, his remains were placed in the central tower so that it was transformed into a temple-tomb, a bakong. In 1934 archaeologists recovered an empty stone container from this tower that may have once held Suryavarman's body or his bones. It was placed beneath a statue of Vishnu, where worship of the dead king would have begun as soon as his spirit had entered the stone image.

King Jayavarman VII portrayed as a bodhisattva

Angkor was at the peak of its glory under Suryavarman II. He re-established diplomatic relations with China; extended Khmer influence into what is now northern Thailand, in the west to the border of Pagan, and southwards as far as the Malayan peninsula; and, finally, overran Champa and sacked its capital Vijaya, near modern Da Nang. He even got the better of the Vietnamese, whose kingdom of Dai Co Viet the Chinese had grudgingly accepted as an independent state in the late tenth century. Yet Angkor's supremacy was not to last. The Chams recovered enough strength to assault Angkor itself in a seaborne invasion, sailing up the Mekong river and across the Tonle Sap. Jaya Indravarman V, the Cham king, launched this surprise campaign against the Khmers in 1177. A Chinese source relates how

the king attacked the capital of Zhenla without warning with a powerful fleet, pillaged it, and put the king of Zhenla to death without listening to a single peace proposal. Not surprisingly, these events produced a lasting hatred.

And the "fruit" of this deep hatred "ripened" in 1190, when Jayavarman VII returned the compliment with an equally unexpected and devastating invasion of Champa.

Prince Jayavarman was away from Angkor when he heard that his father had died and a cousin who succeeded him had been killed by a non-royal usurper. Perhaps it was not entirely such a misfortune for the prince that the Cham king Jaya Indravarman V decided to take advantage of the situation and attack Angkor then, for his execution of the usurper left the way open for Jayavarman VII to ascend the throne four years later. Having restored the capital, encircling it with the moat and walls that now constitute Angkor Thom, the new king prepared to wreak vengeance on Champa.

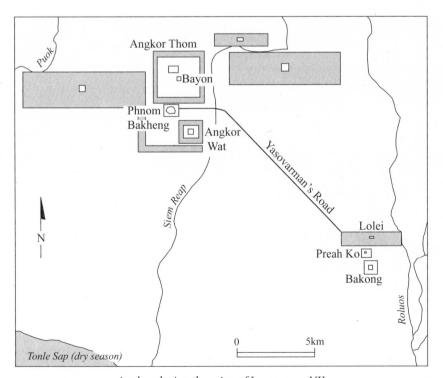

Angkor during the reign of Jayavarman VII

Everyday scenes at Jayavarman VII's Bayon

The walls of Angkor Thom, or "Great Angkor", are about 3 kilometres long on each side, and are pierced by elaborate entrances, which lie at the end of a row of gods and demons engaged in a tug of war using as a rope a nine-headed serpent, or naga. This reference to the myth about the churning of the ocean is unmistakable. In it Vishnu's incarnation as the tortoise Kurma permits the recovery of soma, the elixir of immortality that was lost in the deluge. Without this miraculous drink, neither the gods nor the demons could long survive. Usually the tortoise acts as the support for a mountain around which the gods and demons pull a serpentine rope so as to churn the cosmic ocean, and thereby obtain soma. Characteristically Hindu here is the idea of the interdependence of both sets of immortals: the concern of Vishnu is not to destroy the demons but, on the contrary, to restore them as the necessary opponents of the gods. Their perpetual antagonism, a balance of forces that gives the universe its dynamic, greatly appealed to the Khmers, whose own spirit-haunted world had to be reordered by their semi-divine kings from time to time.

Within Angkor Thom, Jayavarman VII restored the old royal palace and its surroundings, but at its centre he raised the Bayon, his own temple-tomb. It has rather unkindly been labelled "a forest of heads" because the king looks down on his subjects from every direction. But the heavy-lidded eyes signal an inner calm rather than any attempt at surveillance. While Jayavarman VII was an absolute monarch as far as the aristocracy permitted, he was also an ardent Buddhist, a belief he may well have inherited from his father. Besides the gigantic royal heads above the temple gateways, it must explain the Bayon's other extraordinary feature—the fact that instead of depicting incidents from Hindu mythology, the bas-reliefs concentrate on historical events. In addition to battle scenes celebrating Jayavarman VII's victories, subjects cover every aspect of daily life. Ordinary people are depicted buying and selling, gambling, raising children, picking fruit, cooking and eating, fashioning timber, attending the sick, and travelling on foot or in ox-carts.

Less impressive though the Bayon's carvings are than those at Angkor Wat, they do offer a rare insight into Khmer society that is comparable with Zhou Daguan's commentary. In it he wrote of the simplicity of ordinary families:

One of the gigantic royal heads at Angkor Thom

... they have houses but nothing else by the way of tables, chairs, jars, or buckets. They use an earthenware pot to cook rice in, and make sauce with an earthenware saucepan. For a stove they sink three stones into the ground, and for spoons they use coconut husks.

While the poor had only clay utensils, Zhou Daguan notes, the rich used "silver or even gold for everything". Like other Southeast Asian peoples, except for the China-influenced Vietnamese, the Khmers "[ate] rice just with their hands".

Separately Jayavarman VII constructed for Buddhist monks at Angkor three walled enclosures, each surrounded by a moat. Farmers were detailed to support these monasteries whose membership ran to many hundreds. As with other Khmer monarchs, Jayavarman VII paid proper attention to Shiva, Vishnu and other Hindu deities in addition to his personal worship of the Buddha. An inscription at Angkor Thom of the warm welcome given to a brahmin named Hrsikesa, who arrived from Pagan, confirms this. So learned was the newcomer in the Hindu scriptures that the king immediately appointed him chief priest, an office he continued to hold under two other kings. In spite of his own faith, Jayavarman VII was never surrounded by Buddhist prelates, his preferred advisers being brahmins such as Hrsikesa.

In 1203 Jayavarman VII subdued Champa and put his own nominee on the throne. At the same time he incorporated southern Laos into the Khmer kingdom. His territories were linked by roads constructed on embankments a couple of metres high. Without these all-weather means of communication, his troops could not have moved any distance in monsoon rain. Bridges, rest houses and first-aid stations completed the network. But towards the close of his reign signs of decline were already apparent; the burden of incessant warfare and construction work was beginning to take its toll on the Khmer people.

From Angkor to Lovek

After the death of Jayavarman VII in 1218, later kings found it impossible to maintain the unity of the kingdom, and as early as 1220 troops had to be withdrawn from Champa. Worse was to follow as the incoming Thai pressured the northern and western frontiers, causing the abandonment of one province after another. The arrival of Zhou Daguan in 1296, as a member of a Mongol mission sent to collect tribute, actually coincided with Angkor's defeat by the small Thai state of Sukhothai, situated to the southeast of present-day Chiang Mai. Zhou Daguan exactly summed up the country's plight: it was "a land ruled by an old man beset with enemies". They proved too much for the elderly Jayavarman VIII, who abdicated in favour of his son-in-law, Indravarman III. The retired ruler lived on in peace, dying at the ripe old age of 104. But he has the distinction of being the last Khmer king to have commissioned a stone building.

The political crisis of the thirteenth century may well have been a factor in the Khmer conversion to Theravadan Buddhism. For the upheaval that affected Southeast Asia in the wake of the Mongol conquest of China, coupled with growing Thai power, must have had an impact on the religious outlook of Angkor. The Thai were already Theravadan Buddhists and their constant success on the battlefield put Hindu-inspired kingship in the shade. If Jayavarman VII really was an ardent Buddhist, it is not difficult to see why Khmer rulers followed his example. He was, after all, the last effective Khmer king.

Spectacular rituals continued to punctuate Angkor's calendar because pomp served to remind its inhabitants of the divinity residing within the monarch's breast. As in other Southeast Asian states, ceremonial was the driving force of court politics and not simply a means of shoring up the power of the throne. The Khmer king still remained at the centre of the universe, albeit on a much reduced scale in Angkor. Zhou Daguan describes the royal procession at one such event.

> Troops march at the head, in front of banners, flags and musicians. Several hundred palace women, wearing flowered cloth and flowers in their hair, follow holding lighted candles, even in broad daylight... Officials and princes ride on elephants topped by red umbrellas. They are followed by wives and concubines of the king in chairs and carriages, or on horseback or elephants. Their umbrellas are flecked with gold. Behind them is the ruler himself, standing proudly on an elephant, sword in hand. The tusks of this creature are covered with burnished gold.

All this was in marked contrast to Beijing where, following Chinese practice, the rare movements of the conquering Mongol emperors outside the palace entailed a general clearance of the streets. Ordinary people were never allowed to look upon the Son of Heaven.

Behind this splendid display there were telltale signs of exhaustion that indicated Angkor's days were numbered. In 1393 the Thai king of Ayudhya, a powerful state established in the lower Chaophraya valley, besieged Angkor and captured the city. By 1431, Thai overlordship was so irksome that the Khmers abandoned Angkor altogether, moving their capital downriver to Lovek, north of present-day Phnom Penh, where one ruler seriously considered Christian baptism as a means of securing military aid from Spain.

3

EARLY VIETNAM

The Vietnamese easily become rebellious and are difficult to control. District officials therefore act with dignity but are careful not to provoke them.

A third-century Chinese visitor

No one living in early Vietnam could have anticipated its present-day shape: the entire southern half of the country was not added until after the conquest of Cham territory beginning in the fifteenth century. Right up to the end, the Indianized Chams fought with such energy that only following the disappearance of several of their kingdoms was it clear how they had acted as a southern barrier to Vietnamese expansion. Once removed, the Cambodians found themselves uncomfortably wedged between the advancing Vietnamese and the newly arrived Thai.

Because of China's own movement southwards we know more about the Vietnamese than any other Southeast Asian people. Only the ancient Greeks and Romans rivalled China in their concern for history. Dynastic chronicles and accounts left by Chinese visitors provide a means of piecing together an account of the Red river valley, the core area of Vietnam. Even the name of the country was decided at Beijing. When envoys from the newly founded Nguyen dynasty went there to establish diplomatic relations in 1803, they claimed to represent Nam Viet, the Vietnamese pronounciation of Nan Yue. But Chinese officials objected to this reference to the kingdom of Nan Yue, which a rebellious imperial commissioner had set up in the 190s BC. So they changed the name to Viet Nam. In spite of a certain amount of annoyance at the

Irrigation schemes have always been important
in the Red river valley

time, Vietnam came to be accepted by the Vietnamese as the name of
their country during the colonial period.

Annam, "the pacified south", was first used by the Tang dynasty in the
670s to describe northern Vietnam, then a protectorate at the extreme
south of the Chinese empire. A euphemism for an area subject to internal
unrest as well as external attack, and indeed a backwater in the eyes of
most emperors, Annam remained under China's control until 939.
Within forty years it had persuaded the Song dynasty about the value
of a loyal but independent ally, then called Dai Co Viet. The country's
name combined the Chinese word dai and the Vietnamese word co,
both meaning "great", a clear indication of how the two languages were
being used side by side. So an imperial edict announced that the proper
relationship between the new nation and China was that of an obedient
son and a benevolent father. Annam reappeared in 1164, when the Song
dynasty recognized Ly Anh Tong as ruler of Annam. And it remained the
country's name in Chinese eyes until 1803.

Champa, on the other hand, was a generic name of several coastal kingdoms that developed in central Vietnam from the third century onwards. Ultimately the name Champa derived from a kingdom in the Ganges river valley that is mentioned in the Indian epic the *Mahabharata*. It appears first in Sanskrit inscriptions at My Son, south of present-day Da Nang. This sixth-century use of Champa is by no means understood because the Chams were then divided into several kingdoms, although there is a distinct possibility that it refers to a paramount ruler who was recognized by lesser kings. As far as the Chinese were concerned, the Cham kingdom they acknowledged was Linyi, meaning "forest city". Its origin may have been an uprising in the southernmost part of Chinese territory, but by spreading southwards in central Vietnam, Linyi transformed itself into a powerful state. In 268 its forces were strong enough to raid Chinese holdings, the start of a pattern of aggression that would endure for centuries. When China flexed its muscles, however, Linyi sent tribute like the other coastal kingdom of Funan.

Southern Yue

Peripheral though northern Vietnam might have been to the Chinese empire, there was no sharp ethic or cultural division between the Red river valley and the southern provinces of Guangdong and Guangxi. They were indeed administered as a whole and called Lingnan, meaning "south of the ridges". That the chain of low mountains separating the far south from the rest of China is mentioned at all indicates its late conquest. Not until 210 BC did China's earliest imperial dynasty, the Qin, reach the coastline near present-day Hong Kong. While the southern peoples were still not firmly controlled, they were now irrevocably tied to the empire: except for the Vietnamese who were to achieve independence a thousand years later. Even then, Ngo Quyen, the first Vietnamese ruler, looked northwards for the model of his new kingdom; as an sinicised aristocrat, he could envisage no alternative.

Under early Chinese rule, local Vietnamese leaders were enrolled as members of the imperial administration, a looser system than prevailed elsewhere in the Chinese empire. Their good behaviour must explain the development of this semi-feudal arrangement under the Han dynasty, which replaced the Qin in 202 BC. During the turmoil that accompanied the overthrow of the Qin and the establishment of the Han, an imperial commissioner by the name of Zhao Tuo declared himself the king of Nan Yue, or Southern Yue. The upstart ruler not only displayed total contempt for the new Han emperor and failed to send any tribute to the Chinese capital, but he even refused to stand up when an imperial official travelled south to reason with him. What galvanized Zhao Tuo into obedience, however, was the threat of the standard punishment for rebels: he learned that his entire family, including his parents and near relations, were to be executed if he did not accept Han suzerainty. Zhao Tuo's belated submission was enough to save him, because a greater danger existed on the northern frontier where the Xiongnu had breached the line of the Great Wall. Possibly the Huns who later assaulted the Roman empire, these nomads and their equally ferocious successors always remained China's prime anxiety before the modern era.

The southern frontier never posed such a danger for China. Zhao Tuo's subjects were regarded as "no more than a few tens of thousands, all barbarians, precariously perched between the mountains and the sea, comparable to a single Han commandery". For nearly a century Han emperors left matters as they stood, but civil conflict in Lingnan eventually led to intervention and direct rule. By 110 BC it had become part of the Chinese empire with northern Vietnam divided into three commanderies. Cultural assimilation was the key to China's success in expanding its empire, especially in the southern provinces where a variety of peoples lived. It received positive reinforcement from a legal system that proclaimed everyone was equal and, even more, that the throne was restrained by convention and precedent. At court it was the onerous task of ministers to speak out against inappropriate imperial policies. "If it becomes necessary to oppose a ruler," remarked Confucius, "withstand him to his face, and don't try round about methods." This firmness of principle was the cardinal duty of the imperial civil service and high officials often perished at the hands of impatient emperors, only to be admired for generations afterwards.

Another benefit arising from Confucius' teachings was a balanced view of government. He advocated keeping taxes and labour requirements to a minimum, promoting virtue, and providing assistance to those in distress. In theory at least, a benevolent approach to ruling Chinese

As in the rest of Southeast Asia, the Vietnamese reverence the spirit of the earth

and non-Chinese subjects meant freedom from arbitrary exactions and outright oppression. That it comprised imperial policy in northern Vietnam can be deduced from the opening of schools whose curriculum was based upon the Confucian classics, even though its emphasis on patriarchal lineage jarred with indigenous matrilineal traditions, a feature of many Southeast Asian societies.

There were signs of resistance to the process of assimilation even before the rebellion led by the Trung sisters. An influx of Chinese settlers may have encouraged officials to show less tolerance towards the indigenous way of life; particularly worrying was the absence of stable families. Men between the ages of twenty and fifty and women between the ages of fifteen and forty were therefore ordered to pick a partner. And local officials were ordered to pay the wedding expenses of those too poor to afford them. On a single occasion a thousand marriages took place. Slanted as this account of social progress may appear, the effect of Chinese attitudes on Vietnamese society was far-reaching, not least because it aimed at two things: Chinese-style families and farming communities. Abandonment of a subsistence economy of hunting and fishing was felt to be essential for the integration of northern Vietnam with the rest of China.

Dissent came to a head in the rebellion of the Trung sisters between 40 and 42. An incompetent governor precipitated the crisis by ordering the execution of a Vietnamese aristocrat named Thi Sach, the husband of Trung Trac. Trung Trac—described as having "a brave and fearless disposition"—joined with her sister Trung Nhi in stirring up the nobility in a general uprising that allowed the sisters to proclaim themselves joint queens. But the rebellion was dealt with harshly. General Ma Yuan crushed the rebels and sent the heads of the two sisters to the Chinese capital. A mass surrender to Ma Yuan after the decisive battle shows how far northern Vietnam had changed during the century and a half of imperial rule. Though the rebels were still prepared to follow women leaders as of old, their support wavered when a major reverse occurred. The patriarchal values introduced from China had their effect, a later Vietnamese historian wrote, because "her followers, seeing that she was a woman, feared Trung Trac could not stand up to the enemy and consequently dispersed".

Ma Yuan's Legacy

Ma Yuan's expedition represents a watershed in Vietnamese history. The general realized how different China's climate was to that of Vietnam. Just before his victory over the rebels he noted with dismay the impact of the monsoon. "Rain poured down, vapours rose from the ground, and the heat was unbearable," Ma Yuan said, "and I even saw a sparrow hawk fall into a pond and drown." Clearly what was required here was an administration with clearly defined southern limits. Garrison troops stationed to the south of the Red river valley were likely to suffer from fatal tropical diseases, which explains China's reluctance to occupy any of the lands belonging to the Chams, no matter the regularity of their raids. It also explains why northern Vietnam was destined to remain the centre of political gravity in a country that would eventually extend as far as south as the Mekong delta. The north, the area covered by Ma Yuan's administration, is still today in many respects the political and cultural core of the Vietnamese nation.

Ma Yuan's legacy was a full Chinese administration. The feudal aristocracy ceased to exist and local customs were subordinated to imperial regulation. We are told that

> wherever he passed, the general promptly established prefectures and districts to govern walled towns and their environs, and dug ditches to irrigate the fields in order to feed the people living in those places.

Soldier-farmers were settled to protect officials, whose task was to implement the regulations that would bind the Vietnamese to the Chinese empire. The provision of land gave troops an incentive to put down roots both in an agricultural and social sense. They not only raised crops for themselves but also for their families as increasingly they married local girls. As news spread of Ma Yuan's restoration of order, Chinese immigrants arrived in large numbers, some of whom married into prominent Vietnamese families and formed the basis of a new upper class that replaced the dispossessed feudal aristocracy. Among these educated newcomers was the Ly family from northern China. In the sixth century it produced Ly Bi, the leader of a Vietnamese uprising that seriously challenged Chinese power.

The permanent settlement of Chinese soldiers and civilians had long-term implications for the pattern of land ownership. The indigenous arrangement seems to have been communal with Vietnamese nobles receiving goods in kind from dependent villages. But after Ma Yuan there was a marked tendency, as in contemporary China, towards the concentration of ownership within a rich landlord class. Imperial demands for labour and taxes caused many peasants to sell their land and become tenant farmers. So influential were the great landowners in China that a year before Ma Yuan's expedition, they had prevented the throne from conducting a survey of cultivated land for the purposes of reassessing tax. They could do this because the restoration of the Han dynasty, after a short usurpation, had relied on their support. Even a patriot like Ma Yuan could comment: "In present times, it is not only the emperor who selects his subjects. The subjects select their emperor too."

The tremendous wealth of landowning families has been uncovered by archaeologists in their brick-built tombs in China as well as northern

Confucius, Vietnam's most enduring import from China

Vietnam. That they are identical in structure indicates how quickly sinicisation took place. The people buried in these tombs had settled on the rich plains of the Red river valley with no intention of returning to China. This was now their home.

According to the Han emperor Ling Di, who ruled from 168 to 189, assimilation to Chinese ways among the entire population was sufficient for Vietnamese residents to hold appointments in the imperial civil service. Yet this advancement depended as much on ability as a willingness to collaborate. In the case of Ly Bi, it was his failure to make the grade in 541 that turned him into a rebel. Of course, not all Chinese immigrants were well educated people. Many farmers and artisans were attracted by frontier opportunities; consequently they worked alongside native Vietnamese and within one or two generations spoke the language fluently. And because Chinese immigration was never overwhelming, intermarriage at all levels of society did not destroy Vietnamese traditions. Understanding the Chinese language was essential for the socially ambitious, because study of Chinese literature was a prerequisite for an official career, but there was no reason to give up speaking Vietnamese. As a result, a strong non-Chinese point of view continued to exist.

When Emperor Ling Di died in 198, the Han dynasty was already in disarray, and it was during this chaotic period in China that rebellions broke out in northern Vietnam. The son of a district official, Ou Lien by name, killed the magistrate in the vicinity of modern Hue and declared himself king. Exactly who the rebel leader was remains a mystery, but most of his non-Chinese supporters were the Chams, who had embraced Indian culture. Here was in fact a major line of cultural cleavage: it marked the border between Chinese-style civilization and a civilization

Lao Zi, the founder of Daoism, whose ideas were so
attractive to Din Bo Linh in the tenth century

derived from India. As a result of Ou Lien's successful revolt, the kingdom
of Linyi was founded. Over time this new polity grew strong, extending
northwards to threaten Chinese authority in northern Vietnam and
southwards until it reached the borders of Angkor.

A contributory factor in the emergence of Linyi was the virtual
autonomy of Lingnan, cut adrift from the three kingdoms into which
China had split in 221, after the fall of the Han dynasty. Careful though
the governors of Lingnan were to show deference to the most powerful of
these separate states, nevertheless they had to manage on their own. No
longer could an imperial army led by a second Ma Yuan be expected to
march south in an emergency. During this period of quasi-independence
for northern Vietnam there was almost great family self-rule, a regional
freedom of action that became gradually more pronounced and
culminated in Ly Bi's open rebellion against the imperial government. The
character of the landowning class underwent constant change in response
to dynastic fortunes in China, which from 316 to 588 was divided into
two halves. While the northern provinces were ruled by a succession of

Central Asian kings, in the south at Nanjing six Chinese dynasties hung onto the remaining territories of the empire. The inability of Nanjing to impose an effective land tax on the Red river valley had benefits for landowners and tenant farmers alike. Their avoidance of its full burden progressively drew them together and permitted the growth of a regional consciousness that was basically Vietnamese.

Like Korea on the edge of northern China, Vietnam received Chinese civilization without losing its own identity. After several generations in Vietnam, Chinese settlers, despite their loyalty to the ideals of imperial China, could not help being influenced by the values and ways of Vietnamese society. Typical of this transformation was the family by Ly Bi, established on the north bank of the Red river near Tan-xuong, in the shadow of Mount Tam-do. This was a strategic location on the upland frontier of the Red river plain, where the Ly family seems to have exercised semi-military duties. As a young man, Ly Bi went to the Liang court in Nanjing but was unable to obtain an official post. "Unable to attain his ambition", we are told, "the disappointed candidate went home determined to improve his own prospects". At the time the Liang emperors were trying to reassert their control over what remained of the Chinese empire and the provincial reorganization they introduced served to stoke discontent among those excluded from local appointments. As there were never enough posts to go round, Ly Bi was not alone in his disappointment.

Ly Bi's personal ambitions were also favoured by the local situation because the governor, a nephew of the reigning emperor, had angered the population by his patent greed and cruelty. In 541, Ly Bi was fortunate to gain the support of Trieu Tuc, "who yielded to the talent and virtue of the would-be ruler". Easily Trieu Tuc raised enough men to drive the corrupt governor away and rallied other discontented Vietnamese to his colours: the entire Red river valley soon fell into Ly Bi's hands. The Liang dynasty response was swift but poorly prepared. An expeditionary force was repulsed and pursued northwards into present-day Guangdong province. But south of the Red river valley Ly Bi was threatened by another invasion from Linyi. It is not known if the Cham attack was prompted by Liang diplomacy, since it may have simply exploited the turmoil in northern Vietnam for the purpose of a raid. In the event, this attack was repulsed as well.

After this, Ly Bi could begin to organize his realm, taking the imperial title of Thien-duc, "heavenly virtue". He built a palace, established a court and named Trieu Tuc as his chief minister. The inner core of Ly Bi's supporters were frontier guardians, many of whom had traced the steps of the new ruler to the Liang court and returned home with a similar sense of frustration. Only Trieu Tuc had not journeyed to Nanjing in hope of preferment, because his influential Vietnamese family looked upon its position as perfectly adequate. The rapacity of the Liang government was the spur for his active involvement in Ly Bi's rebellion. What Trieu Tuc contributed to the court was sponsorship of the Buddhist faith, for Confucian-inclined though Ly Bi was in his outlook, he gave his blessing to the spread of Buddhism. A temple was erected in the main citadel at Gia-ninh, close to the king's family estates.

Incense sticks offered to a temple guardian

In summer 545 a Liang army at last reached the Red river valley, where it defeated the rebels. A year later, Gia-ninh fell to the Chinese, but Ly Bi managed to escape into the nearby mountains among Lao tribesmen. He rallied his scattered forces, along with a number of Lao chieftains, and came down from the mountains with an army of 20,000 men. Once again Ly Bi suffered defeat, yet he escaped and prepared for another showdown. It looked as if his genius for survival would outlast the determination of the imperial generals, but the rebellion faltered with Ly Bi's execution by the Lao, who exchanged his head for Chinese gold.

With the reunification of China in 588 by the Sui Dynasty, the return of northern Vietnam to the Chinese empire was inevitable. Sui armies marched south, brushing aside local resistance, but they were merely the vanguard of even stronger forces belonging to the Tang emperors. The Sui dynasty, which lasted from 581 to 617, was almost a repeat of the short-lived Qin, the founder-dynasty of the Chinese empire. Its repressive regime provoked another nationwide rebellion that handed the throne to the Li family, whose dynasty was called the Tang. Of Sino-Turkish origin, the Li gave China a stability that had been missing for centuries and brought Chinese cultural achievement to one of its peaks.

The Protectorate of Annam

The Sui official who had been sent to serve as governor of northern Vietnam was able to maintain order even after the collapse of the Sui dynasty. Because of the honesty of his administration, the new Tang emperors continued the official as commander-in-chief of the Tang forces deployed there until his death in 637.

The protectorate of Annam, "the pacified south", as north Vietnam was soon called, represented an admission on the part of the Tang dynasty that the majority of the inhabitants were barbarians. Non-Chinese people in frontier areas were put under the authority of a protector-general, who in northern Vietnam oversaw eight provinces. The same arrangement prevailed in Central Asia, where the Tarim basin was "the pacified west", in "the pacified north" of Mongolia, and "the pacified east" in northern Korea. A large degree of self-government was permitted, especially in tribal areas where the Chinese authorities preferred to work through chieftains or councils of elders. We are informed how, in 669, the "uncivilized Lao" were encouraged to settle down and cultivate empty land. A Chinese chronicle tells us how they were "beckoned and soothed".

The administrative centre of the protectorate of Annam was Giao province in the lower Red river valley. Here a large agricultural population came under intense Chinese influence and ambitious families ensured that their sons received a thorough Confucian education. Austere courtyards and plain buildings in his temples underlined the simplicity of Confucius' family-oriented philosophy; its fundamental principles were on display in large black characters—filial piety, brotherly respect, loyalty, honesty, politeness, righteousness, integrity and chastity. There were no images, no priests and, above all, no divination. What Vietnamese men studying in temple libraries encountered was a this-worldly approach

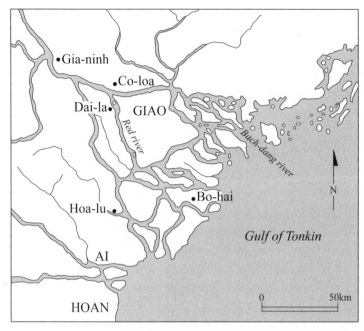

Tenth-century Vietnam

to life, quite divorced from the indigenous spirits that were propitiated in their own homes. In Buddhist temples, however, the native deities found shelter, because Giao province was also the centre of Vietnamese Buddhism. Today at the Van Mieu, "the temple of literature", this double legacy is evident in Hanoi. Although this temple is no longer a seat of learning, a statue of Confucius dominates its main courtyard; and this large statue is accorded the reverence usually reserved for a deity, with offerings from those who seek aid with their studies. On special slabs, set in the backs of eighty-two stone turtles at the Van Mieu, are carved the names of all the Vietnamese scholars who came first in government-sponsored examinations between 1442 and 1779. That the heads of the turtles have been rubbed black suggests how they are regarded as another source of success for examination candidates.

During the Tang occupation, Vietnamese people living in the Red river valley may have drunk deeply from the well of Confucian wisdom, yet for China the protectorate of Annam remained no more than an isolated imperial outpost. Tang census returns show how Chinese authority was secure only in Giao province where over half the total of all tax-paying families were registered. An estimate of the population is almost impossible now, because census figures do not include non-tax payers and a significant number of Vietnamese who chose to live in places where imperial control was relatively weak. But it is not impossible that the total number of people living in the protectorate had already reached one million by the end of the eighth century.

According to Vietnamese historians, Tang rule was the worst of any Chinese dynasty, and a series of revolts seems to confirm this view. Increased taxation was the reason for the first rebellion of 687; before this date its level was always kept much lower than in China because of the problems inherent in ruling a non-Chinese population. This uprising was a peasant revolt, pure and simple, against official demands for a greater share of agricultural wealth. Before their suppression, the rebels stormed the provincial capital of Giao, the city of Dai-la, present-day Hanoi. In spite of its failure, the uprising of 687 began a cycle of unrest that gradually picked up momentum and led to Vietnamese independence. In 722 the so-called Black Emperor defied the Tang army before fleeing to the mountains, where he died. Because of his dark complexion, the rebel leader Mai Thuc Loan adopted this title and at one stage commanded thousands of armed followers. In contrast to the rebellion of 687, however, the Black Emperor's supporters included many non-Vietnamese mercenaries attracted by the prospect of plunder.

There can be no question that the internal crisis of the Tang empire aided the movement towards Vietnamese self-rule. In 756 the Chinese capital fell to the rebellious general An Lushan and imperial troops were recalled to deal with the disturbance. The Tang fight back was a slow and humiliating one for Emperor Su Zong, who needed the aid of the Turkish cavalry to regain his position. But even this assistance was not enough to preserve the capital from the Tibetans who looted its treasures in 763. It was fortunate for China that Tibet was soon wracked by internal troubles of its own, when a dispute between its warlike king and the great Buddhist monasteries left the latter dominant in Tibetan society.

The Tang empire, though now much reduced, continued for another century, but interest in such a remote protectorate as Annam waned over the years. Not only was there another major uprising over taxation in

The Van Mieu founded by Emperor Ly Thanh Tong
in 1070 as Vietnam's national university

791, but even more the Yunan-based state of Nanzhou invaded the Red
river valley. A chronicler expressed Chinese frustration when he wrote
that "in Annam were treacherous people who often rebelled", preventing
the collection of taxes and complicating the task of dealing with foreign
incursion. The situation became critical in 862, when Nanzhou launched
an invasion aimed at total conquest. Only a determined counter-attack
dislodged the invaders, who then shifted their attention to other parts of
the Chinese empire.

Vietnamese Independence

For the Vietnamese the conflict with Nanzhou represented a painful
prelude to independence; because the fragmentation of China after the
fall of the Tang dynasty in 907 lasted long enough for Ngo Quyen to

declare himself an independent ruler. He ruled from 939 to 944, but after his death there was anarchy until Dinh Bo Linh restored order in 968.

The initial Vietnamese response to the collapse of Tang authority, and China's temporary breakup into the Ten Kingdoms, was prudent inaction. A landowner from Giao named Khuc Thua Du had been appointed as military governor in 906 and, when he died two years later, his son took over his responsibilities. By posing as loyal servants of the Chinese empire, the Khuc family was able to administer Vietnam until 930. That year an army arrived from Guangdong, where a local warlord had set up a kingdom named the Southern Han. The twenty-five years of peace under the Khuc administration allowed the Vietnamese to ponder their own destiny. As one poet put the case for freedom:

The mountains and rivers of Viet are old;
The men of Tang are new.

It was time for the Vietnamese people to be "no longer pressed down". Even though they had learned to use chopsticks, the habit of chewing betel was never abandoned. Southeast Asian customs were too deeply rooted in peasant life to be changed by Chinese manners, notwithstanding the great landowners' fascination with Confucianism.

It was Ngo Quyen, a member of a prominent landowning family from Ai, south of the Red river delta, who secured Vietnam's freedom. Because a strange light shone from him at birth, and there were three black moles on his back, he had been named Quyen, "power and authority". Ai and nearby Hoan were Ngo Quyen's power base, and the forces that he raised there repulsed a seaborne assault from Southern Han in 937. Familiarity with coastal waters obviously helped, when his soldiers planted a barrier of large poles in the bed of the Bach-dang river, one of the tributaries to the Red river delta. The tops of the poles reached just below the water level at high tide and were sharpened and tipped with iron. When the Chinese fleet appeared off the mouth of the river, Ngo Quyen sent out shallow-draft boats to provoke a naval engagement and lure the Chinese vessels upriver. As soon as the tide fell, these warships were damaged by the submerged poles and they became easy targets for the Vietnamese, who slew half of the soldiers and sailors on board.

In early 939, Ngo Quyen took the title of emperor, but he was careful to attribute his elevation to Phung Hung, the leader of the abortive rebellion that came to an end in 791. This immortal rebel had appeared to Ngo Quyen in a dream as "a hoary-headed old man in formal attire, holding a feathered fan and a bamboo staff": he told Ngo Quyen to intercept the enemy on the Bach-dang river. During the engagement the Vietnamese heard the sounds of horsemen galloping in the air and as a thanks-offering for the victory, Ngo Quyen

patronized Phung Hung's cult. He erected temples and shrines, enhancing old rituals, and also supplied feathered fans, yellow banners, brass gongs and deerskin drums for all the ancient dances with sword and battle axe, as well as sacrificial oxen.

Indian-inspired sculpture from central Vietnam, where the Chams adopted Hinduism

The new ruler also moved the capital from Dai-la, the Chinese administrative centre, across the Red river to Co-loa, a location redolent with Vietnamese associations. This nod to a pre-Chinese past did not stop Ngo Quyen, however, from basing his court on Chinese etiquette. A thousand years of belonging to China could hardly be jettisoned overnight.

When he died in 944, Ngo Quyen's four sons were too young to occupy the throne and their guardian seized power. There was anarchy when others challenged this usurpation and peace only returned with the elevation of Dinh Bo Linh in 968. Dinh Bo Linh was born at Hoa-lu village, some 35 kilometres from the sea. As a boy, Dinh Bo Linh's conduct impressed the villagers enough for a palisade to be erected to keep him safe. When two yellow dragons were observed hovering over him, the village knew that here was someone who would "benefit his generation and bring peace to the people". Other folk tales underline his contempt for the Vietnamese ruling class and a preference for merchants who were capable of funding his bid for power. Though he patronized Buddhism by endowing monasteries and building temples, Dinh Bo Linh was deeply interested in Daoism because its ideas were close to traditional Vietnamese reverence for the spirit world. The indigenous belief of China, Daoism had—in competition with the imported Buddhist faith—developed into a full-blown religion without losing touch with shamanism. Daoist adepts never gave up magic or the quest for the elixir of life.

Because Dinh Bo Linh was very conscious of his humble background, he seems to have been trying to put a distance between his dynasty and the Confucian-inclined Vietnamese upper class who regarded him as an upstart. Through Buddhism and Daoism, Dinh Bo Linh may have attracted the loyalty of his ordinary subjects, like the villagers among whom he grew up. There is some truth in the suggestion that his rise to power had the backing of a peasantry tired of the squabbles of the great landowners.

The first decision facing Dinh Bo Linh in 968 was where to place his capital. The old centres of Dai-la and Co-loa were unattractive to him. Eventually he settled upon his birthplace at Hoa-lu, a virtually impregnable site in a valley whose approach was guarded by easily defended passes. Because continued disorder caused Dinh Bo Linh anxiety, he subsequently placed in the palace courtyard a big kettle and a tiger in a cage. Then he decreed that "those who violate the law will be boiled and gnawed". It is recorded that "all were afraid and obeyed; no one dared to ignore his commands".

Dinh Bo Linh was surrounded at Hoa-lu by tough men like himself and his court retained the atmosphere of a military camp. This could hardly be avoided at a time when Vietnam remained unstable and China was in the process of reunification under the Song dynasty. After the surrender of Southern Han to a new imperial house in 973, Dinh Bo Linh sent envoys laden with tribute to the Chinese capital, where they were well received. Song recognition of Dinh Bo Linh as an independent king saved many lives because his timely submission to China formed the pattern of Sino-Vietnamese relations down to modern times.

Yet Vietnamese independence was effectively established by two early dynasties, the Le and the Ly. The former began in 980, after Dinh Bo

Linh's death, with the enthronement of Le Dai Hanh, a general who was backed by other senior commanders still worried about China. But his two sons were such a disaster that in 1010 the throne passed to Ly Cong Uan, whose posthumous title was Ly Thai To.

Ly Cong Uan was born in 974 and raised by Buddhist monks as a temple orphan. His coup seems to have been achieved with Buddhist aid. In 1010 he was commander of the palace guard at Hoa-lu, where the conduct of Le Dai Hanh's youngest son Le Long Dinh scandalized the entire court. Having seized the throne, Le Long Dinh took sadistic pleasure in cutting sugarcane with a heavy knife, using the head of a monk as a chopping block. The worst was when he missed, and he missed more often than not. To erase this painful memory, Ly Cong Uan moved the capital to the old Tang administrative centre of Dai-la and gave it the new name of Thang-long, "city of the soaring dragon".

Sniffy though later Confucian scholars were about the Ly, which had its succession problems like other Vietnamese dynasties, the fact was that its emperors were as sympathetic to classical Chinese learning as they were to the teachings of the Buddha. Ly Cong Uan indeed looked back to pre-imperial China, to the Shang and Zhou kings who were renowned for their respect of traditional values. A rather self-effacing ruler, he let the great landowning families collect taxes on behalf of the government, provided they remained loyal. Quite different in character was Ly Cong Uan's son, who took the title of Ly Thai Tong; he was both a powerful warrior-king and a great reformer. Not only did he put down rebellions and deter attacks by the Chams, but he also curbed palace intrigue, supervised court appointments, reorganized the palace guard and brought order to the Buddhist establishment. His humanity was evident in the softening of methods used in the arrest of suspected criminals and their interrogation; the matching of penalties to the nature and magnitude of the crimes committed; the improvement of living conditions in prisons; the treatment of slaves, especially their sale; and the tax breaks offered to veteran soldiers and impoverished peasants. Ly Thai Tong is even credited with the setting up of a postal service. Perhaps his concern for responsible government is most transparent in the comparative frugality of the palace itself—he limited the number of consorts and concubines to thirteen, attendants to eighteen, and musicians and dancers to one hundred.

In 1039, a famous debate was held at court about the nature of good government. While Ly Thai Tong insisted that it was the result of firm imperial leadership, his advisers politely suggested that vigorous rule could overburden what was still a rudimentary administration. Ly Thai Tong took their point, and established a Chinese-style civil service, which was strengthened by his successors. One of them, Ly Thanh Tong, founded in 1070 the Van Mieu as the country's first university and dedicated it to Confucius. Respect for Confucian learning lasted long enough for Ho Chi Minh to despair at its continued use to recruit officials in the early 1900s. Typically, the revolutionary leader gave up such study and began to learn French, "better to know the colonial enemy".

Above all, the Ly dynasty shaped Vietnamese institutions after the withdrawal of the Chinese. Mahayana Buddhism was affirmed as the measure of civilized behaviour; a pantheon of indigenous spirits became the kingdom's guardians; the Chinese theory of a heavenly mandate

The giant turtles upon whose backs are the slabs recording the names
of Van Mieu's top graduates; a student rubbing the head of a "turtle
of honour" in the hope of gaining examination success

to rule was borrowed to justify "a southern emperor" in Vietnam; and an examination system selected those who would staff officialdom. The country might have descended into chaos on occasion, but it was set on a course that not even a century of French colonial rule would fundamentally disturb. Annam had come of age.

After the Ly dynasty died out in 1225, the well-connected Tran family seized power. To regularize the succession, the Tran kings installed a single consort chosen from their own relations, insisted upon primogeniture, and abdicated in favour of their eldest sons while retaining power behind the scenes. In order to break the power of the great landowning families in the Red river valley—something the Ly had never really accomplished—the Tran later favoured officials recruited through the examination system, even though Vietnam remained essentially an aristocratic society where birth, favour and followers counted for everything. Courtiers who could not read a word still held key posts. The fact that the Tran descended from Chinese immigrants perhaps explains their use of an educated civil service to give balance to court politics.

Whatever the shortcomings of government by Chinese imperial standards, the Tran gave early Vietnam a dynastic stability rare in Southeast Asia. This was fortunate because the Mongols severely challenged Vietnamese independence. In 1257, after having conquered the state of Nanzhou, the Mongols advanced from Yunnan down the Red river valley to encircle the Song dynasty that was still holding out against them in southern China. The Tran thwarted this Mongol strategy, but once Kubilai Khan overcame the last Song emperor and brought the whole of China under his control in the late 1270s, he sent envoys to Thang-long demanding submission. Emperor Tran Nhan Tong refused and commissioned a history to be written demonstrating how he had inherited a status equal to that of the deposed Chinese emperor. When in 1284 the Mongols attacked from four directions, two overland and two by sea, the Vietnamese fought hard to prevent these attacking forces from linking up: the southern force that had landed in Champa and marched north was destroyed in a pitched battle, while elsewhere the invaders were harried by guerrilla warfare.

General Tran Hung Dao, a member of the imperial family, refused to submit to the invaders and his indirect strategy used ambush and surprise attack to weaken the Mongol resolve. "When the enemy comes, everyone must fight them," he said, "but if you are not strong enough ro resist them, you should flee and never surrender". Despite Thang-long being temporarily abandoned by the Vietnamese for six months, the Mongols tired of the campaign and withdrew on the onset of the monsoon. In 1287 a final Mongol invasion was defeated after the Vietnamese navy captured the invader's supply fleet. General Tran Hung Dao's soldiers, who had tattooed on their arms this triumphant slogan: "Death to the Mongols", inflicted heavy casualties on the Mongol army as it struggled back to China.

Unused to any defeat, the Mongols were preparing to settle accounts with the Vietnamese when Kubilai Khan died in 1294. The Mongol court then decided to leave Southeast Asia alone. Rival princes had already brought the political violence of the steppe to China and inaugurated a series of coups, murders, poisonings and purges that would tear the Mongol dynasty apart. Kubilai Khan's successor, Timur, struggled to impose his will on the Mongol tribes, not to mention his leading subjects. Drunkenness may have been a cause of his problems. His grandfather Kubilai Khan had reservations about his suitability as a ruler, but with no better candidate in sight, Timur Khan became China's second Mongol emperor. The timely release of prisoners taken by the Vietnamese must have come as a welcome relief to this lethargic ruler.

The Tran kings who ruled after the Mongol wars gradually lost their taste for action. Fortunate though they were in the decline of Mongol power on the northern frontier, they faced a determined enemy in the Chams who ravaged the south and even sacked Thang-long. With the Tran dynasty crumbling away, the threat from Champa only subsided in the 1390s after the death of its aggressive warrior-king Che Bong Nga, as the Vietnamese knew him. We remain unaware of his Cham name.

Champa

Indianized Champa was always a thorn in the side of Vietnam. Inscriptions from an early date indicate that the Chams spoke an Austronesian language entirely distinct from Vietnamese. As early as the fourth century, the founding of the temple complex at My Son, close to present-day Da Nang, marked the beginning of an attempt to achieve some unity among the various Cham chiefdoms that were located in the

A Cham king portrayed as Shiva, "the great lord"

river valleys dotted along the coastline of central Vietnam. Because the land suitable for cultivation was restricted in comparison with the Red river valley available to the Vietnamese, Cham agriculture could only feed a modest population and other means of support had to be sought. Despite occasional disruption of the trade route to China through pirate attacks, the Chams derived much of their wealth from the export of luxury goods from the forested interior, such as aromatic woods, ivory and rhinoceros horn. And the ports at present-day Hoi An and Nha Trang provided welcome shelter and fresh water for ships sailing on the India-China run, especially after Funan ceased to be actively involved in international commerce.

An additional source of wealth was undoubtedly warfare. Raids on Chinese holdings in northern Vietnam, then independent Vietnam, and Angkor provided rich pickings for followers of adventurous war leaders. So annoying did the northern raiding become that in 446 a Chinese army crushed Linyi, the earliest Cham kingdom to have received recognition from China. As a consequence of this invasion, Cham power shifted southwards from the vicinity of modern Hue, and eventually settled around Da Nang. There the My Son temple complex first refers to Champadesha, although as far as the Chinese knew this country was still Linyi. According to visitors from China,

> the people living in this country build the walls of their houses with baked bricks covered with a layer of lime, and the houses are supported by a terrace... The people themselves have deep-set eyes, straight prominent noses, and black frizzy hair. Women wear their hair in a knot at the top of the head... Both men and women wear nothing but a length of cloth wrapped around their bodies. They pierce their ears so that they can have small rings in them. The upper classes wear leather shoes, while the common people go barefoot... Their king wears a tall cap with flower embroidery in gold, decorated with a silk tassel.

There were two other things that the Chinese noticed. One was the fact that people with the same family name were not forbidden to marry each other; an absolute prohibition on such liaisons existed in China, lest they had the same ancestors. The second Cham singularity was disposal of the dead, because the practice of cremation was in vogue here as elsewhere in Indianized Southeast Asia. "The body is carefully shrouded, carried to the sea-shore or the bank of a river to the sound of drums and the accompaniment of dances, and then delivered to the flames on a pyre prepared by the mourners. The bones which survive the flames are placed in a container and thrown into the water. The parents of the dead follow the procession and cut their hair before leaving the river, this being the only sign of a mourning period which is brief."

The contrast with the tombs and rituals of mourning conducted by the Chinese in the worship of their ancestors could not be more dramatic. Little seems to have changed in Champa by the arrival of Zheng He's fleet at the start of the fifteenth century. The chronicler Ma Yuan, who went on several of these Ming ocean voyages, noted how

> most of the men take up fishing for a livelihood; they seldom go in for agriculture, and therefore rice and cereals are not abundant. The people ceaselessly chew betel nuts and leaves. When men and women marry, the

only requirement is that the man should first go to the woman's house, and consummate the marriage. A half moon later, the man's father and mother, with their relatives and friends, to the accompaniment of drums, escort the husband and wife back to their home, where they drink and enjoy music.

Equally baffling to Ma Yuan was the abdication of each king after a reign of three decades. He tells us how the ex-king then became a priest and lived in the depths of the mountains, while his closest relatives ruled in his place. Should he have offended the gods during his time on the throne, the ex-king expected to be devoured by wolves or tigers. "If, after the completion of one whole year, he remains still alive," Ma Yuan relates, "he ascends the throne once more to the acclaim and jubilation of his subjects." An intimacy with natural forces is just as evident in this ordeal as in the method of settling intractable legal disputes. Whenever officials were unable to reach any final decision, they made "the two litigants ride on water-buffaloes across a crocodile pond. As the crocodiles only devour the unrighteous, the person whose cause is just survives the crossing".

King Bhadravarman I built the earliest Hindu temple at My Son around 380. His capital was to the east of this important religious centre at present-day Tra-kieu. Here in the very heart of Champa is unequivocal proof of early Indian influence along lines similar to that experienced by the Khmers. Again it is the cult of Shiva that dominates, with the close association of the ruler and the linga. Inscriptions honour Shiva as Maheshvara, "the great lord", and also mention the gods Vishnu and Brahma as well as the goddess Uma, Shiva's consort. The royal linga at My Son is in fact the oldest known example of Shiva worship in Southeast Asia. Reasonable agricultural resources, along with several well-sheltered harbours, allowed Bhadravarman's kingdom to flourish and extend its influence as far as south as Ty Hoa, some 50 kilometres away. How much control he exercised over this distant area is uncertain, but a king of Funan did complain to China in 484 about Cham pressure on its borders. But it seems unlikely that a unified Champa preceded the campaigns of King Rudravarman, who sent an embassy to the Liang emperor in southern China around 530. An unusual inscription discovered to the northwest of Tra-kieu associates Bhadravarman with a nagaraja, "king of the nagas", a serpent deity. As in pre-Buddhist Pagan, serpents must have once received worship at the highest levels of Cham society. Even though the Tra-kieu inscription contains Sanskrit words, it is written in Cham and represents the earliest text in any Austronesian language.

In 529 a new dynasty had been founded by Rudravarman that would last for over a century. He had only a tenuous relationship with his immediate predecessor, but China recognized Rudravarman as the legitimate ruler of the Chams. Yet this did not stop him launching raids on northern Vietnam, like other Cham kings. The weakness of the southern Chinese dynasties at Nanjing was too tempting an opportunity to miss. His son and successor, Sambhuvarman, also took advantage of the political situation and sought to free himself from every form of subordination to China. But when he saw how the power of the Chinese empire was reborn under the Sui dynasty, he thought it prudent to renew relations and presented the emperor with tribute in 595.

But the Sui never forgot Cham impudence and, after the recovery of northern Vietnam, an invasion of Champa was ordered. Sambhuvarman could not stop the invaders who sacked his capital at Tra-kieu and carried away an enormous amount of booty. After the withdrawal of the Chinese, the shaken king regained control of his country and begged pardon from the Sui emperor, sending tribute in 623, 625 and 628 to the Tang dynasty that had replaced the Sui in 618.

Sambhuvarman was succeeded in 629 by his son Kandarpadharma, whose reign was peaceful since good relations with Tang China were maintained by the regular dispatch of rich presents. During this period the Buddhist faith appears to have spread among the Chams, although the extent of conversion is hard to judge. Whereas Hindu texts were often inscribed on stone, Buddhism was disseminated through the use of palm-leaves, the less durable writing material common to India, Sri Lanka and Southeast Asia. Even though Shiva was regarded as the chief deity and Shiva's linga always remained the focus of royal ritual, the Cham king could also be presented as a Shiva-Buddhist entity.

As at Angkor, Indian gods and goddesses fused with the indigenous spirits who protected certain localities. At the Po Nagar complex, near present-day Nha Trang (in Cham Ya-tran, in Sanskrit Kauthara), the largest surviving tower is dedicated to Po Nagar, the mother goddess of

The Po Nagar complex at Nha Trang, constructed in 813 by Harivarman I

Champa; her identification with Uma turned this indigenous spirit into Shiva's mate. Kautharesvari, "the blessed sovereign of Kauthara", was once portrayed as half-man, half-woman but, after the Chams were pushed out of Nha Trang, the goddess reverted to her primordial condition, a faceless protector of the Earth. A Cham hymn of praise for Kautharesvari, composed around 1050, speaks of the "magic power" of the goddess as being essential for good harvests. Because the soils are poor and the rainfall low in this part of central Vietnam, Po Nagar-Kautharesvari must have received fervent worship from the Chams, who were still forced to supplement their livelihood through trade.

The Po Nagar complex was constructed in 813 by Harivarman I. A decade earlier he had launched a successful expedition against Annam, but in 809 he renewed the attack with less success. Around this time, at

A Cham king whose royal cult did much to bind his people together

the start of Jayavarman II's reign at Angkor, the Cham king raided Khmer territories as well. The next ruler of Champa, Virantavarman II added further temples at Po Nagar and erected Buddhist as well as Hindu temples elsewhere. During the ninth century the Cham capital moved between several locations, but finally settled at Vijaya, in modern Binh Dinh province. This site was certainly chosen as a means of relieving pressure from independent Vietnam, in whose internal affairs the Chams had interfered in 979. A descendant of the first Vietnamese ruler Ngo Quyen persuaded King Paramesvaravarman I to assist then in the restoration of the original Vietnamese dynasty. But the seaborne expedition was sunk in a gale, with the exception of a single warship. So as to avoid a second invasion, the Vietnamese sent an embassy to Champa: but Paramesvaravarman kept the envoys prisoner and provoked Dai Co Viet into an invasion of its own. This obliged the Chams to move their capital to the less vulnerable site of Vijaya.

It is often assumed that Champa suffered an inexorable decline in the face of Vietnamese pressure from the 982 invasion onwards. In spite of some revivals, it is argued, events in Champa represent no more than the history of the retreat of Indian civilization before that of China. Such a view is incorrect. In the first place, it ignores the arrival of Islam in the early eleventh century. Through contact with Arab and Indian traders, some leading merchant families converted to the new religion, which is a solace for many of the Chams who live in Vietnam today.

The Cham kingdom based in Vijaya was more powerful, populous and influential than any of the states that had preceded it. War with the Khmers even culminated in the sacking of Angkor in 1177, the revenge for which exacted by the warrior-king Jayavarman VII seems to have permanently weakened Angkor. In 1220, the Khmers were forced to evacuate Champa and place on the throne Angsaraja, who had been raised in the court of Jayavarman VII. Angsaraja, who took the title of Paramesvaravarman II, spent most of his time restoring the kingdom's irrigation systems, which had been neglected under the Khmers. He also repaired temples that had been damaged, re-establishing "all the lingas of the south save those of Po Nagar". Towards the end of his reign, he came into conflict with the Vietnamese, whose Tran dynasty protested about a revival of Cham piracy. When Paramesvaravarman II said that his cooperation depended upon the return of lost territories, Champa was again invaded from the north.

Realization that the Mongols now posed the most dangerous threat to Southeast Asia led the Chams to seek better relations with the Vietnamese. No less than four embassies went to Thang-long between 1266 and 1270. But Champa still had to endure a Mongol attack when, in 1284, an expeditionary force landed on its coast in order to assault northern Vietnam from the south in a four-pronged invasion. According to Marco Polo, the Cham king Indravarman V

> was of great age and had not an army to match that of Kubilai Khan in a pitched battle; but he maintained a stout defence of cities and fortified towns without fear of any foe. The open country, however, and the villages were all ravaged and laid waste. When the king saw the havoc that was being wrought to his kingdom, he was deeply distressed. He promptly sent his emissaries to the Great Khan with this message: "Sire, the king of Champa salutes you as his lord. He sends you word that he is a man of great age and has long ruled his kingdom in peace. He is ready to be your faithful servant and to send you every year elephants and aromatic woods. He begs you courteously, imploring your mercy, to recall from his country your commander and your forces who are ravaging his kingdom."

Kubilai Khan "took pity on the king" and ordered the Mongols out of Champa, which afterwards sent annually "a quantity of timber and twenty elephants" as tribute. Marco Polo adds that Indravarman V had "356 children, male and female, including over 150 men of an age to bear arms".

Following the Cham monarch's death shortly afterwards, information about Champa is scarce until a new conflict with the Vietnamese ended in

1318, when a pro-Vietnamese ruler was installed at Vijaya. But this client king was unwilling to be a vassal of either the Mongols or the Vietnamese, and by 1326 he had achieved this aim. The Franciscan friar Odoric of Pordenone, who travelled by sea as a papal envoy to the Mongol court, reports that Champa was then "a very fine country, having a great store of victuals and of all good things". Splendid catches of fish ensured that the people were well fed and healthy. Less impressed was the friar by the Hindu custom of sati, whereby "on the death of a man, they bury his wife with him, for they say that she should live with him in the other world as well". It is clear that he never witnessed the self-immolation of a widow on her husband's pyre, or Odoric would have described the ceremony, and his mention of "the other world" means that he also missed Cham belief in reincarnation.

By taking advantage first of all of the decline of the Mongols and later coming to an agreement with the first Ming emperor, who recognized him as the king of Champa, the great Che Bong Nga was able to lead a series of victorious campaigns against the Vietnamese. Three times he sacked Thang-long. After the death of Che Bong Nga, one of his generals usurped the throne in 1390 and ruled for a decade. But it was soon discovered that the Chams could no longer match the strength of the Vietnamese and had to rely on Chinese assistance to keep the peace. From 1406 to 1427 China campaigned in Annam, having intervened at the request of a survivor of the Tran family, most of whom had been killed off by a usurper in 1400. The Ming emperor Yongle was keen to reassert Chinese influence abroad after the humiliation of the Mongol conquest, and so he ordered an intervention that was thwarted by the death of the surviving Tran prince in confused fighting there. Once they appreciated the strength of Vietnamese resistance to their return though, the Chinese prudently withdrew and left the Chams to deal with the Vietnamese on their own.

When hostilities resumed between the Chams and the Vietnamese, Champa therefore had to face Vietnam without outside assistance. The only possible ally were the Khmers, but they had not forgotten Cham attacks on Angkor. And so it was in 1471 that the Vietnamese captured Vijaya and annexed the area around modern Da Nang. A small Cham kingdom struggled on at Nha Trang until 1653, but the thousand-year-old polity of Champa was no more.

4

EARLY INDONESIA

The profits from maritime commerce are enormous. If such trade is properly managed, the revenues earned total millions of strings of cash. Is it not better than taxing the people?

The Southern Song emperor Gao Zong in 1145

The collapse of the Han dynasty in 220, and the consequent disruption of the overland trade route to China, led to the gradual replacement of the Silk Road with a maritime means of supplying exotic goods. During the partition of China from 317 until 588, when the northern provinces were ruled by Central Asian kings, seaborne trade became the sole method of meeting demand at the courts of the five Chinese dynasties that in turn struggled to maintain what was left of the empire south of the Yangzi river. Their stronghold Nanjing, "the southern capital", stood almost 600 kilometres south of the previous capital at Luoyang. Its separation from the historical core of China, the great plains of the Yellow river, was in itself an encouragement to look south, and this new outlook was certainly strengthened by existing friendly contacts with Southeast Asian states.

Under the Tang emperors, whose dynasty lasted from 618 until 907, a reunified China could enjoy once again products brought by caravans along a revived Silk Road as well as those carried by vessels plying the South China Sea. Periodic weakness connected with dynastic change, however, has always tended to threaten China's overland commerce. For nearly two hundred years the Song dynasty kept open the Silk Road to Central Asia, India, Persia and Europe, but with the fall of its capital at Kaifeng, in 1127, this supply line was shut tight. In a repeat of the earlier partition of the Chinese empire, the Song court fled southwards from the Yellow river valley and at Hangzhou fended off the invading Jin, the nomadic forerunners of the Mongols who were destined to conquer the whole of China in 1276. It was Gao Zong, the first emperor of the Southern Song, as the fugitive dynasty was known, who rallied the southern Chinese against the Jin invaders. He refused to accept defeat and secured the independence of south China during his thirty-year reign.

With the loss of the northern provinces, Gao Zong appreciated how the truncated empire needed to use the Yangzi river and the sea as a new Great Wall. A headquarters was set up near modern Shanghai to organize a navy of eleven squadrons and 3,000 men, soon rising to twenty squadrons and over 50,000 men. Some vessels were armoured with iron plates, all were capable of discharging gunpowder rockets and bombs.

Even though the immediate cause of this new sea-mindedness was pressure from the peoples of the Central Asian steppelands, the economic and political centre of the Chinese empire had been shifting for centuries from north to south, from the great plains of the Yellow river to the Yangzi delta. By the Southern Song period, the southern provinces were both the richest and most populated parts of China. A result of this southward movement of the imperial capital, and the precariousness of overland trade routes, was a remarkable increase in seaborne commerce, an expansion which actually coincided with a more relaxed official attitude towards merchants, who traditionally occupied a lowly position in Chinese society.

The choice of Hangzhou as the Southern Song capital was not solely a matter of chance, as the location was safer than that of other Yangzi river valley cities. Its approach was dotted with lakes, rivers, streams and paddy fields, formidable obstacles to the deployment of Jin cavalry. Summer heat and rain also caused problems for these steppe warriors, when in 1130 they gave up their pursuit of Gao Zong: he had sailed to an offshore island, only returning to Hangzhou on the news of the Jin withdrawal north of the Yangzi. Neither Gao Zong nor his six dynastic successors showed much enthusiasm for living at Hangzhou. Later Marco Polo incorrectly translated its name Kinsai as "celestial city", not realising that this actually meant "temporary residence". Regardless of whether they liked Hangzhou or not, the Southern Song emperors had to make the

A seventeenth-century view of Palembang, once the Srivijayan capital

best of it, because at the very least the city's vibrant economy was able to sustain the imperial court.

Although the huge influx of courtiers, officials and scholars altered the character of Hangzhou, it by no means eradicated its commercial heritage. The city remained China's greatest trading centre and, for the very first time, the imperial bureaucracy gave thought to increasing the volume of international commerce. A maritime commission even fostered contacts overseas by sending officials with gifts of silk for rulers in Southeast Asia and encouraging merchants to arrange trade missions of their own. As more ports were opened to international shipping, Gao Zong sent naval squadrons to deter pirate attacks in Chinese waters. Their success prompted officials responsible for coastal security to adopt permanent measures, including regular naval sweeps of rivers and bays, plus the registration of all merchant shipping. Any vessel found without authorisation was liable to be seized and its cargo forfeited in an attempt to prevent collusion between private ship owners and pirate captains. Gao Zong's navy initially comprised converted merchantmen, but these were quickly replaced by purpose-built warships.

Chinese Tributary Relations

These unprecedented measures soon paid off, as the amount of seaborne trade doubled, trebled and kept on growing to the benefit of businesses and the imperial exchequer. But this upsurge rested upon a pattern of commerce in which several maritime polities had long played an active role: they enjoyed trading privileges as tributary states which acknowledged the authority of the Chinese emperor as the Son of Heaven. Initially stimulated by Arab traders who brought frankincense to Sumatran ports, exchanging this perfume for other goods, the onward China trade came to dominate the Southeast Asian market. Early Arab and Indian merchants, who joined in the east-west exchange, have left no trace of their presence, but Chinese sources note that Srivijaya held great quantities of frankincense in its warehouses. "At both Guangzhou and Srivijaya", we are told, "officials examine the amounts of the perfume and establish its value."

Of the six earliest tributary kingdoms of Indonesia, Srivijaya was almost the last to make diplomatic contact with China. Prior to the Tang dynasty selecting the Srivijayan kingdom from among its rivals as the favoured Southeast Asian maritime state, China had close trading relations with Java. The king of Heluodan sent seven missions between 430 and 452 to the second Chinese dynasty established at Nanjing, following the Central Asian occupation of northern China. It has been suggested that this western Javanese ruler began to dispatch missions only when he was in trouble. Possibly the cessation of missions after 452 does mean that a neighbouring king had ended its independence, but Heluodan's primary interest in cordial relations with China was trade, since even a reduced empire represented a massive market for its goods, which included handicraft items as well as perfumes and drugs. Camphor was always sent as tribute because the Chinese court particularly valued its aromatic qualities.

In the report of the 430 trade mission, King Visamvarman of Heluodan was said to live in fear of his enemies both inside and outside his realm, and thus requested diplomatic assistance and iron weapons from China. As there were no local deposits of iron, Visamvarman obviously hoped to regain the initiative through superior armament. That the king addressed the Chinese emperor as "the protector of the weak everywhere" is remarkable, because it is assumed that China would always

Early Indonesian ships carved on the walls of Borobudur

Seventh-century bronze figurines unearthed at Palembang:
Avalokitesvara (left) and the Buddha

be concerned about the maintenance of peace in maritime Southeast Asia. Whereas India was looked upon as the source of religious ideas, China was expected to play a political role. Successful Indonesian kings clearly felt the need to underline their entitlement rule by demonstrating China's approval. Heluodan, as the Chinese called western Java, could well have fallen under the sway of King Purnavarman, the ruler of the Tarum river basin just to the east of modern Jakarta. From Sanskrit inscriptions discovered near the shore there, we are aware that this early kingdom was Tarumanagara, whose prosperity rested upon improved drainage near the coast. It appears that Purnavarman diverted the course of the Tarum river in order to find a better outlet to the sea. These downstream schemes anticipate those of eastern Javanese kings in the Brantas river valley, and especially the water control and irrigation network developed by Erlanga in the eleventh century. Unlike the paddy fields this energetic ruler restored and extended in the eastern part of the island, western Java still grew dry-rice.

Other inscriptions refer to Purnavarman's own identification with Vishnu, whose vehicle is the golden sun bird Garuda. What attracted Purnavarman most, however, was Vishnu's incarnation as a brahmin dwarf, when the great Hindu saviour deity worsted the demon Bali. At the behest of the other gods and goddesses, Vishnu approached the demon in this apparently innocuous form and requested a boon. Bali consented to this request when the dwarf asked for the ownership of a tiny patch of land, as much as he could measure with three strides. Whereupon the diminutive priest waxed into a cosmic giant, and with two strides crossed the universe, his third crushing the head of Bali. These great strides were evidently considered a parallel of Purnavarman's own impressive expansion of the borders of Tarumanagara. It is quite likely that the river project also had a connection with international trade, since increased rice harvests upriver would have allowed the export of this grain to Srivijaya, a rising star in Southeast Asian commerce. Replacement of the east-west trade route, which ran across the Isthmus of Kra and along the coast of the Gulf of Thailand towards Funan, by a sea passage through the Straits of Malacca, brought benefit to merchants living in Purnavarman's kingdom, but nothing like the commercial edge it bestowed upon the Sumatran port of Palembang.

Srivijaya

Strategically situated to take full advantage of the new east-west trade route, Srivijaya's capital city of Palembang in southeastern Sumatra stood on the Musi river some 65 kilometres from the swampy coast. Near the confluence of three other rivers—which allowed valuable jungle products to be ferried down from the island's interior—the Srivijayan capital possessed a fine natural harbour that ships could easily reach with the help of the tide. Even in the nineteenth century, the largest ocean-going steamers had no difficulty in reaching Palembang. Although none of the early ports close to the Straits of Malacca could boast agricultural resources comparable to those of Funan, the Palembang area did have the unusually wide, slow and silt-bearing Musi to sustain intensive cultivation. Arab merchants reported that the soil was "as fertile as any land can be". Yet imported Javanese rice always remained crucial for Srivijaya's growing population. This Sumatran state would dominate seaborne commerce around the Straits of Malacca, including western Java and the Malayan peninsula, from the seventh to the eleventh centuries.

The founders and rulers of the Srivijayan kingdom were local Malay-speaking chieftains. And the Sanskrit name that they chose for their realm means "great victory" or "glorious conquest", doubtless in recognition of that kingdom's sudden rise to prominence. By the arrival of the Buddhist monk Yijing in 671, on his voyage from China to India, Palembang was already the centre of a prosperous kingdom. He stopped there for six months so that he could master Sanskrit grammar. Then he relates

> there were more than 1,000 Buddhist monks whose minds were entirely turned to study and good works. And they consider every possible subject. If a Chinese monk wishes to travel westwards and consult the original scriptures, he should stay here for a year or two and prepare himself for the journey to India.

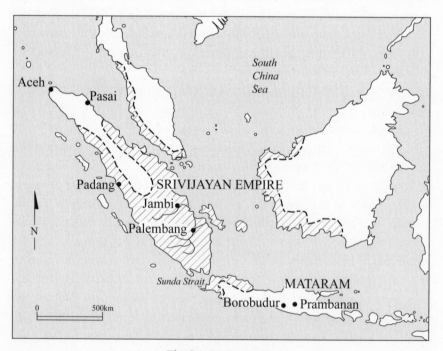

The Srivijayan empire

On his return from India, Yijing remained in Palembang for another four years, during which time he translated Buddhist texts into the Chinese language. In 689, after a brief trip to Guangzhou, where he recruited four assistants, he returned to the Srivijayan capital and set up a translation school. Yijing was still a resident when the ruler of Srivijaya first paid tribute to the Chinese emperor in 695.

Yijing's voyage in 689 was involuntary. He tells us that he went on board a merchant vessel in the Musi estuary so as to send a request to China for the dispatch of assistants and writing materials. A wind suddenly sprang up and carried the ship away from the coast, with Yijing still on board. The monk had heard that it was about to sail, and hurried downstream on the ebb tide to deliver his message. But the favourable wind was a gift that the ship's captain could not afford to miss, since it was part of the monsoon system which aided vessels sailing to China.

There can be no question that Chinese monks travelling by sea to India provided valuable intelligence about both China and Southeast Asia. One Sumatran ruler, whose kingdom was a forerunner of Srivijaya, dreamt of a Buddhist pilgrim who gave him this advice:

In China there is a very devout ruler. Over the next decade the Law of the Buddha will prosper greatly in that country. If you send envoys with tribute and pay your respects now, your kingdom will become rich and happy and merchants and travellers will multiply a hundredfold.

When the Chinese empire was stable, it could absorb such a volume of maritime trade that Southeast Asian kingdoms were bound to be enriched. The Tang emperors in particular were concerned about ensuring a smooth exchange of goods at Guangzhou, and in the 690s regulations for the provisioning of foreign shipping were issued. This was the duty of the Superintendent of Merchants, a post established shortly before 714. But when dynastic instability troubled China, the returns that Srivjayan traders earned swiftly diminished. They ceased altogether during the rebellion of Huang Chao, from which the Tang dynasty itself never really recovered. In 880 this bandit leader even captured the Chinese capital of Chang'an, while his followers sacked a large number of cities including Guangzhou. The massacre of foreign merchants in this port made Southeast Asians reluctant to trade with China for several years. After the eventual defeat of Huang Chao, international commerce resumed at Guangzhou, but its volume remained low until the Southern Song emperor Gao Zong's enthusiastic sponsorship of seaborne trade raised it to a level never attained under the Tang emperors.

Because any increase or decrease of the China trade profoundly affected the maritime states in early Southeast Asia, it is obvious how tributary relations were viewed by their rulers as the effective means of gaining access to the Chinese market. China's interest in "the pestilential lands"—as Southeast Asia was often called—rested upon its supply of exotic products; not only Arabian frankincense and myrrh, but more so indigenous plants that could be used as medicine. The second Tang emperor Tai Zong, having failed to respond to treatment for chronic diarrhoea, had been cured by a preparation of milk and "long" pepper. Apart from its use as incense, frankincense was also discovered to have valuable medicinal properties, although Chinese doctors sometimes prescribed Sumatran pine resin as a substitute.

According to Yijing, the rival Sumatran state of Malayu came under Srivijayan control around 671. Its capital of Jambi lay to the north of Palembang, and commanded the only other important river system on this strategic coast. The earliest inscriptions in Malay—a group of five discovered in southern Sumatra and on the nearby island of Bangka—indicate how the king of Srivijaya was then winning supremacy over his neighbours. Having conquered Malayu and Bangka, he decided to launch an expedition against Java. The king was almost certainly Jayanasa, who is named in two of the inscriptions. His prowess was such that Srivijayans accepted Jayanasa's publicly stated claim to possess the supernatural power capable of ensuring the kingdom's prosperity. We are told how "the king expressed his wish that all cleared land should be planted with crops, that all animals should be carefully tended, and that all servants should be faithful and industrious. No scope was ever to be given, the king insisted, for thieves, ruffians and adulterers, but instead only the teachings of the Buddha and the worship of the monks should prevail".

The king most likely to have sent the embassy to China in 695 was also Jayanasa, who had succeeded in combining the Malay seafarers of Sumatra into a very powerful fleet that consisted of warships as well as merchantmen. In large measure Srivijaya became prominent because Jayanasa was prepared to buy out the pirates. He made an agreement with enough of them so that in return for a share of Palembang's revenues, they would not attack ships at sea. These new seaborne allies were deployed to patrol local waters and ensure the safe movement of merchant vessels. They could also act as peaceful traders themselves. As long as there was sufficient income from customs dues and commercial profits to retain the services of the Malay pirates, Srivijaya's position was secure. But should these regular payments ever cease, then the Malay sailors would revert to raiding on their own account, or in alliance with rival Sumatran ports.

An ornate Buddha from Palembang, where Yijing was amazed at royal support for the Indian faith

Thus King Jayanasa was able to dominate the Straits of Malacca, the main artery of east-west trade. The excellence of Srivijaya's location is echoed by the Portuguese traveller and diplomat Tome Pires in his description of Malacca, which had become the key port during the fifteenth century. The capture and fortification of Malacca in 1511 gave Portugal a stranglehold over the Europe-bound spice trade and Pires noted that

> whoever is lord of Malacca has his hand on the throat of Venice. As far as from Malacca, and from Malacca to China, and from China to the Moluccas, and from the Moluccas to Java, and from Java to Malacca and Sumatra, all is in our power.

Unfortunately for Pires, who arrived at Guangzhou as a Portuguese ambassador in 1521, the Chinese took a slightly different view. The building of a fortress at Malacca was one thing, the construction of another downstream from Guangzhou something else, especially when its commander hindered merchant vessels entering and leaving the port. This typical Portuguese method of coastal domination so annoyed the Ming court that it denied Pires an audience. Ordered home, the Portuguese envoy was arrested in Guangzhou at the same time that Chinese troops destroyed the rogue fort. Pires did not survive imprisonment and his fellow countrymen were obliged to trade by subterfuge. They had to remain below decks while hired Malays or Thai dealt with the exchange of goods and paid customs dues.

The unsatisfactory situation was only resolved when a very small Portuguese settlement at Macao, near present-day Hong Kong, received Chinese toleration. However its swift growth caused the local Chinese authorities some uneasiness, and in 1574 they placed a wall right across the isthmus connecting Macao with the mainland, posting soldiers to guard a single gateway, above which was written: "Fear Our Greatness, Respect Our Virtue". Following this, movement through the gate was denied to foreigners lacking official Chinese passes.

Like the Portuguese, the Malay rulers of Srivijaya secured their hold over international shipping through the acquisition of ports: soon revictualling stations in peninsular Malaya and in southern Thailand came under Srivijayan control. So great was the flow of wealth derived from domination of the Straits of Malacca that Srivijaya was indifferent to the annexation of territory away from the coast. Neither the Acehnese in northern Sumatra, nor the Minangkabau to the west of Palembang, ever fell under the sway of Srivijaya. Their independence must explain the distinctive character of each, and especially in Minangkabau lands where a matriarchy still exists today.

Another reason for the limitation of Srivijayan authority in Sumatra was the absence of any pan-Sumatran identity. The Malays were but a single ethnic group living on the great island, where even now they number less than seven million. Only in present-day Malaysia and Brunei do Malay-speakers constitute the majority community. Small groups are to be found in southern Thailand, Singapore and Kalimantan, but these total no more than four million. Given the many hundreds of languages spoken by Austronesian peoples, it is not difficult to see

A typical Minangkabau house

why Srivijaya's political impact on early Indonesian history was so transitory. Only its location permitted this riverine kingdom to grow rich from international trade, before Emperor Gao Zong's initiatives opened up commercial opportunities in the rest of the Indonesian archipelago. Once populous Java fully responded to increased Chinese demand, Srivijaya's influence was bound to decline without the status of China's favoured trading partner in maritime Southeast Asia.

Where a Srivijayan legacy survived was in the use of Malay, or Jawi, as the language of communication and learning. The Arabic-based script facilitated inter-state contact and, after the arrival of Islam, it gained prestige as the courtly speech of sultans. During the seventeenth century, one Cambodian king abandoned Buddhism and embraced Islam. Taking the name of Ibraham, he married a Moslem, compelled his courtiers to sport krisses, and used Malay in correspondence. Rather like Latin and French in medieval Europe, an understanding of Malay was then considered to be a sign of an educated person.

Although the Javanese referred to the whole of Sumatra as "Melayu", they were fully aware of the island's ethnic diversity. The sturdy independence of Aceh was quite beyond interference by Srivijaya anyway, while the singular social structure of Minangkabau remained aloof from the Buddhism propagated at Palembang. And the hill tribes of the interior, here as on other Indonesian islands, were left to their own devices. All the Srivijayans wanted from the latter were the farmed and harvested forest products they traded down the tributaries of the Musi river.

As the Minangkabau highland valleys enjoy volcanic soils and dependable rainfall, a large population lived there from early times. The name Minangkabau comes from a legend about a victorious buffalo, a menang kerbau. Once an invading army appeared in the highlands and demanded submission from the inhabitants. The locals suggested that, rather than settle the question by force of arms, the two sides should stage a buffalo fight, which they did to the disadvantage of the invaders. To their complete surprise, the champion buffalo they fielded was killed by a starving calf, whose sharpened horns tore into its stomach in a desperate attempt to suckle. Whether this folk tale—or a similar one concerning the repulse of an attack by the Javanese kingdom of Majapahit—represents an historical event is impossible to determine, but it does indicate how Minangkabau maintained its freedom by ingenuity, not warfare.

William Marsden in the late 1700s believed that the Minangkabau highlands were the ancestral home of the Malays. An English East India Company official stationed in western Sumatra, Marsden's idea impressed Thomas Stamford Raffles enough to mount an expedition from Padang during his governorship of Java. Raffles writes that at the village of Suroaso, he visited "a palace, a small planked house about thirty feet long, on the banks of the Golden River. Here we were introduced to the Tuan Gadis, or Virgin Queen, who administered the country". That Raffles was disappointed in not discovering the ruins of a Hindu kingdom, which was supposed to have shaped Malay culture, is hardly surprising because that role had been performed by Srivijaya.

Propitiation rituals remain central to all Southeast Asian societies. Alongside Hinduism, Buddhism, Confucianism, Islam and Christianity,

The so-called Telaga Batu stone, which was used
for swearing a loyalty oath to the Srivijayan monarch

there is felt to be a need to placate the invisible spirits, whether these
unseen powers are directly related by ancestry or indirectly through
their habitation of the environs of a town or village. Whereas imported
faiths appear more concerned with social harmony and the afterlife, local
beliefs focus exclusively on the here and now. This emphasis is nowhere
clearer than in the water ritual conducted daily by Srivijayan monarchs.
Styled "lord of the mountain", each occupant of the throne claimed a
special authority granted by the ancestral spirits who dwelt on the upper
slopes of Sumatra's volcanoes. As "lord of the isles" though, the king was
also believed to enjoy the favour of the turbulent forces of the sea. We
do not know the Sumatran equivalent of Ratu Lara Kidul, the Javanese
sea goddess whose body comprises the hair and bones of her drowned
victims, but such was the fear she inspired in the minds of Srivijayans that
each day they expected their ruler to cast a gold bar into the Musi river as
a peace offering.

Maritime Southeast Asia is of course a world of water, and without
safety on rivers, along coasts and across seas not only travel but
commerce would be impossible. Since Srivijaya was above all a trading
state, good relations between its rulers and the denizens of the deep were
held to be crucial. Despite fluctuations in the China trade really being the

An inscription in Tamil and Chinese recording the consecration
of a Shiva temple at Guangzhou in 1281

decisive effect on early Indonesian polities, the islanders looked upon their kings as guarantors of prosperity and peace. The Srivijayan monarch was therefore regarded as the vital link between the holy mountains and the fruitful sea, a Musi-like figure whose magic powers protected people from flood, ensured fertility in the fields and, last but not least, warded off evil influences. In the latter case, the king's unusually generous patronage of Buddhism is perhaps explained; only at Nalanda in northeastern India, the most famous of all centres of Buddhist learning, was a greater number of monks supported. Buddhism provided extra magical strength which underscored the monarch's legitimacy as well as enhanced his international prestige. Yijing mentions with awe the elaborate celebrations held in honour of the Buddha, when the people paraded images of Buddha through Palembang's streets and monks offered prayers to local divinities.

That Srivijaya grounded traditional Malay ideas about a leader's magic powers in Buddhist conceptions of kingship is evident from a ceremonial stone that was protected by seven carved serpent heads, representing the seven-headed Muchalinda. This gigantic naga's hood had prevented the Buddha from being disturbed on the eve of his attainment of supreme consciousness. Significantly the oath of loyalty sworn on the Telaga Batu stone by the king's most important followers involved the drinking of water.

Because stone was in scarce supply locally and bricks were reserved for religious purposes, archaeology has turned up little at Palembang. The contrast could not be greater between the islands of Sumatra and Java: between the 730s and the 1020s there was a construction boom in central Java that saw Buddhist and Hindu monuments planted on hillsides and plains in their hundreds, the most magnificent of which is the massive granite stupa of Borobudur. Fine wooden carving apparently satisfied Srivijayan kings, evidence of whose devotion to the Buddha relies largely on the testimony of bronze figurines.

In the light of Srivijaya's devotion to Buddhism, the Chola attack of 1025 on Palembang came as a shock. An inscription at the Tanjavur temple in present-day Tamilnadu praises King Rajendra Chola for having launched that year "many ships in the midst of the rolling sea, catching the ruler of Kedah by surprise, together with the elephants of his glorious army, and seizing his treasury", and afterwards "overwhelming the extensive capital of Srivijaya with its gateway resplendent with large jewels". The inscription goes on to list other ports in peninsular Malaya and Sumatra which the Chola navy had raided.

Rajendra I's mighty expedition was a unique event in India's history and its otherwise peaceful relations with the states of Southeast Asia which had come under the cultural influence of India for almost a millennium. India was, after all, the holy land of Buddhism and Hinduism. The reasons for the unexpected attack are by no means understood, although growing Tamil involvement with the China trade may well have been a motivating factor for the overseas expedition. The Chola kingdom had firmly established itself in southern India during the tenth century, and then extended its control over a large part of Sri Lanka as well. The father of King Rajendra had brought Chola fortunes to a peak, so that his ambitious son may have thought it was time for him to exploit the potential of the navy that was developed during the Sri Lankan wars. A trial run could have been the annexation of the Maldives, over 900 kilometres south of the Chola naval base at Nagapattinam. Because Chola rule was marked by constant warfare, and kings were judged by their exploits on the battlefield, it is not difficult to see why Rajendra was driven to seek fame abroad.

Relations between the Srivijayans and the Cholas were deteriorating before 1025. Perhaps to ensure continued favour in Song China, Srivijaya sent in 1003 envoys with a message that a Buddhist temple was being specially erected at Palembang with the purpose of praying for the long life of the emperor. So appreciative of this gesture was the Chinese court that the envoys were presented with bells for the temple, which was given the name "Heavenly blessings forever". Two years later Srivijaya entered into the same kind of diplomatic relationship with the Chola kingdom, when finance was provided for the construction of a monastery at Nagapattinam. Srivijaya was obviously trying to maintain and strengthen its privileged position in east-west trade.

Yet Srivijaya overplayed its hand. In 1017 a Tamil tributary mission returned home from China with the news that the Chola kingdom was regarded by the Chinese as a dependency of Srivijaya. Nothing could have put out the nose of Rajendra more than this Srivijayan assertion of his subordinate position. Having just come to the throne, Rajendra was in no mood to tolerate such an insult. And the Chola king would have had the support of Tamil merchants intent on expanding their share of the China trade. But the 1025 assault does not seem to have weakened Srivijaya's power in the Straits of Malacca. Another Chola invasion was deemed necessary in the 1070s, again with little practical effect.

It is not a little ironic that Srivijaya was undermined by China, not India, once Emperor Gao Zong decided to promote unrestricted seaborne trade. Tamil inscriptions in Aceh and Barus, modern Lobu Tua, reveal how quickly southern Indian merchant guilds penetrated the Sumatran market in the twelfth century, while even more at Guangzhou the dedication of a temple for Shiva, the favourite Chola deity, indicates that the southern Indian kingdom was no longer perceived by the Chinese authorities as an unimportant tributary state. Palembang did not cease being a trading port because its excellent harbour was too conveniently situated to be ignored altogether, but the old Srivijayan capital never regained its former glory.

Java and Bali

The Srivijayan realm had lasted for nearly four hundred years. Not until the tenth century was there serious competition with eastern Java, whose most powerful states were located in the Brantas river basin. Although the Chola sack of Palembang in 1025 represented a setback for Srivijaya, it was the emergence of Java as the key Indonesian island in the international network of commerce that temporarily ended the importance of the Straits of Malacca. Only with the foundation of the port of Malacca itself would the main east-west trade route shift westwards

A portrait of a Javanese queen from Prambanan,
the great Hindu rival to Borobudur

once again. That Malacca's rulers purposely linked their genealogies
to Srivijaya is a testimony to the contribution that Palembang-based
monarchs were believed to have made in the development of Southeast
Asia's early maritime states.

Before the advent of aggressive kingdoms such as Singhasari and
Majapahit in eastern Java, the political and cultural focus was Mataram,
the name of the heavily populated centre of the island. Thanks to its rich
volcanic soils and a year-round growing season, central Java sustained
kingdoms older than Srivijaya, but they hardly enter the historical record

until the rise of the Sailendra dynasty, whose devotion to the Buddha was reflected in the construction of the great stupa at Borobudur on the Kedu plain, north of modern Yogyakarta.

One of Java's earliest Indian-influenced dynasties, the Sanjayas, had already raised Hindu temples on a plateau situated to the north of the Kedu plain. Looking upon this elevated area as the cloud-covered abode of the gods, King Sanjaya Canggal erected there in 732 a linga in honour of Shiva, Brahma and Vishnu. Already sacred to Javanese deities, the plateau brought indigenous beliefs into direct contact with imported religious ideas. The king seems to have deliberately fused existing cults in Shiva's worship, so that he became himself a semi-divine figure in a potent new cult. Through this special relationship, an inscription informs us that Sanjaya Canggal "ruled the Earth in peace and prosperity, banishing fear among the people of Mataram".

The Prambanan temple complex which developed from Sanjaya Canggal's foundation has not been satisfatorily dated. While some temples are older than Borobudur, others were clearly built to celebrate

The great stupa of Borobudur in central Java

the later decline of the Buddhist faith in central Java. The remains of 244 temples in various states of repair have been identified at the huge complex. Pride of place belongs to the largest temple, which is dedicated to Shiva: the god's statue still stands on a richly decorated plinth. That the Prambanan sculptures are somewhat superior to those of Borobudur most likely have a connection with the material

Plan of Borobudur

used—sandstone which is more easily carved than rock-hard granite. In all probability, the Hindu temples were intended to serve as mausoleums for members of the royal family in a similar manner to the temple-tombs constructed for the Khmer kings at Angkor.

If Prambanan is the Javanese apotheosis of Hinduism, then Borobudur is that of Buddhism. The name Borobudur may have originally meant "many Buddhas". Architecturally, it is unlike anything else in Java because a whole hillside has been clothed in stone, and topped with a stupa, while seventy-two smaller stupas are arranged in concentric circles below. Seen from a distance, the granite structure looks, as its designer obviously intended, like one gigantic stupa. Started in 778 but not finished until 824, Borobudur's incredible number of carved reliefs and the painstaking way in which they were executed explain the length of time required for the project. When the lower basement was uncovered in 1885, the care with which this work had been undertaken could be seen in the guidance inscribed there for sculptors: they were instructed to carve scenes that touched upon karma, the cause and effect of reincarnation.

What the Sailendra kings wished to show their subjects was the path that each individual must tread to follow in the footsteps of the Buddha. The basic idea at Borobudur is an exposition of the faith by means of a journey through the Buddha's previous lives; pilgrims walk around its terraces and view the bas-reliefs before arriving at the top, the level of nirvana, "the enlightenment" which abolishes the craving that leads to the endless round of rebirths. In the ascent of the stupa, groups of pilgrims would have been guided by learned monks who explained the meaning of the bas-reliefs. But the beauty of the stupa's natural setting, the richness of the imagery and, above all else, the serenity of the statues on the terraces of Borobudur could not have failed to move Buddhist worshippers, just as it continues to cast a spell over visitors today.

At first, the Sailendras were just an obscure regional dynasty. When they emerged in the early seventh century, their realm was one of a number of small kingdoms in Mataram. Instead of trying to subordinate neighbouring kings, the Sailendras preferred to bask in the international fame which arose from their sponsorship of Mahayana Buddhism, once Borobudur acted as a magnet for pilgrims. Given Srivijaya's generous patronage of the faith, ties between the two courts developed to the extent that around 850 a Sailendra prince sat on the throne at Palembang. Benefit though they did from the export of surplus rice, Sailendra kings were unenthusiastic about trade. They allowed farmers to take their crops to market, where they acquired other goods in exchange. From these inland markets wholesalers transported the rice to merchants in the ports, where it was sold on to shippers who delivered cargoes to places such as Palembang. Not until the rise of larger kingdoms in eastern Java would rulers combine a volume of trade equal to that of Srivijaya with agricultural resources comparable to Mataram. A pioneer of this economic transformation was King Erlanga, who took advantage of the Chola-Srivijaya conflict to establish a new entrepot near modern Surabaya.

The sudden decline of Mataram in the tenth century is still unexplained, but there is no uncertainty about its depopulation and the shift of economic and political activity into eastern Java. Centred on the Brantas river basin, the new states established there could draw upon wide areas for cultivation which were untouched by volcanic eruptions, the favoured explanation for Mataram's abandonment; a heavy layer of ash would have been sufficient to disrupt agriculture for decades. In the 930s an east Javanese king by the name of Sindok encouraged the migration of farmers eastwards, and also welcomed foreign merchants to Brantas river ports. It was during Sindok's reign that the *Ramayana* first appeared in the Javanese language. The Indian epic extols Vishnu,

The upper levels of Borobudur, close to the attainment
of nirvana, "complete enlightenment"

whose periodic incarnations result in the defeat of demonic forces on
Earth. In the *Ramayana*, Vishnu is incarnated as the hero Rama, who,
with assistance from the monkey god Hanuman, overcomes on Sri Lanka
the demon Ravana. The translation of Sanskrit texts greatly widened
the appeal of Hinduism in Java and allowed its spread to Bali, the only
Indonesian island faithful to this religion now.

Bali was actually drawn into Java's cultural orbit by King Erlanga,
sometimes rendered Airlangga. Born around 1000 on the island, he was
the son of King Udayana and the Javanese princess Mahendradatta, the
great-granddaughter of Sindok. As a young man, Erlanga was invited
to the east Java court, where he married one of King Dharmavamsa's
daughters. As a royal son-in-law, he was then most likely charged with the
administration of a province, because he seems to have been absent from
the capital in 1016, when invaders destroyed the palace and killed the
king. The perpetrators could have been the Srivijayans, still smarting from
a Javanese raid on Palembang in 992 and not yet at war with the Cholas.

King Erlanga portrayed as Vishnu,
seated on Garuda, the slayer of serpents

As a result of the sack, Dharmavamsa's vassal rulers swiftly asserted
their independence. It was indeed their interminable feuds that slowed
Erlanga's efforts to restore the kingdom. Doggedly progressing from
smaller to greater victories, he realized his objective after thirty years
of fighting and eastern Java was, in 1037, reunited once more. "Having
placed his feet on the head of his enemies", we are told, "Erlanga took his
place on the throne of lions, decorated with jewels". Kahuripan, the site
of his new capital, has still not been identified. Already he had brought
a recovered Mataram under his sway. Yet Erlanga's devotion to Vishnu,
whose incarnation he was believed to be, did not stop him confiscating
temple lands and employing this accumulated wealth to regenerate a

stricken economy. Most of all, he is remembered by the Javanese with gratitude for finally developing effective water-control schemes. By the placement of dams on the Brantas and other rivers, Erlanga prevented flooding and provided a regular supply of water for irrigation, long a Balinese speciality. In Bali, the bounty of nature was always most apparent in the water that flows down from the great lakes next to its centrally-sited volcanoes. Water temples still distribute this life-giving resource, which the Balinese call "the purifying gift of the water gods". Particularly sacred are the springs located high on Mount Agung, home of both the gods and deified ancestors. Although it is doubtful whether Erlanga managed to transplant Bali's belief in the sanctity of water to Java, this energetic ruler did return the island to prosperity.

Not only was agricultural output increased along the highly fertile Brantas river, but even more the ports of eastern Java grew rich through international trade, an entitlement Erlanga was pleased to guarantee by means of charters engraved on metal sheets. These documents mention foreigners who were welcomed as traders and taxed like local residents. Archaeological findings confirm the presence of Chinese, Indian and Arab merchants, revealing how Erlanga's initiatives soon put eastern Java on par with Sumatra. The king showed an unusual capacity to maintain religious harmony among his people. His chronicles invariably suggest a great esteem for monks and priests who functioned as advisers or witnesses of royal decisions. Even though Hinduism was embraced by the majority of his subjects, and considerable sums were spent on temples and shrines as soon as the economy recovered, Erlanga was careful to preserve the Buddhist heritage of Mataram.

Despite growing commercial rivalry, some kind of reapproachment may even have been achieved with Srivijaya. Erlanga's dedication of a Buddhist monastery named Srivijayasrama points in this direction, as indeed does the presence of a Srivijayan princess in his court. But from 1042 onwards, Erlanga lived as a hermit, having determined to divide his kingdom between two sons of different queens, in the hope of avoiding civil strife after his death. His ashes, enclosed in a stone casket, were buried in 1044 beneath the pool of a sacred spring on the slope of Mount Penanggungan: an obvious reference to the end of the *Ramayana* when Rama disappears in a river, water being the favourite element of Vishnu.

Mongol Intervention

Both of the states bequeathed to Erlanga's sons were eventually absorbed into Singhasari, and later Majapahit, the last and greatest of the seaborne empires before the arrival of the Europeans. Of the two states established in 1044, the one located on the lower Brantas and known as Kadiri had most influence on Javanese history. This was because the Kadiri kings made the pinnacle of their realm a sanctified court rather than a temple complex. That the heightened focus on the court was accompanied by a further elevation of the ruler's status, must explain the unprecedented powers claimed by Kertanagara, whose actions were to draw the Mongols into Indonesian politics. In Java, Erlanga had been the first monarch to be regarded as a world saviour, a figure combining in equal measure spiritual and secular authority. His descendants in Kadiri went another step up the spiritual ladder; inscriptions never mention a ruler's name but refer only to "the dust of His Majesty's sandals", drawing an indelible line between a divine king and his human subjects.

This exalted status did not preclude uprisings led by commoners though. An adventurer named Ken Angrok took control of eastern Java in 1221, establishing the kingdom of Singhasari. Ken Angrok even married the wife of the deposed ruler, and assumed the throne under the name of Rajasa. But neither he nor his successors were able to fully dominate this part of the island. Not even the powerful ruler Kertanagara, whose reign lasted from 1263 to 1292, could entirely have his own way. He was killed in a rebellion shortly before the arrival of the Mongols. By the time Kertanagara's father abdicated in his favour, Indian religious ideas had totally fused with indigenous beliefs, making the ex-king into a multiple deity. As a result, his ashes had to be divided between several shrines.

It was, however, Kertanagara who really took royal spirituality to an extreme. He even erected a huge statue of himself as the Buddha. In the person of the king the combined essences of every religion were now thought to reside, an awesome power that Kertanagara was going to need in dealing with the Mongols, whose envoys he gratuitously insulted in 1289. Instead of executing them like King Narathihapate at Pagan, Kertanagara tattooed the faces of the ambassadors, sending them back in disgrace. Kertanagara felt himself strong enough to resist the demands of the distant Mongols, who had ordered that a member of the royal family

A scene from the *Sutasoma* tale painted on the ceiling of
the audience chamber at the Klungkung palace in Bali

be sent as a hostage to the court at Beijing. Kertanagara's expansion of
Singhasari's authority into Sumatra, where Palembang had been attacked
in 1272, the Malay peninsula, Borneo, and Bali may have been part of
a plan to form a grand alliance against Kubilai Khan. Because of this,
Kertanagara was always careful to stay on good relations with the Chams.

Inheriting the political role of the Chinese emperors, Kubilai Khan
resented the unopposed growth of Kertanagara's influence in Southeast
Asia, a reaction that would have been strengthened by the complaints he
received from small tributary states in the Indonesian archipelago, who
were fearful of the aggressive policy adopted by Singhasari. So often did
their envoys raise this concern that in 1292 Kubilai Khan dispatched a
fleet of 1,000 ships to humble Kertanagara. Having overcome the Javanese
navy and landed near modern Surabaya, the Mongol expeditionary force

King Kertanagara's father portrayed as Shiva, although he was regarded as a multiple deity

moved on Kertanagara's capital, unaware that the king was already a casualty of a local conflict. Amazing though it seems, Kertanagara's own son-in-law, Raden Vijaya, persuaded the commander of the expedition that he should punish those who had killed Kertanagara and restore the situation. Thus Raden Vijaya ascended the throne of the new state of Majapahit, allowing the Mongols to carry away vast quantities of booty without becoming involved in a costly guerrilla war. As in northern Vietnam, they would have found how the jungle terrain gave plenty of scope to the Javanese for protracted opposition.

The Empire of Majapahit

Opinion was always deeply divided about Kertanagara, who laid the foundations of Majapahit's seaborne empire. In the *Nagarakertagama*, an epic poem composed by the Buddhist monk Prapanca under the patronage of Majapahit's kings, the story does not begin with the establishment of Majapahit, but with the reign of the controversial Singhasari monarch, Kertanagara. According to Prapanca, Kertanagara was a serene and compassionate ruler. The fifteenth-century *Pararaton*, on the other hand, portrays him as a drunkard and womaniser. Kertanagara seems to have sustained his spiritual powers by means of Tantric rituals which involved sexual exercises, a practice then common to Hinduism as well as Buddhism. Along with the consumption of alcohol, they brought on the trances that are said to have inspired his leadership.

Perhaps Kertanagara's real triumph was to be declared a jina, the Javanese term for someone who has achieved enlightenment. In the *Sutasoma*, a fifteenth-century tale of a Buddhist prince, the king actually appears as a divine incarnation: he is described as having "the jewel mind and wise body" of an utterly perfect man. If Kertanagara were not

The Pura Tama temple at Mengui,
the ancestral shrine of a Balinese royal family

included as Sri Jnanabajreswara, the teacher of Sutasoma, the *Sutasoma* would be no more than another account of gods and mythical kings with extraordinary powers locked in the timeless struggle between good and evil. That the young prince was a jina himself only serves to strengthen the impression of the Singhasari king's supreme accomplishment: an understanding of the scriptures that disclosed ultimate truth. As Prapanca insisted in the *Nagarakertagama*, Kertanagara followed the path of a faultless Buddhist.

The roots of Majapahit's imperial ambitions were nourished in Singhasari. Foolhardy though Kertanagara undoubtedly was in his defiance of the Mongols, he set the agenda for the seaborne empire that Raden Vijaya established in 1293–94. His capital at Majapahit, which gave its name to the new state, was located 40 kilometres upriver from Surabaya on the coast. By readily accepting the status of a tributary king, Raden Vijaya was able to hurry the Mongol expeditionary force out of eastern Java. And he was more than fortunate that the successor of Kubilai

A shrine dedicated to Dewi Sri, the indigenous Balinese rice goddess

Khan, who had died shortly after the Javanese expedition put to sea, was uninterested in overseas ventures. To maintain the peaceful relations, nonetheless, Raden Vijaya sent at least four tributary missions to Beijing during his reign. The return of political stability to maritime Southeast Asia was of great benefit for Majapahit because the Mongols recognized its commercial connections with the Indian Ocean, where the rapidly expanding European market had increased demand for spices.

When Raden Vijaya's son died without an heir, he was succeeded by his mother Rajapatni, the great-granddaughter of Kertanagara, and finally by the queen's daughter's son, who reigned from 1350 as King Hayam Wuruk. Behind these intricate successions stood the famous chief minister Gajah Mada, who handled day-to-day administrative affairs. Acting in the name of the queen, Gajah Mada consolidated the dynasty's position in eastern Java as well as the nearby island of Madura. Royal relatives and trusted courtiers took charge of the pacified provinces, which from 1343 onwards encompassed Bali as well. So steady was Gajah Mada's hand on the tiller of state that the visiting papal envoy Odoric of Porberone was deeply impressed by the strength of Majapahit, which had the alliegence "of seven crowned kings... The king himself possesses a marvellous palace, and many a time the Great Khan has come off worst in his wars against him". Although this last remark seems to refer to Raden Vijaya, it is not impossible that Majapahit pursued a policy of armed resistance to the declining authority of the Mongols.

The year 1284 had first seen Bali become subject to foreign rule when Kertanagara invaded the island. This king's death granted half a century of renewed independence but there was no escaping the rule of Majapahit, whose culture replaced indigenous traditions. Even today, the pre-Majapahit era has an aura of unreality and mystery among the Balinese themselves. Only in the unique construction of their temples is there an echo of the earliest religious outlook. Towering pagodas resembling stacked megaliths are a reminder of the importance once accorded to rocks and mountains, while in the openness of temple sites is preserved the ritual descent of gods and ancestral spirits.

The extent of Gajah Mada's cultural imperialism is recorded by Prapanca, who says the "vile, long-haired princes of Bali" were wiped out and that "all the customs changed to those of Java". In spite of too sweeping a claim about an easy conquest, the chronicler-monk is right to describe the break in tradition as decisive. A client king was the means by which Bali was bound to Majapahit, and the tremendous emphasis placed on his person formed the basis of royal Balinese government down to the early twentieth century. In addition to this Singhasari-style elevation of the throne, the introduction of the Hindu caste system gave ten per cent of the population social superiority. Anyone in this top group, the wong jero or "insiders", could aspire to rule as a Balinese king but the importance of royal lineage effectively limited access to power. State ceremonies turned into a kind of metaphysical theatre: performances designed to express the fundamental nature of reality and, at the same time, draw society into actual contact with that reality. It was in part a survival of early Balinese belief in magic, but also a public affirmation of the divinity of the ruler, whose court was considered to be nothing less than the axis of the world. As we are aware from the report compiled on Angkor by the Mongol envoy Zhou Daguan, the motor of early Southeast Asian power was state ceremony in which the king's divine entitlement to command obedience was always the central theme.

Gajah Mada turned Majapahit into a second Srivijaya with outposts as far east as New Guinea and as far north as the Philippines. He regularized the spice trade by the collection of annual quotas as tribute. A chronicler relates how Majapahit's "empire grew prosperous, people in vast numbers thronged its capital, and food was in plentiful supply". Most telling of all is the statement that "from the shores of the Southern Ocean envoys came from everywhere for an audience with the king, bearing tribute and presents".

Majapahit seemed set for a long period of dominance in east-west trade. Officials in China noted how the use of copper, silver and gold assisted its commercial activities. Copper coins with holes in their centres for easy handling on strings may have been Chinese in origin, or locally minted copies of this universally accepted currency. So large were the quantities of spices imported by China, especially pepper, that there was a massive outflow of its copper coinage to Java. Due to this transition to a money economy, Majapahit's taxes were collected in cash as well as kind: officials, soldiers and sailors were often paid in both. As European demand for spices steadily increased, there was also a major inflow of gold and silver from the West.

Arguably the expulsion of the Mongols from China in 1368 marked the turning point in Majapahit's fortunes, because three years later the new Ming dynasty invited Palembang to send a tribute mission once again. The revival of the Straits of Malacca as the focus of Southeast Asian maritime commerce was the last thing that Majapahit wanted. Warships sailed westwards to prevent this happening, just as Thai pressure stripped Palembang of any remaining ambitions in the Malayan peninsula. Unnoticed at the time was the foundation of Malacca.

Shortly after Hayam Wuruk's death in 1389, a certain Paramesvara set himself up as the ruler of this new port. A native of Palembang and the husband of a princess from Majapahit, Paramesvara first seized the island of Singapore, then a Thai possession. After being expelled by the navy of Ayudhya, he moved northwards to the site of Malacca. Had Paramesvara not alienated the island's Malay inhabitants by killing their chieftain, it is quite possible that Singapore rather than Malacca would have been the target of the Portuguese. A war of succession undermined Majapahit in the early 1400s, when Malacca was beginning to develop its role as the main entrepot for Southeast Asian maritime trade. Another bonus for the fledgling state was the prevention of either Thai or Indonesian interference afforded by the great Ming admiral Zheng He, who made use of a temporary naval base at Malacca during his ocean voyages. In 1405 a tributary mission to China was rewarded by Emperor Yongle with the recognition of Paramesvara as "king of Malacca".

LATE
SOUTHEAST ASIA

5

LATE BURMA

It was civilly intimated that we ought not protrude the soles
of our feet towards the seat of majesty, but should endeavour
to sit in the posture that we observed by those around us.
With this desire we would have complied, if it had been in
our power, but we had not yet learned to sit upon our own
legs: the flexibility of muscles which the Burmans... possess,
is such, as cannot be acquired by Europeans.

Envoy Michael Symes at Amarapura in 1795

After poisoning his father King Narathihapate of Pagan in 1287, Prince
Thihathu then murdered three of his brothers, a not untypical action.
Although the best known example of violence occurred at Mandalay in
1878, when King Thibaw oversaw the slaughter of some seventy siblings
and close relations, the outside world was still shocked in 1947 by the
killing of the entire cabinet three months before the date of Burma's
independence, when assassins machine-gunned Aung San and his
ministers. The perpetrators of the massacre were quickly brought to
justice, and a period of national mourning lasted several months. Yet
blood has always been the stuff of Burmese politics.

Thihathu's triumph was short-lived. He died at Pegu, where consumed
with fury by the city's refusal to accept his usurpation, Thihathu mortally
wounded himself with an arrow. A surviving nephew tried to reassert
Burman authority at Pagan, even sending tribute to China, but Shan hillmen were in no mood to tolerate a subordinate position any longer and
they set up a kingdom of their own at Ava, upriver from Pagan. Already

At Pagan the Buddha is shown cutting off his Burman hair-knot,
as King Tabinshwehti did to please his Mon subjects

the Shan occupiers of Upper Burma had shown their disdain for Pagan's religious traditions: they executed prominent monks, pillaged temples, and burned Buddhist scriptures. Shan violence also badly disrupted agriculture, prompting a large-scale Burman migration to Toungoo in the remote Sittang river valley. This tiny principality was destined to form the nucleus of national revival when, with the assistance of Portuguese mercenaries, the second Toungoo king, Tabinshwehti, conquered the whole of Lower Burma and was crowned in 1541 at Pegu.

The arrival of the Portuguese in the sixteenth century had enhanced Lower Burma's position both commercially and militarily. The Portuguese capture of Malacca in 1511 diverted Moslem traffic to other ports where Southeast Asian products could be obtained free of Portuguese interference. Anti-Portuguese Aceh began to supply commodities to Lower Burma, which attracted Indian merchants unwilling to run the Portuguese gauntlet during the long voyage to Indonesian ports. In the 1550s Moslem traders resident at Pegu were permitted to build the city's first mosque.

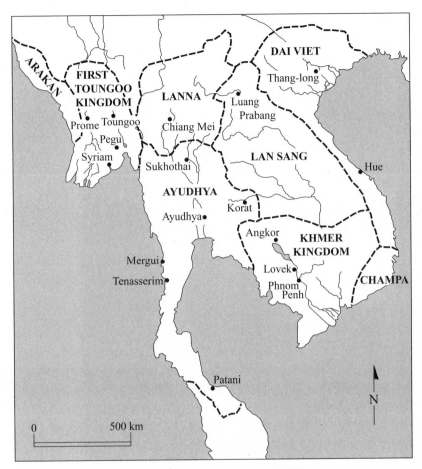

Mainland Southeast Asia around 1540

However, the chief contribution of the Portuguese to Lower Burma's ascendancy was not commercial, but military. In the 1530s, bands of Portuguese freelance soldiers competed to offer their services to local rulers, who recognized how their weaponry outclassed handguns and cannon of Indian or Chinese manufacture. Tabinshwehti was indeed the first Burman king to employ these ruthless, hard-bitten men who fought alongside equally tough Moslem mercenaries from Java and India. Matchlocks supplied by Portuguese soldiers of fortune proved superior in accuracy, ballistic weight and rapidity of fire. The expansion of Toungoo to the coast actually coincided with the cusp of a transformation in arms, which Tabinshwehti and his successor soon turned to their advantage. By the 1550s Portuguese and Moslem cannon had forced a shift from wood to brick and stone fortifications.

The First Toungoo Dynasty

Toungoo's growing commercial links with the coast had persuaded Tabinshwehti of the strategic advantage to be gained from uniting the ports of Lower Burma with the interior. On inheriting the throne of Toungoo, he had chosen to attack southern Pegu rather than northern Ava. After seizing Pegu, Tabinshwehti moved his court there and patronized Mon culture. The commercial wealth of this riverine city allowed the Toungoo monarch to send even more mercenaries against

Even though the Mon origins of the Shwedagon stupa are obscure,
King Bayinnaung inaugurated a tradition of royal worship there in 1556

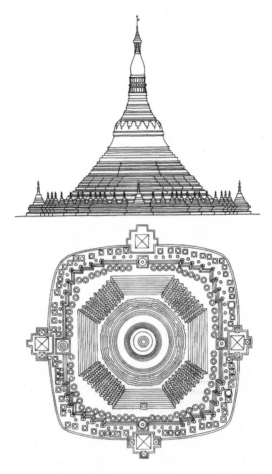

The elevation and plan of the Shwedagon. It was Bayinnaung
who raised the stupa to its present height of 90 metres

rival ports and inland centres. Portuguese cannon overcame Martaban
in 1541, Prome in 1542, and threw back a Shan attack in 1544. The last
victory demonstrated the weakness of Ava, which had not retained any
of Pagan's coastal dependencies, thereby cutting off the Shan from the
supply of improved weapons.

The strength of Chittagong, for instance, was enough to deter the
Portuguese, who were obliged to settle as traders, not overlords as
in Malacca. The premier port on the eastern side of the Bay of Bengal,
Chittagong was then part of Arakan, a kingdom which successfully

thwarted the territorial ambitions of the Toungoo dynasty for many years. But Arakanese kings still found defending a long and exposed coastline a difficult task. Whilst remaining Buddhists themselves, these rulers accommodated Islam by the use of Moslem titles, a diplomatic tactic that kept the peace with India until they became entangled with Mughal politics.

Quarrels within the imperial family had troubled the Mughal empire almost from its foundation in India during the late 1520s. No exception to the bitter conflict between fathers and sons was the usurpation in 1658 of Aurangzeb, whose popular name was Alamgir, "Seizer of the Universe". Not only did he imprison his father Shah Jahan, who spent the last years of his life gazing from the Agra Fortress at the Taj Mahal, the splendid mausoleum which he had constructed for his favourite wife Mumtaz-Mahal, but Aurangzeb also sought to eliminate his brothers. One of them, by the name of Shuja, managed to flee to Arakan laden with treasure. Perhaps it was the sight of the gold and jewels he had brought with him as much as the enormous bribe offered by the Mughals for Shuja's extradition that complicated matters. In the event, Shuja tried to depose the Arakanese king but, with few followers, he failed and was killed. Aurangzeb himself would have executed Shuja, though not his women. They had been added to the Arakanese king's harem. So annoyed was the Mughal emperor by this presumption that the governor of Bengal was ordered to raise a fleet and capture Chittagong, which fell after a furious assault. Notice was given that only Aurangzeb had the right to deal with imperial kinsmen.

After the repulse of the Shan in 1544, Tabinshwehti could have conquered Ava and reunited the Irrawaddy basin. He chose instead to direct his energies against prosperous Arakan and Ayudhya, the Thai capital city. It seems that his objective was gaining control over international commerce in the region. Both campaigns failed miserably. Tabinshwehti's guns were matched at Ayudhya as well as the Arakanese capital by those belonging to rival Portuguese mercenaries, while his Burman and Mon levies proved inadequate for investing these well-fortified cities. Siege warfare was a risk, especially if kings took part themselves. There was always the likelihood of rebellion at home. For this reason Bayinnaung, Tabinshwehti's successor, was forced to end his

An enormous chinthe guarding the Shwedagon stupa

siege of Prome after only one month. Such assaults thus involved heavy stakes for both the besieger and the besieged: the former had to reduce the city as soon as possible while the latter needed to hold out until an event caused the abandonment of the siege. And a robust defence also made it much easier to negotiate reasonable surrender terms, something Bayinnaung learned during the frantic effort to secure his own succession following Tabinshwehti's sudden death.

King Tabinshwehti had switched Toungoo's territorial expansion to Lower Burma once he appreciated the extent of Pegu's riches. That he was just as interested in acquiring Mon manpower for his army is evident in his making a Mon princess the chief queen and cutting off his Burman hair-knot in favour of a Mon hairstyle. Whereas Mon grew their hair atop but shaved the sides and back parts of their heads, Burmans wound their long hair into topknots. In the famous Ananda temple at Pagan there is even a sculpture of the Buddha cutting off his topknot, before setting out

Colossal Buddhas at Pegu before their recent restoration

on the quest for enlightenment. Even though Tabinshwehti's gesture of conciliation was unprecedented, it did not prevent his Mon bodyguards from murdering him in 1550, after luring him into the jungle with reports of a white elephant, a creature highly prized by Southeast Asian monarchs.

The Mon had clearly become exhausted through almost continuous campaigning. Bayinnaung was himself putting down a rebellion farther south when the assassination happened. At first, Bayinnaung was a king without a kingdom because a usurper took over Pegu and the great vassals sat on their hands. The tide only turned in his favour when the tyranny in Pegu alienated the capital's inhabitants and Bayinnaung rallied his Shan, Burman and Mon followers for an assault. A small company of Portuguese soldiers lent him support too. The usurper was in fact killed by a Portuguese bullet, but it still took a tough fight to regain control of Pegu.

King Bayinnaung was not slow in appreciating the necessity of reinforcing his army with Thai-speaking highlanders, the Shan and their newly arrived Thai cousins. Having captured Ava in 1551 after a five-day artillery barrage, Bayinnaung then moved against Chiang Mai, capital of the northern Thai kingdom of Lanna. Succession disputes had plunged Lanna into such an acrimonious civil war that there was not a great amount of resistance to this invasion. By 1558 the whole of Lanna was subdued, beginning two centuries of Burmese suzerainty. Yet Burmese overlordship was never peaceful, because the Toungoo dynasty used Lanna as a staging post for prosecuting its long war with Ayudhya, which had been founded two centuries earlier.

Down to Ayudhya's destruction in 1767, Lanna remained a disputed territory, and it only stopped changing hands after the present-day Chakri dynasty established itself at Bangkok in 1782, reviving Thai fortunes sufficiently to liberate Chiang Mai a decade later. Twice Bayinnaung captured Ayudhya. On the first occasion a divided Thai court quickly surrendered, in part because it was overawed by the size of the artillery train the Burman king had brought with him. But the 1569 victory followed a fierce bombardment. The difficulties that Bayinnaung had faced in reducing rebel strongholds after Tabinshwehti's death made him very conscious of the need for large-calibre cannon. During the siege of Chiang Mai, Bayinnaung had also deployed incendiary devices to set fire to the upper works of the defences as well as numerous rockets. Yet it was mines that successfully ended the siege at Ayudhya: the breaches they opened in the masonry fortifications permitted the besiegers to attack in force.

Bayinnaung also extended Burma's influence in the east over the Thai kingdom of Lan Sang—modern Laos—and in the west over Manipur, a kingdom on the borders of India as yet unaffected by Hinduism. The Manipuris were later to defy Burma and suffer several invasions as a consequence of these bids for freedom. In 1724, however, they inflicted a serious defeat on a Burmese expeditionary force. *The Glass Palace Chronicle* has no hesitation in putting down this unexpected reverse to the incompetence of its commanders.

Comparison of Bayinnaung's achievements is sometimes made with those of Sultan Agung, who in the early 1600s led Mataram in its resistance to Dutch pressure on the island of Java. He also drew upon the commercial revenues of coastal cities and strengthened his forces with European weapons. Although less successful than Bayinnaung in

As did the Pagan kings, the Toungoo dynasty
spent vast sums on temple construction

his sieges, Sultan Agung twice invested the Dutch port-city of Batavia without forcing a surrender, even though its defenders were anxious when a Portuguese fleet was rumoured to be headed for Batavia as well. Antagonism between Portugal and Holland gave the Javanese king a useful ally at sea, but the Portuguese were unable to assemble enough warships to decisively intervene. Despite the brilliance of Sultan Agung's reign, however, the Java-wide empire he created was as inherently fragile as that of Bayinnaung, because it comprised no more than a collection of semi-independent territories linked to the court through personal ties with the sovereign. Outlying areas were entrusted to governors or local rulers who could appoint subordinates, maintain armed retainers, and raise taxes for their own use as well as Sultan Agung. As long as Bayinnaung and Sultan Agung remained invincible, the loyalty of these people was assured but, after both these rulers passed away, central authority declined sharply.

Responsibility for the decline of the Toungoo dynasty is blamed on Bayinnaung's determined son, Nandabayin. According to *The Glass*

Palace Chronicle, so fixated was the new king with the reduction of Ayudhya that he ignored everything else. The actual cause of renewed conflict with Ayudhya was Naresuan, a Thai prince who had been taken to Pegu as a hostage in 1564; he had been allowed to return to Ayudhya in 1567, when his sister took his place. Later Naresuan returned to Burma and paid homage to Nandabayin, who had succeeded Bayinnaung in 1581. There he must have observed at first hand how factionalism and jockeying for position troubled Nandabayin's court. The weak position of Toungoo kings had resulted from adopting similar administrative arrangements to Pagan, since only the area immediately surrounding the capital was under their direct rule. The rest of the kingdom was controlled by virtually autonomous vassals, who were prepared to exploit any faltering of royal power. At last, thought Naresuan, an opportunity existed to throw off Toungoo suzerainty.

Even before he sat on the Ayudhyan throne, Naresuan's defiance of Pegu had led to punitive expeditions being sent against him. Because Naresuan repulsed them all, Nandabayin decided to launch in 1592 a massive invasion via Martaban. It advanced to within a 120 kilometres of Ayudhya, only to meet with an ignominious defeat at Nong Sarai. Overconfidence on the part of the Burman commander was a factor in the rout, but just as critical was Naresuan's generalship and the aid of Portuguese volunteers. The latter had agreed to join a general call-up at Ayudhya.

After Nong Sarai, Nandabayin sought to prepare fresh invasions, but men of arms-bearing age fled his recruiting officers. Some hid in the jungle or roamed around the countryside as vagabonds, others entered Buddhist monasteries to avoid military service. And not a few mortgaged themselves as debt-slaves to nobles who could shield them from royal manpower demands. So angry was Nandabayin at this mass desertion that he ordered the branding or tattooing of men in order to assist identification. When he started an investigation into the monastic order, so as to laicize all but the most pious and learned, senior Mon abbots who objected to this interference were exiled to Upper Burma. A reign of terror quickly ensued as the distraught king struck out at those who appeared to oppose his will. A sign of Nandabayin's loss of divine favour was believed to be a plague of giant rats which ravaged the fields around the capital, and then broke into the city and swarmed over its granaries, no matter the strenuous efforts made by soldiers to kill these enormous creatures with spears and swords. A terrible famine then followed, the first of a series that converted Lower Burma into a virtual desert.

Had he been prepared to leave Ayudhya alone, Nandabayin might have still kept his kingdom. When his undiminished resolve to continue campaigning became generally known in 1599, however, the king found himself besieged in Pegu by rebellious vassals and kinsmen, who enjoyed the assistance of troops from both Arakan and Ayudhya. The king of Arakan had been invited to join the civil conflict because he possessed a fleet capable of sealing off the seaward approaches to Pegu. The Arakanese landed in force at Syriam and marched northwards to combine with the Burmese rebels. After Pegu fell and Nandabayin was killed, the kingdom split into a dozen petty states, some which were held by Bayinnaung's other sons, most notably Nyaungyan at Ava.

The Arakanese deported large numbers of Peguans, who had been reduced to cannibalism during the protracted siege. They also carried away huge amounts of loot as well as many cannon, plus a daughter of Nandabayin who was enrolled in the harem of the Arakanese king. Left behind at Syriam was a garrison of Portuguese mercenaries under the command of Filipe de Brito e Nicote, who temporarily exploited the problems of Lower Burma for his own personal benefit.

The Restored Toungoo Dynasty

Perhaps it was a horoscope predicting future kingship which served to foster Nyaungyan's ambitions. Another reason may have been the special favour that he was believed to have been shown by the nats, the indigenous spirits associated with trees, large rocks, fields and waterfalls. Sacrifices to these hidden powers were offered in every town and village by shamans, who were usually transvestites or women. To propitiate the nats at Ava, Nyaungyan erected a sacred enclosure, where his troops camped on the auspicious earth and made sacrifices before the start of each campaign.

But the restoration of Toungoo rule was not achieved by Nyaungyan as the horoscope seemed to predict: it was his son Anaukpetlun who restored the fortunes of the dynasty. This determined prince seized the

Guardian chinthes, known to the British as "Chindits", the name of
Orde Wingate's long-distance penetration groups during World War Two

palace at Ava and proclaimed himself ruler, before his brothers could
learn of Nyaungyan's death. During his father's funeral, Anaukpetlun
administered the oath of allegiance to all the mourners. Shrewd though
this move was, his military prowess would have in all probability secured
his succession anyway, but Anaukpetlun was taking no chances with his
immediate family, nor more distant relatives who had set themselves up as
independent rulers. His campaigns should therefore be seen as the logical
fulfilment of his father's plans. Both understood that the subjection of the
Shan was a prerequisite for the recovery of Lower Burma and the revival
of the kingdom. Whereas Bayinnaung had reunited the coast with the
interior, Anaukpetlun began his reconquest from Upper Burma, the seat
of the first Burman centre of authority at Pagan.

After subduing Prome, the weakest of the successor states to emerge
after the deposition of Nandabayin, in 1610 Anaukpetlun attacked his
cousin Natshinnaung at Toungoo. Realising that there was no possibility
of defeating the combined forces of Upper Burma, the Shan kingdoms
and newly captured Prome, Natshinnaung submitted without a fight. On
meeting his cousin, Anaukpetlun expressed regret that they had not been

able to engage in combat. Natshinnaung replied that he too had looked forward to such a contest, but alas, a painful sore prevented him from sitting in one place, much less riding a war elephant.

The levity was not long to last. Discovering how Natshinnaung was plotting with the Portuguese to recover Toungoo, Anaukpetlun had his cousin's chest cut open. The involvement of Arakan in the Burmese civil war had allowed de Brito to construct a strong fortress at Syriam in the Irrawaddy delta. Before taking up service as a mercenary with the ruler of Arakan, de Brito was a salt merchant resident at Chittagong. Even though affairs on the eastern side of the Bay of Bengal interested Goa very little, the Portuguese viceroy based in this Indian enclave knew it was region into which many underpaid, indeed unpaid, Portuguese soldiers had drifted in search of personal wealth. The travel writer Mendes Pinto places the number of Portuguese mercenaries fighting for the Toungoo dynasty at over 700; but this may be as exaggerated as his claim that 500 fell beneath the walls of Prome, "whose only burial then was in the bellies of vultures and crows that tore them apart bit by bit as they lay scattered in the fields".

Possibly de Brito gave up his share of the spoils from Pegu, or paid the ruler of Arakan cash, for the privilege of retaining in 1601 a stronghold at Syriam. The suggestion that he ransomed the crown prince of Arakan is far-fetched. Had this young man fallen into de Brito's clutches, there was nothing to stop the Arakanese monarch from mounting a rescue operation by sea. Rather the enterprising de Brito took advantage of a power vacuum left in Lower Burma after the fall of Pegu, and then gained the support of the Portuguese authorities in Goa for making his base at Syriam into a customs house. He pointed out how a small squadron of ships stationed there could easily levy taxes on matritime trade between Burma and the Indonesian archipelago.

De Brito's motive was undoubtedly a desire to rejoin mainstream Portuguese society. Because the political situation in Lower Burma appeared favourable to the Estado da India, the name given to Portugal's Asian empire, the viceroy not only lent de Brito his support but also married one of his daughters to him. Ennobled and awarded the title of captaincy of the Syriam fortress for life, de Brito returned with his bride to Lower Burma, together with six ships and military supplies. Should they

The Konbaung court at Amarapura, where Michael Symes was unable
to secure any agreement on a border with British India

have a son, then the entitlement to act as a semi-independent ruler would
be inherited by him. Such was his authority that de Brito could pardon
the crimes of Portuguese living along the shore of the Bay of Bengal, even
when deserving a death sentence.

In 1612 de Brito cooperated with the ruler of Martaban, then a vassal
of Ayudhya, in an assault on Toungoo, whose reduced population was
unable to man the city's walls. This legacy of Natshinnaung's intrigues
convinced Anaukpetlun that something would have to be done about de
Brito, whose other actions included interference with coastal trade, the
melting down of bronze bells stolen from Buddhist temples for founding
canon, and a conspicuous patronage of the Catholic church.

Anaukpetlun's attack exposed the weakness of de Brito's position.
It is true that the defenders of Syriam ran short of gunpowder and were
unable to use effectively their excellent cannon. Yet it is most unlikely
that European weapons alone could have halted the siege. With no more
than 400 Portuguese and Indian followers, and perhaps four or five times
that number of local auxiliaries, de Brito had little hope of resisting the
100,000 men that Anaukpetlun had assembled. Scepticism about the size

King Bodawpaya's white elephant,
a creature prized by Southeast Asian monarchs

of the Burmese army is misplaced, because we know that the stockade
built by the besiegers was much larger than the Portuguese fortress.
Besides surrounding Syriam by land, Anaukpetlun also blocked the arrival
of reinforcements and new supplies of gunpowder through the stationing
of his own ships south of Syriam, manned by Moslem sailors.

With the fortress subject to almost continuous assault, de Brito's local
troops stole away until his remaining men could no longer maintain a
proper defence. As a punishment for looting Buddhist temples, de Brito
was impaled on an iron stake, where he lingered for two days in full view
of his men. But Anaukpetlun spared the lives of these cowed professionals,
settling them in villages northwest of Ava, where for over a century their

descendants were responsible for the Toungoo artillery. They were later joined by sailors and gunners captured from ships which arrived unaware of Syriam's fall. De Brito's wife's point-blank refusal to enter the harem of Anaukpetlun saw her reduced to the status of a palace menial.

What the fate of Syriam demonstrated was the limit of European power during the late era when confronted by the manpower resources of organized Asian states. The first European power to arrive in Southeast Asia, Portugal never had sufficient men to do more than plant fortresses at strategic locations and conduct regular sweeps of the sea. The total number of Portuguese soldiers and sailors in Asia at the height of the Estado da India's power never topped 10,000 men.

The restored Toungoo dynasty exercised a firmer grip on Burma than any of its predecessors. Donations to Buddhist monasteries were curbed so that too much wealth would not escape taxation; senior princes had to live in the capital at Ava under palace supervision; and appointed officials took charge of outlying territories in order to check separatist movements. Above all, Toungoo kings eschewed foreign adventures with the consequence that Lower Burma lost its importance as a staging post for assaults on Ayudhya. Anaukpetlun's successor Thalun, who was crowned in 1629, underlined the primacy of Upper Burma by identifying himself with Burman as opposed to Mon traditions, despite the Burmans still comprising less than 50 per cent of the kingdom's population.

But the price of firm central government was the gradual erosion of royal power. Well before Thalun's death in 1648 the growth of ministerial authority had greatly reduced the monarch's control over policy, while his son and successor Pindale proved incapable of dominating the court, and was eventually driven from the throne. His low birth did not help: Thalun had no sons by queens, for Pindale and his half-brothers were born to concubines. Another complication was incursions by Ming loyalists. Refusing to accept the Manchu conquest of China in 1644, these die-hards endeavoured to carry on resistance from Upper Burma. But their violent behaviour alienated the Burmans and the Shan so greatly that high officials and military commanders turned to Pye, one of Pindale's half-brothers. Although Pye promised to spare the dethroned king, ministerial pressure obliged him to drown Pindale, along with his family, in the Chindwin. "There cannot be two suns in the sky", Pye was told by his backers.

The coup of 1661 was accomplished by ministers and generals shifting their allegiance from a discredited ruler in favour of a prince who could deal with the Chinese intruders. Effective though Pye certainly was on the battlefield, the new king owed his position entirely to his senior advisors, a dangerous situation for the Toungoo house because ambitious backers might in future be tempted to promote weak princes instead of strong ones. In fact, this happened after the brief reign of Pye's sickly son and successor Narawara. As soon as this king expired in 1673, the palace was sealed off from the outside world while ministers decided which of four possible candidates to crown.

According to *The Glass Palace Chronicle*, they rejected three as unsuitable: one was too slow-witted, another was too fond of cock-fighting and drink, the third was too violent. So a cousin of the late king by the name of Minrekyawdin was chosen for his quiet disposition. When two of the rejected candidates protested during the coronation, they were summarily executed. An attempt to dethrone Minrekyawdin by another discontented kinsman was prevented shortly afterwards. The corridors of the palace were said to be haunted by the ghosts of those who fell in the bloodbath then.

How unsatisfactory Toungoo rule became under such overbearing ministers is well described by an English report in 1750. It relates how

> The Government... at present has a King, without experience, and entirely ruled by Ministers, without any other knowledge but a bare private Interest, which makes the Country in general wish for a change, because every petty Governor of Towns and Cities, if he can satisfy the Minister at Court, can at his pleasure oppress the people under him, without any fear of Punishment.

Already apparent even in Thalun's day, such a development inevitably led to disorder and the emergence of alternative centres of power. To protect their people, headmen erected stockades around villages and formed alliances with other strongmen. Unable to slow the trend towards local autonomy, Mahadammayaza Dipati, the last Toungoo king, tried to gain control of it by the bestowal of titles on leading figures, who were allowed to amass arms and men in their own districts. Ava's weakening hold over non-Burman peoples marked the final stage of the decline and a Mon revival that led in 1752 to the capital's destruction. An armada pushed up the Irrawaddy to Ava in concert with an army marching northwards. It seemed that Pegu was about to be reborn as a Mon capital where, a local chronicler proclaimed, its kings, would once again "receive homage from umbrella-bearing rulers".

The Konbaung Dynasty

That Mon expectations were rudely disappointed was due to Alaungpaya, a well-to-do Burman from Shwebo. For generations his forbears had been local leaders, who claimed descent from an important fifteenth-century chieftain. From the far north, where irrigation systems remained still largely undamaged, Alaungpaya began the reintegration of Burma by force of arms. Hand in hand with his military successes went administrative reforms that placed resources solely at his disposal. As his soldiers gathered Burman refugees together, Alaungpaya awarded them rice, clothing and land allotments in return for military service. Recruitment of lower-level officials from the old Ava administration, who had fled to their native villages on the capital's fall, provided much-needed expertise in ceremonial, religious and legal affairs. When in 1754 the Mon tried to halt Alaungpaya's revival of Upper Burma, an offensive was repulsed with considerable loss of life. Within two years his own forces had penetrated Lower Burma, capturing many towns and cities, but they were halted at Syriam by its strong walls and French ships trading there. Alaungpaya attempted to play off the European powers against one another, but the English East India Company declined to supply cannon.

A Burmese monk with his begging bowl

The arrival of large Burman and Shan reinforcements allowed Alaungpaya to blockade Syriam, which was starved into submission. Afterwards he announced his own buddhahood and his entitlement to rule as a great king like Asoka, the famous Mauryan emperor. Dressed up as a divine prophecy, this Konbaung claim to universal authority harked back to the ideology of the Pagan kings.

An unexpected bonus at Syriam was an arsenal of European weapons, which was supplemented when two French vessels, laden with military supplies from Pondichery, were captured shortly after the fortress fell. So much a godsend to Alaungpaya was this extra armament that he spared the lives of the crews. They were decently treated, given Burmese wives, and added to the king's army. This elite group served Alaungpaya well and, when too old for military action, they were comfortably retired in Upper Burma. There, with a Catholic priest, they ended their days, far from their original families in France. With this enhanced expertise and firepower, Alaungpaya moved against Pegu, some 50 kilometres to the north of Syriam. It still took a five-month siege to take the Mon capital.

British troops occupying Lower Burma in 1824

The Konbaung royal barge. Such teak vessels proved
no match for the paddle-steamer *Diana*

The thoroughness of the sack, coupled with edicts that encouraged the adoption of Burman manners and speech, did much to hasten the decline of Mon culture. A further acceleration occurred through migration to present-day Thailand, following the destruction of Ayudhya in 1767, after a fourteen-month investment.

Infuriated by the prolonged resistance, the city was subjected to several weeks of wholesale destruction—houses, monasteries, temples, the great palace itself, went up in flames. Most of the inhabitants were slaughtered or enslaved, while the city walls were razed to the ground, so that Ayudhya might never be restored as a Thai capital. Because of the sheer quantity of the loot that fell into Burmese hands, Thai chroniclers said that gold, silver and jewels constituted the real reason for this final assault. It seems to have been triggered, however, by Burman suspicions of Mon-Thai cooperation.

At the same time this happened, the Konbaung dynasty also staved off an invasion from China. The Manchu emperor Qian Long, in 1765, decided to reassert China's authority in Southeast Asia. The four-year campaign in Upper Burma ended in a stalemate, with the kingdom paying the same tribute to China as before. Much to Emperor Qian Long's anger his army was compelled to conclude hostilities by melting down its cannon, more easily to take the metal home. The withdrawal confirmed Konbaung rule but brought no peace to the royal household, because in 1782 thirty-seven-year-old Bodawpaya, the fifth son of Alaungpaya, seized the throne.

The erratic behaviour of his predecessor Singu Min, who was addicted to alcohol, had given Bodawpaya his opportunity. Having slain this drunken cousin, the new king initiated what was called "the massacre of the kinsmen", in which all his rivals perished along with their wives, children, retainers and servants. Many of the women were burnt alive, holding their babies in their arms. Perhaps to compensate for this savage

Nor would these fortifications offer much protection
when the British finally reached Mandalay

blood-letting Bodawpaya deliberately enlarged the royal family during his long reign: his fifty-three queens and concubines produced no less than 120 children.

A year after coming to the throne, Bodawpaya moved the capital a short distance away from Ava to another site at Amarapura, on the earnest advice of his chief astrologer. It was not to be the last Konbaung capital, since for not dissimilar reasons its last king moved in 1857 the court to Mandalay. If these two relocations were meant to guarantee the longevity of the dynasty, its kings suffered disappointment. Trouble came to Burma from the annexation of Arakan, because it led to conflict with Britain, even though the Burmese were invited by Arakanese aristocrats to restore order in their country. Relations with British India deteriorated through the refusal of Arakanese opponents of the take-over to respect international frontiers altogether. Anticipating the renewal of war with France, Governor-General Sir John Shore feared that unless some agreement was reached with Amarapura over border incidents in Arakan, Bodawpaya might be tempted to allow the French to use his ports. His concern encompassed the timber trade as well: vast quantities of Burmese teak were exported to India for shipbuilding purposes. So in 1795 a mission headed by Michael Symes arrived at Amarapura, but without being received by the king himself. Impressed though he was by the pomp of the Konbaung court, but not as much as by the "solemn and ceremonious" conduct of the Chinese envoys encountered there, all Symes achieved was a vague acknowledgement of the governor-general's concerns. After the failure of a second mission in 1813, Symes recommended that British influence should forcibly be imposed on Burma.

Relations between the English East India Company and Burma reached the explosive phase during the early 1820s. It was King Bagyidaw, the grandson and successor of Bodawpaya, who obliged the British to go to war by failing to restrain his military commanders. General Thado Maha Bandula had pursued Arakanese fugitives far into English East India company territory and killed its tiny garrison at Chittagong, then under company protection. Bandula believed that a show of strength here would consolidate Burma's western border. How wrong he was became transparent when a British seaborne force easily occupied Rangoon in 1824.

Yet the British found themselves masters of a deserted town. Except for a cellar of brandy, on which British regulars swiftly got drunk, there was nothing to sustain the expedition. Although Bandula's attempt to storm Rangoon with an army of 60,000 men failed, the British were in no condition to advance inland, as poor diet and tropical disease soon took their toll. The situation only improved when bullocks arrived from India and the local inhabitants began to reappear and offer assistance.

At Danubya, northwest of Rangoon, Bandula made a stand, his army reinforced with the royal cavalry. But he was killed by an exploding shell and his troops dispersed under heavy bombardment. Doubtless having a gilt umbrella carried above his head turned the Burmese general into a tempting target. The decisive moment occurred on the Irrawaddy, however, with the capture of teak war-boats sent to check the British advance up river: these vessels were nearly 100 metres long, with a crew of sixty oarsmen and 330 musketeers. They also carried small cannon. Their fate was sealed by the paddle-steamer *Diana*, a tugboat brought over from Calcutta harbour. By 1826 the *Diana*, which the Burmans called "the fire devil", had reached Amarapura and peace was hastily agreed. When the terms were announced at court, in "an unbounded rage" King Bagyidaw ordered "the wretched minister who explained the treaty to have his mouth cut from ear to ear". The payment of £1 million, and the cession of Manipur, Assam, Arakan and Tenasserim was hardly onerous: the war was the most expensive war ever fought by the English East India Company; it cost £5 million and the lives of 15,000 British and Indian soldiers.

It was quite by chance that the *Diana* took part in the First Anglo-Burmese War. But the ability of this steamer to penetrate rivers was not lost on the English East India Company, whose subsequent purchase of steamers conferred an easy supremacy in Asian coastal waters. The *Nemesis* would confound China in 1840, when its demolition of the forts protecting the approach to Guangzhou made this iron warship more feared, according to her captain, "than all the Line-of-Battle ships put together".

6

LATE THAILAND
AND CAMBODIA

The king is by no means a tyrant, for it is not in his nature. The
income derived from customs throughout his kingdom is set
aside for certain pagodas as charity. Consequently, the duties
paid here are very low; for since the pagodas are not allowed
to accumulate wealth, the merchants are only asked to pay
what they wish, by way of charity, of their own free will.

Mendes Pinto on the Ayudhyan monarchy

Political disintegration in mainland Southeast Asia after the intervention
of the Mongols provided the Thai with their chance of power. The
Indianized states based at Pagan in Upper Burma and at Angkor in
Cambodia were already in decline by the close of the thirteenth century.
Although Khmer authority did not collapse with the dramatic suddenness
of the Burmese kingdom in 1287, there was a lack of dynamism at Angkor
that no amount of ceremony could disguise. And it was a misfortune
for the Khmers that the decline of Mongol power happened to coincide
with even greater Thai pressure on Angkor, because it meant during the
fourteenth century they were left to wage a losing conflict on their own.

Yet Thai migration predated the Mongol conquest of Nanzhou in
1253, a belligerent kingdom based on the Thai homeland of Yunnan.
Incorporation of Yunnan province into the Chinese empire certainly gave
impetus to the southern movement of the Thai but the myth of Khun
Borom is a memory of a much earlier dispersal. The bringer of agriculture,

handicrafts, manners, learning and ritual, this semi-divine hero ruled the plain around Dien Bien Phu, in northern Vietnam for twenty-five years. From there, he sent his seven sons to rule over the numerous groups of Thai-speakers already spread across mainland Southeast Asia. They comprise today the Shan, Khun, Lu, Lao, Yuan and Thai. Their survival depended upon two things: martial ability and irrigation skills.

A patchwork of Thai principalities then stretched from Vietnam across the Mekong and Chaophraya rivers to the Gulf of Martaban. None of these jostling kingdoms ever attained sufficient power to dominate their neighbours, and it was not until the foundation of Ayudhya in 1351 that any sign of regional strength appears. A rare exception to this general weakness was Lanna, meaning "a million ricefields", whose capital of Chiang Mai was founded in 1296 by Mangrai, a Thai leader with some Mon-Khmer blood. An astute and energetic king, he took advantage of Angkor's weakness after the death of its last powerful ruler Jayavarman VII to acquire new territory at the expense of the Khmers. Mangrai was so esteemed by his Thai neighbours that he settled a bitter dispute between Phayao and Sukhothai. Even though the king of Phayao would have been within his rights to kill Sukhothai's monarch for seducing his queen, Mangrai persuaded him to accept instead an apology and an indemnity of 990,000 cowrie shells, then the standard medium of exchange.

Yet Mangrai's desire to keep the peace on his southern border may have had more to do with foreign policy than any Buddhist concern to avoid unnecessary bloodshed, because in 1281 he conquered the northern Mon kingdom of Haripunjaya. Eight years later he extended his influence to Pegu, the chief Mon city in Lower Burma. Already freed by Mongol arms from Pagan's overlordship, the Peguan king was pleased to offer a daughter in marriage and conclude an alliance, according to a local chronicler, so that "the Thai and the Mon, of great and small villages, form a single people".

From Upper Burma Mangrai seems to have imported craftsmen for the embellishment of his new capital at Chiang Mai, which still remains the political centre of northern Thailand today. His growing power was noticed by Beijing and in 1301 an army of 20,000 men, reinforced by Mongol archers, marched against Chiang Mai. The expedition achieved nothing, diplomacy eventually settling relations between the Mongols and

A bronze Buddha from Sukhothai, whose conversion to
Theravada Buddhism opened new perspectives for the Thai

the Thai through the despatch of tribute to China from 1315 onwards.
Two years later Mangrai suddenly died, leaving a succession crisis that
lasted until 1324. Lanna survived the period of instability, but soon found
itself a pawn in the prolonged conflict between Burma and Ayudhya, a
powerful Thai kingdom established in the lower Chaophraya river valley.

Ayudhya

To the south of Lanna, Sukhothai had put together a network of alliances
similar to Mangrai's. A Chinese envoy to Angkor in 1295 reported that
Sukhothai had just laid waste large areas of the Angkorian kingdom,
forcing the Khmer king to introduce universal military conscription.
Remembered for the development of an Indian-inspired script suited
to the Thai language, Sukhothai kings worshipped Hindu deities such
as Vishnu and Shiva as well as the Buddha. Though strongly influenced

by Theravada Buddhist traditions from Sri Lanka and Burma, the art of Sukhothai is notable for its distinctive Thai appearance, especially in the representation of the Buddha's face.

A sharp decline in Sukhothai's fortunes during the 1320s was in fact the prelude to the rise of Ayudhya. The core of what was to become this new Thai kingdom had been Angkor's western provinces centred on Lopburi. Inspired by Sukhothai, with whom they were close allies, the rulers of Lopburi sought to grow at the expense of Angkor and obtain the recognition of China: tribute missions were sent to the latter between 1289 and 1299 because, like Indonesian kings, they appreciated how tributary relations gave access to the Chinese market, by far the biggest consumer of trade goods.

Lopburi was in itself unable to exploit the growing weakness of Angkor, but it produced a leader who could do so. This was the adventurer U Thong, whose name means "Prince Golden Cradle". Though he was born around 1314 into a rich Chinese merchant family, it was his marriage to a Thai princess that laid the basis for Thailand's future strength: an effective combination of Thai arms with Chinese commercial enterprise. One account of U Thong's elevation as King Ramathibodi mentions an outbreak of smallpox, a vacant throne and the removal of the capital from Lopburi to Ayudhya. This new city, built on a downstream island, was named after the hero Rama's stronghold in the Indian epic, the *Ramayana*: Ayudhya or Ayutthaya. Although the Chinese called this kingdom Xian, which the Portuguese converted into Siam, here Ayudhya is used in order to distinguish it from the Thai power based later upon the city of Bangkok.

The kingdom of Ayudhya consolidated its position by means of a tactical alliance with Sukhothai, which managed to remain independent until 1438 when it was converted into an Ayudhyan province. Proximity to the remnant of the once mighty Khmer empire undoubtedly inspired imperial ambitions in King Ramathibodi and, between 1351 and 1431, there was an almost permanent state of war between Angkor and Ayudhya. He may have even temporarily occupied Angkor, deporting some of its inhabitants to his own kingdom. But armed rivalry did not preclude admiration for Khmer kingship, and the court at Ayudhya adopted its protocol wholesale, thereby inaugurating the process by

A magnificent Buddha of unknown date from northern Thailand

which Thailand came to absorb so much of Cambodian tradition. There can be no question that Ramathibodi had already imported a Khmer-style administration from Lopburi.

Ayudhyan society was divided into a strict hierarchy, presided over by royal officials from leading families. As a foreign community, the Chinese exercised political influence by assisting one court faction or another to increase its wealth and make diplomatic contacts abroad. Despite a great deal of assimilation, this behind-the-scenes influence continues nowadays, so that with a degree of truth modern Thailand could be described as a Sino-Thai corporation, owing allegiance to a royal house. Quite different is the situation in present-day Malaysia, where Islam is such an effective wedge between Malay and Chinese citizens that discriminatory legislation has even been introduced to bolster the social and economic position of the Malays. There is additionally no central figure to unify society like the Thai monarch, who is believed to possess the essence of the Buddha himself. Kindly benevolence and impassivity are its outward signs, a reason for portraits of the Thai king never showing a smile or a frown, since these would imply an unnecessary attachment to worldly objects. In Malaysia, on the other hand, a number of Malay sultans entirely associated with Moslem tradition take it in turns to be king.

The duties of royal officials were defined by King Borommatrailokanat, who ruled from 1448 to 1488. The acquisition of new territories prompted

A "spirit" house dedicated
to the "lord of the place"

the setting up of an administration that was capable of controlling provinces at a distance from the capital. Following Khmer practice, Trailok (as he is known) centralized government, distinguished between civil and military landholders, amalgamated local forces into the royal army and replaced tribal leaders with princely governors. His legislation dealt with every level of society to the extent of determining the fines and punishments appropriate for all his own subjects' misbehaviour. If a peasant assaulted an official, for instance, it was regarded as more serious than an assault on a slave, because the crime represented an affront to the king from whom the official derived his status. Trailok's chief concern appears to have been the regulation of human inequality in the interests of the smooth operation of Ayudhyan society. The outcome of Trailok's legislation was a stability unsurpassed anywhere else in late Southeast Asia. His system lasted with minor modifications right down to the nineteenth century when Western-style reforms were urgently adopted to modernize Thailand. Even then, the government remained until 1932 the preserve of the nobles. That year a constitutional revolution finally abolished absolute monarchy.

Externally, Trailok was challenged by two Thai kingdoms, Lanna and Lan Sang. Angkor was no more, and not for another century would Toungoo Burma become the main threat to Ayudhya's existence. With the accession of King Tilokaracha in 1441, Lanna felt strong enough to move against Lan Sang, whose capital was located at Luang Prabang on the middle reaches of the Mekong river. The new king of Lanna would seem to have been trying to increase his reserves of manpower and draft animals for the major war with Ayudhya that he realized was coming.

According to Lao legend, the son of a ruler of what later became Luang Prabang fled to Angkor and married a Khmer princess, Keo Kaengkana. He was Fa Ngum, a Lao prince who claimed direct descent from Khun Borom. With the aid of Khmer soldiers, Fa Ngum fought his way back up the Mekong and in 1353 installed himself at his forefathers' capital, which he was to name Luang Prabang, as the rightful king of Lan Sang, which means "a million elephants". After the death of Queen Keo Kaengkana, however, Fa Ngum is said to have become so dissolute that he was deposed in 1373 by his own disgusted son, who then reigned as an exemplary king for the next forty-three years. He is remembered as the "King of Three Hundred Thousand Thai", recalling the census of 1376 which discovered that there were 300,000 Lao men who were eligible for military service in the kingdom, besides 400,000 non-Thai inhabitants. That Lan Sang managed to survive in conflict-ridden Southeast Asia had much to do with its remote location. As the Jesuit missionary Gian Filippo de Marni astutely pointed out:

> The Laotians have used the advantages which their country got from nature
> to declare war on the Emperor and cease from obeying him; and with the

The riverside location of Luang Prabang,
the royal residence of Lan Sang, present-day Laos

help of other peoples which live in the mountains, they have preserved
the liberty and independence which they still enjoy.

This reference to China should be no surprise, given how close Luang
Prabang itself actually is to the Chinese border. Yet it would be the
Ayudhyans and the Burmese, not the Chinese, who eventually forced the
removal of the Lao capital in 1563 from Luang Prabang to Vientiane, a site
even more easily defended against outside attack.

Sukhothai rebelled in 1462 against Ayudhya, whose war with Lanna
was not then going very well. Recognising the need to maintain a strong
presence in the north of the kingdom, King Trailok transferred his
capital to Phitsanulok, near the city of Sukhothai, and appointed his son
Itharacha to act as regent in Ayudhya. But soon tiring of the conflict
with Lanna, and unable to reach a satisfactory peace agreement, Trailok
abdicated and entered a Buddhist monastery which he had constructed
near Phitsanulok. With a great deal of reluctance, the monk-king
agreed in 1466 to resume the kingship at Ayudhya. But the restoration
proved unnecessary because a Vietnamese invasion of Lan Sang obliged
troublesome Lanna to look to its eastern frontier and seek tributary

A Luang Prabang Buddhist monastery

status with China. After Trailok's death at Phitsanulok in 1488, Ayudhya experienced a significant expansion of seaborne commerce that coincided with the development of Malacca as a key hub for Southeast Asian trade. Ayudhya was then the major supplier of rice to Malacca, which may have accepted the overlordship of both Ayudhya and China.

This dual tributary relationship must explain why the Portuguese immediately sent a mission to Ayudhya, following their capture of Malacca in 1511. They obviously thought that the port was a Thai vassal. Because Ayudhya's earlier seizure of Tavoy and Tenasserim had been motivated by a desire to exploit the international commerce of the Bay of Bengal, some kind of overlordship of Malacca was intended to allow its involvement with the trade passing through the Straits as well. This interest was of course bound to put Ayudhya on a collision course with Burma, once the Toungoo king Tabinshwehti had reunited this country. Although he failed to take Ayudhya himself, Tabinshwehti's son and successor Bayinnaung did so in 1564 and 1569. Thai independence was not fully restored until the accession of Naresuan in 1590: he annoyed Burma before this date, but once a puppet ruler no longer sat on the Ayudhyan throne, Naresuan could plan a concerted defence against further Burmese attacks.

One of the greatest took place in 1592–93, when the Toungoo king Nandabayin's army negotiated the Three Pagodas Pass and descended upon the strategically important town of Kanchanaburi, some 120 kilometres west of Ayudhya. Rather than withstand a siege, Naresuan decided to risk a pitched battle. The Portuguese traveller writer Mendes Pinto tells us how news of the invasion resulted in a general call-up. Foreigners were given thee days to rally to the colours or leave Ayudhya altogether. Pinto declares

with regard to Portuguese residents, who had been shown the highest respect, the king sent a minister, the governor of the capital, to ask them to voluntarily join his army, in view of the reputation they had, for he was desirous of having them serve as his personal guards since from what he knew about them, they were better suited for it than all others. Considering the nature of this message, which was accompanied by liberal promises and expectations of high wages, favours, honours, and above all,

permission to build churches in his kingdom we felt so deeply obligated to
him that, out of the 130 of us Portuguese who were there at the time, 120
agreed to go with him.

Encouraged by this timely support, Naresuan marched with his own
Thai troops towards Kanchanaburi at the beginning of 1593.

Although heavily outnumbered by the Toungoo army, a Thai chronicle
relates how Naresuan found comfort in the appearance of auspicious signs
such as the relics of the Buddha, which glowed in the sky. Yet he really
placed his hope of victory in the effectiveness of "the lotus array", a battle
formation comprising a vanguard supported by powerful wings. During
the engagement at Nong Sarai, his troops were thus deployed when a
small Thai force sent forward to reconnoitre the enemy's position was
driven back in considerable disorder. Instead of going to its aid, Naresuan
decided to stand firm and let the Burmese advance in the belief that the
Ayudhyans were abandoning the battlefield. An uncoordinated pursuit
handed the advantage to Naresuan's men, although they still had to fight
hard to avoid envelopment by a larger Burmese army.

Pinto mentions how cleverly Naresuan adjusted his tactics after the
initial contact, but makes no mention of the encounter between him and
the Toungoo commander, whom he slew with a long-handled sword from
the top of his favourite war elephant. More important still, Pinto omits
a singular Portuguese action: a shot fired by one of the volunteers killed
Nandabayin's eldest son, thereby contributing to a succession struggle
that for a generation would cripple the Toungoo dynasty.

To meet the continued threat from Burma, Ayudhyan kings
understood how they had to improve their weaponry. The Chinese had
first introduced firearms to the Thai, but from the seventeenth century
onwards they looked to Europe for the latest models. A Portuguese
from Macao was even charged with the casting of cannon, a calculated
response to the incorporation of Portuguese gunners into the Toungoo
army following the fall of Syriam in 1613. Besides noticeably improving
its artillery, Ayudhya also imported firearms in great quantities. When
the city finally fell to the Burmese in 1767, its armoury contained 12,000
muskets inlaid with gold and silver tracery and more than 10,000 ordinary
muskets.

Roof finials on a Laotian temple

Of all its kings, Narai was possibly most aware of the need to keep Ayudhya's armed forces up to date. Although Naresuan had almost single-handedly revived Ayudhya on the battlefield, this was not enough to preserve the kingdom's independence. Having seized the throne in 1656 with the aid of Moslem backers but not the Dutch, who refused to become directly involved in Thai politics, King Narai maintained friendly relations with Dutch traders but looked to France for outside support, at the instance of Constantine Phaulkon. This Greek adventurer arrived at Ayudhya with the English East India Company, learned to speak Thai fluently, and then acted as an interpreter for Narai's court. As French Jesuit missionaries, already resident in Ayudhya, had made themselves useful by their advice on the construction of fortifications, it was not unnatural for Narai to look to Paris for further assistance. A recent convert to Catholicism, Phaulkon seems to have believed that the king himself might be converted through a closer relationship with France. A French mission arrived in 1685 with this purpose in mind, but there was competition from a Persian mission already trying to win Narai's conversion to Islam.

Neither mission achieved their aims. That Narai would never convert was obvious to one French observer, who realized that Christianity would never sit easily with Ayudhyan kingship.

> Oh my God, how he made me feel sorry for this poor King, when I saw him with this pomp, passing in front of 200,000 people at the river's edge, who with their hands joined and their faces bowed to the earth, gave him divine honours! How could such a poor man accustomed to such adoration not conceive himself to being above humanity? And how difficult it will be to persuade him to submit to all the humiliations of the Christian religion!

Missed entirely here was Narai's genuine desire to understand the outside world. His curiosity to learn about Christianity as a part of foreign, European culture was genuine: the Jesuits were wrong to assume that he never intended to embrace the faith. They simply failed to convince the king that conversion was worthwhile.

The French connection was not, however, without its uses to Narai. Rather than defend the port of Mergui against the English East India Company, he handed it over to France in 1686. But the presence of French troops was as unpopular in Ayudhya as the king's reliance on Phaulkon, with the result that anti-foreign sentiments encouraged a palace coup in mid-1688, just before Narai died. The king's terminal illness provided a prominent commander by the name of Phetracha with the perfect opportunity for the elimination of Phaulkon and any rivals to the throne. Some help may have been forthcoming from Buddhist monks, although they were not motivated by fear of Catholicism, since it had gained no following among the people at large. King Phetracha did nonetheless seek to strengthen his position by conspicuous patronage of Buddhism. His dislike of the French, and to a lesser extent the English, left the Dutch as Ayudhya's favoured European trading partner. Friction between Ayudhya and Batavia, Holland's permanent trading post on the island of Java, was never entirely overcome though, because both wanted to extract the greatest possible profit from international commerce. In the end, the Dutch did not really benefit from the French absence because, without a French threat, there was less reason for Phetracha to rely on Dutch support.

The French presenting a letter from Louis XIV to Narai in 1685.
A prostrate Phaulkon gestures the ambassador to raise it higher

In spite of being a usurper, Phetracha survived unrest in different parts of the kingdom, and one of his sons succeeded him in 1703. Yet not for another six years would peace return to Ayudhya, with the crowning of King Phumintharacha, better known as Thai Sa: literally "the end of the lake", a reference to the moat surrounding his palace. During King Thai Sa's long reign there was a trade boom with China, which from 1727 opened its southern ports to the import of Thai rice. The withdrawal of the Dutch from Ayudhya left this profitable seaborne trade in the hands of Chinese merchants, whose wealth encouraged integration with Thai

European gunners, mercenaries in great demand by Southeast Asian kings

society. Even leading court families were now prepared to give their daughters in marriage.

King Thai Sa had strictly forbidden Catholic priests to proselytize, but his successor Borommakot took a more relaxed view of religion—his name can be translated as "the king in an urn", that is, the one awaiting cremation. Borommakot even permitted Europeans to view a footprint of the Buddha, without showing any reverence for its sanctity. While some courtiers were deeply annoyed by this, the king reasoned that "who is not faithful to his god, is not faithful to his master". And he had other worries such as the problem of balancing kingly and princely power against the nobles who ran the administration. By creating more but smaller government departments, Borommakot hoped to prevent any future seizure of the throne.

Borommakot endeavoured to ensure a smooth succession but once again the crown was fought over, and a civil war could not have happened at a more dangerous moment, since Ayudhya was about to be attacked by the newly established Konbaung dynasty of Burma. There had been street fighting in the city prior to Borommakot's own coronation, and now princely executions and the abdication of his short-lived successor took the kingdom to the brink of collapse. The last king of Ayudhya had no chance at all of uniting his subjects against another Burmese invasion. The city would have been captured in 1760 had not one of the besiegers' guns burst, fatally injuring King Alaungpaya. As this founder of the Konbaung dynasty died on the way back to Burma, the task of destroying Ayudhya fell to Alaungpaya's second son, Hsinbyushin, who subdued Lanna and then Lan Sang before he was ready for the final assault. As if epidemics and famine were not enough to break the spirit of the Thai, a fire burned down 10,000 houses in the city just before its walls were breached. Without mercy, the Burmese army raped, pillaged, and plundered, and finally led away thousands of captives as slaves. Left behind was a devastated kingdom, a Thai chronicler sadly recounts, "afflicted by countless ills".

A Thai princess on an elephant accompanied by armed guards

A Dutch map of Ayudhya, "the Venice of the East"

Siam

Appalling though the Burmese sack was in 1767, its long-term result was ironically the unification of Thailand, for the territories covered by the kingdoms of Ayudhya, Lanna and Lan Sang were incorporated under the long-lasting Chakri dynasty. The present Thai king, Bhumibol Adulyadej, who ascended the throne in 1946, is the ninth member of this incredibly long dynasty to reign, his title being Rama IX.

The country's saviour was a second U Thong, whose charisma offset a Chinese ancestry. The son of a Chinese father and a Thai mother, Sin had been adopted by a Thai noble family. At the time of the fateful Burmese invasion, he was serving as governor of Tak province: hence his preferred name, Taksin. Having shifted the capital downriver to Thonburi, a small port on the west bank of the Chaophraya river across from modern Bangkok, he established himself as a benevolent and effective ruler. We are told that he "showed a generous spirit. The needy were destitute no longer. The treasury was opened for their relief".

King Taksin claimed that his new kingdom restored the traditions of Ayudhya, but in reality his court was cosmopolitan with the sons of Indian, Persian, Cham, Malay and Chinese families joining those belonging to old Thai ones. From his startling successes on the battlefield probably stemmed Taksin's personal problems towards the end of his reign. By 1779 it was clear that all was not well at court. French missionaries reported how Taksin increasingly devoted himself to religious exercises: "He passed all his time in prayer, fasting, and meditation, in order by these means to be able to fly in the air." What they saw as nothing more than black magic, or at best Southeast Asian eccentricity, was actually the serious pursuit of immortality, a will-o'-the-wisp that had attracted more than one Chinese emperor. Confirmation of Taksin's aim comes from his insistence on being called a Buddhist saint, even a deity; monks who refused to accord him this singular honour were either flogged or sentenced to hard labour. Alienating the Buddhist monks, the old Thai families, the royal officials and the Chinese merchants, Taksin's fate was sealed when he was deposed and, with sandalwood clubs, beaten to death inside a velvet sack, which was then cast into the Chaophraya river. Violence can never be directly inflicted on the body of a Thai king. Following Chinese practice, royal victims were strangled in Vietnam, never decapitated. Drowning appears to have been the preferred method of execution in Burma, although the last king of Pagan accepted poisoned food rather than face death by a Mongol sword thrust.

Taksin's general Chaophraya Chakri ascended the throne in 1782 as Rama I. One of his first acts as king was to move the capital across Chaophraya river to the present-day site of Bangkok, where the restored Thai government would be less vulnerable to a renewed Burmese assault from the west. Convinced that moral degeneracy had caused Ayudhya's downfall, Rama I reaffirmed the religious duties of the laity, whose understanding of the Buddhist faith was enhanced by the translation into the Thai language of important works such as *The Questions of King Milinda*. Not content with this, the king reformed the monastic order, weeding out corrupt monks and requiring others to carry passports for purposes of identification whenever they moved around the kingdom. By the end of his reign in 1809, Thai Buddhism had gathered sufficient strength to ensure its survival into modern times. As significant were his political and military actions, because even tributary states willingly accepted Siamese rule: it guaranteed them protection from Burmese as well as Vietnamese aggression.

That more dangerous enemies were on the horizon was not missed in Bangkok when, in 1786, news arrived of the sultan of Kedah's cession of Penang to the British. This island base was secured by Francis Light, who had assisted Kedah when it was attacked by Indonesian pirates. A grateful sultan believed that the presence of the Royal Navy would more effectively deter opponents than Siam, whose vassal Kedah actually was. Despite the Royal Navy finding the anchorage less than satisfactory, Penang did act as a counter to Aceh, where the French had obtained permission to refit their warships. Before Light died in 1794, the new colony was several thousand strong; many of its residents were Chinese merchants seeking to escape Dutch domination of Southeast Asian trade. The Dutch had taken Malacca from the Portuguese in 1641 and then progressively tightened their grip on commerce in the Straits of Malacca. But it was the Dutch conquest of Riau, in central Sumatra, shortly before the Penang cession which opened up new trading possibilities through its disruption of existing networks of exchange, much to the advantage of Penang. As Singapore was to be later on, Penang was a free port that levied negligible taxes on international commerce.

Encroachment by Britain was feared in Bangkok, especially after the English East India Company acquired Tenasserim in the First Anglo-Burmese War of 1824–26. A common border seemed fraught with danger until an agreement was reached on the new frontier. In a treaty agreed in 1826, Siam was relieved that Britain also acknowledged its suzerainty over the Malay states of Patani, Kedah, Kelantan and Trengganu. The last three, however, would pass under British control at the start of the twentieth century. Only the Malay rulers of Patani failed to shake off Thai overlordship: in 1909 Patani became a Siamese province.

Even though the Anglo-Siamese Treaty of 1826 was useful in establishing a workable pattern for Siam's relations with the West, Siamese kings were under no illusions about the increasingly uncertain political situation in Southeast Asia. Despite Rama III bequeathing to his successors a Siamese empire that was more powerful and stronger than at any previous occasion, he was realistic about its prospects of survival. On his deathbed, in 1851, the king remarked that

The Emerald Buddha's Hall in the Grand Palace at Bangkok
shows the influence of Khmer traditions

there will be no more wars with Vietnam and Burma. We will have them only with the West. Take care, and do not lose any opportunities to them. Anything they propose should be held up to close scrutiny before accepting it. Do not trust them blindly.

The dying king appreciated how the British defeat of China during the First Opium War of 1840–42 had altered the balance of power in favour of Europe. Unable to foresee the rise of a modernized Japan, he believed that nothing could now halt the advance of Western colonialism.

How his brother Mongkut, Rama IV, managed to steer Siam on an independent course remains one of the most surprising achievements of the late nineteenth century. The country's position was far from safe, with Burma and Malaya being steadily absorbed by the British and Vietnam coming under increasing French influence. Treaties signed with Britain in

1855, and France a year after, regularised relations with Siam, although never missing an opportunity for trade, the British gained for its infamous Indian export, opium, the waiving of import duty. The policy of playing off Britain against France was continued by Mongkut's son Chulalongkorn, or Rama V, who was probably assisted in this high-risk game by the desire on the part of both colonial powers to avoid having adjacent territories in Southeast Asia.

Chulalongkorn also followed his father's lead in the modernization of Siamese society. Mongkut had cultivated relations with Europeans, in particular the more reasonable missionaries. Through these contacts he acquired imported books and a grasp of the English language. His

King Chulalongkorn and his son

More Khmer influence is evident in the architecture
of the Regalia Hall at Bangkok

interests ranged from steam technology to the mathematics of astronomy. But it was Chulalongkorn who derived the greatest benefit from the palace governess, Anna Leonowens. Despite the glamour attached to her name by the Hollywood film *The King and I*, she was treated as a servant whose workload expanded dramatically, without any extra financial recompense. After five years' service, she was granted in 1867 a period of "rest" at Singapore. Mrs Leonowens appears to have hoped that King Mongkut would summon her back under more favourable terms, but the king died unexpectedly from malaria and his son, her star pupil Chulalongkorn, made a point of not inviting her to return at all.

Both father and son had contracted malaria on a visit to southern Siam, where they travelled to witness a solar eclipse in 1868. Not long after returning to Bangkok, the fifteen-year-old Chulalongkorn was crowned as Rama V in spite of his precarious health. Once he recovered and his position on the throne was secure, Chulalongkorn began a series of reforms that revealed a concern for progress. Royal decrees sought to speed up justice, reduce corruption, control expenditure, improve the armed forces, develop communications and tackle slavery. In 1905 debt-bondage was abolished, one of the last vestiges of feudalism cleared away by this still absolute king. It was the reigns of Rama IV and V, from 1851 until 1910, that really ensured that the Thai were the only Southeast Asian people to avoid Western colonial rule. But survival came at a price: Bangkok had to trade territory for peace with Britain and France.

Lovek

Nowhere was this kind of trade-off more apparent than in present-day Laos and Cambodia, since France readily established protectorates over both these countries. In 1863 the Cambodian monarch agreed to place his people under French protection, while simultaneously recognising the suzerainty of the Siamese. Once this secret agreement with Bangkok became public knowledge, the king was immediately obliged to accept "all the administrative, judicial and commercial reforms that the French government shall judge, in future, useful to make their protectorate successful". Doubtless a French gunboat at Phnom Penh, anchored within sight of the royal palace, had a salutary effect. In 1893 again, it was the sudden appearance of French gunboats on the Chaophraya river that persuaded Bangkok to let Laos become another protectorate of France.

The abandonment of Angkor in 1431 had really marked the end of Cambodia's political greatness. No longer able to withstand Thai pressure, the Khmers cut their losses and moved towards the sea, where eventually at modern Phnom Penh international commerce sustained a diminished Khmer kingdom. As a maritime orientation developed, the Ayudhyan occupation of Angkor seemed less insulting to Khmer pride, although repairs to some of the ex-imperial city's buildings during the sixteenth century suggests that its glorious past was never entirely forgotten. From his capital of Lovek, a river port not far north of modern Phnom Penh, we know that the Cambodian king Ang Chan made pilgrimages to Angkor before his death in 1566.

According to the Portuguese missionary Gaspar de Cruz, who visited Lovek towards the end of Ang Chan's reign, the people

> dare do nothing of themselves, nor accept anything new without the leave of the king, which is why Christians cannot be made without the king's approval.

More frustrating still for this missionary was the status accorded to the Buddhist clergy, whose "supreme monks precede the king". He marvels that "alive they are worshipped for gods… and so the common people have great confidence in them". Realising that such reverence allowed no scope at all for mass conversion, Gaspar da Cruz quit Cambodia. But thirty years later a Khmer ruler was prepared to contemplate Christianity as a means of securing military aid.

Anxious about renewed pressure from Ayudhya, King Satha II put his trust in a Portuguese adventurer named Diogo Veloso, who promised assistance from Portuguese Malacca. While Filipe de Brito e Nicote enlisted the aid of the viceroy at Goa for his enterprise at Syriam in Lower Burma, Veloso got nothing at all from Malacca, a city already weakened by a shortage of men and money. It was also harassed by the Acehnese, fearful of Ayudhya and, above all, worried by the arrival of the first Dutch and English ships. So an appeal was therefore made to Madrid, since Portugal was then under Spanish control, and in 1596 an expedition sailed from Manila with Veloso on board. In Cambodia, however, a totally different situation greeted him: Satha had been overthrown by a usurper, who was suspicious of foreign aid. After a short campaign, the second son of Satha II, Ton, was placed on the throne. Not

A Thai royal procession. Absolute monarchy lasted until 1932

ungrateful for his elevation, the new king granted privileges to Catholic priests and awarded Veloso an island downriver from Lovek, where he could build a fortress and levy charges on passing merchant ships.

The idea of the second Syriam here appealed greatly to Spain and the necessary funds were supplied for its construction, but whether it was ever built remains uncertain. In 1599, when Spanish reinforcements landed at Phnom Penh, they quarrelled with Malay residents there and in the ensuing fight they were massacred, except for a single Spaniard and a few Filipinos. Veloso himself died in a separate altercation in peninsular Malaya, possibly over a dispute about trading rights. Although Cambodian rulers did not persecute the few Europeans who continued to live in their kingdom after the Luso-Spanish debacle, they no longer favoured them as Satha and Ton had done. Thus a new era of Cambodian history began in which Siamese influence was to predominate until a Vietnamese menace appeared in the south.

That the bloody quarrel with Malay traders at Phnom Penh terminated Spanish ambitions on mainland Southeast Asia is illustrative of Cambodia's progress as a trading state. At Lovek and Phnom Penh there were separate quarters for Chinese, Japanese, Arab, Spanish, Portuguese, Indian and Indonesian merchants, who operated through officials close to the king and members of the royal family, so that a substantial part of the profits from imports and exports ended up in the royal treasury. By marrying into the Khmer nobility, Chinese and Malay traders had reinforced Cambodia's commercial character. A uniquely Khmer Buddhist tradition evolved without entirely discarding the Hindu heritage of Angkor but rather adapting it to new purposes. A prime example of this is Angkor Wat, which makes use of the magnificent Vishnu temple and tomb of King Suryavarman II as a Buddhist monastery.

By the end of the nineteenth century Cambodia had become a backwater, tightly squeezed between Vietnam and Siam. The Vietnamese emperor Minh Mang went so far as to suggest that only colonisation would save Cambodians. He said they needed to "speak Vietnamese, adopt our dress and follow our table manners". The Indian-inspired custom of eating with fingers had to give way to civilized chopsticks, Vietnam's cultural import from China.

7

LATE VIETNAM

There is an abundance of silk in Tonkin. The natives, both
the rich and the poor, all wear silk. The Dutch trade to every
corner where they could yield profit. Every year they ship
away a vast quantity of Tonkin's silk to the Japanese market.

A European observer in 1679

The cordial relations established by the Song dynasty between China
and Vietnam were briefly interrupted in 1407. That year the Chinese
intervened at the request of the son of a murdered Tran emperor, after
the overthrow of that dynasty by one of its own officials. But such was
the strength of the opposition to this, when excessive demands for timber
revealed how Vietnam was being asset-stripped for the construction of
the new Ming capital at Beijing, that massive Chinese reinforcements
were not enough to master Vietnamese resistance. Guerrilla tactics
directed against the occupation force had roused the countryside to
a rebellion so widespread that China had no choice but to accept a
humiliating withdrawal.

Given the relative sizes of the two countries though, the influence
of China continued unabated because Vietnamese rulers could foster
Chinese ways of doing things with more success than Chinese officials.
They were, after all, aware of what their people would tolerate. Yet in
many ways, the twenty-year Chinese occupation marked a watershed
in Vietnam's cultural history. For the Le dynasty which followed this
unexpected event was more inclined to patronize Confucius than the
previous Tran emperors, who had shown special favour to Buddhist

monks. It is almost as if two decades of Chinese rule were sufficient to revive interest in Confucius, whose philosophy was now the yardstick for behaviour in the late Chinese empire. Hereafter Vietnamese rulers mused over Confucian ideals of conduct rather than Buddhist notions of merit and reincarnation. Although Buddhism would remain an important dimension of Vietnamese society, its role was henceforth restricted to concerns about personal salvation.

Had he still been alive, the delight of the Ming emperor Yongle at this revival of Confucianism would have been palpable. Even though an odd mixture of ruthless brutality and moral idealism made him the perfect absolutist ruler, Yongle wanted his subjects to associate his rule with the Confucian ideal of a wise emperor who always listened to ministerial advice. And this was the image of the Son of Heaven that he also wished to project well beyond China's frontiers. The ocean voyages commanded by the eunuch admiral Zheng He were part of this propaganda drive, along with Yongle's decision to annex Vietnam once again. That the latter failed politically, but not culturally, is testimony to how deep-rooted Chinese ideas already were in the Vietnamese psyche.

The Le Dynasty

Following the Chinese withdrawal, the Le dynasty founded in early 1428 proved to be Vietnam's longest-lasting dynasty, only coming to an end in 1788. A painful period of renewal gradually put Dai Viet back on its feet but it was not until the reign of Le Thanh Tong that prosperity returned. Perhaps the greatest Vietnamese emperor, Le Thanh Tong was attributed powers beyond anything Confucius would have recognized. Despite Confucian learning being once again the route to official office, with schools reopened at provincial and district levels, the limits that Confucius had placed on the status of rulers were largely ignored in the case of Le Thanh Tong. Unlike the Chams, and indeed other Indian-influenced peoples of Southeast Asia, the Vietnamese never looked upon their rulers as gods, but Le Thanh Tong's mother claimed that Heaven had sent down a divinity to be her son. Apparently, the future emperor had let it be known, just before his birth, that he considered Dai Viet too small a country to rule, and so he received Champa as well. When this still left him unsatisfied, Le Thanh Tong asked in addition for China. Exasperated

Thang-long showing the riverside English and Dutch factories

by this presumption, Heaven cracked him over the head, which was said to explain why he was born with a scar right across the forehead. That this emperor actually conquered Champa in 1471 probably accounts for the unusual story: he then executed a Cham ruler in whose body a portion of the Hindu god Shiva was believed to reside. The severed head of this semi-divine opponent was prominently displayed on the prow of the Vietnamese emperor's ship during the voyage back to Dai Viet.

Besides pushing the border of Dai Viet southwards through the conquest of Champa, Le Thanh Tong is celebrated for a law code that was inspired by Neo-Confucianism, the classic form of the philosophy. It was Zhu Xi who formulated this new expression of Confucius' idea that virtue comprised self-control and ritualized behaviour. As the mutual dependence of the living and the dead, of ancestors and descendants, had always been a central element of Chinese culture, Zhu Xi's *Family Rituals* concentrated upon the correct observance of cappings, weddings, funerals and ancestral rites. "The most serious instance of filial impiety", he maintained, "is denying a family of posterity". Reprinted many times after the death of Zhu Xi in 1200, *Family Rituals* was gradually expanded by other Neo-Confucian philosophers until it became the late Chinese empire's handbook for social conduct, and by extension that of Dai Viet, for Le Thanh Tong's laws placed emphasis on the family, loyal service, hard work and honesty. For criminal offences there was a range of punishments less severe than those previously handed down, and children were allowed to bear the sentences of their parents. The sick, handicapped, and elderly were exempted from physical punishment altogether.

Zhu Xi had seen himself as fighting off the twin evils of Buddhism and Daoism through moral self-cultivation. He was sure that there was a single correct interpretation of the Confucian classics, that anyone who studied them with dedication and sincerity would arrive at the same interpretation, and this understanding would transform the individual. In other words, literary effort was not just edifying, it was enlightening. This fresh look at Confucian wisdom attracted both Chinese and Vietnamese scholars, whose excitement was akin to that experienced by Buddhists in the contemporary reshaping of their faith. The Le dynasty, it was fervently hoped, would put Vietnamese society on the correct track, now that Emperor Le Thanh Tong's reforms were addressing the lapses from Confucian standards that had been tolerated by the Tran.

Inspired by such moral progress, between 1463 and 1509 more candidates passed the palace examinations than at any other period in Vietnam's history. By doing so, they had reached the apex of the national system of examinations. The social impact of such success is recorded in a poem about a poor scholar who graduated at a second attempt. Having been shunned by his relatives during his initial failure to scale the academic ladder, the graduate is overwhelmed at how "six seals of office jingling on his belt" could alter everything. We are told:

> His parents met him at the village gate.
> His wife, awestruck, admired him with timid eyes.
> His sister greeted him on bended knees.
> His lifetime's ambition he'd achieved.

Reflecting on their complete change of attitude, the scholar-official asked: "You all respect me now—why not before?"

Nguyen Sinh Sac, Ho Chi Minh's father, had a similar experience in the 1890s, when Confucian studies were still the road to official success. He failed to pass the palace examinations, and had to accept a minor

position overseeing a provincial examination centre. Eventually he passed
and the village where he lived built a house for him because it could now
call itself "a civilised spot, a literary location". Although the district had
produced many degree holders, Nguyen Sinh Sac had made it to the very
top, and could anticipate a senior appointment. But his growing disdain
for ceremony, which arose from the plight of the young emperor Thanh
Thai whom the French treated as no more than a tourist attraction,
caused Nguyen Sinh Sac to postpone taking up an official post. He even
declined to participate in a ceremonial welcome from his fellow villagers,
but he did agree to taking a new name: Nguyen Sinh Huy, meaning "born
to honour".

The preparation needed to sit the rigorous tests that led to the palace
examinations under Emperor Le Thanh Tong spread Chinese-style
education throughout Vietnamese society. Whether candidates were

The sea goddess Thien Hau
is widely worshipped in Vietnam

prepared through private tuition or attendance at state schools, it was inevitable that there were scholars who had no chance of joining the imperial civil service. Yet this in no way discouraged literacy in the provinces, once well-to-do families were drawn into the current enthusiasm for scholarship. Even village headmen were now required to be literate. And as in China, there was also the extra incentive of tax exemptions for those who passed the provincial examinations.

Observing the social cohesion produced by this expansion in education, Le Thanh Tong ordered the newly conquered Chams, as well as people of Lao descent, "to correct themselves" by adopting Vietnamese names and taking Vietnamese wives. He realized, however, that public unrest could only be avoided by sustained economic development. Agriculture was therefore improved by the confiscation of untilled fields, the building of new irrigation canals, improving delta dikes, and encouraging land reclamation along the coast, the western foothills, and especially the southern frontier. The upsurge in productivity was enough to feed 5,625,000 people within half a century. Over the long term rising output strengthened a class of wealthy peasants and modest-sized landowners from whom scholars tended to emerge and whose support broadened the authority of central government.

Le Thanh Tong, who died in 1497, had made an immense contribution to the Vietnamese civilization. With the backing of a Neo-Confucian administration, he confirmed the Van Mieu, the "Temple of Literature", as the pinnacle of scholarship, and commissioned historical as well as geographical studies of the country. Le Thanh Tong's patronage did not extend to Buddhism, since he forbad the construction of stupas, temples and libraries, the printing of scriptures, and the casting of bronze bells. He urged his subjects to conduct instead the ritual worship of their ancestors in accordance with Zhu Xi's instructions.

Yet there was a darker side to Le Thanh Tong's reign—the unbridled rivalry between his fourteen sons and twenty daughters. Blind to their intrigues, the elderly emperor dismissed the warnings of his ministers about the trouble that lay ahead. As soon as Le Thanh Tong passed away, his descendents' ambitions caused the predicted pandemonium which tore Vietnam apart. Le Thanh Tong's son and grandson ruled in turn until 1505, when the latter was succeeded by his older brother, who took

The Buddhist goddess of mercy. Though Emperor Minh Mang
tried to impose Confucian values on southern Vietnam, Buddhism
seems to have drawn its inhabitants together

the title of Emperor Le Uy Muc. This ruler was immediately notorious
for violence, a character trait that must have been aggravated by his
delayed enthronement. Besides murdering his grandmother as well as two
prominent ministers who opposed his accession, Le Uy Muc enjoyed the
Thousand and One Nights treatment accorded to court ladies, who were
strangled at dawn after a single night's pleasure. During the day, Le Uy
Muc liked watching the palace guards club each other to death.

Appreciating at last the danger in which these activities placed him,
martial arts experts were hurriedly recruited as the emperor's personal
bodyguards. Their leader was a poor fisherman named Mac Dang Dung.
As soon as he was promoted to an absurdly high position, many ministers
resigned in protest. The court was then taken over by Mac Dang Dung's
followers until a cousin of the king organized a palace coup in 1509. This
solved little because court extravagance continued to undermine imperial
authority, now reliant on an excessive level of taxation which triggered

rebellion in the countryside. The new ruler, Le Tuong Duc built vast palaces as well as special boats for his womenfolk to row on huge artificial lakes. Defying Vietnamese custom and Neo-Confucian precepts, he added to his harem the concubines of his own father. So impervious was Le Tuong Duc to criticism that he had flogged in public a senior military commander, who with the help of two lieutenants later assassinated the wayward emperor. Shortly afterwards, the capital of Thang-long was sacked and power shifted to strong men such as Mac Dang Dung, who briefly became emperor in 1527.

The Mac usurpation started a civil war that lasted until nearly the end of the century and involved four families: the Mac, Le, Nguyen and Trinh. Even though the Mac were crushed in 1592, and a Le ruler was once again enthroned at Thang-long, the restoration of the dynasty was the work of the Trinh, whose leading members remained the power behind the throne. Nine Le emperors reigned with Trinh permission until in 1788 the Tay Son rebellion finally put an end to the family's supremacy.

A Divided Country

A modified version of the Le political system survived the turmoil, but the dynasty was henceforth under the control of the Trinh. In spite of assisting with the overthrow of the Mac pretenders, the Nguyen family decided to put a safe distance between itself and its Trinh rivals and moved southwards to Hue, where it ruled as a separate dynasty, although it never formally declared independence from the Le. This southern state was called Cochin China by Portuguese and Dutch traders, while the Trinh-dominated north was known as Tonkin. The disappearance of the Mac family should have led to the legitimate Le dynasty ruling a united country, but the puppets placed on the throne by the Trinh were not acceptable as emperors to the Nguyen, and so strife between the two kingdoms continued sporadically until 1672.

Vietnam's first direct contact with Europe had occurred in 1535 when a Portuguese ship entered the bay at Da Nang. Within a few years the Portuguese set up a trading post at Hoi An, a port some distance to the south, which for a time became the main point of entry for foreign goods. By the division of the country into two separate states, there were European traders resident in both Tonkin and Cochin China.

Elephant combat with a tiger at Ayudhya, a favourite Southeast Asian royal sport

Although the first European missionaries were Portuguese, they were soon outnumbered by Frenchmen and Spaniards whose efforts met with such success that both the Le and Nguyen courts issued periodic bans on conversion to Catholicism. More welcome were European traders because they offered the possibility of military aid in the conflict between Tonkin and Cochin China.

Whereas the Trinh tried to enlist the support of the Dutch, the Nguyen turned to the Portuguese, who were more forthcoming in return for commercial privileges. A certain Joao da Cruz, a Portuguese cannon founder from Macao, created the Nguyen artillery. The Nguyen had two hundred cannon in 1642, twelve hundred in 1750 and, by 1822, the arsenal at Hue included more than two thousand pieces of artillery. Outnumbered though they were by Trinh foot soldiers, the Nguyen infantry was better trained and equipped with better firearms. Crucial in several engagements was the Nguyen elephant corps, which Dutch traders estimated to be six hundred strong. Wild elephants were quite rare in Tonkin, so the only means of matching Nguyen numbers would have been by tribute or trade. Cochin China, on the other hand, enjoyed the great advantage of being able to breed its own war elephants.

How valuable these great creatures were to the Nguyen can be deduced by the care taken over their training, especially as regards firearms. To accustom them to the noise and flashes they would encounter in battle, the elephant corps

> was confronted by around 500 soldiers with swords, spears and guns in their hands. They stood on the training round 1000 metres away from the elephants. As soon as the signal was given the soldiers ran towards the elephants and fired, but the elephants stood still. Then the bronze drums began beating... and the elephants charged towards the soldiers who all started running to escape from them... This battle enabled the court to distinguish the best and the worst elephants.

Fights were also staged with other animals such as buffaloes and tigers. A regular part of court ritual and display throughout Southeast Asia, these animal contests in Cochin China always had a military purpose.

At the suggestion of the Nguyen minister Dao Duy Tu, a wall was additionally built along the Trinh-Nguyen border at Dong Hoi. From the Portuguese, the Nguyen learned how to deploy maritime cannon, which inhibited flanking movements by sea around this wall. An advantage in firepower undoubtedly aided Cochin China, for Western-style artillery gave Nguyen defenders the edge over Trinh attackers, who still relied upon traditional and Chinese-style weapons. The defenders

Elephant troops in Tonkin

at Dong Hoi had only to persist in a stubborn defence during spring, because the onset of hot and rainy summer weather meant an end to the campaigning season. Thus they frustrated in 1627 a force consisting of 200,000 infantrymen, 500 elephants and 500 warships. Its commander, Trinh Trang, was determined to crush the Nguyen once and for all. Instead, his forces were swept by Nguyen artillery and partly trampled upon by their own elephants, who were terrified by the explosions. At sea the Nguyen navy more than held its own, before Trinh Trang was obliged to order a withdrawal northwards.

Trinh and Nguyen Vietnam

With no immediate Trinh threat in sight, Dao Duy Tu advocated the strengthening of the Dong Hoi defences as well as an advance beyond them, with the result that in 1631 the Trinh governor of the adjacent area was put to death and replaced by a Nguyen general. Because Dao Duy Tu was the son of an actor, always a social inferior in the eyes of both the Chinese and the Vietnamese, he could not sit the national examinations. But one day he appeared uninvited at a meeting of graduates and outshone them all in a scholarly debate. This famous triumph was enough for Dao Duy Tu's recruitment to the Nguyen government.

His greatest contribution as a minister was undoubtedly the system of border defences. Having studied the terrain in the Nhat Le river basin, Dao Duy Tu appreciated how a narrow gap between the foothills and the coastal sand dunes could be blocked by a series of walls built along the banks of the river's tributaries. Barely 5 kilometres wide, the north-south passageway prevented the superior numbers of the Trinh army

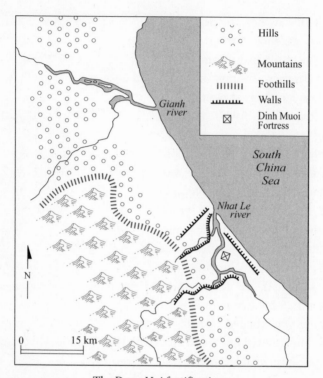

The Dong Hoi fortifications

being brought to bear on the fewer Nguyen defenders, who manned walls 6 metres high with cannon mounted every 12 metres. Another line of fortifications facing the sea ran along the crest of the dunes while an iron chain stretched across the mouth of the river itself to keep out enemy ships during an attack. The entire able-bodied male population of the southern kingdom was mobilized to complete the defensive system in 1630 and 1631. A final feature was the Dinh Muoi fortress in the middle of the rectangle formed by the walls and the foothills.

When the inability of the Trinh to overcome these formidable fortifications and subdue the resilient Nguyen could no longer be disguised, a truce between Tonkin and Cochin China was agreed in 1672 with a border established at the Gianh river. Interestingly, it was almost the exact location of the demilitarized zone between North and South Vietnam in the mid-twentieth century. Popular uprisings had of course played their part in the division of Vietnam, as indeed had the brief Mac usurpation, but the underlying cause of the emergence of Tonkin and Cochin China as separate powers was a revival of regional tensions, which Le Thanh Tong's truly remarkable reign had kept in check. The chief difference between Toungoo Burma's collapse in 1599, following King Nandabayin's stubborn refusal to stop mounting assaults on Ayudhya, and Vietnam was this: whereas the Burmese crisis lasted less than a generation and preceded a more thorough integration of the Toungoo realm, Vietnam's fragmentation went on for almost two centuries.

Geography of course assisted Nguyen independence, once Cochin China had fended off more populous Tonkin, because its extensive coastline was a gift for international trade. The Portuguese traded regularly at Hoi An from the 1540s onwards, and they were joined by Japanese and Dutch traders. So many came from Japan to settle in Hoi An that a Jesuit missionary thought it was "a city of the Japanese". A colleague fluent in the Japanese language, this missionary tells us, reformed "these Christians who were become libertines, and kept women".

Yet relations between Cochin China and Batavia, the stronghold of the Dutch in Java, were strained and often hostile. This antagonism may well have been due to the Portuguese, because from 1580 to 1640 Portugal was controlled by Spain, the implacable enemy of Holland. Lack of success against the Spaniards in the Philippines, where the Dutch suffered a disastrous defeat at Manila Bay in 1617, turned the attention of Batavia to Portugal's overseas possessions and its dominance of the spice trade. The Asian headquarters of the Portuguese at Goa was blockaded for two

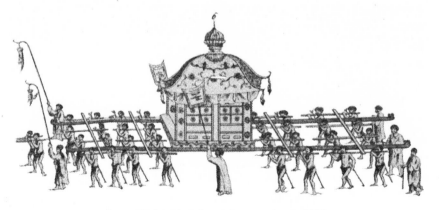

Part of Trinh Tac's funeral procession in 1682

An audience with the Vietnamese emperor, the nominal ruler of Tonkin

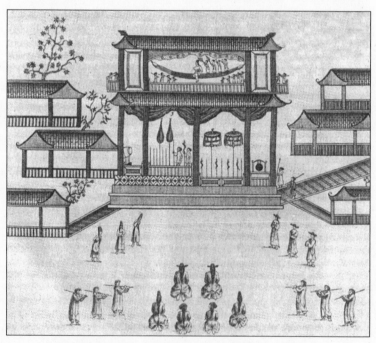

Tonkin's powerhouse, the court of the Trinh generalissimo

years until 1623 and again for six years until 1644, while on one occasion a Dutch squadron managed to prevent any vessel sailing from Lisbon. The seizure of the *Santa Caterina*, a Portuguese galleon carrying goods to Goa from Macao in 1603, revealed for the first time the determination of the Dutch to seize control of Southeast Asian waters. Chinese officials were not surprised when Portuguese traders resident in Macao reported this incident: they knew about Dutch interference with merchants from China buying pepper and spices in Java as well as Sumatra. That is why they preferred to deal with the Portuguese and the Spaniards in the silk trade. Only after the Dutch harassed sea traffic along the southern coast of China did the Ming emperor agree to the Dutch handling of silk too. These depredations had already earned the crews of Dutch ships the name "Ocean Devils".

What both the Portuguese and the Dutch aimed to do with their silk purchases was supply the Japanese market. Pirate raids on China had led to a cessation of direct trade with Japan, opening up a great illicit and lucrative trade for Western entrepreneurs. But Catholic evangelism in Japan had come under suspicion and, in 1612, the shogun Tokugawa Ieyasu issued an edict that stopped samurai from receiving baptism. Not long afterwards the Jesuits were expelled just as compliant Dutch traders conveniently arrived to replace the zealous Portuguese.

Hence the urgent need of the Dutch for silk, which they discovered was also readily available in Tonkin. So grateful were they for this additional source of supply that in 1643 Dutch ships were induced to fight on the Trinh's behalf. A treaty signed in 1651 was supposed to restore peaceful relations between Cochin China and Batavia, but these soured again when the Nguyen learned of Batavia's secret negotiations with the Trinh. One of the Dutch traders temporarily imprisoned as a result of this intrigue was Samuel Baron, the son of a Dutch father and a Vietnamese mother. His description in a 1678 record of the Dutch East India Company as a "Tonkinese half-bred", with all the social stigma this label clearly implied, must explain his defection to the English East India Company when war broke out between England and Holland. At Bantam in Java, his new English employers found Baron "an active, intelligent person with competent abilities for his years", and took advantage of his personal knowledge in setting up a trading station in Tonkin.

A Chinese illustration of a Dutch vessel
whose crew were termed "Ocean Devils"

According to Baron, the Tonkinese were poorly governed, unfriendly and turbulent in spirit, cautious with foreigners, inept at trade, and always hungry. His Protestant belief was particularly offended by "vagabonds that haunt every corner of the kingdom, pretending to be conjurers and fortune-tellers, cheating and misleading thereby the simple and ignorant people". He thought that this happened for the reason that the Tonkinese were really "very credulous, and thereby embrace almost every new opinion they meet withal". Baron was nonetheless impressed by the pomp of Trinh Tac's funeral in 1682, notwithstanding the advice received by his relations from such adepts about the most appropriate time and place for burial. Trinh Tac's son Trinh Can had led without success the seventh and last effort to breach the Dong Hoi defences.

Peace, as far as the Trinh were concerned, did not arise from any urge for reconciliation with Cochin China. They had problems with China

Two views of the famous bridge at Hoi An,
a key port for trade in the South China Sea

itself, following the Manchu overthrow of the Ming dynasty. A common border with the Chinese empire obliged Trinh Tac to renegotiate recognition with the new Manchu rulers, and fighting a war in the south was hardly the best way to go about it. The newly established Qing dynasty, as Manchu rule was known in China, was not without problems of its own and the Trinh had to wait until 1667 for the formal approval of Kang Xi, the second Manchu emperor and the first one to master the Chinese language. As the Nguyen were less concerned about the displeasure of the Manchus, they welcomed many anti-Manchu refugees from China as settlers at Saigon, a port the Nguyen acquired in 1680s. The extension of Cochin China all the way down to the Mekong delta, at the expense of the Chams and the Khmers, inevitably made southern Vietnam much more cosmopolitan than Tonkin. Even today Ho Chi Minh City, as Saigon has been renamed, feels more like a typical Southeast Asian city than Hanoi.

So long as Nguyen eyes were fixed on the struggle with the Trinh, their policy toward their southern neighbours remained accommodating. Thus early Nguyen rulers married princesses to Cham and Khmer kings. But after peace was agreed in 1672 between Cochin China and Tonkin there was much less tolerance of cultural differences so that captured Cham leaders, as during Le Thanh Tong's reign, were told "to change their clothes and follow Vietnamese customs". Similar pressure on Khmer inhabitants brought about a major uprising in 1730 which left 10,000 Vietnamese dead and even reached the outskirts of Saigon. It is likely that Nguyen devotion to Mahayana Buddhism, rather than the strict Neo-Confucianism espoused in Tonkin, functioned as the salve for multicultural woes in the south. Certainly daily contact with Chams, Khmers and upland tribesmen encouraged a diversity of social practices quite unknown in Tonkin. During the early nineteenth century the attitude of southerners so annoyed one Vietnamese ruler that he ordered their correction. Emperor Minh Mang condemned them for "despising the value of rice", by which he meant that too many people were engaged in trade, rather than in agriculture. "Southern Vietnam will be enlightened before long," he insisted, so that "each person realizes what is the proper way".

This unfavourable perception ultimately sprang from Cochin China's great success as a trading state. Hoi An had become the power-house of

From a Japanese scroll recording a voyage to Hoi An.
It took forty days to sail there from Nagasaki

the South China Sea economy by the mid-seventeenth century, and even after the Tokugawa shogunate banned Japanese from travelling overseas, this restriction had little effect on exports to Japan because Cantonese merchants replaced Japanese traders. Like Bangkok, Hoi An attracted a large Chinese population, although the port gradually lost its premier position to Saigon. By the 1750s the Nguyen dynasty derived nearly half of its annual revenue from taxes on maritime commerce.

Lacking such a valuable income stream, Tonkin was unable to match the prosperity of the Nguyen. Oppressed by taxes, and frustrated by incompetent government, the northern peasants rose in a series of revolts that culminated with the famous Tay Son rebellion of 1771. Ironically, the uprising started in the district of Tay Son, in central Vietnam, and only later spread from Cochin China to Tonkin. As it gained momentum, the rebellion undermined government by driving away corrupt officials, destroying tax registers, and redistributing uncultivated land. That it appealed to Chinese settlers in towns gave the Tay Son uprising timely financial support. The first phase of the rebellion, from 1771 to 1776, saw the Nguyen ruling family expelled from Hue and the Trinh annexation of northern Cochin China. During the second phase which lasted from 1776 to 1786, the Tay Son engaged in constant warfare with Nguyen loyalists in the Mekong delta. The final phase of the uprising shifted its focus to Tonkin, where its capital at Thang-long fell to the rebels in 1786. Even though the power of the Trinh family was broken, a Le emperor was still left on his feeble throne. Had his successor, Le Chieu Thong, not sought military aid from China, the dynasty might well have survived. Instead, an army sent by the Manchu emperor Qian Long was defeated by the Tay Son in 1789 at the battle of Dong-da, and once again Beijing was obliged to come to terms with the resurgent Vietnamese.

Yet Qing China chose to recognize the Nguyen dynasty, not the Tay Son rebels. Despite the strenuous efforts made by the Tay Son leaders to maintain the impetus of the thirty-year-old rebellion, Nguyen forces gradually fought their way from south to north, capturing their former capital of Hue in 1801 and Thang-long the following year. Nguyen Phuc Anh now established his family as an imperial dynasty ruling from Hue and, on the completion of his palace there in 1806, he assumed the title Gia Long.

China's acceptance of the Nguyen dynasty as the successor of the Le imperial house owed much to Gia Long's generosity towards its surviving members, who were confirmed in their ownership of land and their privileges so as to carry on with ancestor worship. In another calculated move, he returned to China for punishment a number of Chinese rebels whose recent activities had caused mayhem in its southern provinces. At the investiture of Gia Long, the Chinese officials sent to oversee the ceremony were greeted with three kowtows and nine nods from the assembled Vietnamese dignitaries. There could be no question of the importance that the Nguyen attached to the goodwill of the Chinese empire.

The Nguyen Dynasty

Two modern myths have evolved from the Tay Son rebellion. The first concerns the nature of the uprising, which is seen as a precursor of the August 1945 revolution led by the Viet Minh. To some extent it did resemble this attempt to secure national independence, after the surrender of Japan and before the return of French colonial rule; but, unlike the Viet Minh, the Tay Son rebels never intended to abolish the traditional order. And it should be recalled that the Nguyen restoration of the imperial system was on exactly the same lines as the arrangements introduced by the Le, following the end of the Ming occupation in 1427. Which brings us to the second myth: namely, that the dynasty founded by Gia Long paved the way for the French conquest of Vietnam by virtue of its own weakness. Because the Nguyen dynasty was no different from its predecessors, and indeed ran a more efficient administration than had existed in either Tonkin or Cochin China, it is difficult to comprehend such a view of events. Given the technological backwardness of Southeast Asia in the nineteenth and early twentieth centuries, there was little that could really be done to resist French aggression. If anything, the Nguyen emperors can be blamed for clinging to a Chinese model of government, once the British had exposed the weakness of China's own defences in 1840–42. They even retained Neo-Confucian examinations for recruitment to official posts for several years after the Qing dynasty abandoned the examination system in 1905. Thai monarchs never made the same mistake as the Vietnamese emperors: they realized in a

A community hall belonging to Chinese merchants, who replaced Japanese traders at Hoi An after the Tokugawa shogun placed in 1635 a ban on overseas commerce

Two views of Saigon: the French governor's residence and a row of shop houses

changed world how the only hope for Siamese independence was rapid modernization.

It was the collapse of Tay Son power that allowed the Nguyen to rule Vietnam, which they came to call Dai Nam, "Great South". For the first time the Vietnamese emperor's writ ran all the way from the Red river valley to the Mekong delta. The new bureaucracy which supported this enhanced empire consisted of officials from the south who already served the Nguyen, plus those whose disdain for the Tay Son rebels had compelled their withdrawal from office. Many of these ex-government servants chose school teaching during the Tay Son interregnum in Tonkin. So despised were those who stayed on and served the rebels that one senior official was publicly beaten to death before the Temple of Literature in 1803. But Gia Long's restarting of the national examination system four years afterwards did much to clear the air of distrust, since members of families tainted through association with the Tay Son were also permitted to offer themselves as candidates.

Vietnam seemed on the brink of a golden age. Reunited under a dynasty determined to revive its prosperity, the country could look forward to a period of recuperation after the chaos of the Tay Son rebellion because Gia Long's son, Minh Mang, who came to the throne in 1820, was just as committed to a programme of national revival through bureaucratic initiatives. A Chinese-style administration was set the task of ironing out regional differences by the reduction of centres of local power: the major revolt in the south from 1833 to 1835 served to underline the urgent need for such a reform. Besides reducing regional dangers Minh Mang's officials were able to raise soldiers more efficiently against Siam, which challenged Vietnamese influence in Cambodia and Laos.

Adopting thoroughly Chinese methods of government appeared the best method of ensuring Vietnam's recovery, at least until the arrival of the French. Not to be outdone by Britain, France pushed its way into mainland Southeast Asia, the last remaining colonial prize. French authority was first established in Indochina—the name by which the French knew Vietnam, Cambodia and Laos—after the Anglo-French capture of Beijing in 1860. Even before the Second Opium War, however, the French admiral Rigault de Genouilly had attacked the port of Da Nang, intending to capture it as a prelude to taking the Vietnamese capital of Hue. Ignorance of the terrain and a lack of flat-bottomed boats restricted the operation to the occupation of an offshore island. Heavy casualties from tropical disease rather than fighting forced de Genouilly to direct his gunboats southwards to Saigon, where French missionaries were already firmly installed. He boldly announced:

> The laws and customs of the country will be respected, but the courts and
> the police will act under French authority. The measures which I will take

will bring commerce to the city. The justice of our administration, which will fairly protect the interests and rights of all, will attract numerous residents.

Not until 1862 did the French reach a formal agreement with the fourth Nguyen emperor Tu Duc, when the Treaty of Saigon ceded to France three southern provinces, Bien Hoa, Dinh Tuong and Gia Dinh, as well as the island of Poulo Condore. Although the French colonial authorities hoped that Saigon would develop into a second Hong Kong, they were intent on expanding beyond Vietnam. Disappointed to discover that the Mekong river was not navigable as far as China, they still used its exploration to declare protectorates over Laos and Cambodia.

The coming of the French totally changed Vietnamese politics. Emperor Gia Long had been prepared to accept aid from France against the Tay Son rebels, but an understanding reached in 1787 came to nothing because of the French Revolution. It would have provided the French with economic and territorial concessions in exchange for military support of the Nguyen cause. Despite a willingness to cooperate with a Western ally, Gia Long harboured deep distrust of the French, and especially missionaries whose condemnation of ancestor worship struck at traditional Vietnamese values. The emperor personally experienced this fact in his own family: his heir, Prince Canh, had secretly converted to Catholicism during a stay in France and, returning home, he caused a national uproar by refusing to honour the cult of his ancestors. Perhaps it was fortunate for the dynasty that the crown prince died shortly afterwards on a campaign, allowing Gia Long to nominate as his successor Minh Mang, the son of one of his concubines.

Gia Long told Minh Mang to "treat the French well but never grant them any prominent posts". After the fall of Napoleon, King Louis XVIII had tried without success to demand the implementation of the 1787 Franco-Vietnamese accord. In 1819, Gia Long did allow two French vessels to trade at Da Nang, but Minh Mang continued an exclusion policy, in large measure because he regarded French missions as the advance guard of Western imperialism. Discrimination against Catholic converts tended to make the situation worse. It drove one Catholic priest to throw his lot in with an abortive rebellion started by a descendant

Emperor Tu Duc ceded Saigon to France in 1862 but the port
never developed into a second Hong Kong as Paris hoped

of the last Le king. Father Marchand was, in 1835, among a group of
prisoners judged guilty of treason in Hue. The Frenchman's brutal
execution made the guillotine appear almost humane: he was tortured
with hot irons and sharp knives, before his head was cut off and put on
public display. Hacked into four parts, his body was thrown into the sea.
Soldiers with whips stood ready to lash any executioner who showed the
slightest sympathy for the condemned.

For the rest of Minh Mang's reign, which ended in 1841, Catholic
missionaries went underground and intensified their clandestine
activities. The next Nguyen emperor, Thieu Tri, was almost overwhelmed
by the legacy of Minh Mang. Not only had he to deal with the aftermath
of Marchand's execution, but even more the protectorate that his
predecessor had imposed upon Cambodia fell to pieces. As with
southern Vietnam, Minh Mang decided that a complete Vietnamization
programme was required by the Khmers, since he had three objectives in
mind: to turn Cambodia into a reliable ally; to make space for Vietnamese
colonists; and to get rid of the Indian-inspired customs that had shaped

Cambodian society. Sporadic anti-Vietnamese protests from 1837 onwards were nothing in comparison with the great rebellion of 1840–41, which ended in a hasty Vietnamese evacuation and the revival of Thai influence at Phnom Penh.

Emperor Thieu Tri was firmly opposed to Catholicism but, aware of Western might, he refrained from any action that might provoke the French, who were eagerly looking for an excuse to intervene. His son Tu Duc had less luck in defending Vietnam. By the mid-1850s, France was once again a fully-fledged empire under Napoleon III, nephew of the original emperor. Wishing to avoid a clash with Britain, Paris left Siam alone and instead concentrated on Vietnam, where armed intervention obliged Tu Duc to cede the whole of Cochin China and allow freedom of worship for Vietnamese Catholics. France's progress as a colonial power was inevitably slowed by the Prussian defeat of 1870–71. At the time, the unexpected capture of Napoleon III at Sedan, then the turmoil of the Commune in Paris, left the colonial authorities at Saigon uncertain about the line they should adopt with the ailing emperor Tu Duc.

The policy vacuum was filled by private enterprise once the French trader and arms dealer Jean Dupuis discovered the Red river was navigable as far as Hunan, the Chinese province on which British traders from Burma had set their eyes. He also learned that Vietnamese salt fetched thirty times its price in Hunan. When the Vietnamese authorities in Hanoi attempted to stop Dupuis from towing upriver stolen barges filled with salt, he ordered his band of Chinese ruffians to seize part of the city and run up the French colours. In a somewhat half-hearted fashion, the French colonial authorities came to Dupuis' rescue and, in 1874, it was agreed with Emperor Tu Duc that there would be French concessions in Hanoi as well as the port of Haiphong.

8

LATE ISLAND POWERS

Debts in gold may be settled by payment. Debts in wisdom are
carried to the next life.

The wali Pangeran Panggung

Had Vasco da Gama rounded the Cape of Good Hope seventy years earlier
than his first expedition to India in 1498, he would have found his own
tiny squadron sailing alongside vessels belonging to a Chinese fleet with
an average displacement three or four times heavier than his own. These
great ships were commanded by the eunuch admiral Zheng He, whose
inaugural voyage in 1405 comprised 317 ships with a crew of 27,870 men.
This armada visited Java, Malacca, Sumatra, Sri Lanka and India. Some of
Zheng He's ships possessed nine masts and his treasure ships displaced
1,500 tonnes. Arguments over the tonnage of Chinese ocean-going junks
were settled in favour of such an unusually large figure by the discovery
of an actual rudder post in 1962 at the site of one of the Ming shipyards in
Nanjing. It once turned a rudder blade of at least 100 square metres, big
enough to steer a vessel between 130 and 190 metres in length.

The advanced state of Ming nautical technology derived from a
tradition of invention already a millennium old. The steering oar, used in
the West until the late Middle Ages, put a severe limit on the size of ship
that could be safely constructed, besides giving the steersman a hazardous
task of control in rough weather. In China, it was replaced in the first
century of the Christian era by the stern-post rudder, the prototype of
Zheng He's impressive ocean-going steering system. Other Chinese
advances in shipbuilding were the watertight compartment, which

allowed junks to become large deep-sea craft, and the aerodynamically efficient mat-and-batten sail, whose place of origin was almost certainly Southeast Asia because mastery of the winds had been achieved by the earliest Austronesian mariners. It was the mat-and-batten sail that allowed junks to make headway to windward, something the square-sailed ships of Europe simply could not do.

For this reason Portuguese shipwrights had turned to Arab models when developing long-distance craft. The famous caravela (from the Arabic word karib) had a wide hull displacing little water, with three masts hoisting triangular sails, hung from long spars. They permitted greater mobility in manoeuvring as well as better use of the wind. By the time Vasco da Gama left Lisbon for India with four vessels, his dhow-like caravels had still only increased their displacement from 50 to 300 tonnes. A Chinese invention of direct use to him was undoubtedly the magnetic compass, which had passed westwards through Arab hands. The magnetic compass, along with accurate star charts, allowed Zheng He's fleet to reach southern Africa, touch the northern coast of Australia, and sail widely in the Pacific Ocean.

Malacca and Aceh

Although the Mongol emperor Kubilai Khan used the Chinese navy to send a punitive expedition to eastern Java in 1292, it was not until the reign of the Ming emperor Yongle that ocean-going junks became once again a familiar sight in Southeast Asian waters. Returning a Chinese presence to these seas was critical to this ruler, who adopted a bold foreign policy on both the northern and southern frontiers of China. As the brief reoccupation of northern Vietnam coincided with Zheng He's voyages, it must have appeared that they were part of a Chinese effort to claim hegemony over Asian waters. Such a view would be incorrect if it is assumed that permanent naval bases or the acquisition of distant territories was ever envisaged. For what Yongle wanted was international recognition of China's recovery after the humiliation of Mongol rule, which had come to an end in 1368. Like the Song emperor Gao Zong, he was interested in the diplomatic exchange of gifts alongside state trading, and Zheng He's treasure ships were the means of effecting this extensive business.

Early Jawi script found in Kedah. It refers to Islam

Between 1405 and 1433 Admiral Zheng He commanded seven major voyages which caused the authority of the Son of Heaven to be acknowledged by more foreign rulers than ever before, even remote Egypt sent an envoy. These expeditions were very different in character from those of the Portuguese: instead of spreading terror, slaving, interrupting trade, and planting fortresses, the Chinese fleet engaged in an elaborate series of diplomatic missions, exchanging gifts with kings from whom the admiral was content to accept merely formal recognition of Emperor Yongle's heavenly mandate to sit upon the dragon throne.

This tolerance happens to be most evident at Malacca, which was not strictly speaking an island power even though its primary orientation was towards the Indonesian archipelago. Malacca furnished the Chinese fleet with a temporary base. According to Ma Huan, an official interpreter on several voyages:

> Whenever the treasure ships arrived there, they at once erected a stockade, like a city wall, and set up watch towers for drums at four gateways; at night there were patrols carrying warning bells; inside again, they erected a second stockade, within which they built warehouses and granaries; all of money and provisions were stored in them. The ships which had gone to various countries returned to this place; then they gathered together the foreign goods and loaded them in the ships; and waited for a favourable south wind to return home.

Alphonso de Albuquerque,
whose aggressive policies laid
the foundations of Potuguese power
in Asian waters

Ma Huan adds that the king of Malacca "made a selection of local products, conducted his wife and son, brought his chiefs, boarded a ship and followed the main fleet", so that he could personally "present tribute at the Chinese court".

The nodal position of Malacca, at the meeting point of several major trade routes, was fully appreciated by Emperor Yongle, who entertained its ruler and granted him a war-junk in order to protect his capital from seaborne assault. Between this state visit in 1411 and Zheng He's fourth voyage two years afterwards Malacca had adopted Islam, a faith then being spread throughout Southeast Asia by the permanent settlement of Indian merchants. Ma Huan, a Moslem like Zheng He himself, noted with interest how "the king and all his people follow the new religion, fasting, making penance, and saying prayers". Such urbanity has nothing in common with the religious fanaticism of the Portuguese, whose sense of national identity had been formed through a long battle against Moslem states. When Alfonso de Albuquerque, the second Portuguese viceroy in Asia, took Malacca by storm in 1511, he told his followers that its capture would destroy Islam locally, bankrupt Cairo and Mecca, besides obliging the Venetians to buy spices in Lisbon: a truly wonderful mixture of spiritual and financial gain.

Most of Southeast Asia remained uninterested in Islam before the fourteenth century. The activities of Arab traders barely figure in the propagation of Muhammad's message, because so few stayed any length of time. *The Annals of Semarang* actually credits Chinese Moslems with spreading Islam, but this may be no more than a memory of Zheng He's great fleet calling at Javanese ports, notwithstanding the Sam Po Kong temple complex at present-day Semarang which celebrates the admiral's personal belief. Arguably, the claim of Alfonso de Albuquerque about the damage that Malacca's fall would have on Islam could not be farther from the truth. Because the Portuguese were never able to do more than disrupt the spice trade, Southeast Asians worked hard to keep it out of Christian hands. As a consequence, Islam received a shot in the arm for championing resistance to European encroachment.

That the Portuguese were able to penetrate so far east was the result of China's turning away from the sea. Not all the causes are apparent for this momentous reversal of policy, which left a power vacuum in Southeast Asian waters into which the Portuguese, the Spaniards, the Dutch, the English and finally the French unwittingly sailed. The control that the eunuchs gained over policy making as a consequence of Zheng He's exploits deeply worried the Chinese civil service, which also noticed how the voyages were becoming less profitable as trading ventures and a drain on the imperial treasury. Another consideration was the removal in the 1420s of the capital from Nanjing to Beijing, the site of the former

Portuguese Malacca. Some 4,000 foreign merchants
lived outside the fortifications

One of the gateways of Portuguese Malacca that was saved
from demolition by Raffles

Mongol seat of power. The new Ming palace and city laid out there shifted
the centre of political gravity northwards and concentrated attention on
the Great Wall, now the empire's primary line of defence.

Yet within fifty years of building a fortress at Malacca, the hold of
the Portuguese on trade passing through the Straits was already being
weakened by Aceh, an aggressive sultanate in northern Sumatra. The early
conversion of Acehnese to Islam in 1204 is recorded in the *Majlis Aceh*, or
"Rules for Kings". This handbook of royal ceremonial leaves no doubt over
the central role played by this new religion: Allah's mercy is explained
in terms of the dignity, obedience and fulfilment of the king's wishes.
Whilst the duty of the king is upholding Allah's commands, should he
not follow them himself, his subjects then had the right to rebel. Not that
this prevented Sultan Ali al-Din Ridayatu Shah from staging out a royalist
coup against a restless aristocracy.

According to Captain John Davis, who was a pilot on a Dutch ship
which called at Aceh, the sultan "ended the lives of more than a thousand
Noblemen and Gentlemen, and of the rascal people made new Lords".
Apparently carried out at a feast just after his accession in 1589, the

carefully planned massacre brought to a close a period of acute political instability, in which there had been five Acehnese rulers in ten years, four of whom died violently. Although in 1604 Sultan Ali al-Din Ridayatu Shah was ousted by his son, the deposed ruler died naturally three years later. Perhaps it should be noted that palace turmoil was not typical of Aceh, which in the late seventeenth century was peacefully ruled by four queens over a period of fifty-eight years.

In Patani, situated in present-day southern Thailand, women also sat on the throne for more than a century without ever becoming puppets of the aristocracy; nor were the queens of Patani content to be passive spectators of international affairs. An English merchant by the name of Peter Peloris explains how, in late 1611, the sultan of Pahang arrived in Patani to marry the queen's younger sister. Having at first refused the match, the bridegroom humbly presented himself at the wedding ceremony after Patani had sent "an army of four thousand men and eighty boats... to threaten the sultan". Rajah Hijau, as the Patani queen was titled, was just as successful in keeping Ayudhya at bay. A probable cause of this surprising strength was the relocation of much of Malacca's trade to Patani after the Portuguese seizure of that port in 1511.

But it is on the island of Sumatra that Austronesian matrilineal traditions have survived most strongly. Married men in Minangkabau, in western Sumatra, still remain attached to their mothers' longhouses and are buried in the maternal family graveyard. Fathers are regarded as evanescent figures "like ashes on a burned tree trunk": one gust of wind, and they are gone. That this tradition survived Islam as well as Dutch colonialism only serves to underline the traditional freedom of women in Southeast Asia.

The Spaniards were baffled to learn in the Philippines that women were never the property of men. Equally disconcerting was the ease with which they could be divorced from their husbands. As in other Southeast Asian countries, women played a major role in commerce, especially in market-places. Various late sources record this fact. "In Cambodia", we are told, "the women take charge of trade", while among the Thai "only women are merchants, and some of them trade considerably". Another visitor noted that "moneychangers in Aceh are all women", as in Vietnam where "every man is a soldier, and commercial operations are performed

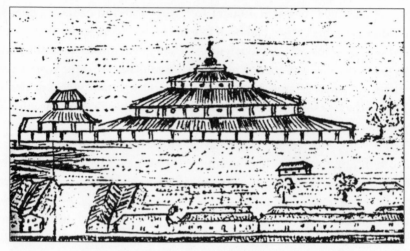

A sketch of the mosque at Aceh, where the ruler's arrival
was announced by a drum

by women". This state of affairs would last into the 1800s, when Stamford
Raffles described during his governorship of Java how "women alone attend
markets, and conduct all the business of buying and selling. It is proverbial
to say the Javanese men are fools in money concerns". Greater involvement
of Westerners in international transactions may have been a cause of the
gradual withdrawal of Southeast Asian women from commerce during
the nineteenth century. But this pre-modern tradition goes some way to
account for the comparative independence they enjoy today.

After the incorporation of Burma in British India in 1886, however,
Western observers still remarked on the independence of Burmese
women in contrast to women living in contemporary India. As the
country's small traders, Burmese women were highly visible to Europeans
in towns and cities. And it is not insignificant that political equality for
women was a hotly debated issue even during the colonial period. In the
1920s, Western-educated politicians argued forcefully that women should
be treated in the same manner as men. But Burmese politicians from
rural constituencies took the traditional view about women's inherent
frailty, arguing that putting men and women in an equal position was
tantamount to "the damnation of women in hell". That this India-derived
pessimism lingered into the 1990s is evident in the case of Aung San Suu

Kyi, whom a military government barred from running the country in large measure because she was a Western-educated woman, despite her political party, the National League for Democracy, winning in the 1990 election 392 of the 447 parlimentary seats contested.

It was during the reign of Ala al-Din al-Qahar that Aceh organized a pan-Islamic counter-crusade against the Portuguese. He even "sent a mission to Istanbul in order to strengthen the Moslem faith", we are told by an Acehnese chronicler, and in response to this request for aid the Turkish sultan "sent various craftsmen and experts who knew how to make cannon. It was at this time that large guns were cast. It was also Sultan Ala al-Din al-Qahar who first built fortifications at Aceh, and he who first fought all unbelievers, to the extent of going to attack Malacca in person". One of the large cannons made then was discovered in the Aceh river in 1874; it has a star on its barrel, suggesting that it might have been intended as a present from the Turkish sultan to Ala al-Din al-Qahar before his death in 1571.

At the height of its military power in the 1620s, Aceh possessed 5,000 large and small cannon. For the attack of 1629 on Malacca, an enormous warship was specially built, known as "the Terror of the Universe". It may well have been the largest wooden vessel ever launched, since its armament consisted of 100 guns, according to the Portuguese who captured the vessel. Frequent though the Acehnese assaults were on Malacca, the Portuguese never countered with any direct blow at Aceh itself, a sure sign of the growing impotence of their Asian empire, the Estado da India.

Mataram

By 1641, the year that the Dutch seized Malacca, Portuguese power ceased to count in Southeast Asia with the exception of Cochin China, where military advice was warmly welcomed by the Nguyen dynasty. News of Malacca's capture delighted Batavia, the Dutch stronghold located in western Java. In 1619, when governor-general Jan Pieterszoon Coen informed the directors of the Dutch East India Company that he had conquered the kingdom of Jayakarta and had started to build a headquarters for the company there, he was instructed to call the new city Batavia, an ancient name for Holland. Not only was it intended to act

Seventeenth-century Java and Bali

as a focal point for trade, but even more a military base in the struggle against Portuguese and Spanish traders already active in Southeast Asia. Great care was taken over Batavia's construction; bricks were brought from Holland as ballast in the holds of ships, along with the prefabricated arches of its gates. The port-city was in fact unique as a settlement built from scratch for the pursuit of profit from seaborne commerce.

Located barely 100 kilometres from the Sunda Strait, one of the main channels between the Indian Ocean and the South China Sea, Batavia catered for an extraordinarily widespread network of shipping, which extended westwards to Sri Lanka, India and Arabia, southwards to Africa and via the Cape of Good Hope to Europe, eastwards to the spice islands of Banda and the Moluccas, and northwards to Siam, Vietnam, China, Taiwan and, last of all, to the man-made island of Deshima in the bay of Nagasaki. In contrast to most other ports in Southeast Asia, Batavia's sheltered bay meant it was an all-weather anchorage, no matter which monsoon was blowing. Except for Britain at the start of the nineteenth century, no European power ever approached the global reach of Dutch trading ventures.

Impressed though Malay rulers were in 1641 by the Dutch capture of Malacca, they soon came to appreciate how its new occupiers were intent on monopolising commerce and paying unrealistically low prices into the bargain. Supplies of spices were withheld and the Dutch East India Company resorted to force. In Perak, then a subject state of Aceh, twenty-seven Dutch, who manned an outpost, were killed in a surprise attack. Despite a blockade of Aceh and Perak, the attackers escaped punishment as the attempt to isolate both came to nothing: the Dutch were frightened to turn back English vessels lest relations became strained in Europe, where between 1652 and 1674 three Anglo-Dutch wars were fought. But as the Dutch East India Company spread out and gained influence over more areas in the Indonesian archipelago, Malacca lost its initial significance for the company.

As soon as more reasonable trading arrangements evolved with the exchange of Indian textiles for Southeast Asian products, Dutch profits ranged from 40 to 100 per cent. Dutch East India Company business in Gujarat, a long-established exporter of Indian textiles, rested entirely on the spice trade. The principal spices sold here in the port of Surat, and farther inland at Agra, where the Dutch had an outlet close to the Mughal court, were cloves, nutmeg and mace. The willingness of the Moslem nobility to pay inflated prices for cheaply procured Southeast Asian spices bewildered Dutch East India Company representatives who considered lowering prices to widen the market. Batavia blocked this move, and stamped out smuggling, in order to make sure the cost of spices should never fall to a level that would be worth their while for English merchants to buy spices in India and sell them in Europe. Throughout the era of their supremacy in maritime Southeast Asia, the sole motive of the Dutch was to extract as much advantage as they could in their relations with local peoples.

Java was the Indonesian island to experience this pressure most because Batavia needed plenty of rice for itself, its ships and its outposts. Hardly unexpected then was the rise of Mataram as Batavia's main antagonist. Situated in the rich agricultural region of central Java, Mataram had begun to emerge in the 1570s around the modern city of Yogyakarta and its first important ruler, Panembahan Senapati Ingalaga, is credited with its forcible conversion to Islam. His son and successor attempted to enlist the aid of the newly arrived Dutch in a war against Surabaya, since Batavia could supply the naval forces that Mataram lacked, but nothing came of this move. The conquest of Surabaya was in fact achieved by Sultan Agung, literally "the great sultan", in 1625 after a series of campaigns which picked off the coastal towns under Surabaya's sway one by one. Now Mataram possessed a northern coastline, along with the revenues that came from seaborne trade.

Like his predecessor, Agung initially thought the Dutch would be useful allies in his war with Surabaya, possibly because they maintained a trading post at Gresik, close to this city. According to Chinese records, the port of Gresik was founded by a southern Chinese, who sent tribute to the Ming emperor Yongle in 1411. It soon developed into a major centre of trade as well as a place renowned for the study of Islam. Nine walis, unorthodox Moslem saints, dwelt near Gresik and they were instrumental in spreading the faith to the islands of Lombok, Borneo and Sulawesi. In what appears to have been a survival of Indian-inspired ways of worship, these saints behaved like the wandering devotees of Shiva, who followed a regime that aimed at unity with the deity. Shiva's followers went naked or wore a single garment, smeared themselves with ashes thrice a day, and spent their lives dancing, roaring like a bull, or simply laughing. Finally, their intense asceticism granted mastery of the senses, allowing them to reside without discomfort on the cremation ground.

Somewhat less extreme a wali was Pangeran Panggung, the elder brother of a north Javanese sultan. Yet his unconventional behaviour scandalised the sultan when it became obvious that Pangeran Panggung was so caught up in the love of Allah that "his worldly goods were lost and, in his actions, he disregarded Qur'anic law". Especially annoying were the two dogs that accompanied him to Friday prayers. The wali is said to have caused "the passions of greed and anger" to emerge from his body in the shape of the dogs: he named the black one Iman, "Faith", and the red one Tokid, "Unity". Other Moslems were furious at the presence of these "unclean" animals in a mosque and even the sultan's brotherly love gave way to a hatred that led to the wali's sentence to death by burning. Taken to the pyre, Pangeran Panggung threw rice into the flames and ordered the two dogs to eat it. When they emerged with fur unsinged, bystanders realized that their master could not be burned either. To make the point, the wali stood in the flames himself while composing a manual for the Javanese people, which the sultan took back to his palace. One of its tenets was that the worshipper must "taste the annihilation of annihilation" to comprehend Allah. This knowledge was vouchsafed only to those who had progressed beyond religious observance and appreciated how fasting and charity were mere "idols".

Moslems unable to understand Pangeran Panggung's mystical approach latched onto his dogs. Missing the full import of his teachings, these admirers of the wali "cherished dogs of all kinds, put collars of

Two views of early Batavia

When the Dutch tired of such trade negotiations, they slew the
Banda islanders in 1624 and replaced them with slave labour

gold coins round their necks, bathed them with care, and provided food
in precious bowls". Though still regarded as an out-and-out heretic by his
more traditional opponents, this criticism does not stop Javanese people
from visiting Pangeran Panggung's grave today. Moslem saints are revered
for the help they can offer the living, and in particular the wali, at whose
tombs spiritual power is said to be heavily concentrated.

Sultan Agung showed great respect for the wali, building in gratitude
for guidance received at the grave of Sunan Tembayat a much better
tomb, surrounded by a high stone-wall. Granite was brought all the way
from Yogyakarta, the construction work being supervised by his younger
sons. Whether or not this saint had advised Agung on his relations with
Batavia is uncertain, but after the fall of Surabaya he besieged Batavia
in 1628 as well as 1629. Considering foreigners who lived in Java as his
subjects, Agung resented the failure of the Dutch to send envoys laden
with presents to his court. In turn, the Dutch East India Company did not
see annual embassies as an obligation and, additionally, disliked the casual

Javanese handling of commercial matters, which were the purpose of all its activities.

But Sultan Agung could be equally impatient with both political and religious opponents. At Gresik, religious leaders annoyed him greatly when they executed the wali Siti Jenar for ignoring the obligation of Friday prayers. Troops were sent against them, but their tombs soon became objects of pilgrimage like those of other Javanese saints. It is hardly a surprise that Pangeran Panggung had been one of Siti Jenar's pupils.

Mataram's two assaults on Batavia were repulsed by the Dutch and their Ambonese, Chinese and Japanese mercenaries. Most worrying for Batavia was a rumour that the Portuguese had reached an agreement with Agung, who realized that Dutch power needed to be checked at sea. Once it was clear that the Portuguese were unable to send a fleet, Agung lost all interest in a third assault on Batavia. But he remained uncompromising in his treatment of Dutch prisoners, shipwrecked sailors and company officials alike. Only those who embraced Islam had freedom to move around; most of those who converted took Javanese women as wives.

These Dutchmen would never be allowed to return to Holland, because race was always an unbridgeable gulf between the Dutch and the Indonesians. Settlers who married local women were not allowed to go home, other than in exceptional circumstances. The ban was then extended to men who used female slaves as concubines, but this did not stop them chasing good-looking Indonesians because so few Dutch women came to live in Southeast Asia. More relaxed was the attitude of the Portuguese and Spaniards, at least until Catholic missionaries arrived in force. At Malacca, St. Francis Xavier was shocked by the moral laxity: one of the Portuguese residents had twenty-three concubines. Yet in persuading them to marry one of their partners Xavier imposed a definite colour bar. "When the woman was dark in colour and ugly-featured, he employed all his eloquence to separate his host from her. He was even ready, if necessary, to find him a more suitable mate". Many Portuguese did not share this racial prejudice, but there were many others who did so that the offspring from such marriages often found themselves poorly regarded. As the viceroy Antonio de Mello de Castro lamented at Goa in 1664, "our decay in those parts is entirely due to treating the natives thereof as if they were slaves or worse than if they were Moors".

A typical fisherman's house
in the eastern Indonesian archipelago

Although peace between Batavia and Mataram had not been concluded on the death of Sultan Agung in 1646, the political situation had altered to the advantage of the Dutch, for with the Straits of Malacca under their control they could harass Javanese ships trading in Sumatran ports. Mataram was under increasing pressure during the reign of Agung's son and successor, Amangkurat I. Whereas his father is remembered as the greatest of Java's late rulers, Amangkurat I is looked upon as the archetypal tyrant. Still remembered with horror is the massacre of 2,000 Moslem leaders and their families in the square before his palace: over 5,000 men, women and children were killed there one day in 1648, for lending support to an attempted uprising by Amangkurat's younger brother.

Further acts of violence during a long reign precipitated the collapse of Mataram. No one was startled by heavy rains out of season, volcanic eruptions or lunar eclipses: they all pointed to the calamity that must result from the despot's rule. It came through a rebellion that was only put down with Dutch support, but at the price of monopolies in the purchase of rice and sugar, the import of textiles and opium, and direct control of the port of Surabaya.

The Dutch East India Company was neither capable of controlling events in Java nor winning wars by itself, but in alliance with local powers it could often tip the balance of a conflict towards those with whom it was allied. Without any agenda other than driving a hard bargain, its officials usually endeavoured to avoid political entanglements. When this proved impossible in 1704 and 1740, intervention meant the propping up of compliant rulers who were prepared to let Dutch traders have a free hand.

That these "company kings" subscribed to Islam was of no concern to Batavia for the Dutch East India Company, with its roots reaching back to the Protestant Reformation, always saw Catholicism as a more serious enemy than the Moslem faith. So when in 1605 the Dutch took Ambon from the Portuguese, they had no interest in converting Moslems living on this island, but Catholic priests were expelled and local Christians

Bali escaped conversion to Islam and was not subdued by the Dutch until 1908

converted to Protestantism. Not until the demise of the Dutch East India Company in 1795, and the passing of its interests to the Netherlands government, would Protestant missionaries be allowed to proselytize but even then colonial officials remained apprehensive about a Moslem backlash.

The spread of Dutch influence in the eastern Indonesian archipelago was haphazard. While Timor was a source of sandalwood, the islands of Flores, Suva and Sumba were of little economic interest. The Portuguese had occupied Flores in 1575 when they stopped during their search for supplies of sandalwood. In 1613, the Dutch took over an abandoned Portuguese fort at Kupang in western Timor, but they made no headway against the "black Portuguese" living in the eastern part of the island.

Portuguese influence lingers in the Flores islands,
which passed under Dutch control in 1859

Outside his front door a Flores boy enjoys the coolness of a relative's gravestone,
while nearby his elders perform a traditional dance of welcome

These Catholics of mixed parentage were reinforced by refugees from Malacca, after this port's capture by the Dutch in 1641. The ethnic mixture actually comprised people of Dutch, Portuguese and Timorese ancestry.

The Portuguese colony of East Timor remained undisturbed until the arrival of the Imperial Japanese Army in 1942. Essentially a backwater of the Dutch East Indies, the eastern islands only became a matter of concern in the mid-nineteenth century through slave-trading and the plundering of shipwrecks. Two Dutch expeditions were dispatched to sort out these problems and, as a consequence, Portugal gave up its claim to Flores in 1859. But Dutch authority remained weak until 1908, the same year in which the island of Bali was also finally subdued. Islam hardly penetrated the eastern Indonesian archipelago with the result that most of its inhabitants are Christian, although tribes living in the rugged mountains of several islands still combine Catholicism with indigenous beliefs.

Brunei

Beyond the island of Java, the Dutch East India Company gradually pushed the Portuguese out of Southeast Asia with the notable exception of East Timor. But it entirely ignored northern Borneo, where the sultanate of Brunei claimed authority. To the amazement of the Spanish survivors of the expedition commanded by Ferdinand Magellan, this superior status was reflected in the rich clothes worn at the sultan's court, where even servants were dressed in silk. Elsewhere they had encountered chiefs wearing cotton, while the attire of ordinary people was made of bark cloth.

There is no question about the influence of Brunei in the Philippines before the advent of Spanish rule. During Magellan's ill-fated visit to the Philippine islands in 1521, the Malay language was even used there for communication, suggesting how an unusual degree of prestige lingered from the glory days of Srivijaya. After all, a refugee prince from Palembang, by the name of Paramesvara, had founded Malacca and one of his descendants moved on to Johor in 1511, when the Portuguese captured that port-city. As a courtier remarked then: "Every country has a Rajah, and if Your Majesty is granted a long life, we can find countries for you." In gratitude for Johor's assistance in expelling the Portuguese

A street scene in Brunei

from Malacca in 1641, the Dutch East India Company agreed that Johor should become the chief trading port in the Straits of Malacca. Because they were inordinately proud of their ancestry, the Johor royal family could never accept the leadership of upstart Aceh, and so it preferred to deal with the Dutch.

From Johor the sultans of Brunei are supposed to have received part of their royal regalia about 1514, shortly before conversion to Islam. Like earlier kings in maritime Southeast Asia who had embraced Hindu-Buddhist beliefs as a means of strengthening their own positions, the ruler of Brunei may have sensed the political advantage then of becoming a Moslem sultan.

Although Brunei's first rulers could well have been sympathetically disposed toward Islam before the Johor gift, close trading relations with China as well as strong links with the Philippines tended to keep them isolated from the Moslem advance elsewhere. Just how favoured Brunei was in the Chinese capital is evident in the tomb specially built for its king, who died there in 1408. So pleased was Emperor Yongle with the Brunei ruler, as a "southern king" who came to present tribute in person, that he was splendidly received at court, expensively buried, and his infant son accompanied home by a Chinese commissioner with instructions to assist the prince during his minority. Today the statuary lining the approach to the royal tomb can still be seen near Nanjing. Whatever the motive for conversion to the Moslem faith, it drew Brunei into the Malay cultural sphere, thereby setting it apart from what was later to be the Republic of Indonesia.

Once the Spaniards had gained the upper hand in the Philippines in 1571, they directed their attention southwards and successfully attacked Brunei, installing puppet rulers of their own. They discovered it was "the Venice of the East", with merchants coming from China, Vietnam, Cambodia, Ayudhya, Patani, Pahang, Java, the Moluccas, Mindanao and Sumatra. In spite of the climate proving too unhealthy for a prolonged stay, the brief Spanish occupation gave the Sulu sultanate in the southern Philippines the opportunity to assert its own independence from Brunei, and indeed encroach on the coast of Borneo. The jungles of the Philippines deterred Spain from planting many colonies on its southernmost islands, but the effect of setting up a stronghold at Manila in 1570 was to thwart the further progress of Islam in the archipelago.

Yet this did not mean an end to Moslem raids on coastal settlements as far north as Luzon, nor was there any reduction of pirate attacks on vessels sailing between islands in the archipelago. Not even the Spanish outpost of Zamboanga, situated on the border of the Sulu sultanate could manage without a high bamboo watchtower, the standard Mindanao method of giving warning of a sudden seaborne assault. How critical defences were around the Sea of Sulu is clear from the description left by the British admiral Henry Keppel, who visited the Sulu capital of Jolo in 1848. He describes its fortifications as follows:

> Passing within the outer stockade, we arrived... at the royal residence. It was walled and fortified; a large space was enclosed by double rows of heavy piles driven into the earth, about five feet apart, and the space between was filled with large stones and earth, making a solid wall of about fifteen feet in height, having embrasures... in convenient places for cannon... A great part of the town was stockaded in a similar way; and the country houses were also walled in, and had guns mounted.

That these fortified compounds, often considerable in size, acted as a shelter for local villagers is an indication of the disturbed conditions prevalent in the southern Philippines.

Elsewhere the Spaniards noted the emergency refuges provided by tree houses, sometimes more than a dozen metres off the ground. These buildings were constructed either in a stout tree or upon tall wooden

A Malay fishing village

pilings, rather like a Borneo longhouse. They were reached by a vine which could be pulled up when not in use. The paths approaching the refuges frequently boasted poisoned stakes to catch an enemy unawares. Despite the Christian-Moslem dimension in the struggle between the Spanish colonial authorities and the Sulu sultans, the widespread existence of fortified settlements and temporary sanctuaries shows how inter-tribal raiding was a Filipino way of life. The Spanish presence at Zamboanga may have disrupted this pattern to some extent in Mindanao, but the small garrison stationed there could never have stamped raiding out completely. The importance of warfare to a paramount chieftain cannot be overstated—the regular capture of slaves and portable goods provided the means of increasing his own following, while at the same time overawing his rivals for political power. Acquiring the labour and resources of weaker chiefs was the only method of preserving a superior position.

The Philippines

After conquests in the New World, where vast territories could be secured through the deposition of a few kings, the Spaniards were quite unprepared for the difficulties of control they encountered in the widely scattered islands of the Philippines, whose peoples were led by competing chieftains and whose languages were mutually unintelligible. The Sulu

The Spanish outpost at Zamboanga

sultanate at first appeared to approximate a polity, until the Spaniards realized that its ruler was little more than a paramount chief himself. Obtaining the consent of local leaders was necessary before concerted action such as large-scale raiding might take place. And because the ability of these lesser chiefs to lead depended upon personal ties with their followers, there was nothing the Sulu sultan could do to command obedience. In Jolo, his authority largely derived from his claim to be the earthly representative of Allah.

This was not an exceptional circumstance in the Philippines. Chiefs and high priests were frequently, though not always, the same person. Unlike Javanese and Balinese kingdoms, where court ceremonial did so much to sustain central authority, Filipino chiefs never found a method of becoming the focus of society. They rose and fell in an almost unending series of conflicts, since plunder was a fundamental preoccupation in the pre-colonial era. Raids aimed at the seizure of slaves, metal, agricultural products and trade goods, while those launched against rival ports were intended to divert foreign traders to safer harbours. Not dissimilar to the piracy of the Chams in southern Vietnam, the purpose of these seaborne assaults was the acquisition of resources sufficient to maintain a chieftain's position. Trade-controlling leaders obviously attracted greater respect, especially if they were able to prominently display luxury Chinese manufactures in the form of silk and porcelain.

During the Southern Song dynasty, we know that Chinese merchants sailed regularly to the Philippines in search of exotic products and that Filipino ships put into Chinese ports as well. In earlier times they had carried goods to Funan, when it was a key port in the India-China trade. The northern Mindanao port of Butuan caused annoyance in China by persistent requests for favoured trade status. When only a minor tributary relationship was offered, it caused such offence that its chieftain sent this message:

> Your humble servant observes that the Emperor has bestowed two caparisoned horses and two large spirit flags on the Champa envoy; he wishes to be granted the same treatment and receive the same gifts.

Notwithstanding the less than a satisfactory handling that Butuan received from Chinese officials responsible for contacts overseas, the

Sulu pirate boats

ability of Butuan's rulers to advertise this connection still ensured that they were recognized as significant members of the Philippine elite.

The earliest Spanish contact with Southeast Asia was in early 1521 when Magellan's ships reached the Philippines. In comparison with that of the Portuguese, Spanish enterprise was a modest affair, not least because it always remained an offshoot of Spain's empire in the New World, being

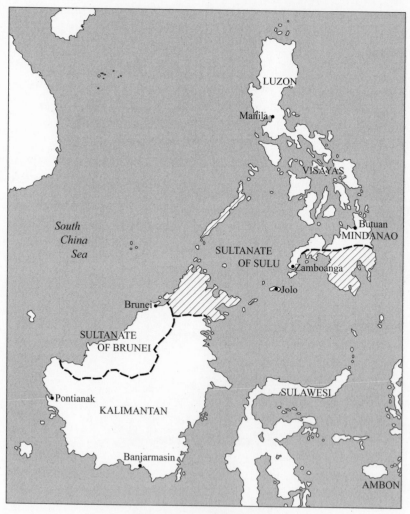

Borneo and the Philippines

A replica in Barcelona of Magellan's ship
which in 1519–22 circumnavigated the globe

under the direct jurisdiction of the viceroy in Nueva Espana, present-day Mexico. The death of its "discoverer", Fernao de Magalhaes (better known as Magellan), hardly acted as an encouragement for settlement, despite the cargo of spices loaded in the Moluccas on the way home more than covering the cost of this expedition. Trying to elevate one chieftain over others as a client ruler of Spain, Magellan had overestimated the advantage of European arms, and fell in an engagement against more than a thousand warriors on the island of Mactan. While very few Spaniards were killed in the attacking force of fifty men, the aura of invincibility was lost, and a tactical withdrawal became necessary.

Born about 1480 in northern Portugal, Magellan had fought in Africa and India before he returned to Lisbon seeking a reward for his period of service. Having no luck there, he decided to assist the king of Spain instead. By sailing to Southeast Asia in westerly direction and rounding Cape Horn, he led his tiny fleet to the Philippines: its subsequent journey home in the same direction completed the first circumnavigation of the globe.

The impetuosity of Magellan was blamed for the expedition's failure to secure a foothold in the Philippines. But other expeditions fared no better until in 1564 five ships carrying 400 men arrived from Mexico, with instructions about "the conversion of the natives and the discovery of a safe route back to Nueva Espana, that the kingdom may increase and profit from trade". On the site of a Moslem stockade at Manila the expedition constructed the first stone fortress in the Philippines. By 1650 its walls had been extended to surround the town which rapidly developed close by.

European powers seeking a permanent place in Southeast Asia always constructed defences in stone. When indigenous settlements on the island of Luzon were fortified with stockades made of wooden posts, and the spaces between them packed with earth, the raising of Manila's Fort Santiago was meant to signal Spain's intention of staying on as a colonial power. So well designed was this fortress, and the stone walls which enclosed the original Spanish settlement, that in 1945 a massive American bombardment failed to dislodge the Imperial Japanese Army. An infantry assault was necessary to overwhelm the city walls, before Japanese soldiers holed up in Fort Santiago were killed with flamethrowers and phosphorus grenades. As one US officer commented, "the artillery alone

Jolo, the seat of the Sulu sultan

The gateway of Fort Santiago in Manila

could not win the fight: as usual, the last battle belonged to the infantry", especially as the Japanese "had decided to sacrifice their lives as dearly as possible".

Because there was no single political or religious authority in the archipelago, the Spaniards were able to secure their position once the healthy climate attracted enough permanent settlers at Manila. The brutality of these immigrants was to a degree mitigated by intermarriage with local converts. The effect of conversion in lowering barriers between the rulers and the ruled would have been even greater had not the colonial authorities decreed that for security reasons only the clergy were allowed to live in the interior. Missionary activity was then seen as a sure method of preparing the indigenous population for acceptance of the Spanish crown. Portuguese and Spanish immigrants were unlike Dutch, French

A Philippine couple

and English arrivals, who tended to see themselves as only temporary residents. As a result, 85 per cent of the Filipinos adopted Christianity and the Catholic church governed large areas, acquiring great wealth as priests collected taxes and sold crops grown by their parishioners. Not until 1825 were friars forbidden from whipping those who showed insufficient faith, often a euphemism for a spirit of independence.

In 1762, Spain's alliance with France in the Seven Years War brought an English East India Company expedition to the Philippines. For a few months, an effort was made to establish company rule but, although Manila had quickly fallen, there was organized resistance in the interior which limited British power to the coastline. Although the English East India Company restored the whole archipelago to Spanish control at the end of hostilities with the French, powerful social forces were already unleashed in the islands. Chinese merchants, totally misjudging the situation, openly supported the occupation, while the sudden disappearance of Spanish authority triggered uprisings by impoverished Filipinos on many islands. The repression of Chinese immigrants had caused unsuccessful revolts at Manila in 1639, 1662 and 1686, so that the arrival of the English East India Company seemed in 1762 to offer a real chance of success.

Expulsion laws had been largely ineffectual in slowing the influx of Chinese settlers, because many escaped repatriation either by bribery or baptism. Nor did the massacres after each rebellion deter newcomers. The Spanish authorities were to sigh with relief when, in the nineteenth century, Chinese families dispersed throughout the archipelago and integrated with Philippine society. After 1762 the Chinese attracted even more distrust than ever from the restored colonial officials, but their lack of enthusiasm for Spanish rule was never as dangerous as the rebellion led by Diego Silang.

Few regretted the return of Spain more than the Filipinos did. In 1660 a major rebellion against the Spaniards had taken place on Luzon, and there were lesser disturbances right until British intervention, when the inhabitants of Manila rejoiced that there would be "no more king, priest or governor". From this moment of euphoria arose Diego Silang's movement for native autonomy. He established in 1762 an alternative government at Vigan, a town quite close to Manila, and rallied supporters there until he was assassinated later in the year at the instance of the local clergy. Diego Silang had tried to interest the English East India Company expeditionary force in his cause but, in the absence of its support, he was soon overthrown and killed, along with his wife.

Although the colony was now bankrupt, after the English East India Company had seized the ships anchored in Manila harbour and departed with whatever bullion it could find, the post-war governors restored order and a degree of prosperity through the encouragement of specialist agriculture such as the cultivation of tobacco and other export crops. Very few Spaniards, however, left the comforts of Manila for farming. Government service remained the chief means of employment, and corruption the quickest route to riches. The dead weight and sheer greed of the colonial bureaucracy virtually paralyzed the government, yet this hardly mattered to land-owning Filipinos who recognized how cooperation with Spain could be socially advantageous. Even though their tenants might feel the strain of meeting annual tax-quotas, and variations in the market prices they received for their crops, there was no chance of a second Diego Silang arising as long as these landowners could safely adopt Spanish dress and enjoy a privileged lifestyle.

PART

Three

MODERN
SOUTHEAST ASIA

9

THE COLONIAL ERA

Indispensable for the future tranquility of our colony is that we have no immediate European neighbour. Siam, which separates us from the English in Burma, will develop and endure, in contrast to the Empire of Annam, which is in rapid decadence and will finish by falling either into our establishment or into that of another foreign power that will seize Tonkin. For the Germans have designs there.

Admiral Marie Jules Dupré in 1872

Modern times began with Asian countries in full retreat. Western encroachment either overland or by sea reduced the majority to the status of colonies, protectorates or client states. Political realities were to alter dramatically after the Second World War, but the technological edge initially enjoyed by the Europeans and the Americans gave them unprecedented dominance over Asian affairs. Nowhere was this clearer than in the humiliation of China, an event which temporarily removed a powerful political counterbalance from Southeast Asia.

The Anglo-French capture of Beijing in 1860 marked the nadir of Chinese influence. Even though the Qing dynasty still tried to assist the Vietnamese in resisting the French, Hue had to accept in 1884 the severance of the historical link with China in the hope of retaining some prestige for its own Chinese-style government. Examinations in Confucian learning remained the means of official preferment, but Ho Chi Minh's father refused an appointment in 1900 after gaining the top qualification. He could not bring himself to serve a puppet Vietnamese emperor.

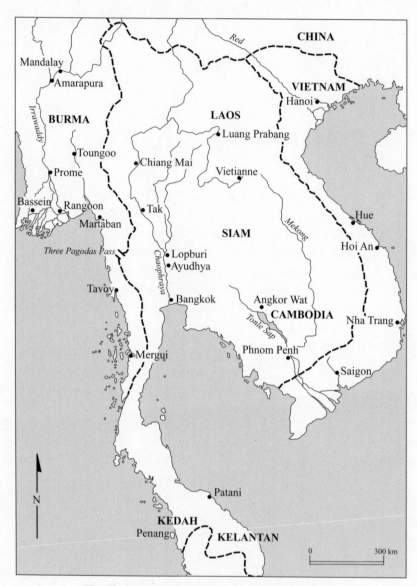

The Thai empire of Rama I with its dependent states

Ho Chi Minh himself came to believe that traditional learning, the Chinese heritage of Vietnam, actually stood in the way of national renewal. In 1905, the year that a modernized Japan defeated Russia, Ho Chi Minh started to learn French, "better to understand the colonial enemy".

Alone in Southeast Asia the people of Thailand were spared a period of colonial rule. Uneasily wedged between French Indochina and British Burma, Thai kings had the difficult and dangerous task of keeping these two Western powers at bay. Their achievement in preserving national independence, however, had as much to do with a desire in both Paris and London to let a shrunken Thai kingdom act as a buffer between their colonies, as with Bangkok's very skilful diplomacy.

The British Possessions

East of India the territorial acquisitions of the British were connected with their struggle against the French. The English East India Company had been looking for years to find a suitable base to protect its China-bound ships passing through the Straits of Malacca, a vital bottleneck for East-West trade. A Dutch campaign in central Sumatra disrupted free passage through the straits in 1784 and, to the consternation of the company headquarters in Calcutta, it was learned that France had obtained permission to refit vessels in Aceh. Strong northeast monsoon winds prevented Royal Navy ships from finding a sheltered harbour

A British stronghold during the Third Anglo-Burmese War of 1885

An ancestral shrine in Penang, a magnet for Chinese traders
in the Straits of Malacca

on the company-controlled east coast of India, forcing them to anchor
off Bombay on the west coast. By contrast, the French could use Aceh
to dominate the Bay of Bengal during the monsoon season. A base was
therefore urgently needed close to the Straits of Malacca, and it was found
on the island of Penang by Francis Light, a soldier who had lent support to
the sultan of Kedah, when he was attacked by Indonesian pirates.

A grateful sultan offered Pulau Pinang as a base, believing that a
Royal Navy presence would deter Kedah's enemies. The English East India
Company called it Prince of Wales Island, but the new name did not take.
Known as Penang throughout the colonial era, the hilly island kept its
association with the betel nut palm, pokok pinang in Malay. Light built a
stockade and a dock, and encouraged settlement by giving land away. To
get the land cleared, he ordered a cannon to be loaded with silver coins
and fired into the jungle: who ever cut down the jungle and recovered the
coins was deemed to be the owner. This policy of granting land to those
who cleared it was popular, as it followed customary practice. Before Light
died there in 1794, the new colony was several thousand strong, many
of its residents Chinese merchants seeking to escape Dutch domination
of trade. As Singapore was to be later on, Penang was a port "free to all
nations", with negligible duties levied on international commerce.

In 1800, a narrow strip of coastline opposite the island of Penang was also handed over to the English East India Company. By means of this acquisition it became easier to intercept pirate raids. The new cession was named Province Wellesley after governor-general Richard Wellesley, the brother of the future Duke of Wellington, Napoleon's nemesis at Waterloo.

Although it was French interest in Burma that finally led to annexation in 1886, trade was again the motive force behind the British advance. More complaints in 1852 from British merchants at Rangoon convinced the English East India Company that Burma had to be taught another lesson. So the Second Anglo-Burmese War commenced with naval forces capturing the ports of Rangoon, Bassein and Martaban, plus the upriver city of Pegu. Grudging acceptance of the loss of much of Lower Burma was not enough to keep the peace in the Burmese court at Amarapura, and a bloody dynastic struggle elevated to the throne Mindon, the half-brother of the deposed Konbaung king.

Mindon's efforts to modernize his kingdom included the sending of subjects to study in Europe: after the defeat of France in the Franco-

Penang shophouses, a typical feature of Chinese quarters
in Southeast Asian cities

Britain secured its hold by building fortresses,
such as Fort Cornwallis here in Penang

Prussian War of 1870, he even sent a general, an admiral and a politician to learn about Prussian military methods. Whether their studies would have proved decisive in the end is difficult to determine, because the British conquest followed soon after, largely as a result of court intrigue rather than fighting in the field. But the drive for modernization did not stop the construction of a new capital at Mandalay, which was intended to revive cosmologically the fortunes of the stumbling Konbaung dynasty. But in 1877 King Mindon fell ill and died without naming an heir, for the good reason that a decade earlier his designated successor had been murdered in the palace by dissident princes. Hardly surprising then was the swiftness of Mindon's successor, King Thibaw, in moving against potentially troublesome members of the royal family. Even their wives and children were taken to a burial ground outside Mandalay, where they were executed by soldiers. Thibaw's complicity in the executions is still hotly disputed but in the eyes of the outside world, they turned the king into a bloody tyrant. While Thibaw chose to ignore the level of international criticism, Britain reluctantly came to the view that an outright take-over was the only solution, especially as the Burmese ruler sought aid from France.

Despite all the talk about Thibaw's repressive regime, London remained worried about popular resistance to annexation, the cost of maintaining a garrison, and the difficulty of administering upland areas nominally under Mandalay's sovereignty. The hesitation was indeed well founded because it took nearly four years and 30,000 British and Indian troops to secure the new territory. The twenty-eight-year-old Thibaw had already boarded the steamer *Thooreah* at Mandalay on his voyage to exile in India. As he made his way to the jetty, a white umbrella of royalty held high over his head, thousands of the city's inhabitants prostrated themselves on the ground. Yet the royal party only slowed down when Supayalat, Thibaw's principal queen, awarded a British soldier in their escort the signal honour of lighting her cigar.

When all opposition to the annexation was finally overcome, the British had to reintegrate Upper and Lower Burma, since the latter had developed commercially following the Second Anglo-Burmese War. Construction was begun as early as 1887 on a railway line from Rangoon to Mandalay, reaching the capital within two years and other remote areas, including the Shan states near the Chinese border, by the turn of the century. Investment in irrigation also did much to restore prosperity to Upper Burma, where years of neglect had depressed rice production. In the countryside though, the colonial authorities feared most of all the activities of Indian moneylenders, who had already made serious inroads in Lower Burma. When in 1935 the Burma Act separated Burma from India, it was decried by Indian financial interests but not the Burmese, whose aspirations for independence were in part driven by a wish to prevent continued Indian immigration. In the Irrawaddy delta, where the most fertile soil was located, Indian moneylenders had by stages taken over land previously owned by the Burmese, and then worked it with cheap imported Indian labour.

The Burma Act went some way in curbing this practice, but the degree of self-government permitted by London failed to satisfy the expectations of university students in Rangoon, among whose number was Aung San, the future nationalist leader. Taking the title Thakins—"the masters" or Europeans—Aung San and these radical students maintained links with the anti-colonial Congress Party in India. Like the Congress Party, they were at first prepared to use constitutional means to achieve their aims. In early 1940, Aung San became general secretary of the Burma Freedom Bloc, an amalgamation of political parties dedicated to the attainment of Burma's immediate independence. Its vocal leader, the experienced parliamentarian Ba Maw, had already argued for this to happen, much to the annoyance of the colonial authorities. In London, there was even an attempt to suppress Ba Maw's proposal in BBC news broadcasts. Britain's gamble in setting up a parliamentary system was about to backfire.

Sir Thomas Stamford Raffles,
the founder of Singapore

Worried by the growing agitation, Sir Reginald Dorman-Smith, the colonial governor, tried to persuade Burmese politicians to amend the existing constitution with a view to the realization of dominion status at the end of the Second World War. What he did not appreciate was that the Thakins were no longer convinced that Gandhi-style civil disobedience would work in British Burma. Hostile though they were to Japan and sympathetic towards the Chinese struggle against the Imperial Japanese Army, now in its fourth year, their growing frustration with the slow-moving independence movement made them easy targets for Japanese agents.

In contrast to Burma, Malaya and Singapore enjoyed calm until the arrival in 1941–42 of the Imperial Japanese Army. Two reasons may have been responsible for this state of affairs. First of all, British penetration of peninsular Malaya was slow and hardly violent. With the exile of Napoleon to St. Helena in 1815, Britain no longer faced a serious European rival in Southeast Asia. When Holland fell under the sway of the French emperor, the Dutch ruler William V had fled from his country to England and took up residence at Kew palace. In what are known as the "Kew Letters", he instructed Dutch colonial officials to surrender their territories to the British, lest they fall into French hands. Armed with this authority, the

English East India Company moved to take over the Dutch East Indies, although at first Batavia flatly refused to comply. Once under English East India Company control there was some discussion about whether this sizeable territory should be added to Britain's Indian empire, but eventually the Dutch were permitted to return to the Indonesian archipelago. Yet the treaty of 1824 did exclude the Dutch from Malaya, where the British established the Straits Settlements of Penang, Malacca and Singapore.

After administering Java during the Napoleonic War, Sir Thomas Stamford Raffles founded Singapore in 1819 because he recognized the value of its first-rate harbour and the possibilities that this new Penang offered for international trade. The second reason for the comparative calm of Malaya and Singapore, prior to the arrival of the Japanese, had much to do with this acquisition because 5,000 Chinese from Malacca and Sumatra swiftly moved there. "In a few years," Raffles commented, "our influence over the Achipelago, as far as concerns our commerce, will be fully satisfied." Singapore's rapid growth through immigration from China itself, and the spread of Chinese settlers elsewhere in Malaya, meant that there was a significant portion of the population more concerned about Japan's attempt to subdue China than any agitation for local independence from Britain. Large sums of money were indeed sent to assist the Chinese war effort. Well might rural disturbances and strikes

An early view of Singapore

in mines be attributed to local grievances, but not the protest from the Malay community that greeted the repeal of a law that restricted grants of land to ethnic Malays. In 1939, Sir Miles Shenton Thomas, governor of the Straits Settlements and high commissioner for the Federated Malay States, decided that rice cultivation should be opened to non-Malays in order to reduce the need for imports from Burma. The Malay-language newspaper *Majilas* described the decision as "an outrage of the Malays' rightful preserve and heritage", which would result in them being "swamped out of the padi fields... literally deprived of their only certain means of livelihood". Although this prediction proved quite groundless, the Malays were to be conspicuous bystanders during the Japanese occupation: they did little to aid either side.

Colonial Malaya was always divided on ethnic lines. Typical in this regard was Sir Frank Swettenham, who rose through the ranks of the colonial service to become governor of the Straits Settlements. He was committed to modernization through improved communications and shipping facilities, but these American- and British-financed projects were for the benefit of international capitalism rather than the local people. Other than the nobility, Swettenham argued that the English language should not be taught to Malays, even though it was becoming essential for any employment outside the villages. In 1890, he wrote in an official report that it was inadvisable "to attempt to give children of an agricultural population an indifferent knowledge of a language that to all but a very few would only unfit them for the duties of life and make them discontented with anything like manual labour".

Towards the Chinese, whose industriousness was a relief after the lack of enterprise shown by the Malays, Swettenham recommended a friendly but distant relationship that underscored who was the master. After all, most Chinese immigrants were either miners or shopkeepers. As for the Indians, who came to work largely on rubber estates, their physical separation from the rest of the population clearly defined their social position. The high mortality rate suffered by Indian estate workers was recognized, however, as a worrying problem. In 1912, one-half of the resident population on a single rubber estate in Selangor died from malaria. It was not until after the First World War that British doctors gained a degree of control over this disease. The wealth of Malaya was

The pseudo-Moslem architecture of Kuala Lumpur railway station
was intended to ease the introduction of Western technology

based on primary products such as tin and rubber, after the planting of
rubber seeds, brought from Brazil via Kew Gardens, cleared vast areas of
jungle.

An arm's length colonial policy suited the Malay sultans, whose
positions were thereby guaranteed by the British. Yet they had to accept
the so-called residential system, which according to Swettenham, aimed

> to preserve the accepted customs and traditions of the country, to enlist
> the sympathies and interests of the people in our assistance, and to teach
> them the advantages of good government and enlightened policy.

In reality, it obliged each sultan to accept the advice of a British resident
at court on all matters other than religion and customary law. Much
of the credit for its smooth operation must go to Hugh Low, whose
administration of Perak between 1877 and 1889 showed how consistent
policies could benefit all its inhabitants. Low had spent thirty years in
Borneo and was a close friend of James and Charles Brooke, whose rule
in Sarawak he firmly believed was based upon a genuine respect for its

various peoples. Cooperation with the Malay ruling class, initially the most hostile towards the spread of British influence, was of course essential for peaceful colonial rule, and it was not long before the financial rewards of sustained economic progress won them over.

Possibly a memory of the divine authority once claimed by the sultanate lingered in the Malay consciousness, because hereditary rulers were to experience a revival of prestige after the end of British rule. Despite the selection by Malaya's first premier, Tunku Abdul Rahman, of a Westminister-style constitutional monarchy, this attempt to retain the non-political role of the sultans that typified the colonial era, did not work. Revelations about the arrogance and misbehaviour of certain sultans barely slowed their political progress until the premiership of Mahathir Mohamad, who imposed a definite check before his retirement

The simplicity of James Brooke's house in Kuching
was at one with his relaxed rule

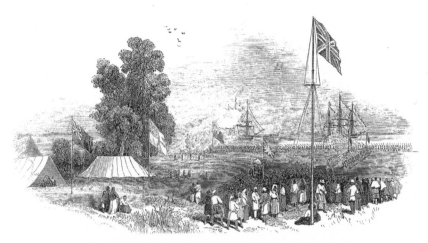

The establishment in 1847 of the small British colony
on the island of Labuan delighted the Royal Navy

in 2003. The absence of sultans in the Borneo states of Sarawak and Sabah, however, may well prove to be the most effective brake on hereditary privilege because their inhabitants look upon the Agung, the Federation of Malaysia's rotating king, as no more than a Malayan invention.

The political implications of the Federated Malay States, which came into being in 1895, were never fully grasped by the sultans. Yet its capital at Kuala Lumpur in the heart of the tin-mining region ought to have indicated British intentions: the creation of a prosperous colony. Although an amalgamation of Singapore with the Malay states was considered in the early 1900s, it was decided to leave the island as the capital of the Straits Settlements. By 1845 Chinese immigrants formed more than half of Singapore's inhabitants, a proportion that would increase as conditions rapidly deteriorated in Qing China. But the migration flow was exploitive, with Chinese men signed on as indentured labourers. They came hoping to make a fortune, send money back to families in their native villages in China and, one day, return home and marry, buy land and enjoy life as prosperous farmers. While some succeeded, most lived and died in Singapore as impoverished labourers, reliant on prostitution for female company and dependent on clan associations, opium dens and gambling parlours. Not that this bothered the colonial authorities, who easily gathered income from the taxes levied on opium, pork, pawnbroking and

By the time Fort Margarita was built in 1879 to command the river
approach to Kuching, Brooke rule was unchallenged in Sarawak

alcohol. As Francis Light had earlier observed in Penang, "the Chinese are
the only people of the east from whom a revenue may be raised without
expense and extraordinary efforts of government".

The same pattern of Chinese settlement occurred throughout
peninsular Malaya and Borneo. In Sarawak, the Malay village of Kuching
was a predominantly Chinese town by 1900. That it happened to be the
capital of an entirely new country as well was the result of a remarkable
example of British private enterprise by James Brooke. Born in India, the
son of an English East India Company official, Brooke tired of commerce
and purchased a schooner, arriving at Singapore with a crew of twenty
in 1839. His inspiration was Raffles' enlightened governorship of Java,
which he thought had revealed a better way forward through positive
collaboration between Europeans and Southeast Asians. He said that

> the experiment of developing a country through the residence of a few
> Europeans, and by the assistance of its native rulers has been never fairly
> tried, and it appears to me, in some respects, more desirable than actual

possession by a foreign nation... above all it ensures the independence of the native princes, and may advance the inhabitants further in the scale of civilisation, by means of this independence, than can be done when a government is a foreign one, and their natural freedom sacrificed.

The English East India Company's preoccupation with the China trade gave plenty of room for Brooke's radical experiment. Having helped put down a rebellion against the sultanate of Brunei by Land Dyaks and Malays, Brooke was installed at Kuching as governor. From the start there was a notably relaxed atmosphere in the town, which had much to do with Brooke's own liking for the local people, whom he considered to be "worthy of attention as the future possessors of Borneo".

Support from British warships in the suppression of Sea Dyak pirates allowed Brooke to consolidate his own position and overawe Brunei, which ceded the island of Labuan. Steam navigation required plentiful supplies of coal, something deposits in Sarawak and Labuan could go someway to meet. London was never really comfortable with Sarawak as a separate kingdom but since its coastline commanded one of the sea routes to China, the Royal Navy insisted upon its protection. The French in Cambodia and Vietnam commanded the other sea route.

Totally different from the Dutch, whose territories in Borneo lay to the south of Sarawak, was the Brooke attitude toward the indigenous population. Charles Brooke, the nephew of James who became the second white rajah in 1868, did not welcome the presence of European women, who might distract his officials from their work and spoil their relations with his subjects. While officials were not allowed to import wives until they had spent a decade in his service, the rajah had no objection to an official keeping a local mistress so long as he behaved discreetly and did not show undue favours to her family. With the old longhouse custom of sexual hospitality accorded to distinguished guests, it was not difficult for district officers to find suitable mates. Children from such unions were usually fitted into junior posts in the administration and formed a reliable element in the community. The Brookes themselves only took Malay girls as mistresses.

The benign rule of the Brooke regime, so unlike the Dutch colonial administration, accounts for the very different reactions to the arrival of the Japanese in 1941. Whereas in Sarawak there was no welcome for the conquerors, with the native peoples as well as Indian and Chinese settlers remaining conspicuously loyal to the Brookes, in Dutch Borneo the Japanese were regarded as liberators from Western domination. There Malays and Dyaks were at first willing to believe the propaganda of the Greater East Asia Co-Prosperity Sphere about restoring "Asia to the Asians". Experience of the Japanese occupation changed this perception, but it never persuaded the peoples of Kalimantan of the desirability of a Dutch return. In northern Borneo, on the contrary, the multiethnic population of Sarawak and North Borneo, together with Brunei, decided after Japan's defeat upon the continued value of British protection.

Because the British government always preferred to have weak European powers as its colonial neighbours, it opposed neither the Dutch conquest of Aceh nor the Spanish conquest of Sulu during the 1870s. A request from the Sulu sultan for assistance against Spain was turned down flat in London: Lord Granville, the foreign secretary at the time, advised the sultan to pray instead. The advice was not misplaced as a Dominican friar in Manila had already preached a Christian crusade against the Moslems living in the sultanate. London was quite happy for the Spaniards to tidy up one of the last corners of independent Southeast Asia, but no other European powers had its permission to intrude.

Lord Granville had already told King Leopold II in no uncertain terms to keep away from the area, when the Belgium monarch tried to acquire parts of Sarawak as a way of establishing a colony. In view of the rapacious nature of that king's autocratic regime in the Congo, the peoples of Borneo were lucky that Leopold gave up such a scheme. It was in this context that the British made their final acquisition in Southeast Asia. Almost a throwback to the English East India Company was the creation of the British North Borneo, which received a royal charter in 1881. The company was expected to remain "British in character", leave foreign relations to Britain, and seek London's approval for its governors.

The Dutch East Indies
Relations between Britain's colonial holdings and the Dutch East Indies were usually good, but in 1824 London warned the Dutch that, although as yet there were no plans to colonize Sarawak, Britain reserved the

Two Javanese crops exploited by the Dutch, sugar above, coffee below.
Notice how the Indonesians were not expected to wear shoes

A Balinese front garden to which revered ancestral spirits descend to the special
abodes, on the right, from Gunung Agung above, Bali's highest volcano

right to do so. The following year a treaty was concluded with Brunei, stipulating that all cessions of territory had to receive British approval; not that these diplomatic moves deterred Holland from expanding elsewhere in the Indonesian archipelago. As late as 1908 Dutch troops used machine guns to overthrow the king of Klungkung, Bali's last independent ruler.

Another massacre had already happened at the Balinese court of Badung two years earlier: rather than surrender to a Dutch expeditionary force, the king, along with his wives, his children, and his courtiers marched straight into the fire of machine guns. It was the refusal of Dewa Agung of Klungkung to tolerate further Dutch interference in Balinese affairs that brought about the 1908 slaughter. Having purified themselves for death, dressed in white, and armed only with spears and swords, the Klungkung nobility charged into battle. Pausing only to dispatch the wounded, the king led his family and followers forward until everyone had perished. Balinese freedom was over in a fashion that baffled the Dutch and horrified the world. Though present-day Japanese tourists may sympathize at Klungkung with this parallel of the glorious self-destruction expected of soldiers in the Imperial Japanese Army during the Second World War, they would be wrong to assume that any military impulse stood behind puputan, or "until the last". Mass suicide in Bali had its roots in reincarnation, an Indian belief that the islanders had acquired from eastern Java prior to the advent of Islam. As rebirth is still thought to be almost immediate on Bali, the acceptance of death at Badung and Klungkung can be seen as part of traditional ritual. The closeness of the seen and unseen worlds remains most apparent in the design of Balinese temples, whose openness to the sky facilitates the descent of the gods and revered ancestors from Gunung Agung, the island's greatest volcano.

A not dissimilar attitude to death has survived among the Javanese, who are able to talk about it without any apparent anxiety. A strong substratum of pre-Islamic belief has obviously modified Muhammad's view of eternal punishment for those who fail to worship Allah. Sampura, or "a perfect death", is espoused now by many Javanese as a way to end life, after which nothing is left but dust.

The sensational Klungkung massacre caused alarm in Holland, where at long last an ethical approach to its colonies was considered desirable. Queen Wilhelmina had admitted in 1901 that the Dutch had an "ethical obligation and moral responsibility", but this was not usually translated as restraint in the Dutch East Indies. Old habits died hard. Slavery was so widespread that Dutch colonial authorities, unlike the British to their north, left the institution undisturbed. Not only did a great demand exist for slave-servants in Java at Batavia, in outposts on other islands and at trading posts along the shipping route to Holland, but the Dutch East India Company itself employed slaves to harvest spices. In the 1620s it had killed or deported all the people living on the small islands forming the Banda group, and then replaced them with Dutch colonists using slaves to collect nutmeg and mace.

Yet the advance of the Dutch in the Indonesian archipelago was not entirely based on violence. In 1859 they purchased the Lesser Sunda islands and a part of Timor from Portugal, then threatened with bankruptcy. But in Sumatra serious fighting was required to subdue Aceh, whose guerrilla fighters held out until 1904. Just how uncompromising the Dutch colonial attitude was can be glimpsed in the advice offered by L. W. van der Berg, a noted specialist in foreign affairs. He recommended that Aceh should be settled by Amboinese, preferably ex-colonial soldiers, in fortified villages. They would gradually take over from the "degenerate" Acehnese "in the same way that savages withdrawal from the spread of civilisation… and die out".

Such an attitude was not missed in the United States. During the 1930s, prominent newspapers asked how it was that a tiny country like Holland could go on plundering the whole of the Indonesian archipelago. President Franklin D. Roosevelt openly complained about the living conditions of colonial peoples and especially those in the Dutch East Indies, despite his own forebears being Dutch. Yet Washington remained anxious about Japan, which it feared might exploit Indonesian nationalism in what was a strategically important area. This gradual shift of American thinking delighted Batavia, which announced that the word "Indonesia" could no longer be used. Relations between the Dutch and the Indonesians then hit rock bottom as police surveillance was stepped up: even the popular village sport of pigeon racing was outlawed to prevent bad news becoming generally known. The fall of the Netherlands to Germany in 1940 could not be kept a secret forever, but the feebleness of Dutch resistance to the Japanese two years later still astonished the local population.

In 1884 French action in northern Vietnam overwhelmed
Chinese forces sent to aid the Nguyen dynasty

French Indochina

Only in French Indochina did the level of unrest threaten colonial rule:
the Vietnamese never accepted the concessions wrung from the Nguyen
dynasty. The reign of Emperor Tu Duc was indeed a turning point,
because by his death in 1883 France was on the verge of imposing its
authority over all of Vietnam.

A last-ditch attempt to halt the French advance was mounted by
China, which still regarded Tonkin as vital to the security of its southern
frontier. Not only had this area once been Chinese territory for a
thousand years, but almost for the same length of time it formed part
of the imperial tributary system as well. Now the French were behaving
as if China's suzerainty had come to an end. Although on his deathbed
Tu Duc refrained from declaring war on France, his officials in Tonkin

Saigon Cathedral:
France transposed to Southeast Asia

issued proclamations calling upon the people to take up arms and offering bounties for severed French heads. Chinese troops dispatched to reinforce this resistance were, however, no match for additional forces sent by Paris, and a defeated China reluctantly signed the Treaty of Tianjin and gave up its long-standing relationship with Vietnam. From Tu Duc to Bao Dai, the last Vietnamese emperor of all, the history of the country is therefore that of French colonial rule, which finally came to a close in 1954–55.

The Cambodian practice of taking Thai and Vietnamese princesses as royal consorts in Phnom Penh inevitably produced two court factions:

one pro-Thai, another pro-Vietnamese. It was the former that blocked a treaty with France in 1856, correctly guessing that the French would help Cambodia to recover the Thai-occupied provinces of Battambang and Siem Reap. In 1863, France got its treaty, which stipulated that the Cambodian monarch had to agree to "all administrative, judicial and commercial reforms that the French government shall judge, in future, useful to make their protectorate successful". Doubtless a gunboat anchored within sight of the royal palace had a salutary effect.

The Thai were also about to discover the same disadvantage of a riverside capital, when the killing of a French officer by Thai troops in Laos brought matters to a head. In 1893 gunboats threatened Bangkok until it was agreed that the kingdom of Laos should become a French protectorate. Already France had tightened its control over Cambodian affairs by persuading its king to nominate his pro-French step-brother Sisowath as heir. At his coronation in 1906, the new king was still considered by Cambodians to be an embodiment of universal order. Sisowath's right eye represented the sun, his left the moon, his arms and legs the cardinal points, the six-tiered umbrella above his head the lower six heavens, and his pointed crown the top of thunder god Indra's palace on Mount Meru, the home of the gods. No matter that his kingdom was so overshadowed by France that it was the French governor-general of Indochina who handed Sisowath his royal regalia, the hallowed throne remained the focus of Cambodian political thought. A decade later, when thousands of peasants gathered in Phnom Penh and requested lower taxes, they quietly returned to their villages at Sisowath's command, in spite of this demonstration coinciding with more drastic anti-French protests in Vietnam.

So pleased were the French to show off Cambodian acquiescence that, shortly after his accession, Sisowath attended the Colonial Exhibition at Marseilles, in the company of his royal dancers. There the king's dancing troop made a tremendous impression and reminded Europe that Cambodia, not Thailand, was the true custodian of Indian cultural traditions in mainland Southeast Asia. The recently arrived Thai had appropriated Cambodian traditions as late as their capture of Angkor. King Sisowath does not seem to have appreciated in Marseilles that he was something of an exhibit himself.

France's last addition to its possessions in Indochina was Laos, a landlocked kingdom at the mercy of Chinese, Vietnamese, Burmese and Thai arms. The Thai had never made any bones about their interest in Laotian affairs and often placed a garrison in the capital, Luang Prabang, situated in the middle of the Mekong river. Their battles with Lanna, a power centred on Chiang Mai, and Lan Sang, the original name of Laos, can be viewed as a struggle for leadership of the migrant Thai. Lan Sang was virtually a Thai kingdom, one of its early rulers called himself Samsenthai, meaning the king of 300,000 Thai. So poor and isolated was Laos that there was no opposition to a French protectorate.

In 1900, the French chose Vientiane as the administrative capital of Laos, from which they hoped to accelerate economic development. But the small population of the country, as did that of Cambodia, precluded

The Treaty of Tianjin confirmed the end
of China's suzerainty over Vietnam

the growth of a sustainable consumer market, for such trade as there was remained tied to the needs of subsistence farmers. Efforts to persuade Vietnamese immigrants to increase agricultural production were soon regarded as a failure, since those who moved to Laos preferred to be traders or hold positions in the French administration. Food supply has remained a persistent problem, the government of an independent Laos being forced as late as the 1970s to import rice because of drought. Apart from the vagaries of the weather, Laotians lack the rich alluvial soils of Cambodia and Vietnam.

So bad were relations between the French and the Vietnamese that in 1906 Phan Chu Trinh wrote a famous letter to Paul Beau, calling upon him as governor-general to live up to the declared colonial intention of modernizing Vietnam. An advocate of non-violent protest, Phan Chu Trinh bluntly told Beau that his administration appeared "contemptuous of the Vietnamese people". Only freedom of speech, the opening of schools, and the introduction of modern methods of production would stabilise the political situation, and make Vietnam more worried about France losing interest in the country than hating its colonial rule. An experienced diplomat, Beau was delighted to arrange for the publication of Phan Chu Trinh's recommendations in several Paris newspapers. But the governor-general found it difficult to implement any of them because of opposition from Vietnamese traditionalists, French colonists, and his own officials. In 1908, the poisoning of the French officers in Hanoi provided Paris with a pretext for Beau's removal and the abandonment of reform.

The year after Phan Chu Trinh's letter was written, the situation in Vietnam grew increasingly intense. Emperor Thanh Thai, who had originally been placed on the throne by the French in 1889, was forced to abdicate on suspicion of his involvement in rebel activities. His son and successor, the eight-year-old Duy Tan, chose as his reign title a Vietnamese word for modernization, thereby associating himself with the Meiji emperor, during whose reign Japan had been the first Asian country to introduce Western-style reforms. But it was probably too late for the subservient imperial court at Hue to do anything constructive. Young Ho Chi Minh had already come to this conclusion: he was expelled from school for joining a peasant demonstration there.

More serious for the French was a plot hatched by Phan Boi Chau, who tried to stage a coup by poisoning French officers attending a banquet at Hanoi: he hoped that rebels in the vicinity could start an uprising during the ensuing disorder and seize control of the city. When the dosage proved inadequate for its purpose, Phan Boi Chau fled abroad where he had a hand in several assassination attempts, before he was captured in Shanghai. Returned to French Indochina, where he expected a martyr's death, Phan Boi Chau suffered no more than the indignity of permanent house arrest.

The efforts of Phan Boi Chau to ferment full-scale rebellion seemed to have failed until the troubles of the 1930s. In addition to containing mutinies then by Vietnamese soldiers in the colonial army, the French were obliged to bomb and strafe peasants marching on Vinh, the capital of Nghe An province, halfway between Hanoi and Hue. Led by nationalist activists, these impoverished farmers were protesting against the greed of landowners as well as merciless tax collectors. Imperial troops were sent to bar the way to Vinh, but it took the French air force to disperse the protesters. A day's attack left the road littered with hundreds of dead and wounded peasants.

The French crackdown after the Nghe An disturbance was severe. Some 2,000 activists were killed and 51,000 of their followers placed in detention. Among them were the wife and sister-in-law of Vo Nguyen Giap, a schoolteacher from Hanoi. His course on Napoleonic history was considered exceptional by his students; after the deaths of these two women, the French and the Americans were painfully to learn that these lessons could be transferred from the classroom to the battlefield. General Giap proved himself to be one of the best commanders of the late twentieth century.

Emperor Bao Dai, who officially ascended the throne in 1925 but went back to resume his studies in France, decided on returning to Vietnam in 1932 that things had to change. Shaken by the naked oppression of the French, Bao Dai endeavoured to persuade the colonial authorities to desist in their efforts to run everyday affairs and return to the looser arrangements that had prevailed after the protectorate treaty of 1884. With the French security service on the trail of revolutionaries, real and imaginary, the governor-general was not inclined to agree. Bao Dai was allowed to press on with the reform of his own administration, provided it was understood by the young emperor that France alone could take key decisions concerning the colony as a whole. The future president of South Vietnam, Ngo Dinh Diem, resigned in 1933 a ministerial post at Hue when French interference showed no sign of abating. His concern for national sovereignty, combined with a lingering disgust for French colonialism, would in 1963 undermine his own relations with the United States. Not even President John F. Kennedy objected to Ngo Dinh Diem's bloody overthrow then by the South Vietnamese military.

The American Colony of the Philippines

The oddest Western colonial adventure in Southeast Asia was the American occupation of the Philippines. Just as Britain had not acquired an empire there by accident, but through intense competition with France, so the United States could not reasonably claim that its annexation of the Philippines occurred in a fit of absentmindedness. Even though it suited President William McKinley to portray the event as an unforeseen consequence of American intervention in the Spanish Caribbean, the truth is that he had already decided to advance his country's position in the Pacific by means of the acquisition of key islands.

In 1899, McKinley disingenuously told Methodist church leaders how he had appealed for divine guidance about the future of the Philippines, and had decided that it was the duty of the United States to "educate the Filipinos, and uplift and civilize them, and by God's grace to do the very best by them as our fellow-men for whom Christ had also died".

American missionaries were soon to be disconcerted by the discovery that the Filipinos were Christians already, having been forcibly converted to Catholicism by Spain. Worse still there remained in the south of the Philippines a sizeable Moslem population whose determination to resist conversion was by no means weakened by the ousting of the Spaniards. Even in post-colonial times, a powerful separatist movement among the Moros on the southern island of Mindanao continues to trouble Philippine democracy.

When McKinley took the presidential oath in 1897, a rebellion against Spain was in progress on the island of Cuba, barely a hundred kilometres from the US coast. Popular support for the rebel cause among

Americans, who saw Spain as a weak colonial power from which they had already taken vast territories on the mainland, allowed the new president to declare war following the explosion in Havana harbour aboard *USS Maine*, which killed 200 sailors. More likely an explosion in the engine room than sabotage, the incident nonetheless set the scene for American intervention.

That Spain was facing a parallel uprising in the Philippines suited McKinley's Pacific policy, because the acquisition of the archipelago would strengthen the position of the United States in Southeast Asia where he feared Japan would soon look to expand its influence. Adroit handling of the Senate and Congress allowed McKinley to consolidate American influence in the Pacific. He annexed Guam, the chief island of the Spanish Ladrones, the present-day Marianas. Guam was in fact the first conquest of the Spanish-American War of 1898–99. Its governor had mistaken the three shots fired by an American warship as a naval salute, apologizing for not returning the courtesy because he lacked any cannon. No news of hostilities had yet reached the island's tiny Spanish garrison. Another McKinley acquisition in 1898 was Hawaii, whose mid-Pacific location provided a vital base for American warships headed towards the Philippines. He was in fact spurred into action by Japanese interest, whose imperial government envisaged some kind of union between Hawaii and Japan. The idea anticipates the Greater East Asia Co-Prosperity Sphere sixty years later, when its imperialist propaganda called for Hawaii's reunion with Asia.

Besides the development of naval facilities at Pearl Harbor, the greatest asset gained by the United States was Subic Bay, southwest of Manila. It remains a vital base today. So depressed was the radical Japanese writer Kotoku Shusui by the fashion of imperialism spreading to the Americans that, in 1901, he asked this question: "If the United States truly fought for freedom and independence in Cuba, why does it try to deny the freedom and independence of the Philippines?"

It was something the Filipinos pondered as soon as Washington's intentions became transparent. Once the rebel leader Emilio Aguinaldo realized that one set of colonial masters was merely being replaced by another, he declared war on "the unmeasured pride of the American Government". The first part of the Philippine-American War ended in

Despite disappointment over annexation by the United States,
the Philippines was destined to be the first Western colony
to gain its independence on 4 July 1946

1899, when Aguinaldo discovered that pitched battles could not be won against the flow of US reinforcements. So he abandoned conventional tactics and dispersed his troops, inaugurating guerrilla warfare. At first, Washington believed its forces could overcome the rebels without difficulty, but thousands of US troops could not contain Aguinaldo's guerrillas as fighting took on a brutality that deeply troubled the American public.

Not even the Gatling gun, whose hand-cranked multibarrel had just dealt such destruction to equally barefoot opponents during the American Indian campaigns, could overcome the hit-and-run tactics of the Filipino insurgents. Treating the Filipinos like "Red Indians" was of course bound to increase the savagery of the conflict, a racial dimension that was not lost on Arthur MacArthur, the father of the Second World War general Douglas MacArthur. Appointed military commander in 1900, the older MacArthur rapidly came to the view that only devolution of power to a civil administration would undermine the insurrection. Cultivating wealthy landowners, who stood to gain from cooperation with the Americans as they had with the Spaniards, he managed to isolate the rebels from mainstream Filipino politics.

After his capture, Aguinaldo swore an oath of allegiance to the United States. "Let the stream of blood cease to flow," he told his followers. Because "the complete termination of hostilities and a lasting peace are not only desirable but also absolutely essential for the well-being of the Philippines".

While many Americans still shied away from the accusation that the treatment of the Philippines was on a par with the colonialism of Britain, France, Holland and Portugal, the missionaries who arrived after the end of the insurrection were less worried about their own role. One of them even branded Aguinaldo as an "oriental despot", whose rule would have been "bloody like that of a Turkish sultan's". They firmly believed that an American occupation was the only means of preparing the Philippines for self-government. What the missionaries had to do was ensure its spiritual success.

A disappointed Aguinaldo had to await the coming of the Japanese for his revenge, yet independence within the Greater East Asia Co-Prosperity Sphere proved not to be the exciting prospect of freedom for which Filipinos had fought Spain as well as the United States. An American campaign to end the embarrassment of colonial rule had already got Congress to pass the Philippines Independence Act, which prescribed a preparatory period during which the colony would be semi-autonomous under the government of Filipinos. The date for independence was actually scheduled for 4 July 1946. The striking contrast between the resistance to Japanese aggression shown by the Filipinos and by the Indonesians was noted by President Roosevelt, who at once began to consider new political arrangements for post-war Southeast Asia. With the active support of a Labour government in Britain, the final curtain was about to be wrung down on the colonial era.

10

THE GREATER EAST ASIA
CO-PROSPERITY SPHERE

In military terms we conquered splendidly, but in the war we were severely defeated. But, as if by magic, India, Pakistan, Ceylon, Burma, the Dutch East Indies and the Philippine islands one after the other gained their independence overnight. The reduction of Singapore was the hinge of fate for the peoples of Asia.

Tsuji Masonobu, staff officer responsible for Imperial Japanese Army operations in Malaya and Singapore

The Japanese always regarded the American colony of the Philippines with a mixture of fascination and frustration. They wondered how the first people to escape from the clutches of European colonialism could presume to restrain Japan's own imperial ambitions while becoming in Southeast Asia colonialists themselves.

Although the Japanese were the first to draw Western blood in the Russo-Japanese War of 1904–05, and thereby gain a foothold on mainland East Asia, the Americans and the British opposed the attempt by the Imperial Japanese Army to conquer China. Beginning in earnest in 1937, the conflict in China was for Japan the start of a nine-year struggle which merged with the Pacific dimension of the Second World War. The challenge to the United States and Britain now seems a reckless gamble. However, its unreality was obscured by initial Japanese successes, just as the hopeless task of subduing a country the size of China failed to register in time for any limitation of war aims. By mid-1939, the Japanese had occupied many of the large cities and towns in China, but in the countryside the Chinese Communist Party had organized the peasants as guerrilla fighters. On the eve of Japan's involvement in the Second World War, the bulk of the Imperial Japanese Army was thus tied down by Mao Zedong's poorly armed combatants.

Unable to reach Chiang Kai-shek's stronghold at Chongqing in remote Sichuan province, or gain control over the countryside, the Japanese turned their attention to the Western colonies in Southeast Asia. An immediate cause of the sudden thrust southwards was American economic pressure. Without imports of scrap iron, nickel and oil products from the United States, Japan could not continue fighting in China. The resources of Southeast Asia therefore offered a tempting alternative source of supply and, with the sweeping German victories in Europe over France and Holland, Tokyo believed in 1940 that a pact with Germany and Italy would put Japan on the winning side. After its defeat, Emperor Hirohito said that the focus of pre-war discussion in Japan was always oil.

A Sudden Rampage

For Southeast Asia the war in Europe had very serious repercussions. The only power to which French Indochina could have looked for aid was Britain but, after the surrender of France, the Royal Navy bombarded French warships in North African ports to stop them falling into German hands, and all diplomatic relations had been severed. Even an attack on the British base at Gibraltar was launched from Vichy airfields in French Algeria.

The Thai dictator Luang Phibunsongkhram (or Phibun as he was known) quickly appreciated the political isolation of French Indochina after the German defeat of France. An admirer of Hitler, he had already changed the name of the country from Siam to Thailand, a move intended to make it attractive to Thai speakers throughout mainland Southeast Asia, and to remind residents of Chinese descent of their place. One reason for Phibun's willingness to side with the Japanese was the support they provided during the Franco-Thai War of 1940–41, which resulted in the recovery of territory lost to French Indochina. When the United

Southeast Asia in 1941

States cancelled the sale of fighters and bombers, Japan stepped in and provided aircraft, guns and torpedoes. A reward for voluntarily joining the Greater East Asia Co-Prosperity Sphere, the name by which Japan's empire was to be known, Phibun calculated, would be the return of Thai territories incorporated into British holdings in Burma and Malaya.

Although Phibun did not openly reveal his intentions, Tokyo was pleased to have gained his goodwill, if not his active assistance, in the run up to hostilities. So Japan asked Germany to lean on the Vichy regime, because a southward advance on Singapore was considered impossible without going through the Malayan peninsula, and to use this land bridge Japan needed airfields and harbours in both Cambodia and Vietnam. Berlin duly forbad the transfer of forces to Indochina, leaving the French colony in no position to refuse Japanese demands for stationing combat units there.

Japan's grand strategy in Southeast Asia and the Pacific relied on Germany and Italy in containing Britain and the United States. Because the Americans were turning their country into a gigantic arms factory and building up their own military strength in the Philippines and Hawaii though, the Japanese reinsured themselves by concluding in early 1941 a neutrality pact with the Soviet Union. It was designed to prevent a Russian attack and release troops for operations outside China. Hitler was not amused at this diplomatic initiative, but for Tokyo it provided considerable relief, before Germany's invasion of Russia later that year.

With Germany apparently vanquishing the Soviet Union, Tokyo thought the moment for decisive action had come. News of the Japanese attack on Pearl Harbor actually reached Hitler when he was handling a major crisis on the eastern front, the unexpected Russian counter-offensive before Moscow. In spite of the dire military situation there, Hitler immediately ordered German submarines to sink American ships and hurried back to Berlin, where he declared war on the United States.

"We are all astounded over Japan", wrote an official in London's Foreign Office. "We never thought she would attack us and America at once. She must have gone mad." Even though this response arose from a long-standing underestimation of Japan, and a consequent belief that the Japanese could be contained, it was still true that Tokyo laboured under a severe disadvantage. With the war in China already draining Japan's strength, no matter how far total mobilization went it could never match the combined manpower of the Allies. That is why the Japanese placed all their hopes on a swift advance, and in early 1942 they seemed to have achieved just this. The Imperial Japanese Army and the Imperial Japanese Navy had secured a defensive perimeter around the western Pacific and the South China Sea, within which a self-sufficient Greater East Asia Co-Prosperity Sphere would be able to fight a protracted war.

On 7 December 1941 the Imperial Japanese Navy launched a surprise air attack at Pearl Harbor, crippling the US Pacific Fleet. A stroke of bad luck for the Japanese, however, was the absence from port of the prime naval targets, three aircraft carriers. Two of them, the *Lexington* and the

Enterprise, were about to play vital roles in Japanese reverses at the battles of the Coral Sea and Midway. Admiral Chester Nimitz, the victor of the second engagement, said it was a blessing for the United States that not only were the aircraft carriers spared but even more that the Japanese had hit the battleships at their moorings. If they had been sunk at sea, they would have been a total loss. With the single exception of *USS Arizona*, the battleships were rebuilt to the latest standards, with sufficient anti-aircraft guns to supplement the air cover that was henceforth recognized as essential for their safety.

In the Philippines, however, the Americans were slightly more alert. General Douglas MacArthur readied his troops for a possible invasion and took the opportunity to draw Washington's attention to the limited forces available for the defence of the colony. But the Japanese drive southwards was relentless, most of the objectives being gained in less time than the planners in Tokyo had allowed. Malaya, Singapore, Borneo and the Dutch East Indies were all taken over before the end of March 1942. Having captured Rangoon, the Imperial Japanese Army also advanced into Upper Burma so as to cut the Burma Road, the main supply route for Western aid to an embattled China. The Americans did not finally surrender in the Philippines until May, although MacArthur had left for Australia in March. This whirlwind advance amazed the world, but nothing in its irresistible path matched the unconditional surrender of 85,000 men in Singapore. The fall of this supposedly impregnable fortress was a blow from which British colonial power in Southeast Asia never fully recovered.

The first Japanese assaults struck Thailand and Malaya. A British plan to pre-empt the occupation of the Kra isthmus was never put into action, and Japanese troops landed virtually unopposed in southern Thailand at Singora. Yamashita Tomoyuki, the general in charge of the Malayan campaign, was disappointed that there were no good airfields around Singora, and so he decided to occupy better ones in northern Malaya, thereby catching British forces in still incomplete defensive positions. The speed of the Japanese onslaught was to be the decisive factor during the whole campaign. "Mr. Quickly-Quickly", as Yamashita Tomoyuki was called by his men, wanted to achieve victory in time for Emperor Hirohito's birthday, which he did.

Without hesitation Phibun reached an agreement with the Japanese that guaranteed Thailand's continued independence. At first, the people of Thailand were enthusiastic about the war and proud of being the only fully independent Southeast Asian state in alliance with imperial Japan. But the export of Thai rice, rubber and tin to Japan brought nothing in return because the Japanese economy was entirely geared to war production. The Imperial Japanese Army's overprinting of the Thai currency as a way out of this dilemma merely added runaway inflation to Thailand's woes. Well before hostilities went badly against the Japanese in 1944, conditions in the country had already degenerated to the level of a black market economy, with recurrent shortages of basic commodities. Phibun fell

Churchill's gunboat bluff. The arrival of *HMS Prince of Wales*
in Singapore was not enough to stop the Japanese onslaught

from power and a US-sponsored Free Thai movement prepared to deal with the post-war situation.

In his account of the Malayan campaign, staff officer Tsuji Masanobu contrasts the landings at Singora and Kota Baru, the capital of Kelantan. At Kota Baru, the British pillboxes along the beach "were well prepared, and reacted violently with such heavy fire that our men lying on the beach, half in and half out of the water, could not raise their heads". Japanese transports were also attacked from a nearby RAF base and two of the three were sunk. It cost the Imperial Japanese Army 320 men killed and another 538 wounded to penetrate the beach defences and then capture the troublesome airfield. That some airfields were in Japanese hands made these losses worthwhile, however, for it permitted Yamashita Tomoyuki to call in his own planes and gain air superiority over Malaya.

Japan's advantage in this aspect of war had already been demonstrated at sea. Ignoring naval advice, premier Winston Churchill sent two capital ships, the newly commissioned *Prince of Wales* and the *Repulse*, to Singapore as a deterrent. He said of the *Prince of Wales* in a telegram to Roosevelt, "there is nothing like having something that can catch and kill anything". The original plan called for the dispatch of the battleship and the battle cruiser along with the aircraft carrier *Indomitable*, but the latter ran aground during fog off Jamaica. Since no other carrier was readily available, Force Z arrived at Singapore with only anti-aircraft guns to protect it from aerial assault. Locally, the condition of the Royal Air Force was pitiful. Of its 246 fighters and bombers the most modern was the lumbering Brewster Buffalo, which never matched the agile Japanese Zero fighter.

Three days after Pearl Harbor, off the east coast of Malaya, Force Z was intercepted by Japanese aircraft flying from airfields in French Indochina and within hours both the *Prince of Wales* and the *Repulse* were sent to the bottom. Only the presence of three escorting destroyers enabled as many as 2,000 sailors to be saved. As Terence O'Brien, an RAF pilot who was later transferred to Singapore, commented: "Without air cover, they were nothing but sacrificial lambs."

Churchill's gunboat bluff had ended in disaster. After the fall of Singapore, Churchill said that Britain had given to the Soviet Union what was really needed for the defence of Malaya. This was a lame excuse. Just as the sinking of Force Z reflected an outdated approach to naval warfare, so on land the complacency of the British garrison almost ensured a Japanese triumph. It was erroneously believed that the jungle was impassable for large numbers of troops and that the situation was therefore overwhelmingly in favour of the defenders. Only a threat from the sea was considered dangerous before the outbreak of hostilities.

But it was the jungle that Yamashita Tomoyuki so brilliantly exploited. He realized the potential for outflanking movements when he saw it for the first time near Saigon. Unlike him, nearly all British senior officers thought that everything depended on holding roads. The shining exception was Ian Stewart, the commanding officer of the 2nd Battalion Argyll and Sutherland Highlanders. He took his men on training exercises designed to accustom them to both the advantages and disadvantages of fighting in primary as well as secondary jungle. In the process, the Argylls banished any fears they had about plants and animals. This familiarity saved the battalion from destruction on several occasions: it also helped inflict an early reverse on the apparently unbeatable Imperial Japanese Army at Grik Road, inland from Penang. There the Japanese were shocked by counter-attacks delivered from the jungle on each side of this thoroughfare. So effective were Stewart's preparations that an Argyll prisoner of war was disbelieved when asked by a Japanese officer how many men were in the rearguard on the Grik Road. When the Argyll scratched on the ground with a stick "35", the Japanese officer added two noughts. He was annoyed when these were scratched out, because the troops he had led down that road were held up for a couple of days by this tiny rearguard.

Yet as Stewart later commented: "New tactics cannot be learnt in the middle of a battle." And so the transport-dependent defenders were outmanoeuvred and pushed down the Malayan peninsula to the island of Singapore, whose northern defences the colonial government had been unwilling to strengthen, because it was believed that their fortification would undermine civilian morale.

This serious defensive shortcoming was compounded by the faulty dispositions of Gordon Bennett, as the battle for Singapore was lost in the northwestern part of the island, where Bennett's 8th Australian Division was supposed to hold the coastline. Not only did he fail to

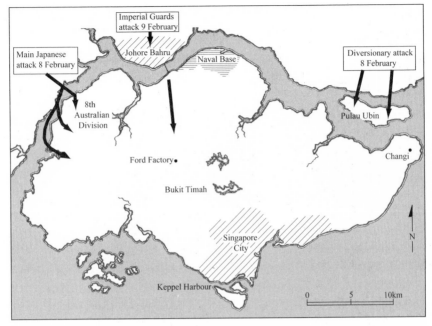

The Japanese attack on Singapore

incorporate a rear defence line into his overall plan, to deal with Japanese infiltration, but worse Bennett refused to listen to advice from his chief of staff over troop movements. After the war, this experienced soldier said that the Australian general "would never admit he was wrong". Other extraordinary decisions taken by Bennett towards the end of the siege were to order his men to surrender, without bothering to tell the commander-in-chief Arthur Percival; and then to leave them behind as prisoners of war while escaping himself on a fishing boat to Australia, where he had the temerity to claim that he, and not Stewart, was the first person who got to grips with the jungle. The errant general was never appointed to a command again.

After the surrender agreement was signed by Percival in the Ford Factory at Bukit Timah on 15 February 1942, Yamashita Tomoyuki admitted that Singapore's capture was a close-run thing. The campaign in Malaya and Singapore had lasted just seventy days, a month less than Tokyo calculated was necessary for the entire operation. In overcoming the island of Singapore, the Japanese general said the assault was

Japanese soldiers celebrate the capture of Singapore in February 1942

a bluff that worked. I had 30,000 men and was outnumbered by more than three to one. I knew that if I had to fight for long for Singapore I would be beaten. That was why the surrender had to be made at once. I was very frightened that the British would discover our numerical weakness and lack of supplies, and force me into disastrous street fighting.

For the people caught up in the surrender, civilian and military alike, conditions under the triumphant Japanese were appalling. The new name that the Japanese gave to Singapore could not have been more inaccurate: it was never Syonan, "the city of Light and Peace in the South". As in China, Japanese soldiers went on the rampage and, though the scale of atrocity was not in the same league as the 1937 rape of Nanjing where at least 260,000 died, the violence again fell largely on the Chinese population. Thousands of men between the ages of fifteen and fifty were either thrown overboard to drown at sea or executed in improvised prison camps. Despite his protestations of alarm at such brutality, Tsuji Masonobu did nothing to protect Singapore's residents.

Most feared of all was arrest by the Kempeitai, the Japanese military police. An unsettling aspect of Japanese rule was the arbitrariness of its repression. Failure to show proper respect to a soldier was often enough to merit detention or death. When Sinozaki Mamoru went to the Kempeitai headquarters in the YMCA building on behalf of the vice-president of the Overseas Chinese Association, an approved society in Singapore, a warrant officer in charge of the case wanted to arrest him as a Japanese traitor. He was uninterested to learn that Sinozaki Mamoru's official role was the protection of civilians. Had a passing Kempeitai officer not recognized him, Sinozaki Mamoru would have been locked in a cell. He reflected uneasily how "many Japanese soldiers thought like this warrant officer... I felt sad, lonely and dispirited until I remembered myself that the lot of the Singapore people was far worse than mine". At least his severed head would not appear on a pole, a gruesome practice the Kempeitai first introduced at Kuala Lumpur. In Singapore, the heads were invariably Chinese.

Churchill called the fall of Singapore "the worst disaster and largest capitulation in British history". Yet he never grasped the island's vulnerability from a land assault; nor did he realize how weak were its air defences. Air Vice-Marshall Pulford's air force, including the fifty-one hastily assembled Hurricanes that arrived crated barely a month before the surrender on 15 February 1942, were outnumbered by well over four to one. "God knows we did our best with what was given," the Air Vice-Marshall said. What was given could never be considered enough: no tanks, almost no modern planes, and few properly trained troops.

So inadequate were the resources available to meet the Japanese onslaught that when Kuching, the capital of Sarawak, was subjected to a fierce air raid, its inhabitants were told to endure such events like any English town. The absence of Allied aircraft for Kuching's protection had of course an adverse effect on civilian morale, especially in relation to a colonial people wavering between support for the Brooke government and possibly the enemy. In Burma the impact of the Japanese advance was even more dramatic, because the Thakin organization was able to provide the Imperial Japanese Army with devastatingly accurate intelligence. But the honeymoon period between the Japanese invaders and the Burmese nationalists was short-lived. The announcement of a Japanese military administration for the British colony meant that Japan had broken its promise of independence. Switching to the Allied side was unavoidable, Aung San told General William Slim: "If the British sucked our blood," he said, "the Japanese ground our bones."

The Failure of Japan's New Order

With the British retreat into India, Japan became the sole colonial power in Southeast Asia. Portugal held on to East Timor for as long as it could, but Lisbon was unable to stop Australian troops from conducting guerrilla operations against the Imperial Japanese Army right across the island.

The change in colonial fortunes was emphasized by the Imperial Japanese Army's favourite policy of humiliating Westerners before local populations. In Malaya, British and Australian captives, stripped to the waist, were made to tackle manual work as a reminder that before the Japanese came, Westerners never undertook these tasks. So annoyed was the Imperial Japanese Army at prolonged resistance in the Philippines that American and Filipino prisoners of war were subjected to one of its notorious death marches, during which 2,250 servicemen died. Japanese

In Brooke Kuching the Anglican girls school behind this Chinese temple
housed a brothel for the Imperial Japanese Army

soldiers were particularly cruel to the Filipinos, whom they regarded as
colonial lackeys. This indifference to suffering on the part of the captors
became patently obvious in the last months of the Pacific War. At
Sandakan, in British North Borneo, 2,428 Allied prisoners were marched
to death in mid-1945. Only six emaciated Australians managed to escape
on the march and survive. Even though their liberators seldom exacted
revenge for Japanese atrocities, on this occasion the 9th Australian
Division averted its eyes from the way in which Dyak head-hunters
dealt with disarmed Japanese. In Kuching, where at Batu Lintang stood
the largest detention centre on the island of Borneo, the prisoners were
lucky to have been earmarked as porters for a Japanese withdrawal inland,
where they were to be liquidated. The sudden end of the war saved them.

An unavoidable aspect of Japanese rule was its repression, but in the
end such severity was self-defeating: it failed to win over Southeast Asian
peoples. As one Borneo colonial officer reflected in 1946:

> What use was it for an officer to make a speech on the iniquities of the
> British, when on the same day, a sentry assaulted a Mohammedan woman
> for failing to bow to him?

A Dyak bamboo cigarette box.
Self-sufficiency allowed the indigenous peoples
of Borneo to survive the Japanese occupation

For the Imperial Japanese Army, however, strict security was necessary in order to release combat units for operations elsewhere. Troops sent to the Dutch East Indies had to take over the colonial administration as well as put down rebellions among the native population. In Sumatra and Java, attacks on Europeans and the looting of their houses indicated a revolutionary nationalism that would soon embarrass Japan. In Aceh, the anti-Dutch agitation had strong Islamic overtones and the Imperial Japanese Army was forced to intervene to stop a campaign of sabotage that threatened to damage the economy. But its own efforts only tended to add to the confusion, once Indonesia was flooded by occupation currency. Because the new notes were worthless, food requisitioning actually led to severe famines in Sumatra as well as Java.

Agricultural production was adjusted to the benefit of Japan, with crops such as sugar being artificially depressed to the advantage of farmers at home and in its colony of Taiwan. Since sugar estates provided work for landless Indonesians, this policy caused real hardship. Elsewhere, the Japanese brought semi-starvation and deficiency diseases to local populations. In Malaya, children were especially hard hit, as their growth rates failed to keep up with their ages. Children of fourteen years were no taller than those aged seven or eight. So desperate did the food supply become in Singapore that plans were made for the relocation of 300,000 residents, about 40 per cent of the island's population. Sinozaki Mamoru was uncertain about the attitude of the residents towards the proposed settlement of New Syonan at Endau, in northern Johore. He need not have worried, because thousands of Singaporeans applied to settle there, away from the attentions of the Kempeitai. To show their appreciation, they presented the settlement's first crop of rice to the mayor of Syonan. Because Sinozaki Mamoru had persuaded the Japanese authorities to let the Chinese settlers at Endau make their own arrangements for law and order, without any interference from the Kempeitai, it is hardly surprising that the Overseas Chinese Association found "the finest jungle workers in Malaya" to clear the site.

From the outset, the Japanese endeavoured to placate Indonesian religious leaders, whom they feared could be as difficult to themselves as

Sandakan from Government House. From this town in North Borneo the Imperial Japanese Army marched nearly 2,500 Allied POWs to their deaths in 1945

they had been to the Dutch, while at the same time keeping nationalist leaders on a very short leash. Some Indonesians actually hoped that cooperation with the Imperial Japanese Army would lead to a degree of modernization akin to Japan's remarkable industrial progress. What they slowly came to understand was that the Japanese, like their Dutch predecessors, were intent on exploiting Indonesia purely in their own interests. But, if there was one welcome thing that Japan's New Order did bring to the Dutch East Indies, it was an end to the racial discrimination that had bedevilled colonial relations for centuries. For the Indonesians, whom the Dutch preferred to go barefoot, this was a massive social improvement. Yet the contradictions in the New Order were soon apparent in the field of education. Popular discontent resulted from censorship of the curriculum, an emphasis on physical training, and compulsory lessons in the Japanese language.

The future Indonesian president, Ahmed Sukarno, was under no illusions about Japanese intentions, but he took advantage of public platforms to disparage the Dutch and stimulate nationalist aspirations. As he reminded the Javanese in 1943, "the fate of our people is in our own hands and not those of others". Once they recognized that the Allies could not be held at bay, the Japanese asked Sukarno and Mohammad Hatta, another prominent nationalist, to devise a formula for cooperation and a draft constitution for an independent republic. The new state was to incorporate under a strong presidency not only the territories of the Dutch East Indies but those belonging to Britain in Malaya and Borneo as well. The Indonesian leaders did not want independence as a gift from Tokyo, so Sukarno proclaimed the Republic of Indonesia on 17 August 1945, two days after the Japanese surrender.

Because the United States had already promised independence to the Philippines, the Japanese were more cautious in their occupation, except when it came to surrendered Filipino soldiers. Yet there was Japanese frustration over the lack of interest shown in the Greater East Asia Co-Prosperity Sphere. It did not assist constructive cooperation that the Filipino administration in Manila discovered that it had less authority under the Japanese than previously under the Americans.

But one liberation movement sponsored by Tokyo had an unexpected impact on Burma. Its aim was the freeing of India from British rule and its

Rangoon Liberator

SPECIAL EDITION

Wednesday, August 15, 1945   Price Annas 2

JAPAN SURRENDERS UNCONDITIONALLY

S.E.A.C., Hqs, August 15 : (07:05) hrs :—At 7-10 last night the Japanese Minister in Switzerland left a note with the Swiss authorities. At mid-night (G. M. T.) Mr. Attlee made his dramatic. announcement and we are able to tell you that Japan has unconditionally surrendered.

LAST OF OUR ENEMIES LAID LOW

Allied forces in Burma learn of Japan's defeat

instrument was Subhas Chandra Bose, who rejected Gandhi's attachment to non-violence and raised an army of 18,000 Tamil workers from Malayan rubber estates and recruited Indian soldiers captured on the fall of Singapore. Few Indian officers responded to his call, even though they had had to tolerate discrimination themselves before the Japanese victory. A colour bar prevented their membership of Singapore's clubs, unlike British officers from their own regiments.

Whether in Germany, where Bose broadcast and met Indian prisoners of war, or in Japan, to which he travelled in German and Japanese submarines that made a rendezvous off Madagascar, his considerable energy was poured into the establishment of the Indian National Army. In both Germany and Japan, however, Bose had to overlook the less attractive side of their regimes. "The internal policies of Germany or Italy or Japan," he said, "do not concern us." All that mattered for India was the defeat of the British, so it would be an "act of political suicide" for Indians to "remain inactive or neutral" during the war. That Bose misjudged Japan's war aims could not be clearer than in his firm belief that the Greater East Asia Co-Prosperity Sphere was undertaking the "noble task of creating a great Asia that will be free, happy and prosperous". Only "Anglo-American imperialism" stood in its way.

The attempt by Bose's Indian National Army to suborn Indian troops in the British Fourteenth Army met with little success. Once Bose's men were found incapable of taking part in actual engagements in Burma, the Japanese abandoned them altogether. General Slim, commander of the Fourteenth Army, had to issue orders forbidding his Indian and Gurkha soldiers from shooting out of hand any of Bose's men who tried to surrender. The British defeat of the Imperial Japanese Army at Imphal and Kohima was quite unprecedented, with 100,000 Japanese soldiers killed by the Fourteenth Army's recapture of Rangoon in early 1945. A breakneck pursuit of the retreating Imperial Japanese Army had given it no chance of mounting any defence.

The desperate effort to invade the Indian borderlands was almost the last major operation launched by Japan. From mid-1944 onwards the Americans began an island-hopping campaign to Japan that reached the islands of Iwo Jima and Okinawa via the Philippines. Waves of suicide pilots could not halt this advance. The divine wind, the kamikaze, that had thwarted the Mongol invasion of Japan in the thirteenth century was reincarnated to little purpose in the bomb-planes that buzzed around US warships. When Emperor Hirohito was informed of the first kamikaze mission, he said: "Was it necessary to go to this extreme? But they have certainly done a good job." The ferocity of the suicide-pilots struck terror in Allied sailors' hearts, but their aircraft were vulnerable to improved US fighters and whole flights of kamikazes were wiped out well before they could reach their targets.

Yet this fanatical gesture and the mentality it revealed, along with the heavy casualties inflicted on GIs in the suicidal defence of the islands of Iwo Jima and Okinawa, obliged Washington to reconsider its strategy. Instead of a seaborne invasion of the Japan, President Harry S. Truman authorized the dropping of atomic bombs on the cities of Hiroshima and Nagasaki. Even after these terrible events, Tokyo still hesitated to surrender until Emperor Hirohito said how "ending the war is the only way to restore world peace and to relieve the nation from the terrible distress with which it is burdened". Between them, the president and the emperor had liquidated the Greater East Asia Co-Prosperity Sphere at a stroke.

Post-War Decolonization

If Singapore's dramatic surrender in 1942 was insufficient to end Western colonialism, the overwhelming election victory of the Labour Party in Britain certainly was. The 1945 landslide ensured that Britain was spared the agony of colonial wars, unlike the Dutch in Indonesia and the French in Indochina. Prime Minister Clement Attlee's decision to grant India early independence meant that decolonization was bound to follow in Southeast Asia.

British intentions were transparent in the speed with which Burma gained its freedom. Not even the assassination of Aung San, by a political rival, caused Attlee to hesitate, so that in late 1947 Burma became independent, and left the Commonwealth. Its withdrawal was not unexpected, Attlee noted, because murder had removed the one man who could have maintained Burmese membership. Then Churchill savaged the Labour Party's policy of imperial decolonization, but he was more realistic on his return to power in 1951. Point blank, Churchill refused an American appeal to assist the French in Indochina. Believing they were beyond help, the British premier rejected Washington's domino theory of a communist take-over of Southeast Asia. Having got the better of a communist insurgency in Malaya, the British had in Tunku Abdul Rahman an effective premier-in-waiting for their colony. This ex-playboy was the brother of the sultan of Kedah: hence his title of Tunku, or "prince". Yet he knew how important it was to ensure communal harmony and, as a result, he incorporated Chinese, Indian and Malay political associations in his Alliance Party. Washington was deeply impressed by the emergence of a pro-Western outlook in Malaya coincident with the terminal decline of French Indochina. Unfortunately for the Vietnamese, the Laotians and the Cambodians, it was to draw the United States into the devastating struggle of the Second Vietnam War.

If Malaya gave Britain initial cause for concern, the kingdom of

In London, Tunku Abdul Rahman signs the
agreement for Malayan independence

the Brookes in Sarawak represented an imperial anomaly of antique
proportions. There was no sympathy in London for its survival as
a sovereign state, and so the last white rajah, Vyner Brooke, ceded his
kingdom to Britain in 1946. Significantly for post-colonial differences
between the state of Sarawak and the federal government of Malaysia,
most Sarawakians opposed the cession. One British governor was
even assassinated in 1949 and it took all the remarkable skills of his
successor, Sir Anthony Abell, to restore Sarawak to its usual condition
of friendliness. A latter-day James Brooke, Abell's genuine enjoyment
of its forty distinct peoples led to his repeated terms as governor. Not
long after his departure, Sarawak held its first general election, a perfect
opportunity to transform itself into a self-governing state before the
formation of Malaysia.

Having formally transferred power to Tunku Abdul Rahman in
1957, the British had to decide what to do about the Borneo territories
including oil-rich Brunei. There was additionally the need to prevent
Singapore becoming a communist state, given its location at the junction

of key international sea routes. Even in Sarawak the attraction of the People's Republic of China to Chinese youths had caused a worrying exodus to China as well as Indonesia. Those who went to the latter were to fight alongside Indonesian soldiers during Confrontation.

So fresh was Brunei's memory of late greatness that its sultan still exercised almost autocratic powers over his subjects. But as the people of Brunei observed the political and economic development of Sarawak and British North Borneo, both now British colonies being speedily prepared for independence, there was resentment over inefficient health, education and housing policies, not to mention political exclusion. Despite the beginnings of constitutional change in 1959, the pace was too slow for A. M. Azahari, a local politician who also feared that joining Malaysia would scupper his own scheme for a Greater Brunei based on the recovery of lost territories in Sarawak and North Borneo. He had already attracted a large following and served six months in prison for dissent. Because the British distrusted his communist leanings, however, Azahari decided on direct action, supported by funds from Indonesia as well as the Philippines.

But the British intelligence service anticipated the rebellion in late 1962 and, within twenty-four hours of its outbreak, Commonwealth forces were moved from Singapore to regain control in Brunei. Thwarted by this move, Sukarno proclaimed Indonesia's support for Azahari and then announced a policy of military confrontation against the proposed Federation of Malaysia. With some justification, the Philippines argued that the North Borneo Company had leased, rather than purchased, part of the island of Borneo from the Sulu sultanate. But neither Kuala Lumpur nor London was prepared to discuss such an old claim, and eventually the Philippines recognized the Federation of Malaysia as an independent state.

So it came as no small surprise, when in early 2013, a small force from the southern Philippines invaded Sabah, the present name of the Malaysian state which used to be British North Borneo. The invaders claimed to be reasserting the ancestral birthright of Jamalul Kiram III, whose family had ceased to rule Sulu in 1878. Possibly the nominal rent still paid by Malaysia each year for Sabah had become inadequate for the would-be sultan to live comfortably in his Manila flat. Sulu's claim to this part of the island of Borneo ostensibly dates from the seventeenth century, when a grateful Brunei sultan is said to have offered the territory as a reward for assistance in putting down a rebellion. But Sulu's encroachment had actually begun a century earlier during the period of Spanish domination at Brunei.

Once Indonesia called off its border war in 1966, Britain knew that it had solved the problems it faced as the last major Western colonial power in Southeast Asia. For Lee Kuan Yew, Singapore's first premier, joining Malaysia meant a sought-after end to British rule but not its military presence, because he seems to have been uncertain about the long-term effectiveness of the tiny island's economy. He knew that the British provided much of Singapore's foreign earnings, a circumstance that drove him to stimulate development during the 1970s as Britain steadily withdrew its forces. After Singapore quit Malaysia in 1965, this was a matter of urgency, although Lee Kuan Yew reminded Singaporeans how "from 1819 right up to the 1930s there was a prosperous Singapore without either of British naval or air base".

Unlike the British, both the Dutch and the French refused to accept the stark realities of the post-war world. Restoring some kind of imperial presence in Southeast Asia was for them almost a psychological necessity following German occupation. Although it might choose to ignore the uneasy collaboration of Vichy Indochina with Japan, Paris could not discount the Japanese claim to have liberated its three colonies by declaring in 1945 the independence of the royal governments of Laos and Cambodia as well as that of the Vietnamese emperor Bao Dai. The Netherlands was just as keen to resume control, too, in what was about to become independent Indonesia.

Neither the French nor the Dutch possessed the military strength to restore their colonial administrations once Japan surrendered. And the sudden end of hostilities also caught the British unprepared. William Slim, now commander of Allied Land forces in Southeast Asia, observed how in Indochina and the Dutch East Indies:

> Nationalist movements, armed from Japanese sources, had already seized power in the vacuum left by the surrender... In all areas were intact Japanese forces... whose acceptance of surrender was not certain, and

many thousands of British, Australians, Indians, Americans, Dutch and French, starving and dying of diseases in brutal and barbaric Japanese prison camps. It was obviously vital that we should occupy all Japanese held territory at the earliest possible moment, not only to enforce the surrender, but to succour these unfortunates.

But there were just too many demands for Slim's troops to tackle, not to say his depleted air force. Transport planes were in such short supply that British troops arrived at the destinations by a mixture of flight and voyage. The inevitable delays influenced the unfolding of events in the French and Dutch colonies, although Slim was particularly concerned that the vehemently anti-Vietnamese attitude of French settlers could inflame an already uncertain situation.

In Indochina the Viet Minh, "the Vietnamese League", set up in 1941 to advance the cause of freedom, refused to acknowledge the restored Vietnamese emperor and, when the Japanese units surrendered, its members occupied Hanoi and declared a republic. Above the sixteenth parallel, virtually the border until 1975 between the two independent Vietnams, the Japanese were ordered to hand over their arms to a Chinese occupation force; but, because they were short of supplies, Chinese troops sold or bartered the weapons to the Viet Minh. Thus the revolutionary supporters of Ho Chi Minh acquired rifles, light machine-guns and ammunition. Upon the withdrawal of Chinese forces a few months later, the returning French recognized with a great deal of reluctance Ho Chi Minh's communist North Vietnam as a state within the Federation of Indochina and the French Union.

But Paris had no intention of letting go of Vietnam. In the south, an autonomous government was placed under the titular authority of Emperor Bao Dai, while in the north the French thought they could regain control by force of arms. So the scene was set for the First and Second Vietnam Wars. They are only now seen for what they really were: not a communist triumph but a national struggle for a free and united Vietnam.

That the first Vietnam War ended in 1954 with the defeat of France was in large measure due to the military genius of Vo Nguyen Giap. Eschewing pitched battles, Giap tied down superior French numbers by ambushes, lightning attacks and sabotage. Once the French found local recruitment almost impossible, its combat units filled up with mercenaries, whose behaviour only served to alienate the Vietnamese people even more. By 1954, defeat was inevitable despite the United States paying for 80 per cent of the war's cost. In a last gamble to bring the Viet Minh to a decisive battle, the French command allowed the garrison at Dien Bien Phu, a fortified base northwest of Hanoi, to be cut off. It was a mistake because they badly underestimated the resourcefulness of Vo Nguyen Giap, who managed to fire 130,000 shells on French positions. His artillery was entirely American in manufacture, having been taken by the People's Liberation Army from the troops of Chiang Kai-shek in China or from US formations in Korea. When Dien Bien Phu was finally overrun, the area under French control had shrunk to the size of two football pitches. American reporter Howard Simpson, who survived the siege, recalls how "grizzled French veterans were astounded by the youth and nervousness" of their captors.

The garrison surrendered just before an international conference in Geneva recognized an independent Vietnam, partitioned into two states.

French soldiers take cover at Dien Bien Phu shortly before
the surrender of the garrison

Devastated Manila after the American liberation

With the French gone, the United States was left as the sole protector of South Vietnam. When in 1956 South Vietnam's president, Ngo Dinh Diem, refused to hold the elections agreed at Geneva because he feared Ho Chi Minh would win, the Americans were on a collision course with the Viet Minh, which culminated in the devastating Second Vietnam War.

Because Holland had no troops available, London expected the Dutch to negotiate with the nationalists in Java as had happened successfully in Burma. But it had not reckoned with Hubertus van Mook, the governor-general of the Dutch East Indies. He resented the light British touch, wrongly believing that Dutch authority could be restored by the application of force. And he correctly guessed that the Labour government had little enthusiasm for restoring Dutch colonial rule, when decolonization was very much part of its own agenda. Ignoring London's desire for a political settlement, the Dutch strung out talks with the nationalists until it was obvious that they would have to recover Indonesia themselves.

After the British withdrawal, the Dutch tried to subdue the whole of Java and secure economically important areas of Sumatra, by diverting funds provided by the United States for post-war reconstruction in Europe. When this "police action" failed, van Mook was obliged to reopen equally unproductive talks with "a terrorist so-called government". Once the Soviet Union showed an interest, the United States ditched Holland with the result that an independent Indonesia became unavoidable in 1949.

Although the end of the Pacific War should have been a time for rejoicing in the Philippines, the extent of the war damage deeply shocked its people. Burma and the Philippines were in fact the most thoroughly fought over colonies in Southeast Asia, and American determination to recover the latter was so much a matter of national honour that no brake at all was ever applied to the heavy-handedness of General MacArthur's liberation of Manila. It took the lives of 100,000 Filipinos and reduced the city to desolation. As one distraught resident remarked:

> Our home had been ransacked, put to the torch, its ruins shelled again and again... The carpet-shelling by the Americans which went relentlessly on, long after the last Japanese sniper was a carcass in the rubble... So this was the Liberation. I was no longer sure what was worse: the inhumanity of the Japanese or the helpfulness of the Americans.

Painful though the US return was in several Philippine islands, the expulsion of the Imperial Japanese Army soon brought about promised independence.

The Japanese occupation, however, had heightened social, political and economic tensions between peasants and landlords, exiles and captives, guerrillas and collaborators. The Hukbalahap, which emerged as a major guerrilla movement in central Luzon, was essentially a peasant protest against rapacious landowners. The disruption of the Second World War had given the Huks, as these insurgents were popularly called, a rare opportunity to challenge the economic balance of power in the Philippines, and this struggle would define the early years of its independence.

11

INDEPENDENCE:
THE MAINLAND NATION STATES

We all seek a better future for our people. But, given the different circumstances of natural and human resources, agricultural or industrial backgrounds, and industrial and technological competence, we have to chart different courses towards that goal.

Lee Kuan Yew in 1971 at the first Commonwealth Conference to be held in Asia

Even though Southeast Asian countries have had a chequered experience of independence since the end of the Second World War, there is no question about the energy that all eleven of them have expended in pursuing their own destinies. Conflict with external enemies ravaged several, most notably Vietnam and East Timor, while civil strife deeply troubled Indonesia, Cambodia, Myanmar and the Philippines. Apart from Cambodia and Myanmar, however, the political instability of Thailand has been exceptional, King Rama IX presiding over ten successful, and six unsuccessful, military coups during his reign. Considering that Thailand was the sole Southeast Asian country not to have endured colonial rule makes these armed interventions all the more surprising. Several were bloodless, including the 2006 coup led by Sonthi Boonyaratglin, Thailand's first Moslem commander-in-chief.

Elsewhere, serious political differences caused Singapore to quit the Federation of Malaysia in 1965, but inter-state relations were not irrevocably soured by this move, because the tiny island of Singapore has demonstrated a remarkable ability to stand on its own feet as an independent nation state. Whatever the different courses that their recent history has taken over the last half century, every Southeast Asian country has managed to forge distinctive characteristics, making each one a unique addition to the community of nations.

As ever, the interplay of outside influences has had a profound impact on Southeast Asia, situated as it still is at the meeting point of important trade and communication routes, but with the end of the Cold War and the revival of China as the regional superpower, there is now a real possibility of sustained economic growth as well as social progress among its many peoples. That Indonesia is regarded as a potential world power indicates how much has changed since the archipelago gained its independence from Holland in 1949. Even more, a realization that the Republic of Indonesia possesses the natural resources of oil and gas which can sustain a major economy underlines how transformed Southeast Asia really is today. The only brake on Indonesia's development remains an incredible lack of unity among its islanders, a weakness that has allowed military figures to exercise undue authority following the compulsory retirement of President Sukarno in 1965.

The troubles of the colonial era are well and truly over, along with the brief and brutal Japanese triumph. Because it was the first Asian country to modernize its economy, Japan was able to pursue imperial ambitions on a par with those of the Western colonial powers. The Imperial Japanese Navy was the most obvious feature of this new status, which Britain first recognized in the Anglo-Japanese Alliance of 1902. Yet the patent inability of the Imperial Japanese Army to subdue China set the scene for the Pacific dimension of the Second World War: Japan's rash assault on the colonies of the United States, Holland and Britain. Although their ill-prepared defences were quickly overcome, the spectacular Japanese advance was checked at the end of 1942, by which time the promised benefits of the Greater East Asia Co-Prosperity Sphere were nowhere in sight either. And Japan's occupation of Southeast Asia was soon seen for what it was, ruthless asset-stripping on a gigantic scale. Possibly as many as 2.5 million Javanese died of starvation during 1944 when vast stockpiles of rice were being created on the island for a long war.

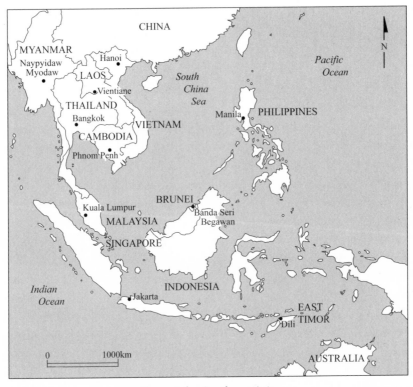

Present-day Southeast Asia

Much as America's atomic bombs brought hostilities to a swift close, it was the singular commitment of Britain to a programme of decolonization that really terminated Western imperialism in Southeast Asia. Holland and France had no choice but acknowledge the wisdom of the British, even though Cold War fears got the better of common sense in Washington to the extent that the United States assumed a neocolonial role in Vietnam. The Second Vietnam War is a salutary lesson of how misconceived were so many actions during the Cold War. The Americans simply failed to grasp North Vietnam's essential aim: the reunification of the Vietnamese homeland. They also became covertly involved in a Laotian civil war because it was wrongly assumed to be another communist-inspired conflict. Yet Washington's worst mistake was to back a South Vietnamese invasion of Cambodia in 1970, which opened the way for the Khmer Rouge's seizure of power. As a consequence of misguided post-war US foreign policy, the countries on mainland Southeast Asia have suffered far more disruption than their maritime counterparts.

Myanmar

Myanmar, formerly known as Burma, is perhaps the strangest Southeast Asian state, because since gaining its independence from Britain in 1947 it has largely chosen to isolate itself from the outside world. Only now is Myanmar starting to welcome foreign visitors and foreign investment. The country has also the dubious distinction of enduring the longest period of civil strife in modern Southeast Asian history.

The Japanese capitulation did not leave the same power vacuum in Burma that occurred elsewhere in French and Dutch Southeast Asia, because Allied forces were already in occupation. But self-government would have to come sooner than the Colonial Office in London planned, and the Labour premier Clement Attlee was quick to recognize this need, agreeing a timetable with Aung San, the most prominent nationalist. The speed with which the colony then moved to independence was breathtaking. Not even the assassination of Aung San, by a political rival, caused Attlee to slow down the independence process: in October 1947, Burma became free, and left the Commonwealth. Its withdrawal was not unexpected, Attlee sadly reflected, because the murder had removed the one man who could have maintained Burmese membership. It also removed the one Burman politician who was trusted by the substantial ethnic minorities living in the country. After Aung San's untimely death, nationalist factions contending for power were only concerned with securing Burman support, thereby reviving age-old ethnic rivalries in their marked indifference to the aspirations of the Karen, Kachin, Shan and Mon peoples.

A fundamental difficulty for the Karens was that they did not all live in the same area, although most dwelt in the hill country adjacent to the Thai border. As a consequence of this dispersal, they demanded a larger area than the Burman leaders could reasonably concede. A compromise of sorts was an agreement to a small but semi-autonomous Karen homeland with its right to secede from Burma after a decade. In the anarchy that engulfed the newly independent country, however, the Karens considered this an inadequate arrangement and, in January 1949, they revolted against Rangoon. The mass desertion of Karen soldiers gave

Premier Attlee with Aung San in London, early 1947

the uprising great strength for, with other hillmen, they had formed the backbone of the resistance movements that grew in strength against the Imperial Japanese Army's occupation of Burma. The British commander, William Slim, recalls in his account of the Burma campaign how the staunchly loyal Karens had fallen upon the retreating Japanese columns in 1945 with untold ferocity. "It was not difficult to get the Karens to rise against the hated Japanese," he wrote, "the problem was to restrain them from rising too soon." It is arguable that a degree of restraint would have helped the Karen cause from the late 1940s until the early 1960s, but Cold War intrigue seemed too good an opportunity to miss. In spite of the prolonged rebellion taking its toll on traditional Karen ways and turning the homeland into an area where warlords rule the roost, the Karens themselves remain no less discontented with their lot today.

Although the other hill peoples, the Shan, Kachin and Chin, lived in more concentrated border communities, the reluctance of Burman leaders in Rangoon to make any concessions meant that insurgency was certain to spread to large parts of the country. In Lower Burma, the Mon had also sought separation from the colony, prior to its independence. What happened was in effect a repeat of the historical pattern of division with

The Sule pagoda was made the hub of Rangoon by British town planners
in 1853. It celebrates the conversion of a malignant nat to Buddhism

Burman armed forces controlling the Irrawaddy river valley, where they
were largely deployed, while insurgents were scattered around its edges.
As a result of this return to Burma's perennial instability, the country
was placed under martial law from 1948 to 1950, but its lifting a year
later did not imply that the armed forces were ready to defeat the rebels.
In response to rebel gains, Ne Win had become commander-in-chief and
begun a dramatic expansion and improvement of the army, although it
remained a poorly equipped infantry force of around 43,000 men.

General Ne Win's efforts to strengthen the country's military capacity,
through large-scale recruitment and the development of a navy as well

as an air force, allowed the recovery of much of lowland Burma and the increasing isolation of the insurgents in pockets around its northern and eastern borders. In the long term, however, this expensive build-up led to military government, when in 1962 tanks rolled into Rangoon and soldiers took ministers into protective custody. The declared reason for the coup was the military's fear that U Nu's government might allow the ethnic minorities to secede from Burma. Ne Win and his senior officers had in fact come to see themselves as latter-day rulers of Pagan, holding the country together by force of arms. One of Ne Win's successors, Saw Maung, even informed his staff in 1991 that he was actually a reincarnation of King Kyanzittha. His own coup three years earlier had restored full military rule, but it did nothing to deal with the country's increasingly severe economic problems. Anxiety about deteriorating finances, coupled with his own heavy drinking and chronic diabetes, prompted Saw Maung to assert his identity as the Pagan king at a golf tournament, but even more threaten with a pistol anyone who dared to deny it. Later on state television the troubled general mentioned King Kyanzittha by name and assured viewers that he had no truck with black magic.

General Than Shwe, who replaced Saw Maung in early 1992, fared no better as a national leader, despite declaring a ceasefire with the Karens. But he retained the name of Myanmar for the country, which had been introduced shortly after Saw Maung's coup. The "Union of Myanmar" was supposed to more correctly signal the country's ethnic diversity than the "Union of Burma". But it seemed a hollow gesture when the military regime was unashamedly carving up Myanmar's commercial assets for its own benefit. In spite of Ne Win's own involvement in corruption, he always paid lip service to social justice. Many people indeed had welcomed his intervention in 1962, when he promised to put an end to the corruption and instability of the previous decade and a half. Since the 1988 coup of Saw Maung, however, the families of the military elite have not bothered to conceal their ill-gotten wealth. They drive expensive cars, bedeck themselves with jewels, and own former state-run enterprises.

The reason for Ne Win's caution was the socialism upon which Aung San had intended to found an independent Burma. But Aung San's successor U Nu was so lacking in political skills that, in comparison with the period 1945–47 when the country had unity but not independence, the post-colonial years of U Nu's government were little short of a national disaster, troubled though they undoubtedly were by the ongoing civil war. Communist unrest had at first appeared to be the greatest problem facing U Nu, but once the ethnic minorities rejected Rangoon's policies as well, there was little chance of progress. In 1948 the Karens and disenchanted supporters of Aung San almost took the capital. Their near toppling of U Nu ensured that suppressing internal disorder would remain a chief priority of every government after independence.

U Nu was not alone in looking upon unbridled capitalism as a serious obstacle to Burma's recovery from the devastation of the Second World War. It was a point of view shared by many, who thought the Burmese experience of capitalism was inseparably interwoven with colonial rule. The drive for independence in the 1920s and 1930s had been not so much about the attainment of democratic freedoms as an escape from the burdens resulting from colonial exploitation. Whilst Aung San neither expected an overnight economic miracle, nor indeed the complete abolition of private property, he did urge the careful construction of a socialist state. Control of the country's natural resources was seen as a first step, something that immediately pitted U Nu against foreign companies involved in oil production, logging timber, and mineral extraction. Rice alone seemed a reliable earner of foreign exchange, but even this traditional crop was subject to painful price fluctuations in the world market. By the late 1950s, Burma's greatly reduced export earnings were made worse at home through inflation and rising costs.

An aspect of this period that is sometimes overlooked was U Nu's energetic promotion of Buddhism. Possibly he believed that it would assist in unifying a country divided on political and ethnic lines. But when the All-Burma Buddhist Association called for the overturning of the provisions in the 1947 Constitution that allowed freedom of religion, U Nu refused. His resolve saved Burma from a conflict similar to the one that has troubled Sri Lanka, where Theravada Buddhists insisted that Buddhism should become the state religion. So divisive an issue has religion become in Sri Lanka that violence is now directed against Hindu Tamils, whose numbers had been augmented by migration from southern India during British rule of the island; against the long-established

Faithful supporters of Aung San Suu Kyi in 2012

Moslem and Christian communities; and against newly arrived American evangelists who are accused of peddling neocolonial attitudes.

Disappointed though the Buddhist establishment was by U Nu's refusal, this did not stop monks taking to the streets in defence of democracy after Ne Win seized power. Soldiers held back from harming monks for a long time, not least because they would earn bad merit and a less favourable rebirth by doing so. In 1988 though, their patience was finally exhausted and monasteries were raided, monks forcibly defrocked, and beaten along with other demonstrators. The worst atrocity was the suffocation of forty-one students in a single police van on a ten-mile journey to prison. In response to a public outcry, the military government said the police were unfortunately short of prison vans that day. Once the police killed several children in Rangoon as well, ordinary people were drawn into the demonstrations and a number of policemen lost their lives in one of the city's markets.

Concerned about the adverse international reaction to these events and increased trade sanctions, the army shuffled the pack with Ne Win's retirement and the assumption of power by Saw Maung, who spectacularly misjudged the situation enough to permit elections to take place in 1990. Rallying behind Aung San Suu Kyi, the daughter of

Aung San himself, the Burmese people gave her party such an overwhelming victory that the armed forces had to prevent her from forming a government. All kinds of constitutional reasons were advanced for the postponement: but one brigadier frankly admitted that "a female should never be allowed to bring ruin to Myanmar". Military repression could of course no longer be disguised and Aung San Suu Kyi had to suffer house arrest until 2010, when her unexpected release coincided with a degree of liberalisation in Myanmar.

The military regime eventually realized perhaps, as Ne Win had in the 1960s, that it could not control the country indefinitely by tinkering with the constitution. The depth of international disapproval was brought home to Than Shwe in the aftermath of Cyclone Nargis, which hit Myanmar's coasts in 2008 with winds of over 190 kilometres an hour. The cyclone left an estimated 150,000 people dead and missing and another 2.5 million homeless and in desperate need of help. Myanmar's new strong man, Than Shwe, did nothing to alleviate the distress of the largely Mon population caught up in the natural disaster, and then refused to accept outside assistance until Western countries threatened to bring him and his fellow generals before the International Court of Justice at the Hague on charges of crimes against humanity. Even the People's Republic of China, a loyal ally of the country, became annoyed at the military regime's indifference to the suffering. The Chinese had provided specialist training for its armed forces and bailed out its banking sector on more than one occasion. By 2001, the People's Republic of China was Myanmar's third most important trading partner, while for Chinese goods its Indian Ocean ports gave better access to South and West Asian markets.

A desperately worried Than Shwe finally agreed to accept international support for reconstruction, although how much of the money handed over went to the people in the devastated areas, and not into the bank accounts of the generals, is unknown. Without doubt some of it was used to finish building a new capital in Upper Myanmar. This change of location formed part of the military's attempt to establish a governmental base at a safe distance from Rangoon and other opposition strongholds. The choice of Naypyidaw Myodaw was also dictated by a desire to associate the move with the memory of Aung San, who launched his independence movement from this Burman town during World War Two.

That Aung San's daughter will never be able to hold a senior political office there was not thought to matter. It is quite possible that the military ended her house arrest in order to ease international pressure by the inclusion of Aung San Suu Kyi in forthcoming elections. After being so long out of active politics, Aung San Suu Kyi was in no position to challenge the well-funded pro-government parties which dominated Myanmar's parliament. Her own party, the National League for Democracy, disappointed many of its members by accepting funds from companies known to support Than Shwe. That Aung San Suu Kyi chose not to speak about a renewed offensive against Kachin rebels, nor the anti-Moslem violence of Buddhists living in what was once Arakan, also persuaded some people that she has sold out to the junta. But she was still a potent symbol of sustained resistance to military rule, a charismatic individual whom the generals needed to try to manage rather than remove from the political arena altogether. It remains to be seen how events unfold in a Myanmar that at long last is opening itself to the world.

Thailand

The chief reason for the military becoming so embedded in Thai politics was the constitutional revolution of 1932, which ended absolute monarchy in Siam. The leaders of this momentous change, and especially twenty-seven-year-old law student Pridi Banomyong, saw the importance of placing the king within the confines of a constitution. What he failed to foresee was how military supporters of this move would take advantage of the new political situation for their own benefit. During the 1930s the People's Party, the author of the constitutional coup, was divided into two groups, roughly identified with civilian and military members and their respective leaders, Pridi Banomyong and Luang Phibunsongkhram. As a result, the future of modern Thailand was seen from two entirely different viewpoints: Pridi's belief in European-style liberty, tinged with socialism, and Phibun's authoritarian approach to nation-building, directed by government regulation.

Phibun and his followers were much attracted to other countries which had a militarized tradition of nationalism, most notably Japan and Germany. In late 1938, Phibun became prime minister, and shortly

Field Marshall Luang Phibunsongkhram

afterwards appointed himself head of the armed forces. As his cabinet was packed with military men, no objection was raised to Phibun assuming the rank of field marshal, which had previously been reserved for the monarch. And his ministers readily endorsed legislation aimed at reforming Thai manners. The new regulations encompassed such daily things as eating, clothes, and family relations. One insisted that husbands kiss their wives before leaving the house each morning, and again on returning from work, so as to show appreciation for their contribution to family life. The most controversial regulation attempted to banish traditional attire altogether. Phibun seems to have been particularly exercised by men who sported their underpants in public: not the skimpy underwear of today, but the knee-length pantaloons then widely worn in Southeast Asia. Such items of dress, or rather undress, were considered inappropriate for a would-be imperial nation.

Field Marshal Phibun's eyes were in 1940 fixed upon a powerful future for Thailand, as Siam was now called. With the support of Tokyo, he won a victory in the Franco-Thai War of 1940–41 and recovered territory lost to French Indochina in Laos and Cambodia. Phibun seems to have imagined that Thailand, serving as Japan's junior partner in driving the Europeans and the Americans out of Southeast Asia, would be rewarded by further territorial enhancement. Although he allied Thailand with Japan during the Second World War, the Imperial Japanese Army still treated the country like an occupied state and stripped its resources without offering anything in return. When in 1944 it became obvious that the Allies were winning, the Pridi group pushed Phibun aside, hoping that the removal of this pro-Japanese figure would improve the chances of negotiating a separate peace.

A poster showing Thai people Luang Phibunsongkhram's dress code: "uncivilized" on the left, "civilized" on the right

They need not have worried. As luck would have it, the Thai ambassador in Washington had already mentioned, well before hostilities began, the likelihood of Phibun supporting the Japanese. Ambassador Seni Pramoj, a great-grandson of King Rama II, even refused to deliver Phibun's declaration of war in 1942. Because he said that Thailand had been betrayed "by one or two men, chiefly the Prime Minister", Seni was able to persuade the Americans to back the Thai people against the military dictatorship and its Japanese ally. The absence of a formal declaration of hostilities between Washington and Bangkok not only saved Thailand from occupation at the end of the Second World War, but even more the British were obliged to accept reparations paid in rice. The United States did insist, however, that Thailand's borders were returned to their pre-war positions.

Phibun's fall brought Pridi back to the centre of the political stage, along with the royalists as a counterweight to the armed forces, but the power which the military had built up proved difficult to hold in check. It was not a little ironic that the anti-royalist Pridi of 1932 should have turned to the royalists for support and welcomed Seni Pramoj back from the United States to take up the reins of government as premier. But the returned ambassador harboured suspicions about Pridi's communist sympathies. That Pridi encouraged the development of trade unions worried the royalists, who also had to cope in mid-1946 with the death of young King Ananda Mahidol, from a gunshot wound. For the king's death, Seni blamed Pridi and eventually three of his followers were executed. Although the event has never been properly explained, it seems likely that the gun-loving monarch accidentally killed himself. Bangkok was gripped with hysteria until towards the end of the year the military stepped in with a coup.

Initially the army leaders continued with a civilian prime minister, but in 1948 he was replaced by Phibun, who once again endeavoured to impose cultural uniformity on the country. Yet Phibun's grip on power was not as secure as it had been before the Second World War, and he was challenged by abortive coup attempts in 1948, 1949 and 1951. The last coup was almost successful because at the time Phibun was participating in a ceremony aboard the *Manhattan*, a vessel which the American government was presenting to Thailand as part of a major increase in its economic and military aid. The Cold War had strengthened the position of the Thai army. Washington readily overlooked Phibun's pro-Japanese past, once the People's Republic of China was founded in 1949, just as France's spiralling decline in Vietnam would later cause it to back any anti-communist regime in Southeast Asia, irrespective of its worth or popularity.

That some of Pridi's supporters in the Thai navy attempted to seize Phibun during the *Manhattan* ceremony opened the way for military rivals to challenge the ageing dictator. The flagship *Sri Ayudhya* was sunk in the Chaophraya river when he was still on board, forcing Phibun to swim ashore. Only intense rivalry between aspiring generals delayed the 1957 coup of Sarit Thanarat, commander of the troops stationed in Bangkok. Phibun went into exile, living in Cambodia and Japan. Pridi was already exiled in China.

General Sarit may have given advance notice of his intentions to Bhumibol Adulyadej, King Rama IX. Between the coups of 1957 and 1958, the second of which consolidated Sarit's position, the general visited the United States where his determination to firmly govern Thailand delighted the US Secretary of State Dulles. Then John Foster Dulles was promoting his notorious domino theory of a communist take-over of Southeast Asia. Britain had already rejected the idea and granted Malaya independence. After the 1958 coup, Sarit declared martial law, dissolved parliament, revoked the constitution, banned political parties, and arrested hundreds of politicians, journalists and activists. Nothing could now stop Thailand from turning into a platform for American air strikes directed against Laos and North Vietnam. Three quarters of the bombs dropped on these two countries during the Second Vietnam War were delivered by aircraft flying from seven bases in eastern Thailand.

An even less attractive side of the American presence was the choice of Bangkok for GIs' R & R ('rest and recreation') tours, with 47,000 visiting by the end of 1967. The explosive growth of the city's sex industry resulting from the arrival of so many soldiers was actually encouraged by Sarit's government, which wondered if the 300,000 prostitutes then at work there were enough to cope with rising demand. While sex for sale was not new in the capital, since floating brothels had existed from its foundation in 1782, unusual in the 1960s was the sheer scale and openness of the sexual exploitation that was permitted by the military. Typical of this period was Sarit himself: he commandeered young women, taking a special interest in beauty queens. A heavy drinker like the Burmese dictator Saw Maung, Sarit died in 1963 of liver failure, leaving an estate worth US$150,000. Despite the confiscation by the state of a large portion of this ill-gotten wealth, there was plenty left over to share among his fifty consorts and their children who came forward to claim their inheritance.

Under the military regime in Myanmar, Rangoon had also maintained its colonial reputation for commercial sex. In 1914 the local police were given the authority to close brothels at their discretion, but this power was rarely used. Health seems to have been the main concern of the British

The enormous Buddha at Wat Po in Bangkok, where the Thai king
is believed to possess the essence of this saviour

colonial authorities, not morality. Troops were required to patronize
establishments near their barracks rather than the less regulated brothels
downtown. The Burmese sex industry gathered many new recruits after
further trade sanctions were imposed by the United States in 2003,
following the renewed house arrest of Aung San Suu Kyi. When textile
manufacturers laid off 60,000 female employees, some went to work in the
red-light district because their families relied on their regular wages. This
recruitment, however, bears no comparison whatsoever with the cynical
expansion of prostitution in Bangkok, where the military wanted to increase
sexual availability for the benefit of the tourist trade, which had reached a
figure of 600,000 visitors in 1970. The generals were worried about the level
of foreign earnings when the United States started to withdraw its forces
from Thailand. Yet their fears proved groundless because the country would
entertain in 2000 more than twelve million tourists.

How scandalous Bangkok became in the eyes of the rest of the
world was evident in 1981, when Chamlong Srimuang said during an
official visit to Australia that the city's brothels should be closed down.

His suggestion won him immediate international recognition. Chamlong was to resign from the Thai army as a major-general in 1985 and win a landslide victory on an anti-corruption ticket in an election for Bangkok's mayor. But his arrest during the crackdown of 1991–92 curtailed his political career, although he remained a member of parliament for another three years. Chamlong's vision of a vice-free Thailand failed as much because of his own political shortcomings as anything else. He thought that his military training and his on-the-job Bangkok experience were all he needed to form a government. Had he bothered to cultivate the business community, government officials and the royal palace, Chamlong might have gained a better understanding of Thailand's political dynamics. Yet his unexpected popularity had an impact on the military, whose political profile became less pronounced until the 2006 coup of Sonthi Boonyaratglin.

But for his own fall in 1973, Sarit's right-hand man Thanom Kittikhachon would have imitated his example of wealth accumulation. The modicum of democracy that Thanom tolerated after the death of Sarit did not augur well for parliamentary government. Students articulated the general disgust with the web of corruption which entangled the state; their disdain for the generals' abuse of power and the total subservience to American foreign policy struck a chord in the population at large, but a desire for change was thwarted by politicians whose personal feuds resulted in a series of unstable coalitions. The abhorrence of military domination, however, was not the same thing as an endorsement for far-reaching reforms, especially at the very moment the 600-year-old monarchy in neighbouring Laos was about to be abolished by the Pathet Lao, the ally of the Viet Minh.

Communist advances in South Vietnam and Cambodia were an additional worry for the Thai monarchy, which along with its most ardent supporters looked upon the student movement as either communist directed or inspired. A firm believer in the US domino theory, Thanom moved against his opponents in parliament, restored military rule in 1971, but banked up enough frustration to cause his own hurried departure from Thailand within two years.

Half a million people joined in a Bangkok demonstration to demand a constitution and parallel demonstrations took place in provincial cities.

In 1992 the Thai army crushes student dissent again in Bangkok

Despite the student-led agitation sending Thanom into exile, they did not really benefit from the military discomfiture because conservative politicians such as the Pramoj brothers, Seni and Kukrit, came to the fore with the backing of the monarch. For Rama IX had emerged as an arbitrator in Thai politics, much to the embarrassment of the generals, when the king declared himself the defender of the weak.

Kukrit Pramoj endeavoured to put Thailand at a distance from the United States, which since 1969 faced defeat in Vietnam. He even met Mao Zedong in Beijing and restored diplomatic relations with China. As important was his scheme to pass development funds to the grassroots level so as to relieve poverty and prevent the spread of unrest in the countryside. None of this pleased the military, whose misplaced fears of the Vietnamese and the Cambodians seeking revenge for Thailand's involvement in the Second Vietnam War brought about another coup in 1975. That year Saigon and Phnom Penh had fallen to communist forces and the Laotian monarchy ceased to exist. These events caused panic among the Thai upper and middle classes, who feared strikes in several companies were a communist-inspired prelude to revolution. Vigilantes attacked strikers and street violence put Kukrit's government on the back foot: in 1976 he was defeated at the polls and Thanom returned to

Bangkok. When two workers putting up posters protesting Thanom's return were hanged, the army radio station declared that Thammasat University should be attacked as the centre of social discord.

The brainchild of Pridi, Thammasat University was intended to train a new kind of official for the post-absolutist era. For the generals the university was never more than a communist stronghold and they sanctioned an attack using anti-tank missiles. A handful of students who tried to escape were burnt alive outside the university. Having broken academic and student resistance at Thammasat, it was announced that there would be a twelve-year gap before any return of constitutional democracy.

Flight from urban repression swelled the numbers of armed guerrillas operating in northern Thailand, but accounts of Cambodia's bloody experience under the Khmer Rouge weakened the resolve for a rural-based revolution. When in 1979 the Chinese attacked Vietnam in response to the Vietnamese invasion of Cambodia, it was transparent that the communist states had returned to the historical pattern of power politics in Southeast Asia. Disillusion, not Thai army operations, ended jungle war in 1983 with an amnesty for the insurgents.

By then Thailand was a different country, anyway. Headlong growth had produced a fully-fledged capitalist economy, strengthened the military dictatorship, revived the monarchy, and extended the influence of the state over society as a whole. The Pridi-Phibun dichotomy, between a liberal democracy and paternal direction, was still of course unresolved. It remains so today, but the easing of Cold War tension in Southeast Asia, after the departure of the Americans from Vietnam, meant that a more relaxed atmosphere typified Thai politics. Generals might still scramble for spoils, and politicians manoeuvre for power, but business prospered and cities grew swiftly. The 1980s boom made Thailand urban, and increased the clout of Bangkok in national affairs. Its inhabitants were already in excess of four million, and would double again by 2010.

From a small, underpopulated state before the Second World War, the kingdom of Thailand was now crowded and overpopulated relative to its economic performance. The country's population rose from eighteen million in 1947, through forty-four million in 1980, to fifty-seven million 1990 and, although there had been a slowdown in the annual growth since

Premier Thaksin Shinawatra claims victory over Thai drug addiction

that date, the social strains were not hard to discern. The most dramatic changes happened in congested and air-polluted Bangkok, whose skyline was no longer punctuated by elegant pagodas but by towering high-rise hotels and office blocks, with one empty and poorly constructed tower block already reminiscent of the leaning Tower of Pisa. Worse still, the decision to fill in the city's network of canals in order to convert canals into roads had wrecked the drainage system, causing extensive floods in Bangkok whenever the Chaophraya river was swollen with monsoon rain.

But the worst crisis in the city occurred in late 1997, when a largely middle-class crowd of protestors obliged the Thai government to acknowledge the country's currency crisis for the first time. What these office workers, many in suits and ties, did was give voice to Southeast Asia's fears about its economic stability. "People are losing their jobs. They see their wages cut," one of the protestors said. "We can't take it any more." Thailand had in a single year ceased to be an admired model of development success and become the victim of a spectacular financial collapse. After a decade of growth, its economy faltered in 1996 through a dramatic fall in exports and the effects of chronic overborrowing. The value of the Thai baht plummeted, losing nearly half its value as a unit of currency.

Though some observers had expressed misgivings about the general direction of development, and in particular a concentration on the property market, the World Bank and the International Monetary Fund were praising Thailand's economic management as an example for other countries to follow right up to the moment of crisis. By early 1998 all this had changed. The economy was in disarray, and a humiliating aid package had been agreed by the International Monetary Fund. Despite balance of payment deficits existing for a number of years in Thailand, Malaysia and Indonesia, their reasonably strong economies and adequate foreign exchange reserves seemed to guarantee safety for foreign investors. This was not the case, however, when anxieties about asset values and exchange rates emerged in Thailand, triggering massive outflows of capital as investors sought to recover their funds.

The shock of the financial crisis created a general demand for political change, not least because many Thai realized that, without stronger institutions, the country would not survive globalism. Even Rama IX admitted that "being a tiger is not important". The idea of tiger economies in South Korea, Indonesia, Singapore, Malaysia and Thailand first appeared in the early 1990s, when the World Bank talked about an Asian "miracle". Rather than seeing a "miracle", the World Bank should have noted how the upsurge was the result of sustained growth, as one economy after another began to accumulate capital, apply up-to-date technology, and deploy workers more effectively for economic development. The slowdown in Thailand, and elsewhere in Southeast Asia, was therefore no more than an adjustment to the global nature of today's markets, in which large amounts of capital can move across borders with great speed.

Such an explanation of the difficulties facing Thailand gave one of the country's most successful businessmen a landslide victory in 2001. The election of Thaksin Shinawatra, the leader of the Thai Rak Thai political party, apparently provided the country with a chief executive who could tackle the consequences of the economic setback. Nationalist though the appeal of Thai Rak Thai, meaning "Thai love Thai", undoubtedly was, Thaksin had the advantage of a new constitution designed to strengthen the position of the prime minister and sustain long-lasting governments. A mixture of efficient business methods in public administration and populist schemes for cheap housing attracted widespread support for Thaksin, who pressed on with a modernization programme intended to assist most of all the commercial sector of the economy. Big business was absolutely delighted and financed Thaksin's re-election in 2005, which produced the highest voter turnout in Thailand's history.

But all was not well. Separatist violence had broken out in the southern provinces of Patani, Yala and Narathiwat, resulting in martial law being imposed upon their largely Moslem inhabitants. Thaksin was criticized for mishandling the uprising when, in late 2004, seventy-eight Moslems died in military custody. The tourist industry was also hit by AIDS, when it became known that several million Thai were estimated to be HIV positive. Added to which the 2004 Boxing Day tsunami had taken the lives of 5,300 Thai and tourists. Although the Thai Rak Thai government had introduced the first national healthcare programme and launched a vigorous anti-drug campaign, Thailand gained an international reputation for a certain lack of personal safety.

This would not have been sufficient to unseat Thaksin, although accusations of corruption, disrespect for the monarch, and selling the assets of Thai companies to foreign investors were taking their toll of his popularity. The inevitable military coup occurred in 2006, when the premier was abroad. Refused asylum in Britain, Thaksin eventually found a refuge in Montenegro. Banned from politics for five years, Thai Rak Thai members of parliament eventually gathered under the banner of the Pheu Thai party, which in 2011 made Yingluck Shinawatra Thailand's first female premier. She had been born at Chiang Mai into the same wealthy Chinese family as Thaksin Shinawatra.

Vietnam

Decolonization in French Indochina took longer and was more violent than anywhere else in Southeast Asia for two reasons. The first is that France tried to hold onto its colonies more stubbornly than the other European powers. The second is that the decolonization process became part of the Cold War, which led to the United States supporting the French and then replacing them in a neocolonial role.

Both the Soviet Union and the People's Republic of China expected the promise of national elections made in 1954 at the Geneva peace conference to be kept. But with the agreement of the United States, Ngo Dinh Diem ousted Emperor Bao Dai a year later and refused to take any steps towards holding elections. With Hanoi bent on internal reform, it did not seem to matter but the dictatorship of Ngo Dinh Diem that followed effectively divided Vietnam into two antagonist states. It is a paradox that the staunchly nationalist dictator should have delivered South Vietnam into American hands. By appealing to US anti-communism and its disdain for France, Ngo Dinh Diem drew Washington fully into Vietnamese affairs. Those who regarded him as no more than a tool of American foreign policy were totally wrong: he deliberately attached the United States to his personal rule, because he knew how without financial aid and military advice, there was no possibility of political survival. The State Department had lost its most experienced Asia experts as a consequence of Senator Joseph McCarthy's witch-hunt against officials with supposedly communist leanings during the early 1950s, and so Washington lacked any real understanding of Vietnam, Laos and Cambodia.

Ngo Dinh Diem came across at first as an anti-communist hero in the United States. It might be thought that his Catholicism would have assisted Ngo Dinh Diem in his relations with President John F. Kennedy, the first Catholic to occupy the White House. Almost the reverse was true. The Vietnamese dictator's elder brother, Ngo Dinh Thuc, actually precipitated the fatal breach in Hue where, as its Catholic archbishop, he forbad in this Buddhist stronghold the traditional display of flags to celebrate the birthday of the Buddha. Soldiers shot nine protesters dead, before teargas dispersed the rest. No one gave credit to the government claim that the deaths were the work of the Viet Cong, the derogatory name by which Ngo Dinh Diem referred to the Viet Minh.

As opposition to Ngo Dinh Diem's American-sponsored regime grew in strength, Buddhists naturally joined the protest movement. Self-immolations of monks on Saigon's streets cost the dictator US support when a reporter heard his sister-in-law draw a parallel between monks, who neither moved a muscle nor uttered a sound when they burned to death with petroleum, and a barbecue, a word her daughter had picked up from American military advisers. Public opinion in the United States reacted so badly to this remark that Kennedy was obliged to press Ngo Dinh Diem to introduce democratic reforms.

Frustrated South Vietnamese generals interpreted Kennedy's anger as their moment to seize power, which they did with the blessing of Henry Cabot Lodge Jr., the American ambassador. On 28 October 1963 at Saigon airport, Lodge gave the go-ahead on the understanding that the plotters would agree to a continuing US presence. Fifteen minutes later when he arrived to catch a plane with the American ambassador and Mrs. Lodge for a short break at the lake resort of Da Lat, Ngo Dinh Diem had no inkling that his fate was already sealed. Within four days, Ngo Dinh Diem and his younger brother Ngo Dinh Nhu were dead, both shot in the head. Archbishop Ngo Dinh Thuc was fortunate to be out of the country at the time: he never returned. Photographs of their blood-splattered bodies dismayed Americans, but not as much as that of Kennedy's assassination in Texas, shortly afterwards.

Although the United States still had a limited role in South Vietnam, a mere 11,000 advisers as compared with the troop deployment of 525,000 men at the height of the Second Vietnam War, a military escalation was already underway. Growing American involvement happened in the same way that so much territory had been colonized by the Europeans in the nineteenth century. Factional struggles led to outside aid and influence, until the United States had taken virtual control of South Vietnam, Laos and, in 1970, even Cambodia. Once this informal colonialism was seen for what it really was, however, the American public insisted on a complete withdrawal. It may well have been that Lyndon B. Johnson, Kennedy's successor, would have been less willing to expand the war had the republican presidential nominee Barry Goldwater, a conservative senator from Arizona, not demanded a tough military response to worldwide communist aggression. Johnson told his jubilant supporters on winning

Protesting against Ngo Dinh Diem's government,
a monk burns himself alive in a Saigon street

the 1964 election that: "I am not going to be the President who saw Southeast Asia go the way China went."

All hopes in Hanoi of South Vietnam self-destructing before the United States could intervene in strength disappeared with the Gulf of Tonkin Incident. A naval confrontation there allowed Johnson to persuade Capitol Hill to give him the right "to take all necessary measures to repel any attack against the United States and to prevent further aggression". It was this blank cheque to use force as he saw fit that brought about the tragedy of Vietnam. Over the next four yours, evidence appeared that the North Vietnamese interception of US ships in the Gulf of Tonkin was not an unprovoked action at all. The Americans were covertly aiding sabotage operations by mercenaries as well as South Vietnamese commandos.

After the incident, Hanoi decided there was nothing to lose by increased military activity in South Vietnam, where between 1965 and 1967 the military hierarchy played musical chairs for the leadership of the country. Two strongmen eventually came to the fore: Nguyen Cao Ky, an admirer of Hitler, as vice-president and Nguyen Van Thieu as president. At last, Washington seemed to have gained leaders who promised political stability, a prerequisite for the safety of the 300,000 US troops then stationed in South Vietnam.

Despite having decided as early as 1959 that South Vietnam would have to be taken by force of arms, the communist leaders in Hanoi could not agree on a timetable for action. Many believed that economic development was a higher priority than military confrontation with South Vietnam and that, in fact, developing a strong economy was an essential first step on the road to victory. This hesitation did not please Le Duan, a working-class communist from the south. He had witnessed at first hand the effect of Ngo Dinh Diem's "denounce the communists" campaign, falling party membership, and the value of American advice on South Vietnamese military operations. A rather uncouth but forceful politician, Le Duan was determined to bring the southern question into the centre of party policy.

In North Vietnam, unlike South Vietnam after its conquest in 1975, communist reforms were generally accepted by its more disciplined inhabitants. Buddhism and Christianity were actively discouraged, while Confucian values were denounced as the mainstay of the pre-revolutionary social order. A notable exception to anti-Confucianism, however, was the justification for rebellion advocated by Mencius, Confucius' greatest follower. In the fourth century BC, he had given philosophical expression to the saying: "Heaven sees what the people see; Heaven hears what the people hear". According to Mencius, this meant that whenever a ruler lost the goodwill of his subjects and resorted to oppression, the so-called mandate of Heaven was withdrawn and rebellion justified. This democratic theory, which had functioned as a kind of safety valve in the Chinese constitution, derived from Mencius' view that sovereignty lay with the people. Heaven granted a throne but succession depended on the people's acceptance of a new ruler. When party cadres discovered in North Vietnam that they could easily slot into the spaces vacated by imperial officials, the political change-over could be explained in such a familiar manner.

The dramatic collapse of the Ngo Dinh Diem regime in Saigon seemed to Le Duan and his followers an ideal opportunity to push for a military solution. Within weeks of Ngo Dinh Diem's death, the central committee of the communist party in Hanoi finally resolved on an aggressive policy of "general offensive and general uprising" to capture South Vietnam. Dissenting party members were rudely brushed aside as North

One-man air-raid shelter in Hanoi during the Second Vietnam War

Vietnamese army units started to move south through the borderlands of Laos and Cambodia.

By the time Johnson opted for all-out war in 1965, the Soviet Union and the People's Republic of China had backed the Hanoi offensive. Arms and equipment poured into North Vietnam, along with specialist military personnel. Chinese troops, for instance, handled air defence, logistics and construction. The communists believed that their disadvantage in weaponry could be overcome by morale, but the cost of this strategy provoked Vo Nguyen Giap to protest about the high casualty rate. He advocated a return to the guerrilla operations employed against the French in order to minimize the effect of superior US firepower. Equally damaging were the American bombing raids on North Vietnam, which seriously damaged its economy.

Whilst the Chinese were sympathetic to Vo Nguyen Giap's point of view, the Russians advocated a battlefield approach alongside negotiations with the Americans. The declining health of Ho Chi Minh, who was always concerned about the destruction being suffered by the Vietnamese people during the fighting, may have been a factor in Hanoi's decision to break the stalemate in 1968 with the Tet offensive. Foreign visitors were struck by how Ho Chi Minh, dressed in a Chinese gown and walking with the aid of a cane, had aged. They noticed that his intelligence was unimpaired and his eyes still had their old sparkle. Yet undisguised now

"Uncle Ho". The leader of Vietnamese resistance
to the French and the Americans, Ho Chi Minh

was his role as a grandfather-figure, spared any details which might undermine his health and prevent him from living long enough to see Vietnam reunited.

Much as Vo Nguyen Giap feared the losses of men and material that would inevitably result from the 1968 offensive, he made thorough preparations for this widespread and simultaneous assault. Down the Ho Chi Minh Trail, which ran through Laos and Cambodia, he despatched tens of thousands of troops and tonnes of supplies destined for the attack on every place of any importance in South Vietnam. To divert attention from the impending action, Vo Nguyen Giap appeared to be interested in the reduction of the American base at Khe Sanh, a possible second Dien Bien Phu. In the United States, press coverage gave the impression that its successful defence would amount to a major victory, so that shortly afterwards the Tet offensive took everyone by surprise, especially as many GIs and half the South Vietnamese Army were on leave. Taking full advantage of the New Year, Tet in Vietnamese, North Korean soldiers and local communist fighters launched a massive assault in which hand-to-hand combat even occurred in the grounds of the US embassy at Saigon.

Communist casualties were in excess of 30,000 men, but US and South Vietnamese losses were just as great. Americans at home were so stunned by the scale of the fighting, which hit towns and cities right across South Vietnam, that the question began to be asked about the final outcome of this undeclared conflict. When Johnson insisted that it could be won, his optimism was shared by few Americans. Most had come to believe the cost of the war, as shown in the increasing number of bodybags being flown home, was unacceptable. Shaken by this decline in popular support, the president was next embarrassed by a request from William Westmoreland, the US commander, for additional troops after the general had claimed that the abortive Tet offensive represented a decisive setback for Hanoi.

Commenting on the event afterwards, Vo Nguyen Giap said that "in spite of the bombing of the North and search-and-destroy operations in the South", it proved "we were stronger in 1968 than at the time of America's commitment of massive forces to the war". More pointedly he added that "our biggest victory" was

> to change the ideas of the United States. The Tet offensive had been primarily directed at the people of South Vietnam, but as it turned out it affected the people of the United States more. Until Tet they thought they could win the war, but now they knew that they could not. Johnson was forced to decrease military action and start to discuss with us around the table how to end the war.

For Americans the futility of the struggle was summed up in the comment of a war-weary US officer, who informed a reporter that during the Tet offensive the utter destruction of the Mekong delta town of Ben Tre was unavoidable. "We had to destroy it," he admitted, "in order to save it."

Although he appreciated the need to keep up military pressure on the Americans, an ailing Ho Chi Minh said in early 1969 that efforts should be made to "conserve human and material resources". That is why he drew attention to the achievement of Tran Hung Dao, whose legendary guerrilla tactics had done so much to hinder the Mongol invaders. Ho Chi Minh's death later in the same year meant that he never witnessed the end of the Second Vietnam War in 1975. His untimely passing also weakened the solidarity of the Vietnamese communist leadership and unbalanced Hanoi's delicate relations with Moscow as well as Beijing, which would have unexpected consequences over the next decade.

In Hanoi, there was genuine relief that Johnson favoured negotiations, although his unwillingness to run again for the US presidency effectively prevented meaningful peace talks taking place. His successor came to power in 1969 with a pledge to "end the war and win the peace", but Richard Nixon's method of winning the peace was to continue direct American involvement in South Vietnam until the beginning of 1973. During the first two years of Nixon's presidency, the US Air Force dropped more bombs than the total tonnage expended by the United States in all theatres throughout the Second World War. The unprecedented bombing was totally counterproductive, because it strengthened North Vietnamese determination not to yield. But Ho Chi Minh's plea for a less conventional pursuit of the conflict had an effect: the Americans were to be allowed to leave without hindrance, while Nixon's "Vietnamization" programme ran its course. There indeed seemed little point in carrying on fighting when it was obvious that the South Vietnamese Army could never survive on its own.

Before Nixon withdrew the troops, however, he backed in 1970 a South Vietnamese invasion of Cambodia, a country hitherto spared the horrors of ground fighting, with the aim of cutting the Ho Chi Minh Trail. The intervention was a disaster for the Cambodian people: once a defeated United States withdrew from South Vietnam, they were left to the tender mercies of the Khmer Rouge. Despite Nixon's reference to the invasion as a "sideshow", the public reaction in the United States was unprecedented. When hundreds of colleges and universities went on strike, the president dismissed the students as "campus bums" until the killing of four protesters by the Ohio National Guard at Kent State frightened him. He was made even more anxious when Wall Street bankers warned him that a wider war was threatening a stock market collapse and a possible financial panic.

A shrine dedicated to the memory of those Vietnamese
who died fighting the French and the Americans

Already becoming enmeshed in the Watergate scandal, Nixon was now desperate to play the China card by becoming in 1972 the first American president to step on Chinese soil. Joseph McCarthy's belief in a united communist block intent on world domination had already been exploded in 1969 by armed clashes between Soviet and Chinese soldiers along the Sino-Mongolian frontier. Reacting to the Soviet invasion of Czechoslovakia the previous year, Beijing was not prepared to bow to ideological pressure from Moscow. How seriously Mao Zedong regarded this threat can be seen in the withdrawal of all Chinese anti-aircraft units from North Vietnam. The frontier clashes marked the nadir of Sino-Soviet relations and the start of Beijing's rapprochement with Washington. Without success, however, the Chinese endeavoured to persuade Hanoi to sever contact with Moscow, a refusal that soured Sino-Vietnamese relations to the extent that in 1979 they were actually at war.

The Shanghai communiqué, issued by Nixon and Zhou Enlai at the end of the president's historic visit, announced that the People's Republic of China and the United States would oppose any country trying "to establish hegemony" in "the Asia-Pacific region". Yet this dramatic turnaround in American policy offered no consolation to the casualties of the Second Vietnam War. More than 300,000 US soldiers were listed as killed, wounded or missing. Of the 58,000 who died in action or related incidents, only 13,000 were regulars. In addition, 4,407 South Koreans, 469 Australians and New Zealanders and 350 Thai lost their lives. South Vietnam's forces sustained losses of 137,000 killed and over 300,000 wounded. Maybe 400,000 civilians also perished while a larger number suffered injury, not just from shells, bullets and bombs but also toxic defoliants such as the notorious Agent Orange. Vo Nguyen Giap admitted 600,000 casualties. In all, nearly two and a half million of the combined Vietnamese population of thirty-two million died between 1967 and 1973, the year in which the Paris peace agreement officially ended the Second Vietnam War.

That all this blood had been shed in vain could no longer be disguised. The following year, in defiance of the Paris accord, Nguyen Van Thieu did away with the American-style constitution, declaring himself a presidential dictator like Ngo Dinh Diem had been earlier. Because he realized how difficult it would be to win the projected 1975 election, the South Vietnamese leader took this risky gamble to stay in power. But the game was up for his military dictatorship once Hanoi, appreciating that no election was ever going to be held, gave Vo Nguyen Giap his head. In a lightning campaign, lasting barely four months, he overran South Vietnam and captured Saigon in April 1975, the end of the conflict as far as the North Vietnamese were concerned. With Nixon disgraced and the Republicans in no position to contemplate further bombing there was nothing to do but quit. Nguyen Van Thieu had already made his own escape by US transport plane, taking his family with him as well as 16 tonnes of gold and silver from the vaults of the national bank.

The First and Second Vietnam Wars were the twentieth century's longest international conflict. If they were not enough to burden the Vietnamese people, two further wars occurred in 1978 and 1979. With Chinese approval and assistance, the Khmer Rouge leader Pol Pot initiated a whole series of attacks across the southern Vietnamese border to expel the Vietnamese population from areas that Phnom Penh claimed as Cambodian. Even though the frontier corresponded with the one that had existed prior to the arrival of the French, it was based on the Vietnamese acquisition of former Cambodian territories in the seventeenth and eighteenth centuries, and especially in the Mekong delta. Exasperated by these incursions, the Vietnamese invaded Cambodia in 1978 and then set up the People's Republic of Kampuchea. The new state was supposed to be a peaceful, independent and non-aligned socialist country.

At this time, Vietnam's own economy was in disarray through the confiscation of private property and the penalization of people with wealth in the south, falling agricultural output, and lack of finance for industrial development in the north. Added to the domestic turmoil was the enmity of Beijing, annoyed at Vietnam's continued reliance on the Soviet Union, its invasion of Cambodia, and the repression of ethnic Chinese residents. Thousands of these "boat people" had already fled abroad. Harsh official treatment of the defeated southerners had pointlessly squandered a potential reservoir of good will that could have contributed to the country's recovery.

Instead, Hanoi had to impose even stricter control over the south and integrate its resources into its militarized economy. The Sino-Vietnamese border war of 1979 was clearly meant to teach Vietnam and the Soviet Union a lesson. In the event, the conflict ended in a costly stalemate or, as far as the Vietnamese saw it, a Chinese reverse. On the battlefield the Chinese performed poorly in comparison with the Vietnamese, who had just outfought the Americans equipped with the latest military technology. The exact origin of the Sino-Vietnamese clash remains hard to fathom, although Deng Xiaoping may have given the go-ahead in return for political support in the run-up to the trial of the Gang of Four. Not until after the public condemnation of Jiang Qing, Mao Zedong's widow, could Deng Xiaoping be sure about his own position. As happened again a decade later in Tiananmen Square, it was timely military assistance that saved his leadership and his reform programme.

Deepening poverty obliged Hanoi to reintroduce incentives for private initiative in agriculture, but little was done to raise living standards in towns and cities prior to the death of Le Duan in 1986. Only with his passing could the more moderate wing of the communist leadership in Hanoi come to the fore. Nguyen Van Linh had always favoured a loosening of state control over markets, religion and cultural activities, and journalism. A southerner like Le Duan but not such a rigorous communist, he understood the need for change. Nguyen Van Linh's opportunity came

The That Luang stupa in Vientiane, where an annual oath
of allegiance used to be sworn to the Laotian monarch

with the disappearance of the Soviet Union, since it allowed him to restore
friendly relations with the People's Republic of China; encourage foreign
investment from Japan, South Korea, Taiwan and Singapore; and, last but
no least, to confront official corruption. Above all else, Nguyen Van Linh
sought to revive traditional Vietnamese culture through village festivals
and religious events. With contributions from a swiftly reviving business
sector, neglected and damaged temples were soon repaired .

Possibly the most surprising event happened in the 1990s, when
China and Vietnam settled their quarrel through a new treaty which
demarcated the land border and the Gulf of Tonkin sea border. Some
Vietnamese believed that the new frontier was too favourable to the
People's Republic of China, others recognized the value of a stable Sino-
Vietnamese relationship. Nguyen Van Linh had already stepped down
from power, but it was his policies that had paved the way for this return
to what only can be seen as tributary relations, the old community of
interest between a benevolent father and a dutiful son. As in the imperial
period, when a Chinese emperor and a Vietnamese emperor enjoyed
mutually supportive contact, so today the evolving communist systems of

both China and Vietnam help sustain each other in what has become a very different world from the 1960s.

Laos

In late 1950 the United States formally agreed to aid the French in Indochina. Despite bearing an increasing cost of the war against communist North Vietnam, Washington discovered that it had no influence over French strategy, so that when in 1953 a crisis occurred in Laos only US airborne assistance saved Luang Prabang. A daring advance by four Viet Minh divisions under the command of Vo Nguyen Giap, accompanied by Pathet Lao soldiers led by Prince Souphanouvong, almost captured the royal city. This American intervention was the start of a covert operation that would last for the next twenty-two years.

The Lao monarchy could trace is origins right back to Fa Ngum, a Lao prince who in 1353 became the king of Lan Sang with Khmer military assistance. The isolation and poverty of this land-locked kingdom in all probability explains its survival down to modern times. Though offered by the defeated Japanese outright independence in 1945, King Sisavang Vong called for France to resume its protectorate after French troops had released him from arrest in his own palace by the Lao Issara, "Free Laos" government. It had been formed to resist the return of the French and had the support of several princes, including Souvanna Phouma and Souphanouvong. After his release, the king granted a constitution that allowed Laotians to elect a government.

Lao Issara forces were no match for the returning French troops and so the rebel government fled. Whilst Prince Souvanna Phouma accepted an amnesty and returned to Laos, where he soon became prime minister, Prince Souphanouvong threw his lot in with the Viet Minh. At Hanoi, Souphanouvong proclaimed the formation of a new resistance government called "the Land of Laos", or Pathet Lao. The prince was never a communist: he was a staunch nationalist who wanted a truly independent Laos, but his dependence upon the Viet Minh gave him little scope for political manoeuvre, with the result that the Pathet Lao was drawn into the Second Vietnam War. Somewhat ironic therefore was the fact that many Pathet Lao recruits came from non-Lao hill tribes, whose dislike of Lao arrogance was only matched by their hatred of the French.

Had the Americans not encouraged the South Vietnamese dictator Ngo Dinh Diem to scrap the 1956 elections agreed at Geneva, and the Viet Minh had won an expected majority, then Ho Chi Minh might well have concentrated on rebuilding a reunified Vietnam. Having achieved his principal aim, Ho Chi Minh would have had little interest in either Laos or Cambodia, not least because these two states acted as a buffer between Vietnam and Thailand, where the Americans were rapidly building air bases. But with the United States replacing France as the dominant Western power in mainland Southest Asia, the whole of Indochina was bound to be engulfed by conflict, sooner or later.

Premier Souvanna Phouma believed that he could work with his half-brother Souphanouvong and wean him away from Hanoi's influence until the United States took exception to left-wingers joining his cabinet. That Pathet Lao candidates had successfully won seats in the Lao Assembly did not concern Washington at all. A frustrated Pathet Lao then resumed an offensive against the government from which Souvanna Phouma had been expelled. Happening to be in Vientiane then, Souphanouvong was arrested for treason. His escape from prison marked a turning point for Laos, because it confirmed the divisions that typified Laotian politics. The Americans never understood this. They regarded the communist threat as a military problem, to be countered by ever more aid, rather than a political problem arising in large measure from the disdain felt by the hill tribes for their indifferent treatment at the hands of the Lao government. As country-dwellers themselves, the Pathet Lao readily made friends with the peasantry, working alongside farmers in the fields and helping them build houses and schools. Such collaboration made the arrival of government forces in disaffected areas look like punitive forays.

The old king Sisavang Vong died in 1959 and was succeeded by the crown prince Savang Vatthana, whose distrust of Souvanna Phouma and his aversion to the Vietnamese did much to weaken the Lao kingdom. That the new king also saw the Pathet Lao as allies of the Viet Minh delighted the United States. When responding to an approach from Souphanouvong, who was keen to end what was essentially a civil war, Souvanna Phouma earned royal disapproval. The Americans immediately cut off their aid programme, but the Soviet Union stepped in with an offer of aid instead. As minister of defence, Souvanna Phouma was well aware

The architect of Laotian neutrality, Prince Souvanna Phouma

of the weakness of the government forces and could see no alternative but a negotiated end to the fighting in Laos.

As Washington and Moscow were then trading allegations about interference in Laotian affairs, the political situation in the kingdom descended into chaos with rival military factions contending for power. Although the United States was unwilling to go to war over Laos, its policy remained the undermining of a neutralist regime while seeking to defeat its opponents. The result was a civil war from 1963 onwards which intensified in parallel with the fighting in neighbouring Vietnam. Increased North Vietnamese support for the Pathet Lao, and use of Lao territory to funnel men and supplies southwards along the Ho Chi Minh Trail, led to a prolonged and ruinous US bombing campaign.

By the early 1970s, the kingdom of Laos was only a nominal nation state. The peace talks in Paris between the United States and North

Vietnam brought about an uneasy ceasefire during which the Pathet Lao extended its influence throughout the country. Areas under government control were kept alive by American airdrops of food, but the writing was already on the wall for neutral Laos. A non-violent communist coup took place in 1975. Arguably it was the consequence of political disillusionment and war fatigue, something even King Savang Vatthana recognized when Souvanna Phouma and Souphanouvong flew to Luang Prabang and obtained his abdication.

The Lao People's Democratic Republic then took full advantage of Souphanouvong's prestige in easing the transitional arrangements for the change from monarchy to republic. Fearing a pro-monarchy uprising, however, the royal family were moved in 1977 to a re-education work camp at Sam Neua, close to the Vietnamese border. There long hours toiling in the fields and inadequate rations caused their early deaths: they were all buried in unmarked graves beside a stream, just outside the camp's perimeter. Both Souvanna Phouma and Souphanouvong died in old age. The latter had given up a political role through ill health in 1991, quietly living in retirement at Vientiane for another four years.

The initial difficulties facing the Lao People's Democratic Republic were largely overcome during the 1980s, although agriculture continued to suffer as ever from the vagaries of the Laotian weather. Yet for all its economic development and social progress Laos remains a desperately impoverished country, still dependent on foreign aid. The unnecessarily prolonged conflict that spilt over from the Second Vietnam War had only served to intensify its deep-rooted problems.

Cambodia

As in Laos, the kingdom of Cambodia was dominated by an elite whose members were mainly of royal descent. While sharing power with these ambitious Cambodians, King Norodom Sihanouk became adept at manipulating the political system and at suppressing opposition, particularly from left-winger challengers. This situation was quite unlike Laos, where power was more fragmented through such regional factors such as the deep-seated discontent of the hill tribes.

In both Laos and Cambodia, however, the institution of monarchy had been much less damaged by colonial rule than in Vietnam, whose last ruler Bao Dai obviously acted under French dirction. Whereas Ngo Dinh Diem easily deposed Emperor Bao Dai in 1955, the Cambodian king proved surprisingly durable throughout the political turmoil of the post-war period. Yet Sihanouk was obliged to temporarily relinquish the throne in order to strengthen his own position. In a tactical master-stroke, he became a "private citizen" so as to lead a political party, leaving his own father, the affable Norodom Suramarit, to reign until he died in 1960. Sihanouk's popularity allowed him to capture 80 per cent of the vote in the 1955 election, and all the seats in the National Assembly.

In spite of Sihanouk's genuine popularity with the electorate, the overwhelming victory meant an end of party politics in Cambodia. The lack of any safety value for discontent in the political arena must explain the build up of pressure against his administration. Growing prosperity and domestic peace were not enough to satisfy every Cambodian, and in 1963 three left-wing ministers resigned from the cabinet and criticized Sihanouk's excessive influence over state affairs. It was a straw in the wind, for already Cambodian communists had staged an anti-Sihanouk demonstration at Siem Reap. Police action dispersed the demonstrators and forced the thirty-five-year-old activist Saloth Sar into hiding. When the Khmer Rouge took over Cambodia in 1975, Saloth Sar started to call himself Pol Pot. Sihanouk had actually coined the term "Khmers Rouges" to distinguish the Cambodian communists from the "Khmers Roses", the pink liberals in the Democratic Party he had defeated so decisively in 1955.

The death of his father came as a shock to Sihanouk, a personal tragedy that nevertheless caused him to frantically search for a satisfactory succession. He sought a political formula that would meet his determination to hold all real power himself, but would also take account of the profound respect felt by Cambodians for the monarchy. Deeply distrusting his royal relatives and fearing the likely establishment of a republic, Sihanouk decided to appoint a Regency Council, as the best solution for his continued "service to the People". He said:

> If I were to resume the Throne I should be far away from you. I must be a simple citizen, a politician who through your will has been made President of the Sangkum. Only in this way can I guide the Country, the People and help the Throne and Religion.

That many of the hundred or so princes who, theoretically entitled to succeed, were incapable of discharging the duties of a monarch there can be hardly any doubt. But their dissolute lifestyles were less worrying to Sihanouk than several competent candidates, who would be less pliant than the late king had been. A Regency Council was therefore a stop gap, but it allowed him to maintain his position as head of state.

Not until 1993 would a seventy-year-old Sihanouk again sit upon the Cambodian throne, once he realized that there was no chance of re-entering politics after his long exile in the People's Republic of China. An unquenched thirst for power and prestige shaped Sihanouk's life and undoubtedly contributed to Cambodia's troubled modern history. Much as he tried to keep his country from becoming embroiled in the Second Vietnam War, this proved impossible and his strategy for doing so actually dragged the country into the fray. Banking on a swift North Vietnamese triumph, he secretly agreed in 1966 with Hanoi that its troops could operate in eastern Cambodia and receive arms shipments via the port of Sihanoukville. This agreement was supposed to benefit Cambodia through North Vietnam restraining the anti-government activities of the Khmer Rouge. Not only were these Cambodian communists disinclined to take orders from Hanoi, but the Americans were outraged by Phnom Penh's cooperation with the Viet Minh.

When in 1970 Sihanouk was overseas, he was overthrown by Lon Nol. Crippled in a road accident through Sihanouk's reckless driving, this Cambodian general had personal as well as political reasons for his military coup. Guessing correctly that his anti-communist credentials would impress Washington, Lon Nol had no difficulty at all in gaining international recognition. With American encouragement he launched attacks on Vietnamese and Cambodian communists alike. But finding the tiny gains out of all proportion to the immense effort expended, Lon Nol fell back on a US bombing campaign. So desperate did he become that he even agreed to a South Vietnamese incursion.

Although President Nixon knew that Lon Nol's chances of survival were slim, he authorized the advance of 32,000 American and 48,000 South Vietnamese troops into Cambodia because this offensive was intended "to protect our men who are in Vietnam and to guarantee the Vietnamization programs". The Ho Chi Minh Trail was disrupted

King Sihanouk of Cambodia in 1941

for a while, but this inconvenience for the Viet Minh was nothing
in comparison with the disruption in the United States caused by
nationwide demonstrations against Nixon's action. If the president was
put on the back foot, however, the Cambodian dictator was bowled over.
Whatever support Lon Nol had enjoyed for his anti-communist stance in
Cambodia, now evaporated. Because the American invasion could not
be consolidated, the Viet Minh soon reoccupied their bases along the
Cambodian border and drove off Lon Nol's forces wherever they were
encountered. Fighting in the Cambodian countryside created a huge
refugee problem, with two million displaced peasants crowding into
Phnom Penh and other cities. By 1975, Lon Nol's authority was restricted

to the capital, fed by airlifted American rice. When the cargo planes came no more, Lon Nol and a few of his advisers, along with the staff of the US embassy hurriedly escaped the country. Those who stayed behind were sent by the Khmer Rouge to the countryside.

The decision to empty the towns and cities seems to have been a long-standing Khmer Rouge intention, possibly because its rank and file, recruited from the poorest sections of the peasantry, saw it as a just punishment for the parasitic rule of an urban hierachy. An impoverished peasantry was no longer prepared to sustain by its unremitting toil a privileged modern capital like some latter-day Angkor. Pol Pot himself justified the emptying of Cambodia's towns and cities in terms of the Paris Commune: this had failed, he claimed, because the proletariat had not exercised dictatorship over the bourgeoisie. Whatever the exact origin of this extraordinary measure, the compulsory resettlement programme decimated the Cambodian people, with as many as three million deaths.

Survivors of Khmer Rouge rule, which lasted from 1975 to 1979, called it samai a-Pot, "the era of the contemptible Pot". What Pol Pot wished to achieve within a very short period was the creation of a socialist Cambodia by collectivizing agriculture and investing foreign exchange earned from agricultural exports in industry. Capital was incredibly expected to be raised in a society where money, markets and private property no longer existed. Typical of this radical change was the ruined national bank, dynamited by the Khmer Rouge shortly after its capture of Phnom Penh. To permit trade to take place without control, Pol Pot argued, would only give a new lease of life to capitalism.

Undue haste and lack of thought doomed Pol Pot's project from the start. Hardly any of the Khmer Rouge leaders had ever planted, transplanted, or harvested rice to feed a family. Their belief that collectivized revolutionary zeal would be enough to treble rice production was unrealistic, especially when town-dwellers had to clear and irrigate forest land before paddy fields could become productive. As the Khmer Rouge was ultra-secretive and Cambodia cut off from the outside world, the tens of thousands of deaths from malnutrition, disease, executions and overwork went unnoticed. Just how indifferent the regime was to suffering can be gauged from this saying: "Keeping you is no gain. Losing you is no loss."

Pol Pot in the countryside where he sent so many Cambodians to perish

Within a year of the drive to increase the output of rice, it should have been transparent that the rising death toll would have an adverse impact on the country. But favourable reports from the countryside, compiled by enthusiastic supervisors, fuelled optimism among the Khmer Rouge leadership, which regarded any criticism of their grand development plan as anti-communist activity. Savage repression was the answer and, in Phnom Penh, this happened at the regime's interrogation facility at Tuol Sleng, a secondary school which still stands today as a terrible reminder of the 14,000 men, women and children who were tortured and then put to death there. In striking contrast to the Vietnamese and Chinese practice, Cambodian communists eschewed re-education and preferred the killing fields close to the capital.

Yet Pol Pot's early confidence did not last and he talked of "microbes" seeping into every corner of the Party, weakening its strength and resolve. Death sentences were handed out to "wreckers", often communists with long records of loyalty to the socialist cause. Even close associates were not safe from arrest, possibly because Pol Pot was always fearful of assassination. On top of these purges, distracting as they were to the on-going revolution, there was now added war with a reunited Vietnam.

Skirmishes and incursions had taken pace on both sides of the border since the fall of Lon Nol, but fighting became intense after the promise of

Chinese military aid to the Khmer Rouge in late 1976. Renewed interest in mainland Southeast Asia, after the death of Chairman Mao, derived from the deteriorating relations between Beijing and Hanoi. The first large-scale attacks by Cambodian forces in early 1977 caught the Vietnamese by surprise. Although a six-division counterattack from Vietnam was repulsed, the Khmer Rouge soon found itself facing an external conflict as well as an internal one, because the Vietnamese decided to lend support to Cambodian forces antagonistic to Pol Pot. They were particularly numerous in the areas adjacent to Vietnam.

By executing large numbers of people who were judged to be sympathetic to Vietnam, the Khmer Rouge forfeited all legitimacy in Cambodia so that, when in late 1978 the Vietnamese invaded in force, no one outside the retreating communist army offered any resistance. After the fall of Phnom Penh, a pro-Vietnamese government was set up in what was named the People's Republic of Kampuchea. A parallel invasion of southern Laos also expelled Khmer Rouge units operating there. For the Vietnamese, the occupation was intended to prevent Pol Pot from regaining power. Until 1989, when Vietnam withdrew all its troops, the People's Repubic of Kampuchea was protected by a garrison of 200,000 men. Relieved though they were to be rid of the Khmer Rouge, Cambodians feared that their country was destined to become a colony of Vietnam, since many Vietnamese settlers stayed on after the withdrawal. They recalled how in the 1830s the Vietnamese emperor Minh Mang had tried to impose a Vietnamization programme on Cambodia. Then it took a war between the Thai and the Vietnamese to free Cambodia, whose King Ang Duong wrote to Napoleon III in the mistaken hope that French protection would not mean colonial subjection.

It is hardly credible now that in 1979 the Thai, the Chinese and the Americans allowed their hostility towards the Vietnamese to cloud their judgement to such an extent that they sided with Pol Pot, whose supporters were given sanctuary in camps situated along the Thai border. For Pol Pot, this unexpected turn of events meant personal security, even plentiful foreign aid for a couple of years. By 1981 the genocidal activities of the Khmer Rouge became too well publicized for the United States to support Pol Pot openly any longer, so other anti-Vietnamese ploys were tried to keep Hanoi's client government in Cambodia isolated. With the

Cold War diminishing in intensity during the rest of the decade, however, there was a significant shift in the power balance around Vietnam. Mikhail Gorbachev's liberal policies in the Soviet Union, Deng Xiaoping's cautious introduction of a market economy in the People's Republic, and a temporary eclipse of the military in Thai politics, all worked against continued confrontation, especially as the Russians lowered the level of their economic and military aid to Vietnam.

Sihanouk had returned to Phnom Penh in 1975 for a short visit but, except for a boat trip on the river, he had been kept inside the palace. When the ex-king noticed that the river banks were deserted, he was told the people were away working in the paddy fields. Under pressure from the Chinese, Sihanouk finally agreed to return home permanently and in early 1976 the Khmer Rouge let him preside over a meeting that endorsed a new constitution for Democratic Kampuchea, as Cambodia was then known. Flown back to Beijing as the Vietnamese were about to enter Phnom Penh, Sihanouk reflected that his "people were liberated from Pol Pot's grip", but these same people now had to be "liberated from the grip of the Vietnamese".

In spite of dogged Chinese support for the Khmer Rouge, Deng Xiaoping met Sihanouk at Beijing airport. Reassured by this show of esteem, and accepting an invitation to reside in the Chinese capital, he decided to wait on events. But Sihanouk had to wait a long time before he could return to the State of Cambodia, the name by which he insisted it should be called in 1989. The People's Republic of Kampuchea, he said, was "a creation and a creature of the expansionist and colonialist Vietnam communist regime". Urged by prime minister Hun Sen, who was concerned to conciliate more reasonable Khmer Rouge leaders under a general restoration of the Cambodian kingdom, Sihanouk became king once more on 24 September 1993, nearly forty years after he had chosen to be a "private citizen". The restored monarch appears to have come to the conclusion that he would wield more influence if politicians had to approach him as petitioners, which of course they did. Several times Hun Sen pleaded with Sihanouk not to step down from the throne again.

Ieng Sary became the first important Khmer Rouge leader to defect. Known as "Brother Number Three", Ieng Sary's wife and the wife of Pol Pot, "Brother Number One" were sisters. At Hun Sen's request, King

Norodom Sihanouk signed for "Brother Number Three" an amnesty without public debate. Even though the king said that he would not grant amnesty to any more Khmer Rouge leaders, it remains as a stain on his record that he never called for any of them to be put on trial. Quite possibly events were already unfolding too quickly for reliance on the law anyway. Learning that political rivals were secretly negotiating with the Khmer Rouge, Hun Sen staged his own Thai-style coup, summarily executing dozens of politicians including two ministers, so as to consolidate his political position. Reaction abroad was unfavourable, especially at the UN General Assembly, where delegates were dismayed by Hun Sen carrying on as if nothing had happened. Even though Ieng Sary avoided trial, Pol Pot went before a people's court at Anlong Veng on the Thai border. Unsurprisingly the eighty-year-old former Khmer Rouge leader was not accused of any crimes committed in the 1970s in which many of those in the audience and among his accusers were themselves implicated. Instead, he was blamed for ordering the murder of Son Sen, a Khmer Rouge comrade whom he considered dangerously disloyal. Throughout the proceedings Pol Pot remained silent.

Sentenced to permanent house arrest, Pol Pot avoided this fate by dying peacefully in his sleep not long afterwards. His body was cremated on a pile of rubbish and car tyres. Even Ieng Sary was shocked by the squalor of Pol Pot's end. Yet it was less undignified than the deaths suffered by countless Cambodians under his rule. As one of his chief accusers commented, Pol Pot "is no more than cow shit. And cow shit is more important than him. We can use it as fertilizer".

Although Sihanouk in the 1990s was as energetic as ever, Hun Sen saw to it that he had only limited authority and little contact with the Cambodian people at large. Chafing under these restrictions, the king spent much of the period abroad. And in 2004 Sihanouk finally abdicated for a second time. When his youngest son Norodom Sihamoni, a childless batchelor, took his place, it seemed clear to many that the days of the Cambodian monarchy were numbered. At the age of 89, Sihanouk died in 2012. His admirers pointed out a unique aspect of his political life: a career in which he made no effort to enrich himself, unlike so many Southest Asian leaders. But his critics simply dismissed Sihanouk as an egoistical autocrat who was fond of flattery and intolerant of dissent.

12

INDEPENDENCE: THE MARITIME NATION STATES

> If we want democracy, it should not be Western democracy, but a democracy that gives a life, that is, political-economic democracy that guarantees social welfare!
>
> *Sukarno at a 1951 rally*

Describing present-day Malaysia as a maritime state may seem odd, but the Malayan peninsula has always been connected with seaborne trade, which reached a peak during the era of Malacca's heyday. At the start of the fifteenth century, the Chinese had recognized the port's potential as a hub of international trade routes in maritime Southeast Asia. It was indeed the timely protection provided by the great Ming admiral, Zheng He, that allowed newly founded Malacca scope to develop its own trade links in peace. His use of the port as a temporary naval base deterred both the Thai and the Javanese.

Since the formation in 1963 of Malaysia, which combined Malaya, Singapore, Sarawak and North Borneo in a single federation, the country has also been spread across a considerable expanse of sea. Had Singapore remained in the Federation of Malaysia, and not become an independent state two years later, then its maritime character would be even more pronounced, because Singapore's development as a port has been phenomenal over the past half century. As Stamford Raffles foresaw in 1819, the strategic location of Singapore island was bound to attract international commerce, once it possessed adequate facilities for shipping.

That its founder also established an almost tax-free regime could not but encourage growth, especially as the Dutch in neighbouring Indonesia were disinclined to offer any concessions. So Singapore became a key anchorage for the Royal Navy whose warships did so much to keep the sea-lanes clear of pirates, as Zheng He had done earlier for the benefit of Malacca.

Independence came early to maritime Southeast Asia. The Philippines was scheduled to become in 1946 an independent state, so that the Japanese occupation had no effect on its attainment of freedom. If anything, the Greater East Asia Co-Prosperity Sphere might have slowed the American commitment to decolonization: but the return of US forces to the Philippines in 1944 put the agreed date for independence back on track. Quite different was the Second World War experience of the British and Dutch colonies, however. The fall of Singapore in early 1942 had shaken Britain and, after the surrender of Japan, a Labour government in London realized how the days of European domination were numbered. Premier Clement Attlee had the vision to see that a Commonwealth of independent nations should replace the British empire. And he willingly accepted Burma's refusal to join the new organization after the assassination of Aung San and his entire cabinet, because he said that membership must be entirely voluntary. The British decision to grant India and Burma early independence ensured that decolonization soon followed in Southeast Asia.

As with the French in Indochina, the Dutch believed that they could re-establish colonial rule in what was to become in 1949 the Republic of Indonesia. They were wrong. Once Britain and the United States ditched Holland, there was nothing to stop Indonesia gaining its independence. While diplomatically referred to as the Netherlands-Indonesian Union, nobody expected any mutual relationship between Holland and Indonesia to last.

Perhaps it was fortunate for the numerous Indonesian peoples that they acquired self-government before the communist triumph in China had a full impact on American foreign policy. Maritime Southeast Asia was spared anything remotely like the fighting that took place in Vietnam, Laos and Cambodia. Notwithstanding disturbances in Malaya, Brunei, Indonesia and the Philippines, the area was largely untouched by the Cold War.

Teluk Bahang fishing village at Penang, now a shadow of its former commercial self

Serious post-colonial conflicts arose from Indonesia's own territorial ambitions. In the 1960s, President Sukarno promoted claims against Malaysia while in 1975 Indonesian armed forces took over the Portuguese colony of East Timor. Because of the abundant sandalwood forests, the Portuguese had established a trading post there in 1642. East Timor's liberation by an Australia-led international peacekeeping force in 1999 marked the last decolonization of all.

Malaysia

With the end of Confrontation, the attempt made by Sukarno to subvert the Federation of Malaysia between 1963 and 1966, the new state could look to its own affairs. But it had already suffered a reverse through the forced secession of Singapore. The idea of including Singapore in a state comprising the Malay sultanates and the Straits Settlements was first floated in 1948, and in protest UMNO, the United Malay National Organization, had been formed to oppose British moves to create a common citizenship.

Communal tensions first erupted at Penang in 1957, the year in which Tunku Abdul Rahman became the first premier of an independent Malaya.

Trouble had been brewing since the break-up of the Straits Settlements and the addition of Penang and Malacca to Malaya. The privations of the Japanese occupation had heightened Penang's sense of difference: its Chinese inhabitants, who had borne the brunt of Japanese brutality, were proud that their island was Britain's earliest settlement in Southeast Asia. Malay residents did not share this view. Despite the creation in 1963 of Malaysia, the Penang Chinese were correct about being marginalized under a mainland government, since there was discrimination in favour of the Malays in the administration, access to education, and financial support. Worse still, Penang's free port status was abolished by Kuala Lumpur in 1968, removing the commercial advantage which Francis Light had bestowed on the island nearly two centuries earlier. And the rapid exit of Singapore from the Federation of Malaysia left Penang stranded by the tide of decolonization, an isolated shadow of its former self.

Given Malay worries about Chinese-dominated Singapore, it was something of a surprise when Tunku Abdul Rahman backed an expanded Malaysia that would include Singapore, Sarawak, Brunei and North Borneo. The Malayan prime minister seems to have come to believe that national security required a political union with Singapore, lest that island was used as a communist base for further insurrection in Malaya itself. And he reassured UMNO colleagues by declaring that indigenous peoples in Sarawak and North Borneo would be regarded as "Bumiputera", literally "the sons of the soil", enjoying the same privileges as Malays. Despite being an effective political argument in 1961, it has not stopped quarrels between Malays and other Bumiputera over the allocation of resources, which was especially transparent in the friction between the state government of Sarawak and federal officials stationed in Kuching.

The government in Singapore at the time of the Malaysia proposal was the People's Action Party under the leadership of a Cambridge-educated lawyer, Lee Kuan Yew. His party had come to power in 1959 on an election platform calling for Singapore's autonomy within some form of association with Malaya. Talks between Lee Kuan Yew and Tunku Abdul Rahman thrashed out an acceptable formula, which preserved Singapore's free port status and gave it special powers over education and labour policies. Over 71 per cent of Singaporeans voted in a referendum to join the new Federation of Malaysia.

The British territories in Borneo were more resistant to the idea of Malaysia, but as fully-fledged colonies Sarawak and North Borneo had to a degree been prepared by the British for inclusion in a larger Malayan federation. Even then, the Kadazan leader of North Borneo, Donald Stephens, rejected federation outright. He said:

> We are against joining Malaysia as individual states, and want the Borneo territories to get together, so that when we talk to Malaysia it will be as equals not as vassals.

Otherwise, Stephens contended, joining Malaysia would inevitably lead to the domination of peninsular Malays. Once the persuasive powers of Tunku Abdul Rahman and Lee Kuan Yew were brought to bear, however, the political perspective shifted so that both Sarawak and North Borneo agreed to become member states. In spite of requiring military assistance from Britain to put down a revolt at the end of 1962, Brunei did not.

But political problems soon arose within Malaysia itself. In the Singapore elections of 1963 and the Malaysian elections of 1964, the Singapore-based People's Action Part did battle with the Malayan Alliance, in large measure because Lee Kwan Yew was determined to prove that his own party alone could speak on behalf of the Chinese. Although no attack was made on UMNO, and Lee Kuan Yew's fire was directed against its coalition partner the Malayan Chinese Association, an intense struggle had actually begun. Once the UMNO-dominated federal government also became a target, the challenge mounted by the People's Action Party had the unfortunate appearance of a struggle between non-Malays and Malays. Candidates endorsed by the People's Action Party, who contested parliamentary seats throughout the Malayan peninsula, might claim to be standing for multiracialism and anti-communism but they looked part of a Chinese-Malay contest.

Worried about the prospect of communal violence, Tunku Abdul Rahman decided that Singapore must leave Malaysia since, without goodwill between its various peoples, "this nation will break up with consequential disaster". Thus secession was pushed through, despite vigorous protests from Singapore's leaders. Lee Kuan Yew and his closest allies, most of whom had been born in Malaya, remained convinced that the destiny of Singapore was inseparable from the economic and political life of the peninsula, after a shared colonial heritage lasting more than a century. Within a couple of years though, Tunku Abdul Rahman would admit that the real reason for Singapore's ejection from Malaysia was "because the Prime Minister of Singapore wanted to be a Prime Minister. There can never be two Prime Ministers in one nation".

The assumption that the Federation's elected leader was by right a Malay, and in the case of the Tunku himself a hereditary prince, points up the very different outlooks of peninsular Malaya and the island of Singapore. It was the difference, according to the People's Action Party, between a "Malaysian Malaysia" and a "Malay Malaysia". Correct though his assault on discriminatory legislation was, Lee Kuan Yew's own political ambition also contributed to the separation of Singapore from Malaysia. Yet even Mahathir Mohamad, Malaysia's controversial premier from 1981 to 2003, came to appreciate towards the end of his long period in office that the entrenched privileges afforded Malays would have to be lessened, with greater opportunities given to Chinese and Indian citizens. Mahathir Mohamad was prepared to say openly that the Malays had frittered away their advantages.

With the secession of Singapore settled, the Alliance government could concentrate its attention on Sarawak and Sabah, as North Borneo was now called. The relative backwardness of these two Borneo states was acknowledged in a longer period of adjustment being allowed for integration into the Federation of Malaysia. Kuala Lumpur was, nevertheless, impatient over any attempt to weaken the newly created union, and Donald Stephens was ousted for his defence of the culture belonging to numerically dominant Kadazan people. What particularly annoyed this Sabahan politician was Tunku Abdul Rahman's open support for Datu Mustapha's plan of Moslem supremacy within Sabah, now that it was part of Malaysia. A Sulu chieftain, Mustapha believed that he could turn the state into a personal fiefdom through playing the Malay card in federal politics, but he alienated so many groups by his declaration of Islam as the state religion, his aggressive programme of Malayanization, and his authoritarian style of leadership, that Kuala Lumpur dropped him in 1976. The last straw was Mustapha's support for the Moros, the Moslem rebels in the southernmost islands of the Philippine archipelago.

The Stephenses in Canberra at Government House in 1968.
Donald Stephens wears traditional Kadazan clothes, while his
wife borrowed a fur coat to deal with the Australian winter

Having got Manila to accept the inclusion of Sabah in the Federation, Kuala Lumpur did not want a diplomatic rift caused by meddling in the internal affairs of the Philippines. Donald Stephens had had to resist objections to Sabah's membership from both the Philippines and local Malays, who yearned for ties with the Moslem-inhabited islands of Palawan and Mindanao, the core of the old Sulu sultanate.

Although Fuad Stephens, as he was known after his conversion in 1971 to Islam, remained powerful in Sabahan politics, he was probably pleased to be appointed as Malaysian High Commissioner to Australia, New Zealand and Fiji. It was tragic that his triumphant return as chief minister in 1976, following the fall of his opponent Mustapha, should have been cut short when the aircraft in which he was returning from a meeting in Sarawak crashed into the sea. Despite the setbacks he had suffered, Fuad Stephens' protection of the Kadazans from exploitation ranks with the best aspects of Brooke rule in Sarawak. His enduring popularity had much to do with his mastery of the various languages spoken in Sabah. Apart from the native tongues, he demonstrated a sure command of Chinese during the hectic election campaign that toppled Mustapha. He was truly a man of Sabah's peoples.

That Sarawak failed to produce a leader of similar stature was a misfortune for its forty or so distinct peoples, although at a moment of crisis in 1966 there appeared from the remote interior an astute conciliator in the shape of the Kenyah paramount chieftain Oyong Lawai Jau. Sarawak's chief minister, Stephen Kalong Ningkan from the state's largest group, the Sea Dyaks, had deeply offended cabinet colleagues by trying to amend the native customary land law. Fearsome though his tiger-teeth ear-ornaments made him look, Temenggong Oyong Lawai Jau was at heart a man of peace who perceived the dangers of indigenous disunity. He is credited with saying that "all problems can be solved if we are patient enough". The chief minister thought otherwise and, with the assistance of Tunku Abdul Rahman, Stephen Kalong Ningkan was replaced by another Sea Dyak, Tawi Sli.

An unexpected beneficiary of this political coup was Abdul Taib Mahmud, a cabinet minister who opposed the new land bill as well. Since 1970 he has managed to dominate Sarawak through a grouping of the Moslem Melanau-Malay parties. To counter this power block, the concept of "Dyakism" has been promoted by the Sea Dyaks as well as the Land Dyaks. When in the 1983 elections the Parti Bansa Dyak Sarawak, the Party of the Sarawak Dyak Nation, did rather well, it was invited to join the administration. Temporarily allied to Abdul Taib Mahmud's political group, the Party of the Sarawak Dyak Nation has since largely gone its own way. The long supremacy of Abdul Taib Mahmud was the result of his skill in continually splitting the opposition.

Such political longevity annoyed the federal government, especially when the stability established by the Alliance Party came under threat. Passions had run high during the 1969 elections and, when the results appeared to diminish the absolute control over the federal government which the Alliance had previously enjoyed, violent clashes erupted in Kuala Lumpur between perturbed Malays and celebratory Chinese. Of equal concern were Alliance losses in the state assemblies, where a Malay vote split between UMNO and PAS, the newly formed Parti Islam Sa-Melayu, had let in opposition candidates. The emphasis placed by PAS on religion appealed to Malay voters in the east-coast states of Kelantan and Trengganu.

According to official figures, some 200 people died and 400 were injured in the Kuala Lumpur riots, but the numbers were certainly higher, with most of the victims being Chinese. The rioting was blamed on unrestrained criticism of Malay privileges and one unseated politician, Mahathir Mohamad, blamed the conciliatory outlook of Tunku Abdul Rahman for all the troubles. Expelled from UMNO for this public criticism, Mahathir Mohamad would eventually return in 1982 to lead Malaysia for over two decades. By then the Alliance had been superseded by a broader coalition of parties, the Barisan Nasional. The Malaysian Chinese Association and the Malaysian Indian Congress remained within this coalition but with their influence much reduced. The other great change under Barisan leadership

Sarawakian elder statesman Temenggong Oyong Lawai Jau, shortly before his death in 1974 at the age of eighty

was headlong economic growth, aimed in particular at improving the prospects of the Bumiputeras. Such a "big government" strategy, involving heavy investment and regular intervention, vastly increased UMNO's power and influence, while the general rise in prosperity to an extent mollified non-Bumiputeras. But their grievances were by no means addressed, and nor would they be under Mahathir Mohamad's authoritarian regime.

An odd mixture of realist and autocrat Mahathir Mohamad was always prepared to speak his mind. Responding in 1986 to criticism over the "barbaric" execution in Kuala Lumpur of two convicted Australian drug smugglers, the Malaysian premier reminded Canberra that many

Australians were descended from convicts. Two years later, when more than one hundred Australian MPs protested about his detention without trial of political opponents, he bluntly replied: "When Australia was at the same stage of Malaysia's development, you solved your aborigines problem by simply shooting them." Despite acting as the champion of the Malays, Mahathir Mohamad was fiercely critical of their growing dependence on government assistance. He said they should do more for themselves and accept that they need to work with non-Bumiputeras in order to develop the country. At the same time, Mahathir Mohamad was criticized for concentrating power in his own hands and, more seriously, ignoring the corruption and the cronyism which had already begun to taint Barisan's reputation.

Undermining the independence of the judiciary and curbing the powers of hereditary rulers were the means by which Mahathir Mohamad enhanced his own personal authority, thus making any assault on Barisan's position virtually impossible. The move against the paramount ruler, Yang di-Pertuan Agung, surprised few Malay politicians when the scandalous antics of the sultanate could no longer be hidden from public view. One sultan even confined a policeman who had offended him to a dog kennel, the ultimate insult for a Moslem. But Mahathir Mohamad waited for the right moment to reduce hereditary power and privilege, because he shrewdly calculated that a growing Malay middle class would soon regard the monarchy as an unnecessary shield. So disconcerted was a retired Tunku Abdul Rahman with Mahathir Mohamad's "irresponsible" policy that he said: "He cares nothing for class, for law, for order, for the Constitution. What suits him, he just does."

But not everything went the prime minister's way. The first setback was the traumatic shock of 1997, when currency woes brought on by the sudden devaluation of the Thai baht spread to Malaysia's financial markets and, within months, precipitated a halving of the value of its own currency, the ringgit, and furthermore a three-quarter slide in the value of the stock exchange. The initial response of Kuala Lumpur was one of denial. There was no crisis. By late 1997, however, Mahathir Mohamad had banned the selling of certain shares, introduced rules to discourage speculation, and propped up share prices by using government funds to purchase them from Malaysian shareholders. In spite of some

A Land Dyak longhouse in Sarawak. The "Head House" above
only boasted four shrunken heads during the 1960s

The Petronas Towers, Kuala Lumpur's distinctive
post-colonial landmark

commentators wondering if these actions marked "the end of a free
market", the Malaysian premier was pragmatic enough to realize that
these emergency measures could only be a temporary solution to the
financial downturn. Even the central bank, Bank Negara Malaysia,
admitted in 1998 that the root cause of the worsening situation was that
Malaysia seemed less committed to reform than its neighbours, then part
of a recovery programme devised by the International Monetary Fund.

A second setback came through the arrest, trial and imprisonment of
Anwar Ibrahim, Malaysia's deputy premier and finance minister. Having
decided that his deputy should not succeed to the premiership, Mahathir
Mohamad accused Anwar Ibrahim of acting incompetently during the
financial crisis and promptly sacked him. Soon afterwards, the police
formally charged Anwar Ibrahim with homosexual acts and corruption.

Taken into custody, he was assaulted by the Inspector General of Police, who was later forced to resign after admitting this offence. The Chinese and Indian communities scrupulously stood aside from the often violent street demonstrations mounted by Anwar Ibrahim's supporters.

Freed in 2004 when the federal court overturned his conviction for sodomy, Anwar Ibrahim was delayed from returning to the political arena for several years because of his corruption conviction. But his rallying call for a government of national unity in 2013 almost swept Anwar Ibrahim into power. A narrow defeat was blamed on election irregularities: Barisan was forced to deny that voters were flown home to vote in their local constituencies, and that rural voters were paid to back the governing party. Whatever the ultimate political outcome of Anwar Ibrahims's challenge, now that Mahathir Mohamad has quit office, the lines of the old ethnic voting blocks had been irrevocably blurred. Even the Barisan coalition, whose Chinese and Indian elements took a hammering at the election, began to think the previously unthinkable—a proper, multi-ethnic party. "The oppression of the ruling clique," Anwar Ibrahim said, "has only strengthened my resolve." Tackling corruption, the chief reason for Barisan's waning popularity, will not be an easy task, whoever holds power at Kuala Lumpur.

Indifference toward proper procedures in government-sponsored business ventures was matched by an equally cavalier approach to the environment, with the result that deforestation in Malaysia surpassed the scale and speed of clearances in the Amazon basin. Since the mid-1980s, when Indonesia also started to cut down its rainforests in favour of palm-oil plantations, an immense haze became almost an annual occurrence in maritime Southeast Asia. Because the cheapest way to clear logged land was to burn it, an acrid smoke spread from the island of Sumatra over thousands of square kilometres. In Singapore, the 2013 level of pollution was so high that Indonesia had to formally apologize. But as much of the area burning in Sumatra comprised peat wetland, which was combustible to a depth of 30 metres, apologies were hardly adequate. As long as the greed that has driven the ruthless exploitation of natural resources in Malaysia as well as Indonesia goes unchecked, the post-colonial era in both countries may well come to be viewed as a self-inflicted environmental disaster.

Singapore

Lee Kuan Yew's political prospects had been boosted in 1957 by US meddling in Indonesian affairs. Determined to overthrow Sukarno, American submarines ran military supplies to rebellious Indonesian troops in Sumatra and American aircraft assisted in a Sulawesi insurrection. Neither rebel group prospered, in spite of Britain reluctantly agreeing to a US task force using Singapore. This concession permitted Lee Kuan Yew—the same man who within a decade lamented London's decision to close its bases there—to label his main political rival "a colonial stooge" and win 43 of the 51 seats for the People's Action Party in Singapore's council election. Very few Singaporeans had any sympathy for Indonesia's insubordinate military. So incensed was Sukarno by the intervention, a CIA report tells us, that the Indonesian president "transferred the full fury of his anti-Dutch complex to the United States and Britain".

The triumph of a left-wing party surprised and worried the British, who were initially unsure about Lee Kuan Yew. They need not have been so concerned because this clever politician was in favour of the Federation of Malaysia as a means of flushing out the radical left-wingers in his own party. Its announcement in 1961 drove these members, along with the communists, into the Barisan Sosialis, or "Socialist Front", an organization set up to oppose Malaysia. Though Lee Kuan Yew and his moderate followers remained in power, they learned to exercise a much tighter control over factions within the People's Action Party and started a grass-roots movement which enabled them to enjoy the remarkable social control that has been Singapore's hallmark ever since.

Overcoming the political and economic consequences of leaving Malaysia in 1965, and then the rapid rundown of a British military presence after 1970, was an absolute for necessity for Lee Kuan Yew, although he reminded Singaporeans how "from 1819 right up to the 1930s there was prosperous Singapore without either a British naval or air base". There is no doubt at all about the pivotal role played by Lee Kuan Yew in Singapore's amazing transformation: today it is no longer a colonial dependency but a thriving entrepreneurial city-state and a major world communications centre. Yet he had the support of a brilliant group of like-minded colleagues, who understood how important it was to forge a new role for their diminutive country, the equivalent in size of a large

Still good friends. Lee Kuan Yew and Tunku Abdul Rahman
during the formation of Malaysia in 1963

European city. Their willingness to sink their differences and work closely together largely explains Singapore's remarkable development, and stands in stark contrast to the bickering and betrayal that typified the political scene in Malaysia, Indonesia and the Philippines.

It was indeed the political uncertainties of neighbouring states that made Singapore so attractive to Southeast Asian investors, while an emphasis on education, and the use of the English language for instruction, drew many students of Chinese descent from Myanmar, Thailand, Malaysia and Indonesia. Discrimination in favour of Malays and Bumiputeras in Malaysia also had the effect of pushing the very best Chinese businessmen onto Singapore island, where they were instrumental in a significant expansion of manufacturing during the 1980s and 1990s. Lee Kuan Yew's government always gave priority to education because it recognized that, without an educated and skilled workforce, there was little chance of sustaining a high-tech economy. British universities were patronized for post-graduate study, while the University of Cambridge enjoyed a special place in Singapore's hierarchy of qualifications. First-class Cambridge graduates were accorded virtually the same respect as those who had passed the palace examinations under the Chinese emperors.

In the mid-1980s there was indeed a conscious attempt to give Confucianism a key role within the national culture. Not quite a modern application of Zhu Xi's *Family Rituals*, the Song reinterpretation of the philosophy of Confucius that formed the yardstick for social behaviour during the late Chinese empire, but by extolling the duty owed to the family and to the state, present-day Singaporeans of Chinese descent were powerfully reminded of their cultural heritage. Arguably, this appeal to Confucian values was not unconnected with a concern about rampart materialism, which manifested itself blatantly in "shopping-mall kids", footloose teenagers who hung around the air-conditioned stores in downtown Singapore.

In looking toward traditional Chinese values, Singapore's leaders were obviously searching for a distinctive national identity, without excluding the traditions of the Malays and Indians resident on the island. Although they were always wary of too close a relationship with the People's Republic of China, individual Singaporeans took full advantage of new business opportunities there, following Deng Xiaoping's encouragement of capitalist enterprise. Considering the extent of Chinese emigration during the nineteenth and twentieth centuries, this renewal of personal contact was hardly surprising. Yet the island city-state was situated in the midst of an un-Chinese maritime world, and so good relations with its neighbours remained essential, for the purposes of trade if nothing else. Should piracy ever prove a problem again in the "Southern Oceans", however, it is not impossible that another Zheng He could exploit Singapore in the same manner as Malacca. The island could become a temporary naval base in order to keep international shipping routes safe. The current revival of Chinese maritime power ought to cause no surprise in the light of the historical pattern of tributary relations, and there is so far nothing to suggest that Beijing entertains territorial ambitions similar to those of the Western colonial powers or imperial Japan.

Brunei

With billions of US dollar reserves and a population of less than half a million, Brunei is maritime Southeast Asia's present-day Kuwait. Substitute jungle for desert and the comparison is even clearer. The family of the sultan, whose new palace cost nearly US$300 million to build, invests its revenues from the export of oil and gas mostly outside the region, with the notable exception of Singapore. Close personal relations with Lee Kuan Yew and his family in part explains this mutually advantageous relationship. Yet Singapore enterprises greatly assisted Brunei, especially in the fields of technology and engineering, for which the tiny sultanate was entirely dependent on outside help.

Qaf Holdings, once managed by the sultan's brother and playboy Prince Jefri Bolkiah, was quickly quoted on the Singapore stock exchange. Originally a conglomerate comprising land, trading, services and oil subcontracting, through its investments Qaf Holdings penetrated every sector of Brunei's economy. The most dramatic event in its development was the 1998 falling out of the twenty-ninth sultan, Hassanal Bolkiah, and his younger brother Jefri. Tens of millions of dollars were alleged to

The coronation chariot of the sultans of Brunei

have been misappropriated by the latter, who denied any wrong doing and refused to show up for a court hearing in 2008. At the time, *The Times* in London commented how the prince had "swapped his notoriously decadent lifestyle of vulgarly named yachts and gold-plated lavatory brushes for a fugitive existence".

The scandal made international news without having the least impact in Brunei on the standing of Sultan Hassanal Bolkiah, whose devotion to Islam binds his subjects firmly together. Nearly 70 per cent of the population is Malay and Moslem. Even though education has made ordinary people more aware of the world at large, there has never been any internal pressure for constitutional development after the abortive revolt of A. M. Azahari in 1962–63. Because oil revenues readily sustain the position of the sultan's family, whose relations hold key posts in the administration and the business community like members of the royal family do in Saudi Arabia, Brunei has been largely insulated from change. And of course Sultan Hassanal Bolkiah could avoid having the bother of an army altogether by paying for the permanent deployment of a battalion of Gurkhas, ostensibly to secure Brunei's oilfields.

A certain nervousness, however, may be apparent in the decision to introduce Sharia law. Flogging, amputation and death by stoning have been added to Brunei's legal code in 2014. But for Moslem offenders it is expected that there will have to be a high burden of proof, and that judges will have some leeway in the choice of punishment handed down. Yet the move to Sharia law does mean a much less relaxed future for the tiny sultanate.

Indonesia

When the Japanese arrived in early 1942, the nationalist leader Sukarno had no hesitation in supporting them, while making it clear that independence for Indonesia was his ultimate objective. He appreciated the imperialist aims of the Greater East Asia Co-Prosperity Sphere, but the overthrow of three centuries of Dutch domination more than compensated for a Japanese occupation which he thought would be short anyway. Collaboration stained Sukarno's relations with some of his followers, since he acquiesced in the conscription of labourers for Japanese projects throughout Southeast Asia. More than 100,000 labourers from Malaya and Indonesia were estimated to have died in building the infamous Burma railway alone. Another 12,000 Allied prisoners of war are known to have perished under appalling conditions, at the rate of one death per every 25 metres of track.

General Imamura Hitoshi, the Japanese commander-in-chief in Java, had no doubt about the reason for Sukarno's helpfulness. "I gained the impression," the general said, "that he was a man of iron resolve. All his thinking was centred on independence, and his passion for it would never desert him." Impressed by the popularity of Sukarno, however, Imamura Hitoshi decided to make use of him in Java, where the island's large population, if restive, could tie down Japanese troops required elsewhere.

Sukarno was adept in exploiting Japanese propaganda for his own purposes. At mass rallies, he told his listeners to look upon Japan as the guardian of Indonesia's freedom. It was an excellent line of argument because it drew upon the genuine desire of Indonesians to be rid of the Dutch and the rash claim of Japan to be freeing Asia for the Asians. By the end of the Second World War, Sukarno had united nationalist factions and raised the demand for independence to fever pitch.

The day after the declaration of independence on 17 August 1945, Sukarno was installed as the Republic of Indonesia's first president with unlimited powers for six months. But the first conflict was with British and Indian troops, who began landing in Java over the next month. At Surabaya, it took them three weeks of hard fighting to gain control of the city, an unexpected contest which convinced the British that the Indonesians were a force to be reckoned with. Equally unaware of the strength of resistance to any return to colonial rule were the Dutch, whose meagre strength on the ground should have dictated a cautious approach. The only troops immediately available belonged to the Royal Netherlands Indies Army. Because these Amboinese soldiers had remained loyal to the Dutch, the Japanese made about 18,000 of them prisoners of war. Thus the British found themselves in the invidious position of acting as the advance guard of restored Dutch colonialism.

A Labour government in London would not tolerate this for long. And it could not afford to do so either, once mutinies broke out among British soldiers, who wanted to return home to civilian life. In Malaya, a refusal to parade led to a mass court martial in 1946: more than 200 men

President Sukarno promising general elections in 1950

of the Parachute Regiment were sent to prison. They had just returned from Java, the focus of the Indonesian insurrection. For Indian troops, the position was even more difficult, especially when the prospect of partition emerged. At the start of 1946, a full-scale mutiny occurred in the Royal Indian Navy, involving 10 naval establishments and 56 ships.

It was Dutch intransigence and British exasperation that finally led to Indonesia's full independence in 1949. More concerned about events in China than maritime Southeast Asia, the United States had no wish to become involved in a colonial war and blocked further aid to Holland. One omission from the independence agreement then was Western New Guinea—or West Irian, as Sukarno called it—where for a time continued Dutch presence was a source of post-colonial antagonism. Not that this represented the limits of Indonesian ambitions, because in the 1960s Sukarno promoted territorial claims against Malaysia, and in 1976 Indonesian forces took over the Portuguese colony of East Timor. Notwithstanding this expansionism, a struggle for unity typified Indonesian independence, which many islands in the sprawling archipelago viewed as no more than Javanese domination. It did not help that economic development was centred on Java, where the overwhelming majority of Indonesians lived. Jakarta, the new name given to Batavia, witnessed unprecedented growth, its population doubling twice between 1945 and 1961.

The Republic of Indonesia was also afflicted by parliamentary turmoil in the 1950s, when party politics descended to a level of mistrust that precluded cabinet government. Moslem reformists and traditionalists split in acrimony, while the communists steadily gained popular support. In Sumatra and Sulawesi, whose foreign exchange earnings sustained Java and the urban elites concentrated on the island, new political forces came to the fore as army commanders forged unorthodox links with local groups as a means of financing their own units and increasing their personal wealth. Smuggling became rife and, in desperation, the powerful general Abdul Haris Nasution either transferred officers or arrested his opponents. So worried did Sukarno become that his slogan, "Guided Democracy", could be viewed as an attempt to head off a coup under Nasution's leadership.

The United States had long been clandestinely supporting outer-island movements in an effort to counter the Sukarno regime's leftist tendencies. Eventually Washington put aside its Cold War anxieties though, and decided it would be wiser to deal with Sukarno than continue the attempt to unseat him, even to the extent of being lukewarm about the Federation of Malaysia, until the British transferred troops to Borneo from Germany, thereby weakening the defence of Western Europe. Then the United States had no choice but to tone down its friendly policy towards Indonesia and recognize Malaysia. But it did not stop the recall home in disgrace of Tom Kajer, a Peace Corps worker who had volunteered to stay at Sipitang during the Brunei revolt, the prelude to Confrontation. Of Czech descent, Kajer assisted its district officer by watching the trails leading from Indonesia to this settlement, near the border between Sarawak and Sabah.

Another reason for the change of US policy was a growing realization in Washington that the Indonesian army was now the key element in the archipelago's politics, and that a post-Sukarno era would be dominated by its senior commanders. While the ill-sorted mixture of central direction, socialist realism and local folklore that constituted Sukarno's democratically guided government seemed to leave the Indonesian president in charge, the truth was that every decision taken resulted from increasing competition between two irreconcilable enemies, the army and the communists. Dutch enterprises might well be nationalized but their administration was often turned over to the military, which soon enjoyed an independent economic power base as well as a monopoly of armed force.

A faltering economy, with hyper-inflation eventually reaching 500 per cent a year, weakened Sukarno's popular appeal in spite of his fiery oratory still being capable of rousing huge crowds. He accused Tunku Abdul Rahman of weakness: the Malaysian leader lacked the courage to quit the Commonwealth with its neocolonial connections. Opposing the Federation of Malaysia had little attraction for Indonesian military leaders once the Commonwealth's rapid build-up of land, sea and air forces was achieved. They were also worried by the unilateral land-reform campaign which the communists launched in 1963, the first year of Confrontation. This directly threatened the interests of landowners, who included military men and, particularly in east Java, scholarly Moslem families. Opponents of the communists fought back, suggesting that support in the countryside was less widespread than expected. But the Indonesian armed forces had to tread carefully because Sukarno's charisma was still far from threadbare.

Only with the sudden illness of Sukarno in August 1965 was there an opportunity for political change. At the end of the next month, an abortive coup was staged by "progressive" air force officers with links to the communists. In one night at Jakarta six generals were killed, although a wounded Nasution managed to escape. General Suharto, excluded from the execution list in the mistaken belief that he was an apolitical figure, swiftly assumed control of the military and ended the coup by force. The Indonesian Communist Party was outlawed, then its members slaughtered in their hundreds of thousands. Skilful propaganda claimed that, prior to the killings, communist women stripped naked had performed a lascivious dance in front of the conspirators and indulged in an orgy after the murdered generals' genitals were severed and their eyes gouged out. The allegations of genital mutilation were bad enough, but in a socially conservative society the naked dancing and group sex reinforced the idea that communist attitudes and Indonesian values were utterly incompatible.

Moslem activists were told to sikat, literally "sweep clean" the country of all communist sympathisers, and a bloodbath duly ensued. During 1965 and 1966 as many as 500,000 people were killed with the approval of the armed forces. General Nasution told a student gathering in Jakarta that since the conspirators had "committed treason, they must be destroyed and quarantined from all activities". Sukarno's recovery of health made no difference at all, because Suharto steadily outmanoeuvred the president and his followers until he was in total control of the country. In 1968 President Suharto introduced his own New Order, which would last until 1998. Washington justified the mass killing in terms of the Cold War as "the most historic turning point in Asia in this decade": entirely overlooked was the fact that Sukarno's overthrow resulted from no more than a bloody military coup.

Although violence was at its worst in Java, the killings spread to other islands including Bali and Kalimantan, Indonesian Borneo. An estimated 80,000 Balinese people were killed during 1965–66, around 5 per cent of the population. The conflict on the island reflected those of the nation at large, with the communists espousing the cause of the peasantry, and the landlords refusing to accept the new land reforms. Yet Indonesian Communist Party supporters aggravated an already tense situation at Klungkung by the attempted desecration of a traditional Hindu funeral. Both troops arriving from Java and local people took a terrible revenge, dumping in the sea or mass graves thousands of victims, executed either with guns or knives.

In West Kalimantan, the province immediately to the south of Sarawak, the upsurge in violence was much more complex in character. It involved collaboration between certain Dyak chieftains and army commanders, the expulsion of Chinese farmers and traders resident in interior villages, and fighting between Dyaks and Madurese, settlers from the poor island of Madura situated off the coast of northeast Java. Even though Madurese migration dated from the late nineteenth century, the first serious Madurese-Dyak violence did not occur until late 1967. The unsettled times were obviously a contributory factor, but the gradual transformation of Dyak unrest to outright rebellion had more to do with the disdain shown for them under the New Order, whose massive logging concessions threatened their traditional way of life. At Pontianak, the provincial capital, the Madurese-Dyak conflict in 1997 was Indonesia's largest outbreak of communal violence in nearly thirty years. Photographs of headless corpses in the city's streets shocked outsiders, ignorant of Dyak headhunting. After the collapse of Suharto's New Order though, there was a greater recognition of tribal peoples' rights, with the first national congress of their representatives held at Jakarta in 1999 amid much publicity. But it remains to be seen whether environmental encroachment slows in Indonesia, given the forest burning which now causes the annual haze.

The involuntary relocation of settlers of Chinese descent in West Kalimantan reflected the uncertain situation in which they lived elsewhere in Indonesia. Inland from Pontianak, the Dyaks showed little interest in empty Chinese land, houses and stores, so that Madurese migrants moved in and soon came to blows with the Dyaks. At the Bandung conference of Asian states in 1955, Zhou Enlai had tried to clarify the position of the overseas Chinese by assuring delegates about China's lack of territorial ambitions beyond its borders. Not unlike the Ming admiral Zheng He, he indicated that the People's Republic was content to accept token recognition of the rightful place it occupied in modern Southeast Asia. This line fell on deaf ears in Washington, where the "domino theory" maintained that any concession to communism was a dangerous move.

Zhou Enlai seems to have struck a chord with his fellow delegates when he reminded them of their common experience of colonial rule. "If we seek common ground," he told them, "and remove the misfortune and suffering imposed on us by colonialism, then it will be easy for us to understand each other." He even said that the People's Republic was prepared to sit down at the conference table with the United States so that they could avoid war. Zhou Enlai added that persons of Chinese descent would no longer be automatically regarded as citizens of the People's Republic. Henceforth the twenty million overseas Chinese would have to become citizens of the countries in which they lived.

This policy change did not ease the lot of Chinese residents in Indonesia. Those whose families had been in the archipelago for centuries

The so-called Puputan monument raised to
commemorate the 1908 Klungkung massacre

opted for Indonesian nationality, others had to choose between the
People's Republic and the Republic of China. Because neither Beijing nor
Jakarta accepted the latter state as covered by the Bandung agreement,
the Chinese were harassed and driven abroad. Opportunist attacks on
Chinese shops also marred the whole episode and pointed to future
violence, such as the extensive looting of commercial premises in Jakarta
immediately after Suharto's enforced resignation after thirty years in office.
A consequence was a surge of capital to Singapore, whose banks were kept
flush by the profits and savings belonging to the Indonesian Chinese.

Suharto's fall was a great disappointment to Washington. Ever since
the removal of Sukarno, a grateful United States had overlooked the less
pleasant sides of Suharto's New Order. The need to favour friends and
supporters entailed the reservation of jobs for members of the armed
forces upon their retirement from active service, thus ensuring their

continued loyalty to the regime. Ex-military men were employed at all levels, from security guards to chief executives. Control of the large public sector of the economy, plus the granting of lucrative monopolies for other commercial activities, gave Suharto and his closest associates access to enormous personal fortunes. That there was no way of hiding the fact that a privileged few were making money at public expense accounts for the criticisms levelled at the Indonesian government in 1998: protestors decried "corruption", "cronyism" and "nepotism".

After ten days of riots which in Jakarta alone destroyed nearly three thousand commercial premises, a reluctant Suharto acknowledged as his successor the sixty-two-year-old Bucharuddin Jusuf Habibie. That Habibie was seen on television kissing the hand of the outgoing president dismayed Indonesians. Javanese rules of courtesy had always required social inferiors to show respect by kissing the feet, knees and hands of their superiors, according to rank. And the Islamic custom of kissing the hand of a man revered for his piety and scholarship was practised throughout Indonesia. No one thought twice about those who kissed the hand of President Abdurrahman Wahid, who briefly followed Habibie in 1999, because he was a well-known religious figure: but offering the same courtesy to a publicly reviled Suharto was an inauspicious start for Habibie's presidency.

This was a pity for the reason that President Habibie was a glimmer of hope for a deeply divided Indonesia. A German-educated engineer who had held a high position in Germany's aircraft manufacturing industry, Habibie seemed to promise more than a military dictatorship. Dependent though he had been on Suharto's good will, from the 1970s onwards he personally led Indonesia's nascent high-tech industries. And Habibie's period in office was characterized by a pragmatism that delighted some but offended others. He released political prisoners and repealed the anti-subversion law; allowed the formation of free political parties and new parliamentary elections; introduced a new press law and issued decrees on human rights; called off military operations in Aceh, whose refusal to accept Jakarta's unlimited authority dated as far back to 1972; offered a referendum to East Timor, where the army had struggled to maintain Indonesian rule since its forcible acquisition in 1975; and, last but not least, reversed the centralization of power in Java which so annoyed the outer islanders. But Habibie had also to cope with the strict conditions imposed by the International Monetary Fund for a US$43 billion rescue loan and find a way of preventing a trial of Suharto that would expose the full extent of official corruption. Caught up in the crisis stemming from the collapse of the Thai baht in 1997, the Indonesian rupiah had lost 80 per cent of its value, the economy swung from rapid growth to rapid contraction, unemployment soared, and the stock exchange virtually collapsed. Foreign investment quickly disappeared and Chinese entrepreneurs fled to Singapore.

In the end, Habibie buckled under the strain and he was forced to stand aside in 1999 from the prospect of re-election. So the frustrated reformer handed over a more restricted presidency to the half-blind Abdurrahman Wahid, a Moslem cleric living in Jakarta. Indonesia's first and second presidents, Sukarno and Suharto, had ruled without constitutional restraints for two decades and three decades respectively. Abdurrahman Wahid came from an impressive political lineage; his grandfather had founded Indonesia's largest Moslem organization, the Nahdlatul Ulama, while his father was the country's first minister of religious affairs after independence. There was no narrowness of outlook in the family, so that the new president was generally seen as the voice of moderate Islam. How great a challenge faced him was transparent from the start. "There was nothing," Abdurrahman Wahid said, "but jagged debris, the ruined wrecks of the former administration." But he made a good start by curbing the influence of the military through sacking the minister of security, a general who was held responsible for many of the atrocities committed by the army in East Timor. Abdurrahman Wahid even travelled to East Timor in order to apologize for them, while working on permanent solutions to the secessionist struggles in Aceh and West Papua. He also sought to give the ethnic Chinese citizens greater political and cultural rights.

Despite many of his initiatives running ahead of Indonesian public opinion, trouble came to Abdurrahman Wahid from his deteriorating health, which by 2001 meant that he often fell asleep during cabinet meetings. When in parliament he was impeached for alleged corruption and incompetence, and his deputy Megawati Sukarnoputri, the eldest daughter of the country's founder president Sukarno, was sworn in as his successor, Abdurrahman Wahid refused to leave the presidential palace. Cutting off electricity and water would not have been sufficient to shift him, but heart and kidney problems drove him to the United States for urgent treatment.

Yet Megawati Sukarnoputri proved to be an even more surprising president than her predecessor. She combined a casualness as regards her responsibilities with an Imelda Marcos-like enthusiasm for shopping in Singapore. Her only major decision was to broaden the scope of the special court already set up to try those behind the violence in East Timor. But there was scepticism that the prosecutions in Jakarta would ever succeed, while cynics speculated about the real motive behind this move. Possibly Indonesia wished to appease international opinion. Decentralization continued apace under Megawati Sukarnoputri, as it did under the former general Susilo Bambang Yudhoyono, the first Indonesian president to be directly elected in 2004. His term of office was immediately marked by a natural disaster, when an earthquake off Aceh produced a tsunami that overwhelmed its capital, Banda Aceh. Either the impact of the disaster or the steady loosening of Javanese control persuaded the Achenese to end their last armed uprising. Released from detention, Irwandi Yusuf was appointed the provincial governor as a result of Aceh's first direct election. *The Jakarta Post* gave the event front-page coverage, because the long-standing contest between state and central governments was over at last, providing of course the Acehnese were left to manage their own affairs. According to Susilo Bambang Yudhoyono, the Acehnese disaster was not the only serious threat that he faced during his presidency. In 2009, an ill-disposed sorcerer sent "revolving clouds" to trouble him, a testimony to the continued use of black magic in the Indonesian archipelago.

East Timor

Just as the outer islanders of the archipelago were never asked if they wished to be part of the Republic of Indonesia, so the East Timorese had no say over their forcible recruitment in 1975. After all, the idea of Indonesia as a description of the Dutch East Indies only emerged in the late nineteenth century, and no pre-colonial maritime state had ever come near to the extent of control exercised by Batavia. It was during the

1920s that nationalists first made use of Indonesia as the name of a single independent Southeast Asian maritime state.

Although the Suharto annexation of East Timor brought terrible suffering to its people, they had already been decimated through the Second World War. This Portuguese colony's troubles had begun in 1942 with the arrival of the Imperial Japanese Army. Seen by Tokyo as the gateway to Australia, Timor was a prime target during the southern advance of the Imperial Japanese Army despite the strenuous efforts of Lisbon to keep out of the conflict. This proved impossible once the largely Australian forces facing the Japanese invaders resorted to guerrilla warfare to prolong resistance right across the island. Members of Sparrow Force, as the Allied contingent was called, fought on for a year because, for all they knew, the Timor campaign was but a prelude to the invasion of northern Australia. But Japanese reinforcements so altered the military situation that the Australian intervention had to be abandoned. Of the 30,000 Timorese who died, the greatest number succumbed to diseases caused by malnutrition. The Timorese sacrifice was never quite forgotten in Australia, notwithstanding Canberra's abject failure to raise any objection to Indonesia's take-over of East Timor. Portugal had resumed control in 1945, and done much to rebuild the colony before independence movements became active. The end of Portugal's dictatorial Salazar regime set the scene for increased agitation and, then in 1975, a unilateral declaration of East Timorese independence. But it also afforded the Indonesians with a convenient opportunity to invade.

At the end of 1975, after a naval and aerial bombardment, Indonesian troops overran Dili, the ex-colony's capital. These men ran amok, killing and raping the civilian population in the mistaken belief that they had been sent to put down a communist threat to the Republic of Indonesia, rather than a people seeking independence from colonial rule. Ardent Moslems in the Indonesian ranks were even told that the invasion was a holy war against infidels. More than 2,000 civilians were slaughtered: two East Timorese men faced a firing squad because their footwear was judged to have a military appearance.

There was no comment at all in Washington in case it embarrassed President Suharto. For six years, the Indonesian army had its brutal way in East Timor, until the killing of 250 Dilians at Santa Cruz cemetery eventually aroused world interest. Some 3,000 mourners were present in 1991 at the interment of an eighteen-year-old East Timorese who had died from injuries sustained in a fight with pro-Indonesian West Timorese. As prayers were being said, a detachment of Indonesian soldiers arrived and opened fire. No shots were returned. Many of those who took shelter behind gravestones, and later escaped the cemetery, sought refuge in the garden of Carlos Belo, the Catholic bishop of Dili. In spite of negotiations with the local army commander, the bishop could not stop a large number of refugees being dragged outside and executed.

Although he found it morally reprehensible that some people could say that those deaths were a necessary sacrifice to draw international attention to a situation that had been previously ignored, Belo threw himself into the cause of independence, whatever the consequences he might suffer himself. Brushing aside death threats and the fears of his closest followers, the bishop managed to garner international support for his downtrodden country.

World attention was then most unwelcome in a Jakarta under acute financial strain because of the severe regional monetary crisis, and also preoccupied with secession threats on several islands: yet there was no real need for concern since American companies with a stake in Indonesia ensured that the Santa Cruz massacre had little immediate impact on Washington's outlook. Not until 1993, when Bill Clinton moved into the White House, would the United States first express its disapproval. Over the next few years, it became obvious that East Timor had no historical connection at all with Indonesia. The award in 1996 of the Nobel Peace Prize to Carlos Belo was crucial, and the citation did not mince its words:

> In 1975, Indonesia took control of East Timor and began systematically oppressing the people. In the years that followed it has been estimated that one-third of the population of East Timor lost their lives due to starvation, epidemics, war and terror.

The bad publicity obliged Washington to acknowledge the plight of the East Timorese. When in 1999, a United Nations team confirmed their wish to separate from Indonesia, Jakarta's tyranny was ended by

The saviour of East Timor, Bishop Carlos Ximenes Belo

an international force from Australia, Britain, Canada, France, Italy, New Zealand, the Philippines, Thailand, South Korea and the United States. Thus was the delayed decolonization of the last Western territory in Southeast Asia accomplished. For the Australian public indeed it seemed more a colonial liberation than a humanitarian rescue mission. For the Indonesians, East Timor's secession served as a warning that, if sufficiently hard pressed, other discontented islands in the archipelago might seek international backing for their own freedom.

The Philippines

The surrender of American and Philippine forces to the Imperial Japanese Army in 1942 posed a dilemma for Filipinos. Should they continue some kind of resistance against Japan, or should they collaborate in the Greater East Asia Co-Prosperity Sphere. Those who chose the former option on the island of Luzon joined the Hukbalahap, the "People's Anti-Japanese Army", or the Huks for short. As one recruit put it, "I believed that the Philippines should be independent. The Japanese had no more right to my land than the Americans."

Even though the Imperial Japanese Army contained the Huks, and indeed other resistance groups that sprang up elsewhere, their subversive activities helped to preserve Filipino self-respect and, just before the American reconquest of the archipelago, they provided intelligence that was important for the US landings. How invaluable such detail as the disposition of Japanese forces was can be deduced from Douglas MacArthur's admonition of an American observer restless for action behind Japanese lines: the general told him, "You're no good to me dead."

Because the United States had already promised independence to the Philippines, the Japanese were more cautious in their occupation, except when it came to surrendered Filipino soldiers. Shortly after Manila fell, talks were held with leading nationalists including Benigno Aquino, Sr. and Jose Laurel. These men eventually called upon their compatriots to accept the American defeat for what it was, a comprehensive Japanese triumph. One Japanese told them: "Like it or not, you are Filipinos and belong to the Oriental race. No matter how hard you try, you cannot become white people."

That Western ideas of superiority had long been part of an armoury used to defend imperialism was indisputable. But the Japanese were by no means enthusiastic about racial equality, for they had a pecking order of their own for Asian peoples. As did European colonialists, they tended to regard their subject peoples as inferior. Southeast Asians were categorized as backward and lazy, but the full venom of Japanese racism was reserved for the Chinese, whose stubborn refusal to submit to the Imperial Japanese Army in China itself had compelled the dangerous thrust southwards against the colonies of Britain, Holland and the United States. Without the oil, rubber and food they could provide for the

Japanese war effort, stalemate in China meant nothing less than defeat.

But widespread collaboration in the Philippines did not result in wholesale convictions after liberation in 1944. There was no bloodbath or purge, internally or externally directed. Ignoring the American reaction to the Bataan death march, Philippine politicians readily collaborated throughout the period of the Japanese occupation, Jose Laurel being appointed in 1943 as head of a separate government. As happened in supposedly independent Burma, the Philippines soon learned any freedom of action was strictly limited. But Tokyo's delegation of some power had its desired effect, since troops released from garrison duties could be redeployed to meet the coming American invasion.

When US forces closed in on Manila in 1944, senior collaborators fled abroad. President Laurel first went to Taiwan and then to Japan, where finally he turned himself in to MacArthur, who was responsible for the Allied occupation of the defeated country. Letting Jose Laurel return to the Philippines was probably a wise decision on the eve of the colony's independence, since political recrimination would have served little purpose then. A footnote to the whole saga was the eulogy delivered in 1959 by Ferdinand Marcos at Laurel's funeral. That Marcos actually assisted him in his dealings with the Japanese seems not unlikely, because the high court opinion that Justice Laurel had delivered in Marcos' favour in 1938, when he was accused of murdering a political rival, suggests that an unusual degree of understanding already existed between them. It is noteworthy, too, that one of the few powerful Filipino families left untouched when Marcos later introduced martial law to strike at his political opponents were the Laurels: unlike so many others, they were allowed to keep their extensive estates, a bank, and a beach resort.

On 4 July 1946, Manuel Roxas became the first president of an independent Republic of the Philippines. Over the next couple of decades, the Philippines gradually recovered from the ravages of war and enjoyed sustained economic growth. Possibly because he had collaborated with the Japanese as openly as Laurel, the new president tried to redeem himself by binding his country to the United States, through a free-trade agreement and granting American companies the right to operate on the same basis as Filipino ones. In return, the Philippines received substantial aid from a Washington reassured by the clampdown on the Huks. The bitter struggle against these agrarian rebels lasted in Luzon and the Visayas until 1954.

A president who really appreciated the legitimate grievances of the peasantry was Ramon Magsaysay, a hands-on leader concerned to alleviate the grinding poverty he had seen in his own village. Born the son of a blacksmith, Magsaysay did not automatically side with the great landowners. Yet he was no friend of the communists and, with the help of American intelligence services, he rooted out left-wingers from key positions in government service. Perhaps Magsaysay's greatest success, before becoming president himself, was the use of the armed forces to ensure the 1951 congressional elections were relatively honest. Soldiers protected ballot boxes, thereby restoring a degree of public confidence in the electoral process.

A clear winner in the 1953 presidential election, Magsaysay lost no time in recruiting an exceptional team of Filipinos and American advisers to help him govern. He was also assisted by the receipt of Japanese war reparations. Having ended the Huk threat through military action and offering amnesty to those who surrendered, President Magsaysay resettled landless peasants from Luzon on the southern island of Mindanao and other undeveloped parts of the archipelago. The arrival of large numbers of Catholic settlers in Mindanao altered the religious balance on the island, contributing to the upsurge of Moslem separatism from the 1970s onwards.

Resettlement postponed but did not cure the ongoing land crisis, which would be a factor in Ferdinand Marcos' rise to power. It was a tragedy for the Philippines, as it was for the Malaysian state of Sabah, that their visionary leaders during the post-war era should both die in plane crashes: Ramon Magsaysay in 1957 on a mountainside and Donald Stephens nineteen years afterwards in the sea. In the Philippines the leadership vacuum was to be filled by Ferdinand Marcos, who in 1965 moved from the Liberals to the Nacionalista party in order to boost his bid for the presidency. Although a large measure of Filipino self-government had existed under American colonial rule, the political pattern was set because large landowners were the chief supporters of the United States. They pulled the strings behind the two main parties, the Nacionalista and the Liberals.

In spite of exploiting the political arrangements of "the old order" to further his own career, Ferdinand Marcos came from a comparatively poor background himself. His family were farmers in the rugged northern area of Luzon. But from the start Marcos made no secret of his ambition. "If you are electing me just to get my services as a Congressman for the pittance of 7,500 pesos a year, don't vote for me at all," he shouted at rallies during his first campaign in 1949. "This is only the first step. Elect me a Congressman now, and I pledge you a President in twenty years." He was duly elected, at the age of thirty-two the youngest member of the House of Representatives; then in 1959 he became a senator with a landslide majority; and finally, well within the timescale that he had set himself, Marcos was elected president in 1965 and re-elected in 1969.

It may be the case that this swift climb to the highest office affected his judgement, since Marcos admitted that he was tired of the chore of elections and spoke of replacing democracy with "constitutional authoritarianism". He used the presidential privilege of declaring martial law in 1972 to overcome the prohibition on a president serving more than two terms. Initially, his dictatorship was not unpopular because the New Society that he advocated seemed to promise land reform, an end to official corruption, and large-scale foreign investment. But even such an astute handler of the American political system as Marcos could not disguise the weakness of his regime indefinitely.

Many thousands of his opponents were imprisoned, the entitlement to a trial suspended, the authority of the courts undermined, press freedom drastically curtailed, and the armed forces unduly strengthened. All these unconstitutional measures were justified to Washington as necessary for heading off a communist take-over of the Philippines, an argument that delighted multinational companies as well. Marcos even managed to persuade some observers that he was a second Lee Kuan Yew, the champion of private enterprise in Singapore. Yet his essential support came from a US-financed army, whose officer corps was given opportunities to acquire great wealth. As a result, the tradition of a non-political military disappeared from the Philippines.

By the late 1970s, though, it became apparent that the New Society was simply a vehicle for Marcos' personal aggrandizement. But growing dissent hardly worried him at all, because he could point to an increase

Mass opposition to President Marcos led to his exile in 1986

in communist activity and moreover to the violent actions of the Moros, whose stated aim was the re-establishment of the Sulu sultanate as an independent state. In 1981, Marcos felt sufficiently confident of his own position to lift martial law. Almost believing he could now walk on water, he did not flinch from the execution of Benigno Aquino, Jr. at the Manila International Airport. After a period of voluntary exile, this serious opponent decided in 1983 that he should rejoin the arena of Filipino politics. How Benigno Aquino was shot in the back of the head by one of the security guards escorting him off the aircraft was never satisfactorily explained.

Whether the murder was ordered by the president, his wife, or the head of the armed forces no one could discover. An inquiry failed to blame anybody. Certainly the Marcoses had much to lose: Imelda Marcos, in particular, was anxious to maintain the family's ascendancy. She was increasingly directing affairs as governor of Metro Manila and minister of Human Settlements. As the Central Intelligence Agency director of operations, Herbert Natzke, remarked of President Marcos, he had two fundamental flaws. "He can't avoid stealing everything in sight, and he can't control his wife."

After the travesty of justice that claimed no one was to blame for Benigno Aquino's assassination, there was a major outflow of capital, as the middle class as well as the rich moved their funds to safe havens overseas. Many Filipinos also emigrated to the United States, taking the total who fled the Marcos dictatorship to 300,000. The flight of brains and money, the loss of confidence in the regime, and the growing impatience of the World Bank, accelerated a financial meltdown. Already US$27 billion in debt, the Philippines was technically bankrupt with cash-strapped enterprises shut or working reduced hours. Nationalisation merely compounded the problem, since the government was loaded with company debts.

Negotiations with the International Monetary Fund and 483 creditor banks took more than a year to complete because few believed that President Marcos would comply with the austerity measures that would be needed for the aid programme. A ploy that the regime used in times of political crisis, such as the aftermath of the failure to bring anyone to book for the assassination, was to print more money. Even Marcos had to acknowledge in late 1984 that "excess liquidity" was becoming a serious inflationary problem.

More worrying for the president was the emergence of Corazon Aquino, Benigno's widow, as the leader of the growing opposition to his rule. And she possessed a powerful ally in the archbishop of Manila, Cardinal Jaime Sin, an outspoken critic whom Marcos could never quell nor silence. With the country's financial position apparently stabilized at last, he called a snap election in February 1986.

It was now obvious even to his close ally Ronald Reagan, the second-term American president, that Marcos had lost his grip. He could no longer deal with either the Moro rebels or the rising demand for a fair presidential contest. Despite widespread vote rigging in the election, there could be no question that Corazon Aquino had won. When Marcos moved towards his inauguration, the people of Manila took to the streets and physically surrounded the presidential palace in non-violent protest. Fearing bloody civil disturbances, the Philippine army abandoned Marcos, who hastily left the country in a US aircraft. The new president Corazon Aquino inherited massive foreign debts, a mutinous army and a growing rebel movement, but for the great landowners it was business as usual. Yet Marcos' downfall was overwhelmingly due to the courage and determination of the Filipino people, many of whom risked their lives to restore democracy.

The leadership of the Catholic Church was quick to recognize the popular mood and lent its support to the new government. Church services almost turned into rousing political gatherings. But during her presidency, Corazon Aquino came to depend on Fidel Ramos, the defence minister and army chief. In 1992 he was the first soldier to be elected president, but with a mere 23 per cent of the votes cast. When six years later Joseph Estrada replaced him, it looked as though the Philippines was following the US example in choosing a former film star. But he was more vulnerable than President Reagan once it was learned how Estrada had accepted bribes. That the 1990s economic crisis was then putting immense pressure on the Phippine peso left him with no choice but to resign.

Troubled though Filipino democracy was by the Marcos and Estrada debacles, its difficulties bear no comparison with coup-ridden Thailand, and since the election of Gloria Macapagal-Arroyo as president in 2004 there has been real progress both economically and politically. The Moros remain restive and their ultimate satisfaction depends on the extent of self-government which Manila will be prepared to concede. The abortive assault on Sabah in 2013 by followers of Jamalul Kiram III, the self-proclaimed Sulu sultan, may be a straw in the wind of future discord. Or, as seems more likely, the unexpected attack was meant to remind the world of an historical dispute that can only be resolved when the Moslem inhabitants of the Philippines feel they are being properly treated.

POSTSCRIPT:
PRESENT-DAY SOUTHEAST ASIA

Notwithstanding the diminutive size of both Singapore and Brunei, not to mention the recent sufferings of East Timor, the modern nation states of Southeast Asia seem destined to remain for the foreseeable future. Internal troubles still preoccupy several countries, most notably Myanmar, Indonesia and the Philippines, but there are signs that some form of political accommodation will be reached. The Burmese military have come to realize that they cannot expect to hold onto power forever; Manila has almost recognized, that unless there is more autonomy allowed in the southernmost islands of the archipelago, the Moro problem will never be solved; and finally the Javanese understand how the outlying provinces have to be reassured that government from Jakarta entails neither neglect nor exploitation.

The 2013 invasion of Sabah by a group of Filipinos loyal to the Sulu sultan, Jamalul Kiram III, is a reminder of disagreements over post-colonial frontiers. Yet the invaders' swift repulse says more about Malaysia's resilience than anything else. The Anwar Ibrahim saga undoubtedly damaged the political process in that country, although the eventual outcome may well be a less ethnic-based approach to government. At sixty-six years of age, Anwar Ibrahim is unlikely to reap any political benefit himself, but his determination to change the system will have an influence on how Malaysians expect politicians to behave in future.

In comparison with Singapore, the politics of Malaysia appear chaotic, for Lee Kuan Yew's legacy to the tiny island state has been a degree of stability rare today. Even now there are commentators who still attribute this social cohesion to the location of Singapore in the midst of a Malay world. While Singapore does in actual fact sit between the western and eastern states of Malaysia, Malay speakers only constitute a small ethnic group in maritime Southeast Asia. Having regard to the diversity of Indonesia, with 300 distinct peoples speaking more than 250 languages, it would be better to say that the Chinese inhabitants of Singapore live in an Austronesian cultural environment. What has ensured Singapore's survival as an independent state are three factors: the immense advantage of its position for international trade, something the English East India Company first noticed; the security of its banks for savers in adjacent countries, and especially the Chinese residents in Indonesia; and, last but not least, the willingness of its people to work hard for the sake of social advancement, a duty owed to one's ancestors which found full expression in Zhu Xi's *Family Rituals*.

Another advantage enjoyed by Singapore has been the absence of street demonstrations. One of the most striking phenomena since the 1980s is the emergence of organized pressure groups, whose direct tactics have to an extent endangered electoral politics. No one would condemn, however, the passive resistance movement that toppled Ferdinand Marcos in 1986, because the Philippine president had blatantly manipulated an election result in his own favour. But the value of similar actions in Thailand and Indonesia is less obvious, in particular when they turn bloody, as in the overthrow of President Suharto. In 1998 the demonstrators opposing Suharto's New Order went on the rampage, looting shops and injuring anyone in Jakarta who tried to defend themselves. Their street violence does not of course bear comparison with that initiated by Suharto as part of his military coup in 1965. Then Islamic groups were encouraged to attack President Sukarno's supporters right across Indonesia, with the result that perhaps as many as 500,000 people may have died.

Corruption was a prime cause of the demonstrations against Suharto's military rule. Protestors deplored "corruption", "cronyism" and "nepotism". Elsewhere corruption remains rife, despite a growing anger amongst ordinary people over the spoils of office. Tawi Sli was almost unique in Malaysian politics since, on stepping down as chief minister of Sarawak in 1968, this Sea Dyak headman was so poor that he applied for a government clerical post in Semanggang, his home town. A pension scheme had to be immediately established for ex-chief ministers.

Singapore stands out as the most conspicuously transparent country for financial affairs. But the island state has not been spared other Southeast Asian trends such as religious enthusiasm. Despite Singapore's elevation of Confucianism as a code of conduct, Christianity is making strong headway now among Singaporeans. The churches there are not politically active as the Catholic one in Philippines. No Cardinal Sin has emerged to chastise a growing materialism in Singapore, or comment on the unusual longevity of the present-day regime. It was the Catholic Church's radio station, and the bishops' pastoral letters read in Philippine churches, that broke Marcos' monopoly of the media. Finally, it was Cardinal Sin who mobilized the people of Manila: they formed a human barrier that thwarted the president's intended use of force.

In both Myanmar and Thailand, there are Buddhists who are prepared to advocate strong government. There was no protest from Buddhist monks when, in 1991, Burmese forces drove 145,000 Moslems out of the Arakan in western Myanmar. As representatives of the official religion, these Buddhists obviously thought they were entitled to monopolize belief. American trade sanctions and protests from Malaysia did have an effect, but religious toleration in Myanmar is a thing of the past. Likewise, in Indonesia a resurgence of Islam caused concern among non-Moslems, although terrorism has been contained by the authorities. Considering that Indonesia is the world's most populous majority-Moslem nation, this Southeast Asian achievement should not be underestimated. Quite likely continued respect for the spirit world had an influence here; because Moslems living in Indonesia always demonstrate a profound dislike for rigid interpretations of the faith. Imams who ignore the spirit-haunted dimension of the Indonesian archipelago are themselves ignored. Only in Brunei Darussalam, "Brunei, the abode of peace", is there a conscious effort to minimize conflict between different faiths. Yet its sultan is so much the leader of Moslem worship that there is no need to worry about non-believers.

Even though Brunei's plentiful oil revenues certainly help to maintain an orderly society, in its foreign relations the sultanate is willing to cooperate closely with a very different state like Singapore. And the wealth that comes out of the ground has allowed Brunei to leave its rainforest intact. The haze from the burning of Indonesia's cleared forests is now little short of an ecological scandal, while in Myanmar, Thailand and Malaysia excessive logging has gone unnoticed because it has not been accompanied by such a primitive method of land clearance. All the countries of present-day Southeast Asia urgently need to conserve their natural resources within a framework of sustainable growth. Perhaps the best example of this approach exists in Vietnam, where the sheer devastation of the Second Vietnam War necessitated serious reflection about the direction that future progress should take. In the longer term though, the impact of global warming may prove to be the decisive factor for Southeast Asian nations, for the good reason that it is one of the world's most vulnerable regions to climate change, with large populations and much economic activity concentrated along most of its coasts.

CHRONOLOGY

42   General Ma Yuan reasserts Chinese authority in northern Vietnam, already part of China's empire for more than a century.

240   Chinese envoys are impressed by the wealth of Funan, the Mekong-delta state later absorbed by the Khmers.

400   The Sri Lankan monk Buddhaghosa brings Buddhist scriptures to Thaton in Lower Burma.

430   The Javanese king of Holotan sends the first of seven tribute missions to China.

443   In response to Cham raids on northern Vietnam, Chinese troops destroy the capital of Champa at Tra-kieu.

547   Ly Bi fails to establish Van Xuan as an independent Vietnamese state.

616   King Isanavarman dispatches the first Khmer embassy to China.

671   The Chinese monk Yijing notices Srivijaya's prosperity as well as its great devotion to Buddhism.

695   King Jayanasa of Srivijaya sends a tributary mission to China.

813   The Cham king Harivarman I constructs the Po Nagar Hindu complex at Nha Trang in southern Vietnam.

824   In Java, the great Buddhist monument at Borobudur is completed.

877   The first great reservoir is dug in the vicinity of Angkor by King Indravarman I.

910   King Yasovarman I is interred on the Phnom Bakheng hill in the centre of Angkor.

939   Ngo Quyen frees Vietnam from Chinese rule.

1010 Ly Cong Uan establishes the Ly dynasty and makes Thang-long the Vietnamese capital.

1025 The Cholas launch raids from southern India on ports in Sumatra and the Malayan peninsula.

1039 Emperor Ly Thai Tong sets up a Chinese-style civil service in Vietnam.

1098 At Pagan, King Kyanzittha proclaims himself as a universal monarch and a Buddhist sage.

1037 King Erlanga restores Mataram's fortunes in eastern Java.

1056 King Anawrahta storms the city of Thaton and transfers its Mon royal family to Pagan.

1070 The Van Mieu, Vietnam's national university and centre for Confucian learning, is founded by Emperor Ly Thanh Tong.

1120 King Suryavarman II commissions the temple, tomb and observatory now known as Angkor Wat.

1165 Pagan's refusal to export any more elephants leads to a seaborne Sinhalese attack.

1167 At Pagan, Narathu smothers his father King Alaungsithu.

1177 The Chams attack Angkor by water.

1181 The last of the great Khmer kings, Jayavarman VII, restores the capital and then wreaks vengeance on Champa.

1220 The Khmers evacuate Champa and leave a puppet king on the throne.

1284 A four-pronged Mongol attack fails to subdue the Vietnamese.

1287 The Mongols capture Pagan and its last king, Narathihapate, commits suicide.

1292 A Mongol expedition arrives in Java to punish King Kertanagara.

1294 Kubilai Khan's successor, Timur, accepts Tran Hung Dao's defeat of the Mongols in Vietnam.

1296 Zhou Daguan records his impressions of Angkor during his visit as a Mongol envoy. King Mangrai founds Lanna in northern Thailand.

1351 U Thong founds the Thai kingdom of Ayudhya.

1353 Fa Ngum is installed at Luang Prabang as the first king of Lan Sang.

1393 Ayudhya captures Angkor, which the Khmers later abandon for Lovek.

1400 A succession dispute undermines the maritime empire of Majapahit.

1405 King Paramesvara of Malacca sends tribute to China.

1407 For a second time, the Ming admiral Zheng He makes use of Malacca as a temporary naval base.

1427 The Chinese abandon their reoccupation of Vietnam.

1438 Sukhothai becomes a province of Ayudhya.

1471 The Vietnamese emperor Le Thanh Tong destroys the kingdom of Champa.

1498   Vasco da Gama reaches India by sea.

1511   The Portuguese seize and fortify Malacca.

1521   Magellan's Spanish squadron arrives in the Philippines.

1527   Mac Dang Dung briefly usurps the Vietnamese throne.

1535   A Portuguese vessel docking at Da Nang is the first
       European ship to reach Vietnam.

1541   At Pegu in southern Burma, Tabinshwehti is crowned as the
       first Toungoo monarch.

1554   The Burmese subdue Lanna in northern Thailand.

1569   The Burmese king Bayinnaung captures the city of Ayudhya
       for the second time.

1571   In Aceh, Sultan Ala al-din al-Qahar dies.

1578   The Spaniards briefly occupy Brunei.

1592   King Naresuan of Ayudhya repulses a Burmese invasion at
       the battle of Nong Sarai. Puppet Le emperors are placed on
       the Vietnamese throne by the Trinh family.

1599   Spaniards are slaughtered at Phnom Penh.

1610   Anaukpetlun restores the Toungoo dynasty in Burma.

1613   After a siege, Filipe de Brito's fortress at Syriam falls to
       King Anaukpetlun's forces.

1619   In western Java, Batavia becomes the headquarters of the
       Dutch.

1628   Sultan Agung of Mataram launches his first attack
       on Batavia.

1641   The Dutch drive the Portuguese from Malacca.

1672 The division of Vietnam into Tonkin and Cochin China is fixed.

1685 French Jesuits try to convert King Narai of Ayudhya.

1709 King Phumintharacha begins his long reign during which Ayudhya's trade with China expands enormously.

1718 The Sulu sultanate halts Spanish expansion in the Philippines.

1752 Alaungpaya founds the Konbaung dynasty in Burma.

1762 The English East India Company occupies Manila, but afterwards Diego Silang's attempt to secure independence from Spain fails.

1767 King Alaungpaya's son, Hsinbyushin, destroys Ayudhya.

1771 The Tay Son uprising breaks out in Vietnam.

1782 General Chaophraya Chakri is crowned as the Thai king at Bangkok and the dynasty he founds lasts until today.

1786 The sultan of Kedah cedes the island of Penang to the English East India Company.

1807 Emperor Gia Long restarts the national examination system in Vietnam.

1819 Thomas Stamford Raffles founds Singapore as a free port.

1820 Gia Long's son, Minh Mang, is enthroned as emperor at Hue and inaugurates a thorough reorganization of Vietnam.

1824 Holland cedes Malacca to Britain. The First Anglo-Burmese War takes place.

1825 Pangeran Dipanagara rebels against Dutch rule in Java.

1826 The Anglo-Siamese Treaty outlines Siam's future relationship with the West.

1843   James Brooke establishes himself as the rajah of Sarawak.
Later Brunei allows the island of Labuan to become a Royal Navy
base as well.

1859   Holland purchases the Lesser Sunda islands and part of Timor
from Portugal. The French take control of Saigon.

1862   The Treaty of Saigon cedes three southern Vietnamese provinces
to France.

1863   Cambodia becomes a French protectorate.

1871   The Anglo-Dutch Treaty of Sumatra clears the way for
a Dutch invasion of Aceh.

1874   The French gain concessions in Hanoi and Haiphong.

1877   King Mindon, the modernizer, dies in Burma.

1879   Spain at last subdues the Sulu sultanate.

1881   The British North Borneo Company is granted a charter.

1884   Vietnam ceases to be a Chinese tributary state.

1886   Upper Burma is annexed to the British empire in India.

1888   Sarawak, Brunei and North Borneo are made British protectorates.

1896   The kingdom of Laos becomes a part of French Indochina.
And the British form the Federated Malay States.

1898   After conflict with Spain, the United States annexes the Philippines.

1901   Queen Wilhelmina announces an ethical policy for the Dutch
East Indies.

1905   Ho Chi Minh starts to learn French better to understand
the colonial enemy. King Rama V abolishes debt-bondage
in Siam.

1906   The Vietnamese patriot Phan Chu Trinh publicly calls upon France to live up to its promise of modernization.

1908   On the island of Bali at Klungkung, Dutch machine guns slay the entire court of the last independent king, Dewa Agung.

1909   Bangkok cedes the Malay states of Perlis, Kedah, Kelantan and Trengganu to Britain.

1924   Planning begins for the Singapore naval base.

1925   Bao Dai becomes the last Vietnamese emperor.

1935   The India Act separates Burma from the Indian subcontinent.

1938   The Singapore naval base is completed but on a reduced scale.

1940   Aung San becomes secretary of the Burma Freedom Block.

1941   A Franco-Thai War ends with a French defeat in Indochina. Afterwards Luang Phibunsongkhram secretly allies Thailand with Japan. Norodom Sihanouk becomes king of Cambodia.

1942   The Japanese overrun Malaya, Singapore, the Dutch East Indies, the Philippines and Burma.

1943   Sukarno tells the Indonesian peoples that they must secure freedom for themselves. In Malaya, Subhas Chandra Bose raises the Indian National Army.

1945   After heavy Japanese defeats at Imphal and Kohima, the British recover Burma. Japan surrenders. Manila is devastated through the American recapture of the Philippines. Sukarno proclaims the Republic of Indonesia.

1946   The Philippines gains its independence. Rajah Vyner Brooke cedes Sarawak to Britain.

1947   Burma becomes an independent state and, to the dismay of Britain, opts to leave the Commonwealth.

1948   A state of emergency is declared in Malaya.

1949   Indonesia gains its independence from Holland.

1953   The Acehnese rebel against Javanese interference in Sumatra.

1954   The French surrender at Dien Bien Phu leads to North Vietnam and South Vietnam becoming sovereign states.

1955   At Bandung, Zhou Enlai reassures Southeast Asian states about the pacific intentions of the People's Republic of China. In South Vietnam, Ngo Dinh Diem ousts Emperor Bao Dai and refuses to hold the elections agreed at the Geneva peace conference.

1957   Malaya is granted independence but the state of emergency does not end for another three years. The reforming president of the Philippines, Ramon Magsaysay, dies in a plane crash. A US task force based at Singapore backs rebellious Indonesian officers in Sumatra and Sulawesi.

1958   General Sarit Thanarat's coup allows Thailand to become later on a US bomber base for operations against North Vietnam and Laos.

1959   Singapore achieves self government. In Laos, Prince Sounana Phouma is excluded from government office.

1962   President Sukarno adds West Irian to Indonesia. The abortive Brunei revolt briefly shakes this tiny sultanate. Ne Win seizes power for the military in Burma.

1963   Malaya, Singapore, Sarawak and North Borneo combine to form the Federation of Malaysia, which Sukarno "confronts" mainly on the island of Borneo. President Ngo Dinh Diem is assassinated in Saigon. The United States intervenes in South Vietnam and the Second Vietnam War begins in earnest two years later.

1965   Tunku Abdul Rahman pushes Singapore out of Malaysia.
Ferdinand Marcos is elected president of the Philippines.

1967   Pushed aside two years earlies, Sukarno is finally ousted by
the Indonesian armed forces.

1968   The Moros living in the southern Philippines rise in revolt.
Despite Vo Nguyen Giap's concern about the extent of
North Vietnamese casualties, the United States is rocked
by the Tet offensive in South Vietnam.

1969   After a long illness, Ho Chi Minh dies in Hanoi.

1970   Washington backs a South Vietnamese invasion
of Cambodia.

1975   Laos abolishes its monarchy, becoming the Lao People's
Democratic Republic. Saigon falls to North Vietnamese
troops. Indonesia invades East Timor.

1976   The Sabahan leader Donald Stephens is killed in a
plane crash.

1978   The Vietnamese occupy Cambodia, after overthrowing
the Khmer Rouge. They establish the People's Republic
of Kampuchea.

1979   A Sino-Vietnamese border war ends in stalemate.

1986   Ferdinand Marcos flees Manila in a US aircraft. Nguyen
Van Linh relaxes communist rule in Vietnam.

1989   When Vietnamese forces evacuate Cambodia, Norodom
Sihanouk returns from exile in the People's Republic of
China and resumes the throne.

1990   Having won a landslide election victory in Burma, Aung
San Suu Kyi suffers house arrest for the next two decades.

1992   Fidel Ramos is the first soldier to be elected as president
of the Philippines.

1997　The Thai baht collapses at the start of a regional currency crisis. Malaysia, Indonesia and the Philippines are also badly affected.

1998　Suharto's New Order is overthrown amid cries of "corruption", "cronyism" and "nepotism".

1999　International intervention liberates East Timor.

2001　President Abdurrahman Wahid is forced from office in Jakarta.

2002　Premier Mahathir Mohamad unexpectedly announces his retirement from Malaysian politics.

2003　Anti-Thai riots convulse Phnom Penh over a claim that Angkor really belongs to Thailand.

2004　Lee Kuan Yew is elevated as "minister mentor" when his son, Lee Hsien Loong, becomes Singapore's premier. A tsunami flattens Banda Aceh, killing 98,000 Acehnese people.

2006　Premier Thaksin Shinawatra is deposed by a military coup while outside Thailand.

2008　Cyclone Nargis strikes the Irrawaddy delta, killing 150,000 people and making another 2.5 million homeless.

2013　Malaysian aircraft bomb Sulanese invaders in Sabah. The haze from Sumatra's burning forests obliges Indonesia to apologize to Singapore.

FURTHER READING

General

Aldrich, R., *Greater France. A History of French Overseas Expansion*, Basingstoke, 1996.

Boomgard, P. (ed.), *A World of Water. Rain, rivers and seas in Southeast Asian histories*, Leiden, 2007.

Boxer, C. R. *The Dutch Seaborne Empire*, London, 1965.

——, *The Portuguese Seaborne Empire*, New York, 1969.

Charney, M. W., *Southeast Asian Warfare, 1300–1900*, Leiden, 2004.

Coedes, G., *The Making of South East Asia*, translated by H. M. Wright, Berkeley, 1966.

——, *The Indianized States of Southeast Asia*, translated by S. U. Cowing, Honolulu, 1968.

Cotterell, A., *Western Power in Asia. Its Slow Rise and Swift Fall, 1415–1999*, Singapore, 2010.

——, *Asia. A Concise History*, Singapore, 2011.

Dreyer, E. L., *Zheng He. China and the Oceans in the Early Ming Dynasty, 1405–1433*, New York, 2006.

Freeman, D. B., *The Straits of Malacca. Gateway or Gauntlet?*, Montreal, 2003.

Hall, R. H., *The History of Early Southeast Asia. Maritime Trade and Societal Development, 100–1500*, Lanham, Maryland, 2011.

Iriye, A., *The Origins of the Second World War in Asia and the Pacific*, London, 1987.

Jones, F. C., *Japan's New Order in East Asia: Its Rise and Fall, 1937–45*, Oxford, 1987.

Lieberman, V., *Strange Parallels. Southeast Asia in Global Context, c. 800–1830. Vol. 1: Integration on the Mainland*, Cambridge, 2003.

O'Reilly, D. J. W., *Early Civilizations of Southeast Asia*, Lanham, Maryland, 2007.

Parry, J. H., *The Spanish Seaborne Empire*, Berkeley, 1990.

Reid, A., *Southeast Asia in the Age of Commerce, 1450 -1680. Vol. 1. The Lands below the Winds*, New Haven, 1988.

——, *Southeast Asia in the Age of Commerce, 1450–1680. Vol. 2. Expansion and Crisis*, New Haven, 1993.

Ricklefs, M. C. (ed.), *A New History of Southeast Asia*, Basingstoke, 2010.

Shaffer, L. N., *Maritime Southeast Asia to 1550*, New York, 1966.

Subrahmanyan, S., *The Portuguese Empire in Asia 1500–1700: A Political and Economic History*, London, 1993.

Swearer, D. K., *The Buddhist World of Southeast Asia*, Albany, 2010.

Tarling, N. (ed.), *The Cambridge History of Southeast Asia. Vol. 1. From Early Times to 1800*, Cambridge, 1992.

——, *The Cambridge History of Southeast Asia. Vol. 2. The Nineteenth and Twentieth Centuries*, Cambridge, 1992.

——, *Imperialism in Southeast Asia. A fleeting, passing phase*, London, 2001.

——, *A Sudden Rampage. The Japanese Occupation of Southeast Asia, 1941–1945*, London, 2001.

Wolters, O. W., *History, Culture and Region in Southeast Asian Perspectives*, Ithaca, 1999.

——, *Early Southeast Asia. Selected Essays*, Ithaca, 2008.

Burma / Myanmar

Allen, L., *Burma. The Longest War, 1941–45*, London, 1984.

Aung-Thwin, M., *Pagan. The Origins of Modern Burma*, Honolulu, 1985.

Burton, R., *Railway of Hell. War, Captivity and Forced Labour at the Hands of the Japanese*, Barnsley, 2002.

Cady, J. F., *A History of Burma*, Ithaca, 1958.

Charney, M. W., *A History of Modern Burma*, Cambridge, 2009.

Hayes, R., *Subhas Chandra Bose in Nazi Germany. Politics, Intelligence and Propaganda 1941–43*, London, 2011

Koenig, W. J., *The Burmese Polity, 1752–1819. Politics, Administration and Social Organisation in the Early Kon-baung Period*, Ann Arbor, 1990.

Lieberman, V., *Burmese Administrative Cycles. Anarchy and Conquest, c. 1580–1760*, New Jersey, 1984.

Maung Htin Aung, *Burmese History Before 1287: A Defence of the Chronicles*, Oxford, 1970.

Stadtner, D. M., *Sacred Sites in Burma. Myth and Folklore in an Evolving Spiritual Realm*, Bangkok, 2011.

Strachan, P., *Pagan. Art and Architecture of Old Burma*, Oxford, 1996.

Thant Myint-U, *The Making of Modern Burma*, Cambridge, 2001.

Cambodia

Bizot, F., *The Gate*, translated by E. Cameron, London. 2003.

Chandler, D. P., *A History of Cambodia*, Boulder, 1983.

———, *Brother Number One. A Political Biography of Pol Pot*, Boulder, 1999.

Coe, M. D., *Angkor and Khmer Civilization*, London. 2003.

Gottesman, E., *Cambodia After the Khmer Rouge. Inside the Politics of Nation Building*, New Haven, 2003.

Higham, C., *The Civilization of Angkor*, London, 2001.

Kiernan, B., *The Pol Pot Regime. Race, Power, and Genocide in Cambodia under the Khmer Rouge, 1975–79*, New Haven 1996.

Mabbett, I. and Chandler, D., *The Khmers*, Oxford, 1995.

Osborne, M., *Sihanouk. Prince of light, prince of darkness*, St. Leonards, Australia, 1994.

Slocomb, M., *The People's Republic of Kampuchea 1979–1989. The Revolution after Pol Pot*, Chiang Mai, 2003.

Snellgrove, D., *Angkor—Before and After: A Cultural History of the Khmers*, Bangkok, 2004.

Zhou Daguan, *A Record of Cambodia. The Land and Its People*, translated by P. Harris, Chiang Mai, 2007.

Vietnam

Ang Cheng Guan, *The Vietnamese War from the Other Side. The Vietnamese Communists' Perspective*, London, 2002.

Blair, A. E., *Lodge in Vietnam. A Patriot Abroad*, New Haven, 1995.

Brocheux, P., *Ho Chi Minh. A Biography*, translated by C. Duicker, Cambridge, 2007.

Chapuis, O., *A History of Vietnam. From Hong Bang to Tu Duc*, Westport, 1995.
——, *The Last Emperors. From Tu Duc to Bao Dai*, Westport, 2000.
Choi Byung Wook, *Southern Vietnam under the Reign of Minh Mang (1820–1841). Central Policies and Local Response*, Ithaca, 2004.
Domen, A. J., *The Indochinese Experience of the French and the Americans. Nationalism and Communism in Cambodia, Laos and Vietnam*, Bloomington, 2001.
Dror, O. and Taylor, K. W., *Views of Seventeenth-Century Vietnam. Christoforo Borri on Cochinchina and Samuel Baron on Tonkin*, Ithaca, 2006.
Duiker, W. J., *Sacred War: Nationalism and Revolution in a Divided Vietnam*, New York, 1995.
Dunn, P. M., *The First Vietnam War*, London, 1985.
Haong Anh Tuan, *Silk for Silver: Dutch-Vietnamese Relations, 1637–1700*, Leiden, 2007.
Issacs, A. R., *Without Honor. Defeat in Vietnam and Cambodia*, Baltimore, 1983.
Macdonald, P., *Giap. The Victor in Vietnam*, London, 1993.
Marr, D. G., *Vietnamese Anticolonialism 1885–1925*, Berkeley, 1995.
Mus, P., *India seen from the east. Indian and indigenous cults in Champa*, translated by I. W. Mabbeth, Caulfield, Australia, 2012.
Simpson, H. R., *Dien Bien Phu. The Epic Battle America Forgot*, Washington, 1994.
Taylor, K. W., *The Birth of Vietnam*, Berkeley, 1983.
——, *A History of the Vietnamese*, Cambridge, 2013.

Indonesia

Anderson, B. R. O'G., *Java in a Time of Revolution and Resistance, 1944-1946*, Ithaca, 1972.
Bastin, J., *The native policies of Sir Stamford Raffles in Java and Sumatra: An economic interpretation*, Oxford, 1957.
Crouch, H., *The Army and Politics in Indonesia*, Ithaca, 1988.
Elson, R. E., *The Idea of Indonesia. A History*, New York, 2008.
Frederick, W. H., *Visions and Heat. The Making of the Indonesian Revolution*, Athens, Ohio, 1989.

Geertz, C., *The Religion of Java*, Chicago, 1960.

——, *Negara. The Theatre State in Nineteenth-Century Bali*, New Jersey,
1980.

Hadler, J., *Muslims and Matriarchs. Cultural Resistance in Indonesia through Jihad and Colonialism*, Ithaca, 2008.

Hobart, A., Ramseyer, U. and Leeman, A., *The People of Bali*, Oxford, 1996.

Hudson, J., *Sunset in the East. Fighting against the Japanese through the siege of Imphal and alongside them in Java 1943–1946*, Barnsley, 2002.

Kahin, A. R. and Kahin, G. M., *Subversion as Foreign Policy. The Secret Eisenhower and Dulles Debacle in Indonesia*, New York, 1995.

Kuitenbrouwer, M., *The Netherlands and the Rise of Modern Imperialism.*
Colonies and Foreign Policy 1870–1902, New York, 1991.

Kulke, H. et al (eds.), *Nagapattinam to Suvarnadwipa. Reflections on the Chola Naval Expeditions to Southeast Asia*, Singapore, 2009.

Lansing, S. T., *Priests and Programmers. Technologies of Power in the Engineered Landscape of Bali*, New Jersey, 1991.

Marsden, W., *The History of Sumatra*, reprinted in Memphis, Tennessee, 2010.

Miksic, J. N. et al, *Borobudur. Majestic, Mysterious, Magnificent*, Yogyakarta, 2010.

Pelras, C., *The Bugis*, Oxford, 1996.

Ricklefs, M. C., *A History of Modern Indonesia c. 1300 to the present*, Basingstoke, 1981.

Rinkes, D. A., *Nine Saints of Java*, translated by H. M. Froger, Kuala Lumpur, 1996.

Vatikiotis, M. R. J., *Indonesian Politics Under Suharto. Order, development*
and pressure for change, London, 1993.

Wolters, O. W., *Early Indonesian Commerce: A Study of the Origins of Srivijaya*, Ithaca, 1967.

Yahaya Jusoh and Kamarul Azmi Jasmi, *A Commentary on the Rules for Kings. Majlis Aceh*, Kuala Lumpur, 2008.

Thailand

Baker, C. and Pusak Phongpaichit, *A History of Thailand*, Cambridge, 2005.

Freeman, M., *Lanna. Thailand's Northern Kingdom*, Bangkok, 2001.

Garnier, D., *Ayutthaya. Venice of the East*, Bangkok, 2004.

Handley, P. M., *The King Never Smiles. A Biography of Thailand's Bhumibol Adulyadej*, New Haven, 2006.

Kobkua Suwannathat-Pian, *Thailand's Durable Premier. Phibun through Three Decades, 1932–1957*, Oxford, 1995.

McCargo, D., *Chamlong Srimuang and the new Thai politics*, London, 1997.

Reynolds, E. B., *Thailand's Secret War. The Free Thai, OSS and SOE during World War II*, Cambridge, 2005.

Stowe, J. A., *Siam becomes Thailand. A Story of Intrigue*, London, 1991.

Wyatt, D. K., *The Politics of Reform in Thailand: Education in the Reign of King Chulalongkorn*, New Haven, 1969.

———, *Thailand. A Short History*, New Haven, 1982.

Laos

Brown, M., *War in Shangri-la. A Memoir of the Civil War in Laos*, London, 2001.

Castle, T. N., *At War in the Shadow of Vietnam. US Military Aid to the Royal Lao Government, 1955–1975*, New York, 1993.

Heywood, D., *Ancient Luang Prabang*, Bangkok, 2008.

Marini, G. F. de, *A New and Interesting Description of the Lao Kingdom*, translated by W. E. J. Tips and C. Bertuccio, Bangkok, 1998.

Stuart-Fox, M., *Laos. Politics, Economics and Society*, Boulder, 1986.

Malaysia

Andaya, B. and L., *A History of Malaysia*, Basingstoke, 1982.

Bijl, N. van der, *Confrontation. The War with Indonesia, 1963–1966*, Barnsley, 2007.

Butcher, J. G. *The British in Malaya 1880–1941. The Social History of a European Community in Colonial South-East Asia*, Kuala Lumpur, 1979.

Granville-Edge, P. J., *The Sabahan. The Life and Death of Tun Fuad Stephens*, Dataram Palma, Selangor, 1999.

Kratoska, P. H., *The Japanese Occupation of Malaya. 1941–1945. A Social and Economic History*, London, 1998.

Pringle, R., *Rajahs and Rebels: The Ibans of Sarawak under Brooke rule, 1841–1941*, Ithaca, 1970.

Reece, B., *The White Rajahs of Sarawak. A Borneo Dynasty*, Singapore, 2004.

Richie, J., *Temenggong Oyong Lawai Jau, A Paramount Chief in Borneo. The Legacy*, Kuching, 2006.

Runciman, S., *The White Rajahs. A History of Sarawak from 1841 to 1946*, Cambridge, 1960.

Sadka, E., *The Protected Malay States, 1874–1895*, Kuala Lumpur, 1968.

Suwannathat-Pian, K., *Palace, Political Party and Power. The Story of the Socio-Political Development of Malay Kingship*, Singapore, 2011.

Wain, B., *Malaysian Maverick. Mahathir Mohamad in Turbulent Times*, Basingstoke, 2009.

White, N. J., *Business, Government and the End of Empire. Malaya, 1942–1957*, Kuala Lumpur, 1996.

Singapore

Collis, M., *Raffles*, London, 1966.

Elphick, P., Singapore. *The Pregnable Fortress. A Study in Deception, Discord and Desertion*, London, 1995.

Josey, A., *Lee Kuan Yew. The Crucial Years*, Singapore. 1968.

Kinvig, C., *Scapegoat. General Percival of Singapore*, London, 1996.

Lee, Kuan Yew, *One man's view of the world*, Singapore, 2013.

Masanobu Tsuji, *Singapore 1941–1942. The Japanese Version of the Malayan Campaign of World War II*, translated by M. E. Lake, Oxford, 1988.

Newbold, T. J., *British Settlements in the Straits of Malacca*, Kuala Lumpur, 1971.

Regnier, P., *Singapore: City-State in South-East Asia*, translated by C. Hurst, London, 1987.

Shinozaki Mamoru, *Syonan—My Story: The Japanese Occupation of Singapore*, Singapore, 1975.

Smith, C., *Singapore Burning. Heroism and Surrender in World War II*, London, 2005.

Brunei

Bijl, N. van der, *The Brunei Revolt. 1962–1963*, Barnsley, 2012.

Chanin, E., *Limbang Rebellion. Seven days in December 1962*, Sydney, 2013.

Ranjit Singh, D. S., *Brunei 1834–1983: The Problem of Political Survival*, Oxford, 1984.

The Philippines

Bonner, R., *Waltzing with a Dictator. The Marcoses and the Making of American Foreign Policy*, London, 1987.

Brands, H. W., *Bound to Empire. The United States and the Philippines*, Oxford, 1992.

Bresnan, J. (ed.), *Crisis in the Philippines. The Marcos Era and Beyond*, New Jersey, 1986.

Connaughton, R., Pimlott, J. and Anderson, D., *The Battle for Manila. The most devastating untold story of World War II*, London, 1995.

Junker, L. L., *Raiding, Trading, and Feasting. The Political Economy of the Philippine Chiefdoms*, Honolulu, 1999.

Smith, J., *The Spanish-American War. Conflict in the Caribbean and the Pacific 1895–1902*, London, 1994.

Steinberg, D. J., *The Philippines. A Singular and Plural Place*, Boulder, 2000.

Warren, J. F., *The Sulu Zone 1768–1898. The Dynamics of External Trade, Slavery, and Ethnicity in the transformation of a Southeast Asian Maritime State*, Singapore, 1981.

East Timor

Kohen, A. S., *From the Place of the Dead. Bishop Belo and the Struggle for East Timor*, Oxford, 1999.

Wray, C. R., *Timor 1942. Australian Commandos at War with the Japanese*, Melbourne, 1987.

INDEX